PRINCIPLES OF ECONOMIC SOCIOLOGY

PRINCIPLES OF ECONOMIC SOCIOLOGY

Richard Swedberg

PRINCETON UNIVERSITY PRESS   PRINCETON AND OXFORD

Library of Congress Cataloging-in-Publication Data
Swedberg, Richard.
Principles of economic sociology / Richard Swedberg.
p. cm.
Includes bibliographical references and index.
ISBN 0-691-07439-9 (alk. paper)
1. Economics—Sociological aspects. I. Title.
HM548 .S94 2003   2002030785

British Library Cataloging-in-Publication Data is available

This book has been composed in Palatino

Printed on acid-free paper. ∞

www.pupress.princeton.edu

Printed in the United States of America

10 9 8 7 6 5 4 3 2 1

For Mabel

Contents

LIST OF TABLES AND FIGURES   ix

PREFACE   xi

Chapter I. The Classics in Economic Sociology   1

Chapter II. Contemporary Economic Sociology   32

Chapter III. Economic Organization   53

Chapter IV. Firms   74

Chapter V. Economic and Sociological Approaches to Markets   104

Chapter VI. Markets in History   131

Chapter VII. Politics and the Economy   158

Chapter VIII. Law and the Economy   189

Chapter IX. Culture and Economic Development   218

Chapter X. Culture, Trust, and Consumption   241

Chapter XI. Gender and the Economy   259

Chapter XII. The Cat's Dilemma and Other Questions
for Economic Sociologists   283

REFERENCES   305

INDEX   357

Tables and Figures

Tables

2.1. The Different "Worlds of Justification," according to Boltanski and Thévenot   50

7.1. Type of Domination and Its Effect on the Rise of Rational Capitalism, according to Weber   170

7.2. Attitudes toward Various Forms of Government Activity in Some OECD Countries   172

7.3. The Relationship between Form of Domination, Type of Administration, and Means of Payment, according to Weber   179

7.4. Percentage of People in Poverty in Various OECD Countries, Pre- and Post-transfer Payments   182

8.1. Possible Variations in Property Rights: The Case of the Rural Industry in China   205

9.1. Reactions to the Pressure for Monetary Success in the United States   236

11.1. Time Spent on Household and Tasks by Full-Time Workers in the United States, Measured in Hours per Week, 1987   274

Figures

1.1. The Subject Area of Social Economics, according to Weber   15

1.2. From Economic Action to Economic Organizations, according to Weber   17

1.3. Different Ways of Organizing the Economy, according to Polanyi   29

2.1. Interest and Social Interaction, according to Coleman   46

3.1. Capitalism and Alternative Ways of Organizing the Economic Process and Economic Interests   58

3.2. The Different Types of Capitalism, according to Weber   61

3.3. Social Networks in Silicon Valley   69

6.1. The Athenian Agora around 400 B.C.   137

8.1. The Role of Law in Society: A Law-Centered View versus a Society-Centered View   191

8.2. The Subject Area of the Economic Sociology of Law,
     according to Weber   192
9.1. From Religious Ethic to Economic Ethic, or How to
     Make a Sociological Interest Analysis, according to
     The Protestant Ethic   231
11.1. Schematic Diagram of Women in Paid Employment
     by Life/Family Cycle Stages. France and Britain,
     about 1850   270

Preface

This book is intended as a general introduction to economic sociology, a field that is relatively new in the social sciences and whose importance is rapidly growing in the United States as well as in Europe. Economic sociology represents a promising type of analysis, and at the rate it has developed over the past ten years it could well become one of the key contenders in the twenty-first century for analyzing economic phenomena—ranking alongside neoclassical economics, game theory, and behavioral economics.

Economic sociology can be defined briefly as the application of the sociological tradition to economic phenomena in an attempt to explain these. Economic sociology shares most of the concerns and goals of economics. On one point, however, it differs sharply from conventional economics; and this is through its direct and strong focus on the role that social relations and social institutions play in the economy. To live in society means to be connected to other people and take part in its institutions—and this deeply affects the economic actions of all economic actors. It affects the way in which such actions turn out individually as well as in aggregate. The patterns of social interaction and the institutions that people create and use in their attempts to make a living and a profit are what constitute the main subject area of economic sociology. As in game theory, there is no isolated *homo economicus* in sociology—only people who interact with one another in their attempts to realize their interests.

My two main goals in writing this book have been to introduce a new perspective into economic sociology and to present its major concepts, ideas, and findings. The new perspective that I wish to introduce centers on the scope of the field: economic sociology should not be concerned exclusively with the impact of social relations on economic actions (which is currently its main concern), but also take *interests* into account, and more generally try to situate the analysis at an interest level, along the lines that Weber did in *The Protestant Ethic and the Spirit of Capitalism*. Indeed, Weber's famous study can be seen as a paradigm and a guide for how to proceed in economic sociology. One starts out by locating people's interests (in Weber's case, religious and economic interests), and then studies the social forces that affect these interests and what consequences this will have. Following the lead of *The Protestant Ethic* will make the analysis sharper as well as more realistic.

The approach I advocate in this book can be described as an attempt to center the analysis around *a sociological concept of interest*. As a quick illustration of what I mean by a sociological concept of interest, I will again refer to Weber, this time to a famous passage in his sociology of religion in which he uses the metaphor of human actions running along different tracks, even when they are inspired by similar motives. Weber's argument, more precisely, is that interests drive people's actions, but it is the way that the actors view the world (including their own interests) that will determine what general direction these actions will take. The passage reads as follows:

> Not ideas, but material and ideal interests, directly govern men's conduct. Yet very frequently the "world images" that have been created by "ideas" have, like switchmen, determined the tracks along which action has been pushed by the dynamic of interest ([1915] 1946b:280).

Weber's argument, I should add, represents only one of a number of different ways in which interests and social relations can be brought together in a sociological analysis. Other suggestions for how to proceed can be found in the works of Alexis de Tocqueville, James Coleman, Pierre Bourdieu, and many others. More generally, the idea that interests should be central to explanations of social behavior is something that has been argued for a very long time—by thinkers such as David Hume, Adam Smith, and John Stuart Mill. According to their analyses, many different types of interest exist—not only economic interests. Interests can oppose one another, block one another, reinforce one another, and so on. Institutions, from this perspective, are not to be understood as rules (which is the popular definition today) but as *distinct configurations of interests and social relations*. What these thinkers worked with was a flexible and powerful type of interest analysis, which it may be time to revive and make use of again. Their recipe for a good analysis was that one should first locate the interests of the actors, and then empirically explore and follow up on the hypotheses generated by this focus on interests. In brief, *follow the interests!*

I have made a conscious effort not to let my ideas about the centrality of interests interfere with my account of the different studies that have been produced in economic sociology. Quite a few of these studies, however, *do* take a stance on interests—they are for or against, openly or implicitly—and this has been noted and commented upon. Still, it is my hope that the reader will find a balanced and fair account of the many different types of work that are currently part of economic sociology.

At this particular moment, economic sociology is in a fluid state, which adds to the difficulty of properly summarizing and presenting its key findings and key concepts. This task has not been attempted before. The way I have chosen to proceed is reflected in the organization of this book. I first discuss the history of economic sociology: its major concepts and its major findings. This is followed by a discussion of capitalism, firms, and markets. The role of politics and law is then explored. The book continues with a presentation of the relationship between culture (including consumption) and the economy, and between gender and the economy. The last chapter is devoted to various questions that are, or should be, on the agenda of today's economic sociology, including the question of whether economic sociology should be a policy science.

Chapters 1 and 2—"The Classics in Economic Sociology" and "Contemporary Economic Sociology"—present the major works in both classical and contemporary economic sociology. In my discussion of classical economic sociology I concentrate on the contributions of Weber, Durkheim, and Simmel. New interpretations include an attempt to highlight the role of interests in the tradition of economic sociology as well as an introduction of Tocqueville as a major economic sociologist. The work of Bourdieu has been neglected in current economic sociology, and I try to change this by giving an account of his ideas. The major message in these two chapters is twofold: there exists a powerful tradition of economic sociology, and economic sociology should not focus exclusively on social relations, as it tends to do today, but also look at the role of interests.

In chapters 3 and 4—"Economic Organization" and "Firms"—I argue that much of economic life can be seen in terms of economic organization or how people, institutions, and material objects are connected to and disconnected from each other. Chapter 3 looks at the way in which the economy is organized on a large scale, from industrial districts to globalization. It also contains a model for conceptualizing capitalism from a sociological perspective. Chapter 4 centers around one particular form of economic organization that plays a key role in today's economy: the modern firm. Economic as well as sociological theories of the firm are presented and commented upon. The main theoretical point in these two chapters is that we cannot fully understand the dynamic of the different types of economic organization without realizing that their structures are determined by a combination of interests and social relations.

Chapter 5, "Economic and Sociological Approaches to Markets," discusses different theories about markets. While economists have mainly been interested in the way in which prices can be predicted, sociologists have tried to develop a theory of markets as social structures or institutions. Chapter 6, "Markets in History," seeks to add to the current state of the sociology of markets. I advocate the introduction of the concept of interest into the analysis and illustrate the potential strength of this concept with the help of historical material. A typology of markets throughout history is presented.

In chapter 7, "Politics and the Economy," I argue that we need an economic sociology of politics. Among the forms that this type of analysis should take are fiscal sociology and studies of the various attempts by political forces to direct the economy—by the state as well as by interest groups. This chapter is complemented by chapter 8, "Law and the Economy," in which I argue that economic sociologists have ignored the role of law in economic life, and that this neglect needs to be corrected. There is typically a legal dimension to economic phenomena, and this introduces a new layer into the analysis. I outline an agenda for an economic sociology of law, centered around such institutions as property, inheritance, and the firm as a legal actor. Law, I emphasize, may block, slow down, or accelerate economic growth.

The issue of culture and its relationship to the economy is discussed in two chapters: chapter 9, "Culture and Economic Development," and chapter 10, "Culture, Trust, and Consumption." No analysis in economic sociology is complete, I try to show, if it ignores culture—something that mainstream economic sociology does today. Culture is defined as values and sense-making. While economists typically ignore culture and take economic interests into account, economic sociologists who advocate a cultural approach tend to do exactly the opposite: they highlight the importance of culture, but disregard economic interests. I also argue that trust and consumption belong to a discussion of culture.

Chapter 11, "Gender and the Economy," notes that gender is largely ignored in current economic sociology, even though scholars among the various social sciences have produced an enormous amount of material to draw upon. Economic sociology has to address the question of how to incorporate the relevant parts of this huge material. I suggest that the following three themes are especially important: the household economy (centered around the idea of a unifying family interest), women and work in the labor market (centered around the idea of separate women's interests), and the role of emotions in the economy. I argue that emotions should not be seen as something that basically disturbs the normal workings of the economy, which is a common viewpoint today, but as an integral part of economic action. The last chapter, "The Cat's Dilemma and Other Questions for Economic Sociologists," introduces four key issues that need to be discussed, as I see it: topics which are currently neglected in economic sociology but which should be part of it; how to handle the issue of reflexivity in economic sociology; advantages and disadvantages with using the concept of interest in economic sociology; and what role economic sociology can play as a policy science. The main theoretical point in this book—the need to look at interests as well as at social relations—is summarized and discussed. Ways to avoid tautology and reductionism in this type of analysis are suggested.

Acknowledgments

Many people have helped me to write this book. First and foremost there is Mabel Berezin, to whom this book is dedicated, with all my love. I also would like to thank Peter Dougherty of Princeton University Press, who inspired the key thesis of this book many years ago. Peter is a truly great editor and knows exactly how to encourage an author. Kevin McInturff, also from the Press, helped with many practical matters. For excellent editing and help with the production of this book, I thank Linda Truilo and Ellen Foos.

A special mention must be made of three close friends and colleagues: Patrik Aspers, Mark Granovetter, and Mauro Zamboni. They are all hereby thanked! I would also like to thank the following people who all have been very helpful: Howard Aldrich, Reza Azarian, Jens Beckert, Rick Biernacki, Anne Boschini, John Campbell, Bruce Carruthers, Frank Dobbin, Malcolm Feeley, Magnus Haglunds, Susan Hanson, Johan Heilbron, Søren Jagd, Erik Ljungar, Thorbjørn Knudsen, Sarah McLanahan, Harry Makler, Robert K. Merton, Eva Meyerson Milgrom, Victor Nee, Trond Petersen, Tiziana Sardiello, Dick Scott, Neil Smelser, Philippe Steiner, Ryszard Szulkin, Michael Woolcock, Hans and Karin Zetterberg, and Harriet Zuckerman.

I am also grateful to the Center for Advanced Study in the Behavioral Sciences in Stanford, where I spent the academic year 2001–02 and where I wrote the main part of this book. My financial support at the center came from Center General Funds and The William and Flora Hewlett Foundation Grant #2000-5633. The center's two librarians, Cynthia Ziegler and Emma Raub, provided me with patient and excellent service. Doug McAdam was a terrific host. The book was completed during my first few months at Cornell University, where I have the pleasure of working with Victor Nee and the Center for the Study of Economy and Society.

While this book was being written my father, Hans Swedberg, died. This took place on July 4, 2001 in Stockholm. I loved him deeply and I often think of him.

Some of the material for chapters 5 and 6 draws on the author's "Markets in Society," forthcoming in Neil Smelser and Richard Swedberg (eds.), *The Handbook of Economic Sociology*, 2nd ed. (Princeton and New York: Princeton University Press and Russell Sage Foundation). A somewhat different version of chapter 8 has been published as "The Case for an Economic Sociology" in volume 10 (2002) of *Theory and Society*.

May 2002, Stanford

PRINCIPLES OF ECONOMIC SOCIOLOGY

I

The Classics in Economic Sociology

THERE exists a rich and colorful tradition of economic sociology, which roughly began around the turn of the twentieth century and continues till today. This tradition has generated a number of helpful concepts and ideas as well as interesting research results, which this and the following chapter seek to briefly present and set in perspective. Economic sociology has peaked twice since its birth: in 1890–1920, with the founders of sociology (who were all interested in and wrote on the economy), and today, from the early 1980s and onward. (For the history of economic sociology, see Swedberg 1987, 1997; Gislain and Steiner 1995). A small number of important works in economic sociology—by economists as well as sociologists—was produced during the time between these two periods, from 1920 to the mid-1980s.

The main thesis of this chapter, and of this book as a whole, is as follows: in order to produce a powerful economic sociology we have to *combine* the analysis of economic interests with an analysis of social relations. From this perspective, institutions can be understood as distinct configurations of interests and social relations, which are typically of such importance that they are enforced by law. Many of the classic works in economic sociology, as I shall also try to show, hold a similar view of the need to use the concept of interest in analyzing the economy.

Since my suggestion about the need to combine interests and social relations deviates from the existing paradigm in economic sociology, a few words will be said in the next section about the concept of interest as it has been used in social theory. This may seem as something of a detour, but the reason for beginning with a general section on interests is that it will help explain why this concept is so useful. This presentation will then be followed by a section on what I call classical economic sociology and that primarily discusses the work of Tocqueville, Marx, Weber, Durkheim and Simmel. A few pages will be devoted to what happened after the classics and before the current revival (which started in the 1980s). The key persons during this period are Schumpeter, Polanyi, and Parsons.

The Role of Interest in Social Analysis

Ever since the Middle Ages, one form or another of what can be called interest analysis has been widely used to study society in the

West. (The history of this type of analysis is little known; see, however, Orth et al. 1982; Hirschman 1986; Holmes 1990; Peillon 1990.) The term "interest" was originally economic in nature (as in "rate of interest") and can be found in such places as Roman law. During this early stage the term "interest" was restricted in meaning and held at best a peripheral place in the discourse of the time. This changed when the concept of interest started to be used in political life. During the seventeenth century interest became a fashionable concept, oscillating between a synonym for ruthless, Machiavellian behavior on the part of the rulers and simply a helpful way of analyzing people's behavior. It was during this time that the maxim "Interest Will Not Lie" became popular. References were also made to various group interests, such as "legal interests," "landed interests," and "monied interests" (Gunn 1968).

During the seventeenth century, especially in French moral philosophy, a psychological concept of interest was developed by people like La Rochefoucauld and Pascal (see Heilbron 1998). Some of the complexity that these authors brought to it can be illustrated by La Rochefoucauld's maxim "Self-interest blinds some, but enlightens others" ([1665] 1959:42). Several eighteenth-century philosophers, most importantly David Hume, were also fascinated by the role of interests in human affairs, as is evident from *A Treatise of Human Nature* (1739–40) as well as from *Essays* (1741). Hume broke, for example, with the idea that interests were somehow fixed, once and for all, and were the product of human nature and biology: "Though men be governed by interest, yet even interest itself, and all human affairs, are entirely governed by opinion" ([1741] 1987:51). On this point he differed from the French philosopher Hélvetius, who a little later stated that "as the physical world is ruled by the laws of movement, so is the moral universe ruled by laws of interest" (cited in Hirschman 1977:43).

That economists also found the concept of interest useful is clear from a number of passages in *The Wealth of Nations* (1776) by Adam Smith. The most famous of these reads as follows:

> It is not from the benevolence of the butcher, the brewer, or the baker, that we expect our dinner, but from their regard to their own interest. We address ourselves, not to their humanity but to their self-love, and never talk to them of our own necessities but of their advantages ([1776] 1976:26–7).

As is well known, Smith also suggests that individual interests somehow end up furthering the general interest, as if guided by "an invisible hand." But even if Smith was fascinated by the positive role of self-interest, he was also well aware that interests other than self-interest drive the individual. In the opening line of *The Theory of Moral*

Sentiments he notes, for example, that "However selfish soever man may be supposed, there are evidently some principles in his nature, which interest him in the fortune of others, and render their happiness necessary to him, though he derives nothing from it, except the pleasure of seeing it" ([1759] 1976:47).

By the nineteenth century the concept of interest made possible a flexible type of social analysis, with interests opposing one another, blocking one another, reinforcing one another, and so on. Individuals had their interests and so did groups; there was "the public interest" as well as the interests of each and every citizen. The concept of interest also plays a key role in the analysis of such subtle thinkers as John Stuart Mill and Tocqueville. Toward the end of the century, however, economists began to restrict the term to mean exclusively "economic interests" and eventually also to replace it with other terms, such as utility and preferences. Economic interest now became part of *homo economicus*, that is, of the isolated, all-knowing, and maximizing economic agent (see, e.g., Persky 1995). Instead of suggesting hypotheses to be explored empirically, the analysis now began as well as ended with (economic) interests. A restricted type of interest analysis, in brief, began to replace the rich and complex type of interest analysis that had been used during the earlier centuries. During the twentieth century this tendency solidified and is still the one that prevails in economics and, to a large extent, in social science as a whole.

One fact that is not mentioned in the histories of the concept of interest is that a *sociological concept of interest* was developed during the late nineteenth and the early twentieth centuries, especially in the works of Weber and Simmel. More will be said about this development later. Here it suffices to note that central to this idea is that interests can only be conceptualized, expressed, and realized in social terms and through social relations—a position that runs counter to that of modern economics.

My own view of interests is close to that of Weber, and I shall therefore start out by saying a few words about what is undoubtedly Weber's most famous statement on interests. It is to be found in a programmatic part of his work in the sociology of religion and has already been cited in the preface:

> Not ideas, but material and ideal interests, directly govern men's conduct. Yet very frequently the "world images" that have been created by "ideas" have, like switchmen, determined the tracks along which action has been pushed by the dynamic of interest ([1915] 1946b:280).

According to this quote, interests drive people's actions but the social element (here, religion) determines what expression and direction these actions will take. Interests can be material as well as ideal (that is, religious, political, and so on). All interests are social in the following two ways: they are part of the society into which the individual is born; and the individual has to take other actors into account when she tries to realize her interests.

There are several advantages to using the concept of interest in a sociological analysis of the economy. For one thing, there is a chance that one would otherwise fail to understand *the strength* that underlies an action. What makes people go to work every day, and what drives each and every private corporation, is first and foremost economic interest. The concepts of power and power resources cover some of the same phenomena as interest, but by no means all. Secondly, interests may help to explain why one route of action was taken, rather than another. While some alternatives may be very attractive to the actor, due to her interests, others may have no interest at all. In other words, interests influence the decision of the actor, or her *choice*.

Similarly, by using the idea of economic interest a *dynamic* is brought into the analysis, which differs from the one that is driven exclusively by social interaction. Interests can oppose each other, they can reinforce each other, and so on. Economic interests, a little like sexual interests, are often to be found somewhere in the background, waiting for an opportunity to be realized. And if they are repressed, they may still pop up—a bit like a black market usually appears if the state forbids the sale of an item. Finally, through the concept of interest, we can establish a natural link not only to the biological side of human beings but also to their environment. Economic interests are ultimately rooted in the needs of the human organism and its dependence on the environment.

Equally as important as introducing the concept of economic interest into economic sociology, I argue, is to avoid the stance of mainstream economics vis-à-vis interests, which is usually profoundly asociological and even naturalistic in nature. Several points need to be made here. First, the notion of interest that I am advocating is close to what Alfred Schutz calls a "construct of the second degree," namely an analytical concept that has been invented by the social scientist to analyze social reality ([1953] 1971:6). The concept of interest, in other words, is an analytical tool.

Second, in realizing her interests the actor has to orient herself to other actors in various ways; the social structure must consequently always be part of the analysis. Third, as opposed to the economists, for whom there only exists one type of interest (which, by assumption, is fully understood by the maximizing economic actor), economic sociology is free to draw on the rich tradition of interest analysis, which goes far back in Western thought. According to this

"Good question. Yes, we have your best interests at heart."

tradition, many different types of interests exist, and these can all enter into different combinations with one another. Finally, in economics the concept of interest is sometimes used as a tautology, and this is obviously something that has to be avoided in a sociological interest analysis.

Once the difference has been properly outlined between the sociological concept of interest and the type of interest that can be found in mainstream economics, it should immediately be emphasized that an extra advantage to using the concept of interest for economic sociologists is precisely that it allows for a natural dialogue with the economists. In economics the concept of interest has been at the very center of the analysis since the days of Adam Smith. If there ever is to be a unified social science of economics, the concept of interest—together with the idea of social interaction—is likely to be its foundation (for further discussion of the concept of interest in sociology, see pp. 297–99).

Classical Economic Sociology and Its Predecessors

The first use of the term "economic sociology" is thought to have occurred in 1879, when it appeared in a work by British economist Jevons ([1879] 1965:xvii). The term was then taken over by the sociologists, and it can be found in the works of Durkheim and Weber during the period 1890–1920 (for example, "*sociologie économique,*" "*Wirtschaftssoziologie*"). It was also during these decades that classical economic sociology was born, in such works as *The Division of Labor in Society* (1893) by Durkheim, *The Philosophy of Money* (1900) by Simmel, and—by far most importantly—*Economy and Society* (written between 1908 and 1920) by Weber. What characterizes classical economic sociology, as I shall call it, is primarily the following: First, there was a sense among Weber and his colleagues of being pioneers and of constructing a new type of analysis. Secondly, there was a focus on such fundamental questions as, What is the role of the economy in society? How does the sociological analysis of the economy differ from that of the economists? To this must be added that there was also an attempt to size up capitalism and understand its impact on society—"the great transformation," as Polanyi put it.

In hindsight there are clearly several works from before the 1890–1920 period that in one way or another prefigure some of the insights of economic sociology. Important reflections on trade and other economic phenomena can, for example, be found in *The Spirit of the Laws* (1748) by Montesquieu. This work also contains a pioneering comparative analysis of the way in which economic phenomena are influenced by different political regimes (republics, monarchies, and despotic states). The role of labor in society is central to the work of Saint-Simon (1760–1825), who also helped to popularize the term "industrialism" (1964). The only two figures before Weber who will be discussed here, however, are Tocqueville and Marx. Tocqueville is of special interest since his analysis of economic phenomena, including its sociological dimension, has attracted next to no attention. Marx is a towering figure in nineteenth-century thought and very much part of a tradition that helped to inspire the creation of economic sociology.

Alexis de Tocqueville

The first contributor to economic sociology whom I shall discuss— Alexis de Tocqueville (1805–59)—had been trained in law, and most of what he knew about economics came from his own studies as a young man (mainly of the work of Jean-Baptiste Say). Later in life he also would learn quite a bit about economics from conversation with friends such as John Stuart Mill and Nassau Senior. Tocqueville was mainly interested in politics, but in his analysis he typically covered all of society and often touched on economic topics. As one of his admirers, Joseph Schumpeter, expressed it: Tocqueville "painted to a considerable extent in economic colors" (1954:820). Tocqueville's most important works, in so far as his analysis of the economy goes, are his two major studies: *Democracy in America* (1835–40) and *The Old Régime and the French Revolution* (1856). Some additional information can also be found in Tocqueville's minor writings, such as "Memoir on Pauperism" (1835).

Democracy in America is important to economic sociology primarily for its analysis of American economic culture in the early nineteenth century and for its attempt to contrast aristocratic and democratic societies, in their political as well as in their economic dimensions. Coming from a society that was highly regulated by the state, Tocqueville marveled at the United States, which he traversed for nine months in 1831–32. The citizens in this "commercial nation" had a totally different attitude to risk than the Europeans; they were also much more tolerant of economic failures and bankruptcies. When Tocqueville described the relationship of Americans to economic matters, he often used expressions that mixed interests with emotions: "commercial passions," "love of wealth" and the like. This did not mean that the Americans were not rational. In a lengthy discussion of what he called "the principle of self-interest rightly understood" Tocqueville argued that Americans thought that it was in their self-interest to behave morally and in accordance with religion—and that this taught them patience as well as made them methodical and efficient in economic affairs: "It is held as a truth that man serves himself in serving his fellow creatures and that his private interest is to do right" ([1835–40] 1945, 2:129). Tocqueville often referred to different types of interest in *Democracy in America*, such as "self-interest," "public interest," "material interest," and so on. He also argued that while the family was the key unit in aristocratic societies, in democratic societies it is the individual with her interests.

Tocqueville was deeply fascinated by the role that organizations played in the United States, again in contrast to France, where the state controlled the right to create organizations. Everywhere he traveled he found organizations—religious organizations, political organizations, economic organizations, and so on. "Americans of all ages, all conditions and all dispositions constantly form organizations" ([1835–40] 1945, 2:114). Tocqueville believed that organizations could play a crucial role in turning democratic societies in a progressive direction, by mediating between the isolated individual and the state. He also observed that by taking part in various voluntary organizations, Americans acquired useful knowledge that they later could use when they wanted to start up an economic organization of their own. On this point Tocqueville is close to some contemporary arguments about social capital.

Let me stress that the dynamic economic culture that Tocqueville encountered in the United States was limited to states without slavery. Wherever slavery was permitted, there was little economic progress. One of the most striking passages in *Democracy in America* describes what Tocqueville saw when he sailed the Ohio River, with Kentucky on one side, and Ohio on the other:

Upon the left bank of the stream the population is sparse; from time to time one descries a troop of slaves moving slowly in the half-desert fields; the primeval forest reappears at every turn; society seems to be asleep, man to be idle, and nature alone offers a scene of activity and life.

From the right bank, on the contrary, a confused hum is heard, which proclaims afar the presence of industry; the fields are covered with abundant harvests; the elegance of the dwellings announces the taste and activity of laborers; and man appears to be in the enjoyment of that wealth and contentment which is the reward of labor. . . .

Upon the left bank of the Ohio labor is confounded with the idea of slavery; while upon the right bank it is identified with that of prosperity and improvement; on the one side it is degraded, on the other it is honored ([1835–40] 1945, 1:376–77).

Also *The Old Régime and the French Revolution* is of much interest to economic sociology, especially for its analysis of taxation and the Physiocrats. Throughout the centuries the French state was always on the lookout for new income and displayed much ingenuity in this pursuit. The result was a multitude of different taxes and fees, levied especially on the nonprivileged strata. An important and unanticipated consequence of freeing the aristocracy from certain taxes and burdens, Tocqueville notes, was resentment, especially among the peasants; and in general the system of taxation set the different classes against one another. Tocqueville also notes that taxes and loans were functional alternatives for the ruler. His portrait of the Physiocrats, finally, has more to say about the political ideals of their leader, Quesnay, and his colleagues than about their economic ideas; and it is precisely in this that his analysis is innovative. The Physiocrats, as it turns out, greatly admired the Chinese bureaucracy, and basically wanted to create a centralized state—exactly what Tocqueville feared and detested.

Karl Marx

The second major predecessor to economic sociology was Karl Marx (1818–83). Like Tocqueville, Marx had been trained in law (and in philosophy), but was self-taught in economics. As opposed to his French contemporary, however, Marx was obsessed with the role of the economy in society and developed a theory in which the economy determines the general evolution of society. What drives people in their everyday lives, Marx argues, is material interest, and this also determines the structure and evolution of society at large. While Marx wanted to develop a strictly scientific approach to society, his ideas were infused by his political desire to change the world. "The philosophers have only *interpreted* the world, in various ways," he wrote in his youth, "the point, however, is to change it" ([1845] 1978:145). The end result was Marxism—a mixture of social science and political ideology, wielded together into a single doctrine.

For a variety of reasons it is obvious that economic sociology cannot accept Marxism on its own terms. Apart from the errors common to most of nineteenth-century thought, Marx's work is much too tendentious and dogmatic to be adopted as a whole. The task that confronts economic sociology today is instead to decide which parts of Marxism can be helpful, and then extract these. In doing so, it may be useful to follow the suggestion of Schumpeter, and distinguish among Marx as a sociologist, an economist, and a revolutionary (Schumpeter [1942] 1994:1–58). By proceeding in this manner, the unity of Marx's thought is no doubt destroyed, as Schumpeter notes. But a wholesale rejection of Marx is avoided, and what is relevant in his work to economic sociology can be salvaged.

As of today, very little effort has been made to extract those parts of Marx's work that may be helpful to economic sociology; and what follows should therefore be seen as preliminary in nature. Marx's point of departure, in his mature work, is labor and production. People have to work in order to live, and this is something that is true for *all* societies. "Labor," to cite a central passage in *Capital*, "is a necessary condition, independent of all forms of society, for the existence of the human race" (Marx [1867] 1906:50). Material interests are universal; and labor is social rather than individual in nature since people have to cooperate with one another in order to survive.

Marx severely criticized the economists for their use of the isolated individual in their analyses; and he sometimes spoke of "social individuals" to make it clear that the individual is always connected to other people (e.g., Marx [1857–58] 1973:84–85). The most important interests are similarly of a collective nature—what Marx calls "class interests." These interests, however, will be effective only if people recognize themselves as belonging to a certain class. Marx notes, for example, in *The Eighteenth Brumaire of Louis Bonaparte* that during the mid-nineteenth century the peasants were "incapable of enforcing their class interest. . . . The identity of their interests begets no unity . . . they form no class" ([1852] 1950:109).

Marx severely criticized Adam Smith's idea that individual economic interests somehow come together and further the general interest of society, as through "an invisible hand." It is rather the case, according to Marx, that classes fight each other with such ferocity that history becomes written in "letters of blood and fire" ([1867] 1906: 786). Bourgeois society is no exception on this score since it encourages "the most violent, mean and malignant passions of the human heart, the Furies of private interest" (15).

In works such as *The Manifesto of the Communist Party* (1848; co-authored with Friedrich Engels), *Grundrisse* (1857–58), *A Contribution to the Critique of Political Economy* (1859), and *Capital* (1867), Marx traces the history of the class struggle, from early times to the future that he envisions. In a famous formulation from the 1850s, Marx states that at a certain stage the "relations of production" enter into conflict with "the forces of production," and the result is revolution and passage to a new "mode of production" ([1859] 1970:21). In *Capital*, Marx writes that he has laid bare "the economic law of motion of modern society," and that this law works "with iron necessity towards inevitable results" ([1867] 1906:13–4).

Economics, philosophy, and law do not represent independent attempts to understand human society, as its practitioners typically believe, according to Marx, but are part of the class struggle and reflect what goes on in the economy. They are part of society's "superstructure," as opposed to its "base" (e.g., Marx [1859] 1970:21). Another way to phrase this would be to say that economics, philosophy, and law express the interests of various classes, but since the practitioners of these disciplines are not aware of this, their areas of study tend to become "ideology."

A positive quality to Marx's approach is his realism and insight when it comes to understanding the strength with which people have been willing to fight for their material interests throughout history. He has also contributed to the understanding of the way in which large groups of people, with similar economic interests, tend to unite under certain circumstances in an attempt to realize their interests. Having effectively linked the concept of class to the economic structure of the economy, he moved without effort from the individual worker to capitalism as a whole. Marx also worked very hard to keep up with economics, and he should be credited with having discovered many areas of social behavior that, contrary to what was thought at the time, are indeed influenced by economic interests. Law, economics, philosophy, and so on are all influenced by economic forces—even if there is more to the story than that.

On the negative side, from the viewpoint of economic sociology, Marx severely underestimated the role that interests other than economic ones play in economic life. His notion that economic interests *in the last hand* determine what goes on in society is impossible to defend. "Social structures, types and attitudes are coins that do not readily melt," as Schumpeter notes in *Capitalism, Socialism and Democracy* ([1942] 1994:12). Marx's attempt, finally, to turn his analysis into a philosophy of history is also unacceptable from the viewpoint of modern economic sociology. There is quite a distance, in other words, between Marx's work and that of economic sociology.

Max Weber

Among the classic authors in economic sociology Max Weber (1864–1920) occupies a unique place. It was Weber who made the first sustained attempt to develop a distinct economic sociology—both to lay its theoretical foundation and to carry out empirical studies with its help (Swedberg 1998). His experience as a professor of economics for many years was no doubt helpful in these efforts. Also very important is the economic as well as social nature of the major research task that occupied Weber's mind throughout his career, namely to understand the origin and nature of modern capitalism. In his own work, Weber drew heavily on the general interest analysis of his time—which he also did much to improve, mainly by making it more sociological.

Weber's academic training was broad in nature, and its main emphasis was on law, with history of law as his specialty. He wrote two dissertations, as was necessary at the time to qualify for a university position in Germany—one on medieval trading corporations and another on the sale of land in early Rome. His adviser for the first dissertation was Levin Goldschmidt, the foremost expert in the nineteenth century on the history of commercial law; and for the other August Meitzen, a well-known historian of agriculture. Both dissertations, it should be noted, covered developments that were crucial to the rise of capitalism: the invention of the firm and the emergence of private property in land.

Weber's two dissertations, in combination with a commissioned study of rural workers, caught the attention of several economists, and in the early 1890s he was offered a position in economics ("political economy and finance"), first in Freiburg and then in Heidelberg. In this capacity he taught a number of courses in economics, even though he primarily published in economic history and on policy questions. Weber wrote, for example, voluminously on the new stock exchange legislation in Germany, which represented a hotly contested subject around the turn of the century (Weber 1999, [1894–96] 2000). A detailed outline for one of Weber's introductory courses in economics has also survived, and it shows that Weber was very familiar with both the analytical tradition of British economics and the social-historical approach of German economics (Weber [1898] 1990). For theoretical tasks, the analytical tradition was very helpful, Weber argued, but once the analysis dealt with empirical topics, it had to be supplemented with insights from the historical tradition.

Toward the end of the 1890s Weber fell ill, and for the next twenty years he would work as a private scholar. It was during these years that he produced his most celebrated study, *The Protestant Ethic and the Spirit of Capitalism* (1904–05), as well as a series of related studies of the economic ethics of the world religions. In 1908 Weber accepted a position as chief editor of a giant handbook of economics, to which a number of prominent German and Austrian economists agreed to contribute, *Grundriss der Sozialökonomik* (*Fundamentals of Social Economics*). From the very beginning Weber set aside the topic of "economy and society" for himself, to complement such subjects as "economy and technology" as well as "economy and population." The work that today is known as *Economy and Society* consists, in its current English version, of material that Weber had intended for publication and of various manuscripts that were found after his death, which the editors of Weber's work erroneously thought should be part of it (for the history behind *Economy and Society*, see, e.g., Mommsen 2000). Just before his death in 1920 Weber had sent off the first four chapters of part 1 to the printer; the rest of the material in *Economy and Society* he would in all likelihood have revised, rewritten, or discarded (Weber [1922] 1978:1–307).

In 1919–20 Weber also taught a course in economic history, which was pieced back together after his death on the basis of students' notes and which today is known as *General Economic History*. Though primarily a work of economic history, *General Economic History* ([1923] 1981) contains much interesting material for the economic sociologist and can be read as a complement to the difficult theoretical chapter on economic sociology in *Economy and Society* (chapter 2, "Sociological Categories of Economic Action").

Much of what Weber wrote in economic sociology can be found in the following two works: *Economy and Society* (1922) and *Collected Essays in the Sociology of Religion* (1920–21). The latter contains *The Protestant Ethic* (in a revised version from 1920), "The Protestant Sects and the Spirit of Capitalism" (1906; rev. 1919–20), and voluminous writings on the economic ethics of the world religions, including *The Religion of China* ([1920] 1951), *The Religion of India* ([1921] 1958), *Ancient Judaism* ([1921] 1952), and a few other texts (see Weber [1920] 1958, [1915] 1946a, [1915] 1946b). According to Weber, the material in *Collected Essays* falls primarily in the sociology of religion but is also of interest to economic sociology. The most important single study is no doubt *The Protestant Ethic* (for a more detailed discussion, see chapter 9).

The quotation that was cited in the preface on how ideal and material interests drive people's actions, but on tracks laid by ideas, comes from *Collected Essays in the Sociology of Religion* and summarizes the way in which Weber uses the concept of interest to understand religion. *The Protestant Ethic* is, for example, centered around an interest analysis of this type, and this is what gives the study its special flavor. The individual believer in ascetic Protestantism is driven by a desire to be saved (a religious interest) and acts accordingly. In doing so, she follows "the tracks" laid out by the worldview of her religion. For various reasons the individual eventually comes to believe that secular work, carried out in a methodical manner, represents a means to salvation—and when this happens, her religious interest combines with her economic interest. The result of these two interests coming together represents, on a collective level, an immensely powerful concentration of human energy, which helps to shatter the hold of traditional religion over people's lives and to release the spirit of modern capitalism.

While he was writing *The Protestant Ethic*, Weber published an essay that nicely summarizes the theoretical stance in his early analysis of the economy, "'Objectivity' in Social Science and Social Policy" ([1904] 1949). Some of the concepts and ideas that are introduced in this essay are still very useful today, such as the idea that the science of economics should be broad and umbrella-like in character (*Sozialökonomik*; 64–65). "Social economics," according to this view, should not only include economic theory but also economic history and economic sociology.

Weber argues that economic analysis should not only cover "economic phenomena" but also "economically relevant phenomena" and "economically conditioned phenomena" ([1904] 1949:64–65; see figure 1.1). Economic phenomena consist of economic norms and institutions, which are often deliberately created for economic ends and are primarily significant to people because of their economic aspect. Examples include corporations, banks, and stock exchanges. Economically relevant phenomena are noneconomic phenomena that may have an impact on economic phenomena. A paradigmatic example is ascetic Protestantism, as analyzed in *The Protestant Ethic*. Economically conditioned phenomena, finally, are phenomena that to some extent are influenced by economic phenomena. The type of religion that a group tends to adopt is, for example, partly dependent on what kind of work its members do. While economic theory can only handle economic phenomena (in their rational version), economic history

"Religious freedom is my immediate goal, but my
long-range plan is to go into real estate."

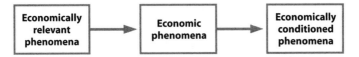

Figure 1.1. The Subject Area of Social Economics, according to Weber.
Note: In his early work Weber saw the study of economics (*Sozialökonomik*) as consisting of the following three parts: the study of the economy ("economic phenomena"), phenomena that influence the economy ("economically relevant phenomena"), and phenomena that are partly influenced by the economy ("economically conditioned phenomena").
Source: Max Weber, "'Objectivity' in Social Science and Social Policy," pp. 64–65 in *Essays in the Methodology of the Social Sciences* (New York: Free Press, 1949).

and economic sociology can also deal with economically conditioned phenomena and economically relevant phenomena.

A somewhat different approach, both to economic sociology and to interests, can be found in *Economy and Society* ([1922] 1978), especially in its key chapter (63–211) on theoretical economic sociology, which Weber wrote in 1919–20. *Economy and Society* represents first and foremost an attempt by Weber to develop a new and stringent approach to sociology; and especially two of the concepts he discusses here are important theoretical building blocks in this effort. These are "social action" and "order" (*Ordnung*). The former consists of two parts: "action," which is defined as behavior invested with a meaning, and "social," which means that the action is oriented to some other actor. An order comes into being when social actions are repeated over a period of time and come to be seen as objective. Orders are also often surrounded by various sanctions, which gives them additional stability and permanency. Economists study pure economic action, which is an action exclusively driven by economic interests—or "desire for utilities," in Weber's formulation ([1922] 1978:63). Economic sociologists, on the other hand, study *social* economic action, or action that is driven by economic interests *and* oriented to other actors. Social economic actions are not only driven by economic interest but by tradition and emotions as well.

If for a moment one disregards single actions, Weber says, and instead focuses on empirical uniformities, it is possible to distinguish three different types: those inspired by "custom" (including "habit"), "convention" (norm), and "interest" ([1922] 1978:29–36). Actions that are "determined by interest" (*Interessenlage*) are defined by Weber as instrumental in nature and oriented to identical expectations. They presuppose, in other words, a social setting where other actors think in the same instrumental way. One example of this would be the modern market, where each actor is instrumentally rational and counts on everybody else to be rational as well.

Weber strongly emphasizes that interests are always subjectively perceived; there exist no "objective" interests beyond the individual actor. In a typical sentence he speaks of "[the] interests of the actors as they themselves are aware of them" ([1922] 1978:30; for the role of meaning in the constitution of economic phenomena, see, e.g., Weber [1907] 1977:109; cf. [1922] 1978:98). Weber also notes that when several individuals behave in an instrumental manner, in relation to their individual interests, this typically results in collective patterns of behavior that are considerably more stable than when norms are imposed by an authority. It is, for example, difficult to make people do something that goes against their economic interests.

Economic actions of two actors who are oriented to one another, Weber argues, constitute an economic relationship. These relationships can take various expressions, including conflict, competition, and attempts to impose one's will on the other (power). If two or more actors are held together by a sense of belonging, their relationship is "communal"; and if they are held together by interest, it is "associative" ([1922] 1978:38–43). Economic relationships (as all social relationships) can also be open or closed. Property, for example, represents a special form of a closed economic relationship.

Economic organizations constitute another important form of closed economic relationships; and Weber introduces a full typology of different economic organizations. This typology ranges from purely economic organizations to those that have as their main task to regulate economic affairs, such as trade unions (see figure 1.2). Weber attaches especially great importance to the role of the firm in capitalism, which he sees as a revolutionary force.

A market, like many other economic phenomena, is centered around a conflict of economic interests—in this case primarily between sellers and buyers (Weber [1922] 1978:635–40). But exchange is not all there is to a market, according to Weber; there is also competition. Competitors must first fight it out to see who will be the final seller and the final buyer ("struggle between competitors"). It is only when this struggle has been settled that the scene is set for the exchange itself ("struggle over the exchange"). Only rational capitalism is centered around the modern type of market (164–66). In so-called political capitalism the key to profit making is that the political authority grants a favor or in some other way assists private economic interests. Traditional commercial capitalism consists of small-scale trading, in money

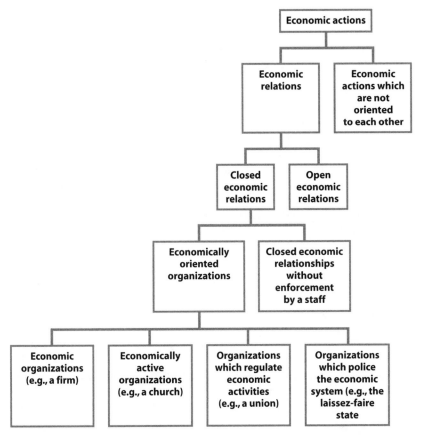

Figure 1.2. From Economic Action to Economic Organizations, according to Weber.

Note: In *Economy and Society* Weber constructs his economic sociology in a systematic manner, starting from economic action and continuing via economic relations to economic organizations.

Source: Max Weber, *Economy and Society: An Outline of Interpretive Sociology* (Berkeley: University of California Press, [1922] 1978), 48–50, 74–75, 340–43.

or merchandise. Rational capitalism, as opposed to the other two forms of capitalism, has emerged only in the West.

This brief overview of Weber's economic sociology is supplemented with several detailed accounts elsewhere in this book. My own opinion is that Weber's work is so rich and complex that it should be experienced firsthand; there is simply no good substitute for exploring his work on one's own. The three texts that I have found to be the most useful in economic sociology are *The Protestant Ethic, Economy and Society,* and *General Economic History.*

Emile Durkheim

It is clear that Emile Durkheim (1858–1917), compared to Weber, knew less about economics, wrote less on economic topics, and in general made less of a contribution to economic sociology. Such a summary, however, fails to signal the most important fact about Durkheim's work in this context, namely that it is deeply original and still largely unexplored in light of economic sociology (e.g., Steiner 1992, forthcoming). While Durkheim was no expert on economics and never taught economics, he had nonetheless studied many of the major works in the field, such as those by Adam Smith, Mill, Say, Sismondi, Schmoller, and Wagner. While none of Durkheim's own studies can be termed a work exclusively in economic sociology, many of them nonetheless touch on economic topics (see especially *The Division of Labor in Society* [1893] 1984 and *Professional Ethics and Civic Morals* [1950] 1983).

Durkheim also strongly supported the project of developing a *sociologie économique* by encouraging some of his students to specialize in this area, and by routinely including a section on economic sociology in his journal *L'Année Sociologique.* In one of Durkheim's articles on the tasks of sociology and its various subfields, he gives the following definition of economic sociology:

> Finally there are the economic institutions: institutions relating to the production of wealth (serfdom, tenant farming, corporate organization, production in factories, in mills, at home, and so on), institutions relating to exchange (commercial organization, markets, stock exchanges, and so on), institutions relating to distribution (rent, interest, salaries, and so on). They form the subject matter of *economic sociology* ([1909] 1978:80).

Even if none of Durkheim's major works, to repeat, can be labeled a study in economic sociology, the one that comes the closest to this is his doctoral dissertation, *The Division of Labor in Society* ([1893] 1984). Its central argument is that Western society has developed from being undifferentiated to having an advanced division of labor. Economists such as Adam Smith, Durkheim emphasizes, view the division of labor exclusively as an economic phenomenon and are especially fascinated by the increase in production that it entails. What the economists fail to see, however, is the social dimension of the division of labor—how it helps to integrate society and make it cohesive, by creating a multitude of dependencies.

As society evolves toward a more advanced division of labor, the legal system also changes. Having been predominantly repressive in nature, and having drawn on penal law, it now becomes restitutory and draws on contract law. In discussing the contract, Durkheim also points out the illusion in believing, as Herbert Spencer does, that a society can function if all individuals simply follow their private interests and contract accordingly. Durkheim notes that "if mutual interest draws men closer, it is never more than for a few moments. . . . [S]elf-interest is the least constant in the world" ([1893] 1984:152). Spencer also misunderstands the nature of the contract. A contract, according to Durkheim, would not be effective in a society where self-interested individuals are allowed to do whatever they want, but only in a society where self-interest is restrained and subordinated to society as a whole. "The contract is not sufficient by itself, but is only possible because of the regulation of contracts, which is social in origin" (162).

A major concern of Durkheim in *The Division of Labor in Society* is that economic advances in Western countries such as France during the late 19th century may wreck society by letting loose individual greed. In Durkheim's work this issue is often cast in terms of the private interest versus the general interest. It is, for example, argued that "subordination of the particular to the general interest is the very well-spring of all moral activity" ([1893] 1984:xliii). In *Suicide* Durkheim also notes that unless the state or some other agency representing the general interest can step in and regulate economic life, the result will be "economic anomie" ([1897] 1951:246, 259). People need rules and norms in order to guide their economic actions, and they react very negatively to anomic or anarchic situations. Suicide, for example, does not only increase when the economy suddenly turns downward, but also when it turns *upward*.

In many of Durkheim's works, including *The Rules of Sociological Method* (1895), one can find sharp attacks on mainstream economics. Throughout his academic career Durkheim firmly believed that if economics were ever to become scientific, it would have to become a branch of sociology. He criticized the idea of *homo economicus* on the ground that it is impossible to separate the economic element from social life and ignore the role of society. As opposed to economic man, he writes, "real man—the man whom we all know and whom we all are—is complex in a different way: he is of a time, of a country; he has a family, a city, a fatherland, a religious and political faith; and all these factors and many others merge and combine in a thousand ways, converge in and interweave their influence without it being possible to say at first glance where one begins and the other ends" (Durkheim [1888] 1978:49–50). The point is not that the economists use an abstract approach, Durkheim emphasizes, but that they have picked the wrong abstractions:

> Is not the use of abstractions a legitimate tool of economics? No doubt—it is only that all abstractions are not equally correct. An abstraction consists of isolating a part of reality, not in making it disappear (1887:39).

Durkheim also attacks the economists for being nonempirical and thinking that one can figure out how the economy works by "a simple logical analysis" ([1895] 1964:24). Economists substitute their own ideas for empirical reality, he charges. They then draw conclusions from these—and present the result as applicable to the society that they chose *not* to study in the first place. Durkheim refers to this type of analysis as "the ideological tendency of economics" (25).

Durkheim's own recipe for a harmonious and well-functioning industrial society is known to most sociologists. Each industry should be organized into a number of corporations, in which the individual will find a true home. The individual will thrive because of the warmth that comes from being a member of a group—"a warmth that quickens or gives fresh life to each individual, which makes him disposed to empathize, causing selfishness to melt away" (Durkheim [1893] 1984:lii).

Durkheim was well aware of the role that interest plays in economic life, and in *The Elementary Forms of Religious Life* he stresses that "the principal incentive to economic activity has always been the private interest" (Durkheim [1912] 1965:390). This fact, however, does not mean that economic life is purely self-interested and devoid of morality: "We remain [in our economic affairs] in relation with others; the habits, ideas and tendencies which education has impressed upon us and which ordinarily preside over our relations can never be totally absent" (390). But even if this is the case, the social element has another source than the economy and will eventually be worn down and disappear if it is not periodically renewed. And it can only be renewed if people forget about the economy and come together in collective activities, just for the sake of being together. If this is not done, society will wither away—and eventually so will the economy.

Georg Simmel

It is not known to what extent Georg Simmel (1858–1918) was familiar with economics. He rarely used references in his works, and at the most there is an occasional mention of Adam Smith or Karl Marx in the text. It is also true that when Simmel discusses economic phenomena, they are often part of some larger, noneconomic phenomena that interested him, as is the case with Durkheim. Still, Simmel's work contains much that is of value to economic sociology. It is also true that Simmel's work—just like the works of Weber and Durkheim—is still very much unexplored in this respect.

One point illustrating this last statement is that Simmel's major sociological work, *Soziologie* (1908), contains an important analysis of interest. In the main theoretical chapter of this volume Simmel addresses the problem of what a sociological interest analysis should be like and why an analysis of interest is indispensable to sociology. Two of his most central propositions are that interests drive people to form social relations and that it is only through social relations that interests can be expressed. To cite *Soziologie*,

> Sociation is the form (realized in innumerable different ways) in which individuals grow together into a unity and within which their interests are realized. And it is on the basis of their interests—sensuous or ideal, momentary or lasting, conscious or unconscious, causal or teleological—that individuals form such units ([1908] 1971:24).

Another of Simmel's key propositions is that interests, including economic interests, can take a number of different social expressions:

> The identical interest may take on form in very different sociations. Economic interest [for example] is realized both in competition and in the planned organization of producers, in isolation from other groups and in fusion with them (26).

Soziologie also contains a number of suggestive analyses of economic phenomena, including competition. In a chapter on the role of the number of actors in social life, Simmel suggests, for example, that competition can take the form of *tertius gaudens* ("the third who benefits"). In this situation, which involves three actors, Actor A exploits the fact that actors B and C are competing for her favor—to buy or to sell something, for example. Competition is consequently not something that concerns only the competitors (actors B and C); it is also related to Actor A, the target of the competition.

There also exists another and much fuller section on competition in *Soziologie*, in which Simmel contrasts competition to conflict. While a conflict typically means a head-on confrontation between two actors, according to Simmel, competition implies parallel efforts, which means that society can benefit from the actions of both actors. Instead of destroying your opponent, as you do in a conflict, in competition you try to do exactly what your competitor does—only better. Simmel also emphasizes the link to the third actor (*tertius gaudens*) in this analysis, and notes how the skillful competitor always tries to figure out what the customer wants, in order to come out ahead of her rivals:

> Innumerable times it [that is, competition] achieves what usually only love can do: the divination of the innermost wishes of the other, even before he becomes aware of them. Antagonistic tension with his competitor sharpens the businessman's sensitivity to the tendencies of the public, even to the point of clairvoyance, in respect to future changes in the public's tastes, fashions, interests ([1908] 1955:62).

The Philosophy of Money (1900) is Simmel's second major sociological work, and it has a somewhat ambivalent status. Durkheim, for example, disapproved of it for its mix of genres, and, according to Weber, economists detested Simmel's way of dealing with economic topics (Frisby 1978; Durkheim [1902] 1980; Weber 1972). Even if it is true that Simmel mixes philosophical reflections with sociological observations in a somewhat idiosyncratic manner; that he draws heavily on anecdotes; and that he supplies no references or footnotes, *The Philosophy of Money* has nonetheless much to give if it is read on its own terms (e.g., Poggi 1993). Simmel's work contains, for example, many insightful reflections on the connection between money and authority, between money and emotions, and between money and trust.

The value of money, Simmel observes, typically extends only as far as the authority that guarantees it—or only within "the economic circle" ([1907] 1978:179–84). Money is also surrounded by various "economically important sentiments," such as "hope and fear, desire and anxiety" (171). Without trust, Simmel argues, society could simply not exist; and "in the same way, money transactions would collapse without trust" (179). In relation to money, he continues, trust consists of two elements. There is first of all the fact that because something has happened before, it is likely to be repeated in the future. People who accept a certain type of money today, for example, are likely to do so tomorrow. This type of trust Simmel calls "a weak form of inductive knowledge." But there is also another type of trust, which has no basis in experience and which can be characterized as a nonrational belief. This last type Simmel calls "quasi-religious faith," and he notes that it is present not only in money transactions but also in those involving credit.

After the Classics

While economic sociology got off to a great start with the classics, it declined after 1920 and would not return to full vigor until the 1980s.

Exactly why this is the case is somewhat unclear and in need of an explanation. One reason is probably that neither Weber nor Simmel had any students who were interested in economic sociology. It was different with Durkheim, who had several students who wrote on economic topics, although the Durkheimian type of economic sociology eventually declined as well.

The most outstanding study by one of Durkheim's students, it may be added, is *The Gift* (1925) by Marcel Mauss. This work contains the famous argument that a gift should not be mistaken for a one-way act of generosity, but implies an obligation to reciprocate. Mauss also comments on the history of the concept of interest and how its meaning has evolved over time:

> The very word "interest" is itself recent, originally an accounting technique: the Latin word *interest* was written on account books against the sums of interest that had to be collected. In ancient systems of morality of the most epicurean kind it is the good and pleasurable that is sought after, not material utility. The victory of rationalism and mercantilism was needed before the notions of profits and the individual, raised to the level of principles, were introduced. One can almost date—since Mandeville's *The Fable of the Bees* [1714, 1729]—the triumph of the notion of individual interest. Only with great difficulty and the use of periphrasis can these two words be translated into Latin, Greek, or Arabic ([1925] 1990:76).

But even if one is justified in talking of a decline in economic sociology during 1920–80, a small number of important studies were nonetheless produced during this period. Of great value to economic sociology are especiallly the studies of Joseph Schumpeter, Karl Polanyi, and Talcott Parsons (for a presentation of other sociologists' contributions during this period, see Swedberg 1987:42–62). All three produced their most important works while in the United States, but it is clear that their thinking had deep roots in European social thought.

Joseph Schumpeter

It is not possible to discuss the work of Joseph A. Schumpeter (1883–1950) without also saying something about the contribution that economists more generally have made to economic sociology. On the whole one can say that the work of several of the early economists is of great interest to economic sociology. One example is Alfred Marshall (1842–1924), whose analyses are all of much relevance to economic sociology ([1920] 1961, 1919; cf. Aspers 1999). There is also Vilfredo Pareto (1848–1923), with his famous sociological analyses of rentiers versus speculators and of business cycles and much more ([1916] 1963; cf. Schumpeter 1951; Aspers 2001b).

The work of Thorstein Veblen (1857–1929) sometimes appeared in sociological journals and is of much relevance to economic sociology. Veblen's most important contributions to economic sociology include his analyses of such topics as consumer behavior ("conspicuous consumption"), why industrialization in England slowed down ("the penalty of taking the lead"), and the shortcomings of neoclassical economics ([1899] 1973, [1915] 1966, [1919] 1990; cf. Tillman 1992). "A vested interest," in Veblen's memorable formulation, "is a marketable right to get something for nothing" (Veblen 1919:100). A final mention should also be made of Werner Sombart (1863–1941), a friend and colleague of Weber. Sombart wrote on the history of capitalism, on the economic temper of his time, and on the need for a "*verstehende* economics" (1902–27, 1930, 1935).

Each of these economists deserves more than a mere mention in a history of economic sociology, but for no one is this more true than for Joseph A. Schumpeter himself (e.g., Swedberg 1991a). Unlike any other economist, Schumpeter succeeded in spanning two periods in modern economics—the period around the turn of the century, when modern economics was born, and the period a few decades later, when it was mathematized and turned into what is known as "mainstream economics." Schumpeter similarly spanned two distinct periods in sociology, through his cooperation with Max Weber in the 1910s and with Talcott Parsons in the 1930s and '40s. Schumpeter is also unique among economists for talking explicitly about economic sociology and for trying to create a special place for it, next to economic theory and economic history. In his effort to open up economics to the other social sciences Schumpeter was clearly inspired by Weber and, like the latter, he referred to this broad type of economics as *Sozialökonomik* or "social economics."

At one point in his work Schumpeter says that while economic theory studies the mechanisms of economic behavior, economic sociology focuses on the institutions within which economic behavior takes place ([1949] 1951:286–87). In *History of Economic Analysis* Schumpeter phrases the same viewpoint in a different way:

> To use a felicitous phrase: economic analysis deals with the questions how people behave at any time and what the economic effects are they produce by so behaving; economic sociology deals with the question how they came to behave as they do. If we define human behavior widely enough so that it includes not only actions and motives and propensities but also the social institutions that are relevant to economic behavior such as government,

property inheritance, contract, and so on, that phrase really tells us all we need (1954:21).

Schumpeter produced three major studies in sociology. One of these is an article on social classes, which is still of interest today partly because of the way in which Schumpeter contrasts economists' use of the concept of class to that of sociologists ([1927] 1991). While economists see class mainly as a formal category, he argues, sociologists see it as a living reality. This is also the only place in Schumpeter's work where he directly links up his economic theory to his sociological analysis. Schumpeter does this by using his theory of entrepreneurs to explain the rise and fall of bourgeois families. As entrepreneurship fades away, after one or two generations, so do the wealth and the status of the family of the entrepreneur.

Schumpeter's second study is an article about the nature of imperialism ([1919] 1991), which stands up very well in comparison to those by Hobson and others. Schumpeter's basic idea is that imperialism is precapitalistic and deeply irrational in nature, and is essentially an expression of a warrior class or stratum that feels it must constantly conquer new areas or otherwise will fall back and lose power. Capitalism and imperialism, he says, have nothing in common. Any imperialism that exists today is a remnant of feudal times.

Schumpeter's third study in sociology is perhaps the most interesting one from the viewpoint of contemporary economic sociology: "The Crisis of the Tax State" (1918) and its content will be discussed in more detail as part of the analysis of the role of the state in the economy in chapter 7. Schumpeter himself characterized this article as a study in "fiscal sociology" (*Finanzsoziologie*), and the main thesis is that the finances of the state represent a privileged position from which to analyze its actions. As a motto for his study, Schumpeter cites the famous line of the father of fiscal sociology, economist Rudolf Goldscheid: "The budget is the skeleton of the state stripped of all misleading ideology" (Schumpeter [1918] 1991:100).

Capitalism, Socialism and Democracy (1942) was not seen as a work of sociology by Schumpeter himself, but its main thesis is nonetheless deeply sociological in nature: while the motor of capitalism is still intact, its institutional structure is weak and damaged, making it vulnerable and likely to be replaced by socialism. On this last point—the triumph of socialism over capitalism—Schumpeter was obviously wrong, and it is also true that his analysis of the forces that are undermining capitalism may seem odd and idiosyncratic to the contemporary reader. Schumpeter argues, for example, that intellectuals are allowed too much freedom to write what they want, and that the bourgeoisie had stopped having families with many children since these were seen as expensive. Nonetheless, Schumpeter should be given credit for suggesting that the way in which intellectuals behave, the way in which the modern family is structured, and so on, *do* have an impact on economic life. Several of the ideas of new institutional economics, it can be added, are to a large extent prefigured by Schumpeter. *Capitalism, Socialism and Democracy* is also shot through with sharp sociological observations about competition, monopoly, and, of course, the key topic of the whole study: *economic change*. With his usual stylistic flair and sense for the contradictory nature of reality Schumpeter referred to this last topic as *"creative destruction."*

The very heart of all Schumpeter's writings is the entrepreneur and how his actions affect the economy (1934: chap. 2). There is no doubt that Schumpeter himself viewed his theory of entrepreneurship as being part of economic theory. More precisely, he saw it as an attempt to create a totally new type of economic theory, which was to be much more dynamic than the one that Walras had created. Nonetheless, many of Schumpeter's ideas on entrepreneurship are sociological in nature and can enrich today's economic sociology. His central idea— that entrepreneurship can be defined as the putting together of a new combination of already existing resources—can easily be given a sociological slant. And so can his idea that the main enemies of the entrepreneur are the people who cling to tradition and resist innovation. Schumpeter's work on entrepreneurship has still much to give and deserves a place in the emerging sociology of entrepreneurship (e.g., Thornton 1999; Swedberg 2000b).

Karl Polanyi

Like many of the early figures in economic sociology, Karl Polanyi (1886–1964) lacked a formal education in economics (e.g., Polanyi-Levitt and Mendell 1987; Polanyi-Levitt 1990). Trained in law, Polanyi later taught himself economics (mainly of the Austrian kind) as well as economic history and economic anthropology. Though he was interdisciplinary in his approach, his main specialty was economic history, with an emphasis on preindustrial economies and nineteenth-century England. Though the work of Polanyi has become quite popular among contemporary economic sociologists, large parts of it are still unknown and other parts have not yet been fully assimilated.

Polanyi's most famous work is *The Great Transformation* (1944), conceived and written during World War II (e.g., North 1977; Block 2001). Its main thesis is that a revolutionary attempt was made in nineteenth-century England to introduce a totally new type of economy, in which everything was centered around the market. No outside authority, be it political or religious, should have any power in economic matters; everything was to be decided by the market ("the self-regulating market"). In the 1840s and 1850s a series of laws were introduced to turn this project into reality, and these transformed land and labor into common commodities to be bought and sold at will. Also, the value of money was taken away from the political authorities and handed over to the market. According to Polanyi, this way of proceeding could lead only to a catastrophe:

> Robbed of the protective covering of cultural institutions [through the operations of the market], human beings would perish from the effects of social exposure; they would die as the victims of acute social dislocation through vice, perversion, crime, and starvation. Nature would be reduced to its elements, neighborhoods and landscapes defiled, rivers polluted, military safety jeopardized, the power to produce food and raw materials destroyed ([1944] 1957:73).

When the negative effects of the market reforms became obvious during the second half of the nineteenth century, Polanyi continues, countermeasures were set in ("the double movement"). These, however, only helped to unbalance society further; and developments such as fascism in the twentieth century were ultimately to be traced back to the ill-fated attempt in mid-nineteenth-century England to turn everything over to the market.

Polanyi casts some of his analysis in *The Great Transformation* in interest terms and argues that in all societies, before the nineteenth century, the general interests of groups and societies ("social interests") had been much more important than the money interest of the individual ("economic interest"). "An all too narrow conception of interest," Polanyi emphasizes, "must in effect lead to a warped vision of social and political history, and no purely monetary definition of interest can leave room for that vital need for social protection" ([1944] 1957:154).

The theoretical, as opposed to the historical, part of *The Great Transformation* is centered around Polanyi's critique of economic theory and his concepts of "embeddedness" and "principles of behavior" (later changed to "forms of integration"). The fullest elaboration of this part of Polanyi's work is, however, not to be found in this work but in *Trade and Market in the Early Empires* (1957), especially in Polanyi's essay "The Economy as Instituted Process." Polanyi criticizes economic theory for being essentially "formal"—for exclusively focusing on choice, the means-end relationship, and the alleged scarcity of things. There is also the "economistic fallacy," or the tendency in economics to equate the economy exclusively with the market ([1944] 1957:270). To the formal concept of economics Polanyi counterposes a "substantive" concept of economics, which is grounded in reality and not in logic. "The substantive meaning of *economic* derives from man's dependence for his living upon nature and his fellows" ([1957] 1971:243). While the notion of economic interest is directly linked to "the livelihood of man" in substantive economics, it is a purely artificial construction in formal economics (1977).

The most famous concept that is associated with Polanyi's work these days is "embeddedness," and it should therefore be pointed out that Polanyi used this concept in a different way than it is typically used today (cf. Barber 1995). According to the current use, an economic action is in principle always "embedded" in some form or another of social structure. According to Polanyi, on the other hand, economic actions become destructive when they are "disembedded," or not governed by social or noneconomic authorities. The real problem with capitalism is that instead of having society decide over the economy, it is the economy that decides over society: "*instead of the economic system being embedded in social relationships, these relationships were now embedded in the economic system*" ([1947] 1971:70; emphasis in original). To set things straight, Polanyi concludes, the economy has to be "reembedded" and political control over the economy reestablished.

Among Polanyi's most important concepts, in so far as economic sociology is concerned, are his so-called forms of integration. Polanyi's general argument is that rational self-interest is, among other things, far too unstable to constitute the foundation of society—the reason being that an economy must be able to provide people with material sustenance on a continuous basis. There exist three forms of integration or ways to stabilize the economy and provide it with the unity that it needs (see figure 1.3): *reciprocity*, which takes place within symmetrical groups such as families, kinship groups, and neighborhoods; *redistribution*, the allocation of goods from a center in the community, such as the state; and *exchange*, the distribution of goods via price-making markets ([1957] 1971). In each economy, Polanyi specifies, there is usually a mix of these three forms and their corresponding institutions: the family, the state, and the market (cf. Granovetter and Yakubovich 2000). Prices and trade may also differ, depending on which form of integration is involved.

Talcott Parsons

Talcott Parsons (1902–79) was educated as an economist in the institutionalist tradition and taught economics at Harvard University for

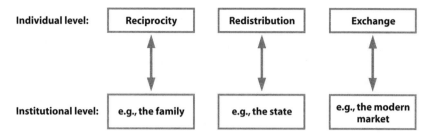

Figure 1.3. Different Ways of Organizing the Economy, according to Polanyi.
Note: The economy can only be organized in a few fundamental ways that all answer to specific institutions: *'reciprocity'*, *'redistribution'*, and *'exchange'*.
Source: Karl Polanyi, "The Economy as Instituted Process," pp. 243–69 in *Trade and Market in Early Empires*, edited by (Chicago: Karl Polanyi, Conrad Arensberg, and Harry Pearson Regnery, [1957] 1971).

several years before he switched to sociology in the 1930s. At this time he developed the notion that while economics deals with the means-end relationship of social action, sociology deals with its value aspect ("the analytical factor view"). In the 1950s Parsons recast his ideas on the relationship of economics to sociology in a work coauthored with Neil Smelser, *Economy and Society* (1956). This work constitutes Parsons's major contribution to economic sociology, even though he produced several other works that are relevant to this field (e.g., Camic 1987; Swedberg 1991b). It should also be noted that it was Parsons who translated much of Weber's work on economic topics into English; he also pioneered an important essay on Weber's theoretical economic sociology in *The Theory of Social and Economic Organization* (Parsons 1947).

The Structure of Social Action (1937) can be characterized as a forceful attack on utilitarian social thought, including the idea that interests represent an archimedean point from which to analyze society. Those who emphasize interests, Parsons notes, cannot handle the Hobbesian problem of order; and they typically try to get out of this dilemma by introducing the assumption that the interests of people do not conflict with one another. Parsons uses an expression by Elie Halévy to refer to this solution: the postulate of "the natural identity of interests" ([1937] 1968:96–97). What is not properly understood by the utilitarians, however, is that norms (embodying values) are absolutely necessary to integrate society and provide order. Interests are always part of society, but a social order cannot be built directly on them (405).

In *Economy and Society* (1956) Parsons and Smelser note that the two disciplines of economics and sociology are very far from each other, and that this is a situation that needs to be remedied. The authors suggest that sociology and economics should both be reconceptualized as parts of the general theory of social systems. The economy itself can be understood as a subsystem, which interacts with the other three subsystems (the polity, the integrative subsystem, and the cultural-motivational subsystem). The idea of the economy as a subsystem, which can be found in Parsons and Smelser's work, is reminiscent of Weber's notion of the economic sphere. While the latter, however, only refers to values, the economic subsystem also has an adaptive function as well as a distinct institutional structure. It may finally be mentioned that *Economy and Society* was not well received by the economists and that it also failed to ignite an interest for economic sociology among sociologists. Smelser's attempt during the next decade to get economic sociology going was similarly unsuccessful (Smelser 1963, 1965, 1976).

Summary

This chapter shows that economic sociology has a long tradition—from around 1900, in the more narrow sense of the word, and from much earlier, in a broader sense. Not only Marx, I argue, can be seen as an important predecessor to this type of analysis, but also Tocqueville. The importance of the concept of interest in economic sociology is illustrated by a discussion of the way in which the founders of sociology used this concept. A brief history of the concept of interest in social theory, from the 18th century and onwards, is also included.

Max Weber is without doubt the most important figure in early economic sociology. He was uniquely trained to launch a project such as economic sociology since he had worked both as an economist and as an economic historian before he turned to sociology. Of the founders of sociology, he was also the only one who tried to lay a systematic theoretical foundation for economic sociology. This is done in chapter 2 of *Economy and Society*. Like the works of the other classic writers in economic sociology, that of Weber is still much in need of study.

Economic sociology came to something of a standstill after 1920 and would not come back to life again until the mid-1980s. Still, some important work was done during the period after the classics—especially by Schumpeter, Parsons, and Polanyi. The current generation of economic sociologists has singled out Polanyi among these three thinkers. Polanyi coined the term "embeddedness" and also supplied some other useful conceptual tools, such as the three forms of integration. The works of Schumpeter and Parsons have, on the other hand, more or less been ignored. While the value of Parsons's economic sociology can be debated, it is clear that Schumpeter's work is of much relevance to contemporary economic sociology. Of Schumpeter's many contributions, especially his theory of entrepreneurship and the analysis of the economy in *Capitalism, Socialism and Democracy* deserve to become part of contemporary economic sociology.

II

Contemporary Economic Sociology

By the 1970s economic sociology had more or less died out. In the early 1980s, however, a few studies appeared, which indicated that something new was about to happen (White 1981b; Stinchcombe 1983; Baker 1984; Coleman 1984). And with the publication in 1985 of a theoretical essay by Mark Granovetter—"Economic Action and Social Structure: The Problem of Embeddedness"—the new ideas found their manifesto. The same year Granovetter gave a talk at the American Sociological Association in which he spoke of the need for a "new economic sociology"—and thereby the new movement also received its name.

Why economic sociology, after decades of neglect, suddenly came alive again in the mid-1980s is not all that clear. Several factors probably played a role, inside as well as outside the field of sociology. By the early 1980s, with the coming to power of Reagan and Thatcher, a new neoliberal ideology had become popular, which placed the economy—and the economists—at the center of society. By the mid-1980s economists had also started to redraw the traditional boundary between economics and sociology ("We analyze the economy and you society"). Forays were made into areas that sociologists by tradition saw as their own territory.

It was also during this period that the work of Gary Becker, Oliver Williamson, and similar authors started to come to the attention of sociologists. The notion that sociologists could reciprocate, by taking on economic topics, may have been in the air; in any case, this is what happened. Finally, the failure of Parsonian economic sociology to create a place for itself, in combination with the decline of industrial sociology in the 1970s and Marxism in the 1980s, had perhaps left a vacuum in U.S. sociology, which made it easier for something like the new economic sociology to emerge.

To some extent this version of what happened is born out by what Mark Granovetter said in his 1985 talk when he introduced the term "new economic sociology." He associated "old economic sociology" with industrial sociology and the economy-and-society perspective of Parsons, Smelser, and Wilbert E. Moore—two approaches, he said, that had been full of life in the 1960s but then "suddenly died out"

(Granovetter 1985a). Parsons's cautious attempt to negotiate a truce between economics and sociology had also been replaced by a more militant tone. According to Granovetter, new economic sociology "attacks neoclassical arguments in fundamental ways," and it wants to take on key economic topics, rather than focus on peripheral ones along the lines that Parsons had suggested. "My position," Granovetter concludes, "is that there is something very basically wrong with microeconomics and that the new economic sociology should make this argument loud and clear, especially in the core areas of market structure, production, pricing, distribution, and consumption" (1985a).

New Economic Sociology

Since the mid-1980s new economic sociology has been quite successful in carving out a niche for itself in U.S. sociology (see box). During the 1980s new economic sociology had only one stronghold—SUNY Stony Brook with Mark Granovetter, Michael Schwartz, and their students—but today economic sociology is well represented at a number of universities, including such prestigious ones as Cornell, Berkeley, Princeton, Stanford, and Northwestern. A good number of economic sociologists can also be found at top business schools. Few economic sociologists work outside of academia, although it should be mentioned that a small number of sociologists can be found at the World Bank.

Many high quality articles and monographs have been produced by these new economic sociologists, such as *Structural Holes* (1992) by Ronald Burt, *The Transformation of Corporate Control* (1990) by Neil Fligstein, and *The Social Meaning of Money* (1994) by Viviana Zelizer. These three works also illustrate the ability of economic sociology to draw quickly on the insights of networks theory (Burt), organization theory (Fligstein), and cultural sociology (Zelizer). The popularity of economic sociology is also demonstrated by the appearance of several anthologies, a few readers, a handbook, and a textbook (e.g., Zukin and DiMaggio 1990; Guillén et al. 2002; Granovetter and Swedberg 1992, 2001; Biggart 2002; Smelser and Swedberg 1994, forthcoming; Carruthers and Babb 2000). All in all, one can say that the new economic sociology has succeeded in laying a solid institutional foundation for its field.

Mark Granovetter on Embeddedness

While several attempts have been made to present general theories and paradigms in new economic sociology, there exists only one sus-

NEW ECONOMIC SOCIOLOGY (1980s–) AS A THEORY GROUP

Programmatic Statement: Mark Granovetter, "Economic Action and Social Structure: The Problem of Embeddedness" (*AJS* 1985).

Basic Approach: Core economic phenomena should be analyzed with the help of sociology. Especially helpful in this enterprise are the following three approaches: network theory, organization theory, and cultural sociology.

Central Theoretical Concepts: "Embeddedness"; "the social construction of the economy."

Signs of Institutionalization: Readers (1992–2001, 2002), a handbook (1994, 2nd ed., forthcoming), ASA Syllabi and Instructional Material (1996, 2nd ed., 2002), Economic Sociology Section at ASA (2001–).

Academic Strongholds: SUNY Stony Brook in the 1980s; today Stanford, Cornell, Berkeley, Princeton, and Northwestern.

Key People: Mitchel Abolafia, Wayne Baker, Nicole Woolsey Biggart, Ronald Burt, Bruce Carruthers, Jerry Davis, Paul DiMaggio, Frank Dobbin, Paula England, Neil Fligstein, Bai Gao, Gary Gereffi, Mark Granovetter, Mauro Guillén, Gary Hamilton, Mark Mizruchi, Victor Nee, Alejandro Portes, Walter Powell, Linda Brewster Stearns, Brian Uzzi, Harrison White, and Viviana Zelizer.

Important Monographs: Mitchel Abolafia, *Making Markets* (1998); Nicole Woolsey Biggart, *Charismatic Capitalism* (1989); Ronald Burt, *Structural Holes* (1992); Bruce Carruthers, *City of Capital* (1996); Frank Dobbin, *Forging Industrial Policy* (1994); Neil Fligstein, *The Transformation of Corporate Control* (1990); Mark Granovetter, *Getting A Job* (1974, 1995); and Viviana Zelizer, *The Social Meaning of Money* (1994).

Note: The term "new economic sociology" was coined by Mark Granovetter in a talk at the American Sociological Association in Washington, D.C. in 1985. The basic message in this talk was that modern economic sociology, as opposed to the "old economic sociology" of the 1960s, should focus on core economic institutions, such as firms, money, and markets. This type of economic sociology started to become popular in the mid-1980s and is today on the road to becoming one of the strongest subfields in U.S. sociology. The concept of theory group comes from Mullins and Mullins (1973) and is used here in a fairly loose sense, more or less as identical to the concept of a school. According to Schumpeter,

> We must never forget that genuine [scientific] schools are sociological realities—living beings. They have their structures—relations between leaders and followers—their flags, their battle cries, their moods, *their all-too-human interests* (1954:815; emphasis added).

tained attempt to elaborate a full theory: Mark Granovetter's theory of embeddedness. As mentioned earlier, this theory was first referred to in Granovetter's 1985 article in *The American Journal of Sociology*. Since the mid-1980s Granovetter has added considerably to his argument and refined it in various writings that are related to two major forthcoming projects: a general theoretical work in economic sociology entitled *Society and Economy: The Social Construction of Economic Institutions*, and a study (written with Patrick McGuire) of the emergence of the electrical utility industry in the United States. (The following material from *Society and Economy* has, according to information from Granovetter, been published over the years: Granovetter 1990, 1992a, 1992b, 1992c, 1993, 1995b). Before discussing Granovetter's theory of embeddedness, it should also be noted that he himself regards this theory as part of a broader theory of "structural economic sociology," which has many of its roots in the work of Harrison White (e.g., Granovetter 2002). Finally, Granovetter's analyses of various substantive topics—such as prices, job seeking, and business groups—can be found elsewhere in this book.

The most important of Granovetter's works discussing embeddedness is his 1985 article "Economic Action and Social Structure," which came to operate as a catalyst for the emergence of new economic sociology and which is probably the most cited article in contemporary economic sociology. A key reason for this popularity is the general sophistication of Granovetter's argument, to which I shall return. Very importantly as well, is the fact that for many readers Granovetter's article opened up a whole new world of research. Some of this enthusiasm was also felt by Granovetter himself, as the following quote from an interview in 1985 demonstrates:

I think that right under our noses there is a gold-mine of subject matter that we [sociologists] can analyze very profitably. In the introduction to the new edition of *Foundations of Economic Analysis* Samuelson talks about the golden age of the 1930s, when mathematics first started to be introduced into economic analysis and all of a sudden all kinds of unsolved problems in economics could be solved that had been fruitlessly debated over the years. Suddenly, with a little bit of application of mathematics, all these problems started to yield. Samuelson says, "It was like fishing in a virgin lake: a whopper at every cast. . . ." That was the golden age and now, of course, things are not so easy. But in those days anybody that could do a little mathematics could jump in and get out with some wonderful results. I think that something like that is true now for economic sociology. I think there is a huge, untouched territory there, a whole "virgin lake"—again— for anybody who knows some sociology (1987a:18).

Granovetter's article on embeddedness from 1985 covers many topics and it is sometimes difficult to follow its central argument. In a first version of the article, however, this argument clearly emerges:

> Critics who have attempted to reform the foundations of economics have mainly been economists themselves. Their attack has typically been on the usual *conception of rational action*. It is my argument here that there is another fundamental feature of neoclassical economic theory that provides more fertile ground for attack: the assumption that economic actors make decisions in isolation from one another—independent of their social connections: what I will call *the assumption of "atomized" decisionmaking* (Granovetter 1982:2).

It should be emphasized that Granovetter in his 1985 article takes a position on embeddedness that on several accounts differs from that of Polanyi. While the latter, claimed that precapitalist economies had always been embedded, unlike capitalist economies, Granovetter argues that *all* economies are embedded—but less so than Polanyi had claimed for the precapitalist economies. This position is elsewhere referred to as a "weak embeddedness position," as opposed to "the strong embeddeness position" (1992b:27–29; Granovetter 1985b:482–83).

Granovetter provides no explicit definition of embeddedness but simply states that economic actions are "embedded in concrete, ongoing systems of social relations" (1985b:487). It should be pointed out that networks are central to his concept of embeddedness: "networks of social relations penetrate irregularly and in different degrees in different sectors of economic life" (1985b:491). A distinction also needs to be drawn, according to Granovetter, between an actor's immediate connections and her more distant ones—what he elsewhere refers to as "relational embeddedness" versus "structural embeddedness" (1990:98–100, 1992b:34–37).

The most important addition to the 1985 article, which one can find in Granovetter's work, has been to connect the embeddedness position to a theory of institutions. Drawing on *The Social Construction of Reality* (1966) by Peter Berger and Thomas Luckmann, Granovetter argues that institutions can be seen as "congealed networks" (1992a:7). Interactions between people gradually acquire an objective quality, and eventually people take them for granted. What is specific about economic institutions, according to Granovetter, is that they involve "the mobilization of resources for collective action" (6).

Granovetter's embeddedness argument has been much discussed and sometimes criticized. An attempt to elaborate on it can be found in the work of Brian Uzzi, who argues that a firm can be "underem-

bedded" as well as "overembedded," and that a firm is most successful when there is a balance between arm's-length market ties and
more solid links (1997). Granovetter's response to Uzzi is that the
attempt to measure the degree of embeddedness may be a less productive approach than to conceive of embeddedness "as [a] kind of
umbrella under which a lot of different and more precise kinds of
research could be done on the ways in which social networks affect
the conduct of the economy, economic behavior, economic actions,
economic institutions" (1998:88–9). Several critics have also pointed
out that Granovetter has left out quite a bit in his analysis, including
culture, politics, and a link to the macro level (see e.g., Zukin and
DiMaggio 1990; Zelizer 1988; Nee and Ingram 1998; Krippner 2001).
Zukin and DiMaggio suggest that to remedy this, one should not only
investigate "structural embeddedness," but also "political," "cultural," and "cognitive embeddedness."

From an interest point of view, one can distinguish between the
micro level and the institutional level in Granovetter's argument. On
the institutional level, as already noted, Granovetter speaks of economic institutions in terms of the mobilization of resources for collective action—a position that goes well with a sociological interest analysis. This is also the case with Granovetter's analysis on the micro
level, but here his argument is somewhat different and more innovative. First of all, he explicitly distances himself from the type of interest analysis that one can find in mainstream economics, on the
grounds that it excludes a sociological dimension. "Any account of
human interaction which limits explanation to *individual* interests," he
notes, "abstracts away from fundamental aspects of *relationships*
which characterize economic as well as other action" (2002:36). He
then adds—and this is where the innovation comes—that economic
actions can never be 100 percent economic but always include noneconomic elements. All social actions, he argues, including economic
ones, are to some extent always infused by "central human motives,"
such as "sociability, approval, status and power" (1992b:26). To sum
up Granovetter's argument on a micro level: economic actions are
never exclusively inspired by economic interests—as soon as the actor starts to interact with other actors, other interests also begin to
intervene, namely social interests.

Contribution I: Using Structural Sociology and Networks

New economic sociology has made contributions to a variety of substantive areas, and, as already pointed out, it has especially drawn on

network analysis, organization theory, and cultural sociology. An increasing effort has also been made to use historical material as well as a comparative approach—two approaches that separate economic sociology from much of mainstream economics. While one can debate whether rational choice sociology should be regarded as part of new economic sociology or not, it is nonetheless true that some rational-choice sociologists, especially James Coleman, have been important to the recent revival of economic sociology in the United States; and that Coleman's work deserves to be highlighted.

While all sociologists who use network analysis do not see themselves as structural sociologists, it is nonetheless true that most structural sociologists use networks and also that structural sociology has played a crucial role in promoting and adding to network analysis in sociology. In general terms structural sociology can be defined as a theoretical approach centered around the proposition that the relations of persons and positions are crucial to the social process (e.g., Mullins and Mullins 1973:251–69). Its practitioners often use a mathematical approach, focus on social mechanisms, and avoid regression analysis and similar methods that use variables as an explanation. The key person in structural sociology is Harrison White, whose work since the late 1960s has inspired many of his Harvard students, such as Mark Granovetter, Scott Boorman, and Michael Schwartz.

White's work on networks, vacancy chains, and markets has been very important to today's economic sociology (for White's work on vacancy chains and markets, see chap. 5). In his major theoretical work, *Identity and Control: A Structural Theory of Social Action*, White begins his analysis by citing people's physical dependence on their surroundings but he also notes that interests are soon embedded in social relations. "Material productions must start the scene," he says, "[and] continuing material productions of all sorts are required in order that social action not cease, but social action itself also induces new productions that mix the social and material" (White 1992:24).

In mentioning structural sociology, it should be pointed out that Mark Granovetter primarily views himself as a structural sociologist, not as theoretician of embeddedness or networks. His embeddedness article from 1985 ends, for example, with a reference to "the insights of modern structural sociology," and in his most recent theoretical statement he explicitly speaks of "structural economic sociology" (1985b:508; 2002:35, 54). The programmatic statement that accompanies Granovetter's book series "Structural Analysis in the Social Sciences" (1987–) contains one of the most concise statements about what this type of sociology wants to accomplish. Granovetter emphasizes that a structural approach rejects methodological individualism

"Yes, I do make things, son. I make things called deals."

as well as the following approaches in sociology: technological and material determinism, the use of variables as an explanation, and explanations that rely mainly on "abstract concepts such as ideas, values, mental harmonies and cognitive maps" (Granovetter 1987b, 1999c). As we soon shall see, Granovetter has on several occasions been criticized for ignoring culture—an issue on which he has partly reversed his position (Granovetter 2000).

With the emergence of new economic sociology in the 1980s, network analysis quickly grew in popularity (for a technical introduction, see Wasserman and Faust 1994). Many interesting studies have, for example, been made of the links that exist between corporations and, more generally, of the social networks that make up industrial districts (e.g., Ebers 1997; Saxenian 1994). In 1992 Ronald Burt published a monograph entitled *Structural Holes*, which analyzes competition, drawing on Simmel's idea that you are in a good position if you can play out two competitors against one another (*tertius gaudens* or "the third who benefits"; Burt 1992). Brian Uzzi's already-mentioned study of embeddedness (1997) also makes use of networks, as do Granovetter's pioneering essays on business groups (Granovetter 1994; 1995a, forthcoming; see also the discussion of Granovetter's *Getting A Job* [1974] in chapter 5, of this book). A multitude of other fine studies could be mentioned (e.g., Powell and Smith-Doerr 1994)—as well as the fact that some critique has been directed at the network approach for ignoring the role that politics and culture play in economic life (e.g., Fligstein 1996:657).

Contribution II: Using Organization Theory

New economic sociology has been very successful in using organization theory to explore a number of important topics in economic life, such as the structure of firms, the links that exist between corporations and their environment, and the like. Organization theory has also inherited many of the concerns of industrial sociology (Hirsch 1975). With several sociologists working in business schools, it has also been common to use organization theory to explore the modern corporation.

Somewhat of a drawback in this context has been the failure in contemporary organization theory to make a sharp distinction between economic and noneconomic organizations. As far as organization theorists are concerned, the relevant unit of analysis is the organization and not the firm. Organization theorists are also loath to acknowledge the existence of anything else in society than organizations, something that limits their capacity to deal with a number of important economic phenomena (e.g., Davis and McAdam 2000). These drawbacks may also be one of the reasons for the reluctance among organizational sociologists to theorize about the role of economic interests in organization.

Modern organization theory contains a number of different approaches, and the following three have been especially important for the development of new economic sociology: resource dependency, population ecology, and new institutionalism. Resource dependency is perhaps the perspective that fits sociological interest theory the most easily, with its argument that organizations are dependent on their environments to survive. An example of a study that draws on this approach is Ronald Burt's *Corporate Profits and Cooptation* (1983). The key argument in this work is that the profit of a firm is determined by the combination of three factors—the number of suppliers, competitors, and customers. The more "structural autonomy" a firm has, Burt attempts to show, the higher its profit will be. Or, to put it differently, if there are many suppliers, few competitors, and many customers, a firm will be in a good position to buy cheaply and sell expensively. Links to other firms may also be used to enhance a firm's position vis-à-vis its environment.

In both population ecology and new institutionalism, interests play a secondary role and are in general undertheorized. In population ecology the main interest that is taken into account is the desire for survival; and analyses typically attempt to show that the diffusion of an organizational form passes through a series of distinct stages. There is first a very slow beginning, then comes explosive growth, and finally there is a slow settling down (Hannah and Freeman 1989). Individual studies of this process in several industries have been carried out, and these clearly fill a void in economic sociology (e.g., Carroll and Hannan 1995). The scope of population ecology, however, is somewhat narrow. It has also been pointed out that "a crucial assumption in this approach is that organizations don't change in important ways over time" (Davis and McAdam 2000:206).

New institutionalism is strongly influenced by the ideas of John Meyer and is centered around what may be called the cultural and cognitive aspects of organizations (for the key texts, see Powell and DiMaggio 1991). Meyer argues that organizations usually try to appear much more rational than they actually are and that specific models for how to organize various activities are often applied to circumstances that they do not fit at all. It has been noted that the strength of new institutionalism resides in its exploration of "factors that make actors unlikely to recognize or to act on their interests," and that it also focuses on "circumstances that cause actors who do recognize and try to act on their interests unable to do so" (DiMaggio 1988:4–5).

New institutionalism no doubt represents an important contribution to new economic sociology, and in some ways to interest theory as well, by pointing out which areas in social life that interest theory is *not* applicable to. It is also possible to combine the insights of new institutionalism with a more conventional type of interest analysis. As an example of this one can cite Neil Fligstein's study of the large corporation in the United States, *The Transformation of Corporate Control* (1990). Fligstein here shows that the multidivisional form spread because of mimetic reasons—but also because this organizational form made it easier for firms to take advantage of new technology and the emerging national market.

Contribution III: Using Cultural Sociology

New economic sociology has from its very beginning been pluralistic in nature and encompassed several different perspectives. In the 1980s it seemed for a while that structural sociology was about to take over and eliminate some of its rivals, especially cultural sociology, Parsonian sociology, and variable sociology. This attempt, however, met with strong resistance, especially from those in favor of a cultural approach.

As already mentioned, advocates of a structural approach have recanted some of their earlier critique of the cultural approach. In today's economic sociology there is, as in the 1980s, only a small group of economic sociologists who are strongly committed to using a cultural approach. But today there also exist many people who find it perfectly natural to refer to symbols, meaning structures and the like, in their studies of the economy (for a discussion of the concept of culture and its relationship to the economy, see chap. 9).

The fact that so many economic sociologists today try to take culture into account in their analyses owes much to the work of the two most prominent advocates of a cultural perspective in economic sociology, Viviana Zelizer and Paul DiMaggio. In a programmatic article from 1988, Zelizer criticized contemporary economic sociology for its tendency to reduce everything to social relations and networks, a position she terms "social structural absolutism" (Zelizer 1988:629). In the work of scholars such as Burt and Granovetter, she notes, "culture lingers on as a relic of a dangerous Parsonian past" (629). But Zelizer also rejects the alternative of reducing everything in the economy to culture ("cultural absolutism"). The goal, she says, should be to take economic *and* cultural factors into account, "to plot a middle course between cultural and social structural absolutism" (629).

DiMaggio has been similarly skeptical about a full-scale cultural analysis of the economy; it has been very important for him to make sure that the analysis includes a "'cultural' component"—but that is all (1994:27; cf. Zukin and DiMaggio 1990:17–78). According to DiMaggio, culture can also be either "constitutive" or "regulative." Culture operates in a constitutive manner through such items as categories, scripts, and conceptions of agency, and in a regulative manner through norms, values, and routines. The relationship of the constitutive versus the regulative dimension of culture to interests is as follows:

> Culture can either affect economic behavior by influencing how actors define their interests (*constitutive* effects . . .), by constraining their efforts on their own behalf (*regulatory* effects), or by shaping a group's capacity to mobilize or its goal in mobilizing (DiMaggio 1994:28).

In this quote DiMaggio is talking about the impact of culture on the economy. That the economy can shape culture, he says, is much more obvious (1994:27).

In empirical studies of the economy, which draw on the concept of culture, Viviana Zelizer's work occupies a central position (see also, e.g., Dobbin 1994b, Abolafia 1998). Her first major work was devoted to a study of life insurance in the United States, with emphasis on the clash between sacred values and economic values that resulted from the introduction of this type of insurance (1979). At first people did not want to accept that a price can be set on a person's life, she argues, but this would later change.

After *Markets and Morals* Zelizer published a study entitled *Pricing the Priceless Child* (1985), where she describes a similar movement, but this time in reverse. Children, who in the nineteenth century had a substantial economic value, would in the twentieth century increasingly be seen in emotional terms and be regarded as "priceless." In her most recent major study, *The Social Meaning of Money* (1994), Zelizer argues that money does not constitute a neutral, nonsocial substance, as is typically claimed, but instead appears in a variety of culturally influenced shapes ("multiple monies").

Contribution IV: Building a Historical and Comparative Tradition in Economic Sociology

As was noted earlier, Max Weber produced a series of studies in economic sociology that were historical as well as comparative in nature, and in doing so he drew on the rich tradition of historical research in Germany. After Weber's death, however, works of this type more or less disappeared from the agenda of economic sociology. In new economic sociology, one can find a few attempts to revive the Weberian tradition of historical-comparative research and to make it flourish once again (e.g., Dobbin forthcoming). But this is a difficult enterprise, which may well take several generations of scholarship to accomplish, as illustrated by the recent attempt by Theda Skocpol and others to create a historical sociology in the United States. Nonetheless, it would seem important for today's economic sociologists to try to rebuild a historical as well as a comparative approach to economic topics. One reason is that Weber and others have shown what solid and important scholarship can be produced in this way. Another reason is that this type of research constitutes an area where economic sociology has a comparative advantage in relation to mainstream economics. Through its assumption that there exists one efficient and rational way of doing things, mainstream economics is nonhistorical by inclination as well as disinclined to use a comparative approach.

A few works in new economic sociology that have already been cited in this chapter draw on historical material (e.g., Granovetter and

McGuire 1998; Zelizer 1979, 1985). To this should be added Bruce Carruthers's study of finance in seventeenth- and eighteenth-century England, and several recent attempts by economic sociologists to challenge Alfred Chandler's account of the rise of the large industrial corporation in the United States. Carruthers is mainly interested in showing not only that economic interests influence politics, but also the opposite: "political interests influence economic action," including actions in the market (1996:7). Using primary material on the trade in shares in the East India Company in the early 1700s, Carruthers establishes that political ambitions clearly influenced from whom you wanted to buy and sell. The critique of Chandler has similarly emphasized that the state played a key role in the emergence of the large industrial corporation. Chandler's key idea—that advances in technology and the emergence of a national market around the turn of the last century made it necessary to reorganize the large corporation as a multidivisional unit—has repeatedly been challenged on this and other grounds (Fligstein 1990; Roy 1990, 1997; Freeland 1996, 2001).

While several historically oriented studies have been produced in new economic sociology, there exist only a few comparative studies. One of the most innovative is *Forging Industrial Policy: The United States, Britain and France in the Railway Age* (1994) by Frank Dobbin. The author shows that industrial policy during the nineteenth century in these three countries differed on several important points, and argues that this shows how incorrect it is to begin the analysis with the assumption that "policy choices are governed by universal laws of interest and rationality" (Dobbin 1994b:1). Political scientists' efforts to analyze industrial policy from the viewpoint of interest group theory is similarly flawed, according to Dobbin, since this approach, too, is unable to handle deep-seated differences between countries.

Contribution V: James Coleman and Interest-Based Sociology

The most radical attempt during the past few decades to develop a sociological interest analysis was made by James Coleman (1926–1995). His effort began in the early 1960s but came to its most complete expression in *Foundations of Social Theory*, which appeared in 1990. In this project he sought to use interest as the foundation for *all* of sociology, and initially he paid little attention to economic sociology (see, however, Coleman 1994). It should nonetheless be mentioned that around the same time as Granovetter's essay on embeddedness appeared, Coleman published a brief article with a similar content in *American Economic Review* (1984).

Coleman's main message in the 1984 article is that economists have failed to introduce social relations into their analysis. He also notes that

> The principal means by which economic theory moves from the micro level of a single actor to the macro level involving many such actors is through the ubiquitous concept of "representative agent." Yet simple aggregation is clearly inappropriate for phenomena such as trust, since trust is a *relation* between two actors (85).

Just like Granovetter, Coleman uses the following three subjects to illustrate the point: trust, the market, and firms.

The key theoretical chapter in *Foundations of Social Theory*, entitled "Actors, Resources, Interest and Control" (chapter 2), contains an attempt to reconceptualize interest theory as well as make it sociological. Coleman's point of departure is that it is not enough to speak of actors and their interests; you also have to add what he terms "resources" and "control." The main idea is that if an actor has something that is of interest to someone else, the two will want to interact. Or, using Coleman's terminology, if actor A has control over a resource that is of interest to actor B, or vice versa, they will interact (cf. Emerson 1964; see figure 2.1). One example of this type of interaction is taking a job and signing over the control of your efforts to someone else, against payment.

Foundations, as well as other works by Coleman, contains a number of analyses that are of much relevance to economic sociology. Three analyses of particular importance deal with trust, social capital, and the modern corporation. Trust is conceptualized by Coleman in a very different manner from Simmel (see chapter 1 of this book). While Simmel emphasizes the side of trust that consists of unthinking belief, Coleman characterizes trust as a conscious bet. You calculate what you can win and lose by trusting someone, and under certain circumstances you go ahead and trust this person (Coleman 1990:99). This way of understanding trust would seem to suit business quite well; even though you trust people, you are cautious in your trust.

Social capital is defined by Coleman as any social relation that can be of help to an individual when she tries to realize her interest. "The function identified by the concept 'social capital' is the value of those aspects of social structure to actors, as resources that can be used by the actors to realize their interests" (1990:305). A firm represents, for example, a form of social capital—even if social capital is usually the unintended result of some action, undertaken for a different purpose. Finally, Coleman is also very interested in the ability of the firm— once people have created it to realize their interests—to develop in-

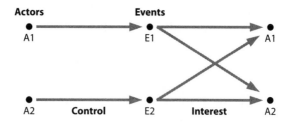

Figure 2.1. Interest and Social Interaction, according to Coleman.
Note: When an actor controls resources that are of interest to another actor, there is an incentive for the actors to interact.
Source: James Coleman, *Foundations of Social Theory* (Cambridge: Harvard University Press, 1990), 30.

terests of its own (see especially Coleman 1974). To Coleman, the firm is basically a social invention, and agency theory is particularly useful for analyzing it.

Recent Developments of Economic Sociology in Europe

New economic sociology is primarily a U.S. phenomenon and has only recently begun to spread to Europe. In Europe, as already mentioned, economic sociology had gradually come to a standstill after the classic writers, even if some of its concerns were later analyzed within the frameworks of industrial sociology, consumer sociology, and stratification theory (e.g., Swedberg 1987). Many of the major European sociologists have, however, written on the economy as part of their general concern with society. This is not only true of yesterday's generation—such as Raymond Aron, Michel Crozier, and Ralf Dahrendorf—but also of today's major sociologists, such as Niklas Luhmann, Jürgen Habermas, and Pierre Bourdieu (cf. Giddens 1973, 1986).

Niklas Luhmann (1927–1998) has, for example, produced a number of interesting essays on the economy, which have been somewhat neglected in the current debate (e.g., Beckert 2002a:201–40). His main thesis in all of these is that "economic sociology can only develop if its approach is overhauled and it sets out . . . from the concept of the economy as a subsystem of society" (Luhmann [1970] 1982:221–22; cf. 1988, 1998). Jürgen Habermas has written much less on the economy than has Luhmann, and Habermas has not shown any particular interest in economic sociology. Nonetheless, his general thesis that in modern society "the lifeworld" of the individual has been uncoupled from "the system world," including the economic subsystem, has been much discussed (Habermas 1984–87; cf. Sitton 1998).

Of all the major European sociologists, however, it is Pierre Bourdieu (1930–2002) who has by far shown the most interest in the economy, from his studies of Algeria in the 1950s to such recent work as his analysis of the housing market in *Les Structures Sociales de l'Economie* (2000). Bourdieu has also devoted several issues of his journal *Actes de la Recherche en Sciences Sociales* to economic topics, such as "social capital" (no. 31, 1980), "the social construction of the economy" (no. 65, 1986), and "the economy and the economists" (no. 119, 1997). His contribution to the relationship of culture to the economy is substantial and is discussed later in this book (chapter 10). Most importantly of all, however, Bourdieu has developed what is the only existing theoretical alternative in economic sociology to the model of embeddedness, namely the idea of the economy as a "field" with all that the term implies.

Bourdieu's foremost study of interest to economic sociology—*Travail et Travailleurs en Algérie* (*Work and Workers in Algeria*, 1963)—can be described as an extraordinarily rich ethnographic study (for a shortened version in English, see Bourdieu 1979; see also Bourdieu and Sayad 1964; Bourdieu 2000b). Some of the strength of the analysis in this work comes from the author's skillful juxtaposition of the traditionalistic habitus or disposition of the Algerian peasants to the rational habitus of people who live in a capitalist society.

While the peasant in Algeria has an intensely emotional and nearly mystical relationship to the land, Bourdieu says, such a relationship is not possible in a society that is dominated by wage labor and capital. Work is not directly related to productivity in Algeria; instead you try to keep busy all the time. The concept of time also separates the precapitalist habitus from the capitalist one on a series of other issues. Money and credit, for example, are not seen in the same way in Algeria as in modern capitalist society, since inhabitants in a precapitalist society have difficulty in relating to an abstract and rational future. Money and exchange are considered inferior to hoarding and barter; and credit, which is tied to the person as opposed to her assets, is only resorted to in rare circumstances, such as deep personal distress. In Algeria commercial ventures are much preferred to industrial ones, since the risk is smaller.

But Bourdieu has not only produced an exemplary study in economic sociology in his work on Algeria; he has also developed a general approach to economic sociology, which rivals and challenges Granovetter's work on embeddedness. This approach can be described as an application of Bourdieu's general sociology, which is centered around the concepts of field, habitus, and different types of capital. In 1997 Bourdieu published an article entitled "The Economic Field," which was revised a few years later and given the new title of "Principles of an Economic Anthropology" (Bourdieu 1997, 2000a, forthcoming). Since Bourdieu is very critical of Granovetter's approach—for ignoring the structural dimension of society, which is strongly developed in the notion of the field—one may well be justified in speaking about *two* rivaling approaches in today's economic sociology.

According to Bourdieu, the economy can be conceptualized as a field, that is, as a structure of actual and potential relations (Bourdieu and Wacquant 1992:94–120; Bourdieu 1997). An industry, a firm, and many other economic phenomena can be seen as a field. Each field has its own logic and interest. The structure of a field can also be understood in terms of its distribution of various types of capital. In addition to financial capital, the following three forms of capital are especially important: social, cultural, and symbolic. Social capital is defined by one's connections; cultural capital, by one's education and family background; and symbolic capital, by various items with a cognitive basis, such as goodwill and brand loyalty (1997; for a general account of the different types of capital—an analysis that Bourdieu pioneered—see Bourdieu 1986). The individual actors in the economic field bring with them their "economic habitus" (or "economic predispositions"), which relates their future actions to their past experience. The idea of *homo economicus* represents, according to Bourdieu, "a kind of anthropological monster" (1997:61). Bourdieu's economic actor does not act in a *rational* way, but in a *reasonable* way.

In addition to field, capital, and habitus there exists a fourth concept in Bourdieu's work that is very important: *interest* or what drives the actor to participate in a field. "*Interest*," according to Bourdieu, "is to 'be there,' to participate, to admit that the game is worth playing and that the stakes created in and through the fact are worth pursuing; it is to recognize the game and to recognize its stakes" (1998b:77; cf. Bourdieu 1990, Bourdieu and Wacquant 1992:115–17). The opposite of interest (or "*illusio*") is indifference (or "*ataraxia*"). Each field has its own interest, even if its masquerades as disinterestedness. Bourdieu criticizes the economists' version of interest for being ahistorical—"far from being an anthropological invariant, interest is a *historical arbitrary*" (Bourdieu and Wacquant 1992:116). The economists are also, in his opinion, wrong in thinking that "economic interest" is what drives everything; "anthropology and comparative history show that the properly social magic of institutions can constitute just about anything as an interest" (117).

Bourdieu terms the error of assuming that the laws of the economic field are applicable to all other fields in society an "economism" (1998b:83). He sums up his position on the concept of interest, as it is used in economics and sociology, in the following manner:

> the word *interest* . . . is also very dangerous because it is liable to suggest a utilitarianism that is the degree zero of sociology. That said, sociology cannot dispense with the axiom of interest, understood as the *specific investment* in the stakes, which is both the condition and the product of membership of a field (1993b:76).

Bourdieu's economic sociology has not been much discussed and explored in today's economic sociology. *Distinction*, for example, has much to say on preference formation and also contains a new approach to consumption (Bourdieu [1979] 1986; cf. Bourdieu and de Saint Martin 1990). Bourdieu's emphasis on economic suffering and his attempt to tie this to the issue of theodicy is also of much interest (Bourdieu et al. 1999). And so is his related effort to discuss the normative aspect of economic sociology, for example, in his recent collection of articles on "the tyranny of capital" (Bourdieu 1998a). All of these topics are discussed later in this book.

It would, however, be incorrect to leave the reader with the impression that Bourdieu is the only economic sociologist of interest in contemporary Europe. There is, for example, also Luc Boltanski and Laurent Thévenot, whose work on the different ways that an action can be justified or legitimized ("worlds of justification") is of great potential relevance to economic sociology. A person who works for a firm may, for example, justify what she does either by referring to efficiency ("the world of the market") or to loyalty ("the domestic world")—with very different results (Boltanski and Thévenot [1987] 1991). All in all there exist six major types of justification in the Western world, according to Boltanski and Thévenot, of which "the market" and "industry" are of special interest to economic sociology (see table 2.1).

Boltanski has also strongly criticized the network approach for being ideological in nature and strongly procapitalistic (Boltanski and Chiapello 1999; cf. Boltanski 1987, 1990). Bruno Latour and Michel Callon have added to network theory by arguing that individuals and organizations not only can be actors but also objects (e.g., Law and Hassard 1999; cf. Callon 1997, 1998). A machine, for example, can determine what kinds of movements a machine operator has to perform and how she must interact with other people in the process of production.

It would seem that France is currently the center in Europe for innovative economic sociology, and to the works just mentioned one

TABLE 2.1.
The Different "Worlds of Justification," according to Boltanski and Thévenot

	Inspired	Domestic	Civic	Opinion	Market	Industrial
Mode of evaluation (worth)	grace, nonconformity, creativity	esteem, reputation	Collective interest	renown	price	productivity efficiency
Format of relevant information	emotional	oral, exemplary, anecdotal	formal, official	semiotic	monetary	measurable criteria, statistics
Elementary relation	passion	trust	solidarity	recognition	exchange	functional link
Human qualification	creativity, ingenuity	authority	equality	celebrity	desire, purchasing power	professional competency, expertise

Note: Boltanski and Thévenot find that people often need to justify their actions, especially when they get into conflicts with each other but also in many other situations. In contemporary society six major bodies of justification exist; and two of these are of special relevance to economic action: "The Market World" and "The Industrial World".

Source: Luc Boltanski and Laurent Thévenot, "The Sociology of Critical Capacity," *European Journal of Social Theory* 2, no. 3(1999): 368.

should add Frédéric Lebaron's study of French economists (2000a, forthcoming), Emmanuel Lazega's study of work in a law firm (2000), and Philippe Steiner's study of different types of economic knowledge (1998, 2001). Also, some French economists produce studies that are close to economic sociology (Heilbron 2001a). This is especially the case with economists belonging to the school of regulation and the economics of convention (e.g., Storper and Salais 1997; Boyer and Saillard 2002). In the former, the emphasis is on the economic system as a distinct socioeconomic unit that needs to be reproduced; the latter stresses the role in economic life of conventions or regularities incorporated into routines (e.g., Boyer 1990:117–23; cf. Lewis 1986). Boltanski and Thévenot's work on "worlds of justification," it should be added, is generally seen as a sociological version of the economics of convention (cf. Favereau and Lazega forthcoming, Jagd forthcoming).

There also exists quite a bit of important research in economic sociology in European countries other than France. Sociology of money and finance has, for example, several skillful practitioners in England and Spain (e.g., Dodd 1994, Ingham 1998, Izquierdo 2001). A comparative study of inheritance is currently being completed in Germany (Beckert forthcoming; see also Beckert 2002b). Industrial districts were rediscovered in Italy and are still being studied there (e.g., Trigilia 2001). A general introduction to economic sociology by Carlo Trigilia appeared in 1998 and has just been translated into English (Trigilia 2002). Karin Knorr Cetina in Germany and Patrik Aspers in Sweden have independently of one another embarked on the project of developing a phenomenological approach to economic sociology (Knorr Cetina and Brügger 2002; Aspers 2001c, 2001d). Finally, the center for rational choice sociology and model building in Europe can be found in the Netherlands, and much of this work is of interest to economic sociology (e.g., Lindenberg 1985; Raub and Weesie 2000).

Summary

From this chapter, as well as the preceding one, it is clear that there exists a distinct tradition of economic sociology, one which has yielded a series of works that all address economic issues from a sociological perspective and that have been produced over a fairly long period of time. The tradition of economic sociology is, however, not a well-integrated tradition, in the sense that later works pick up where earlier ones leave off. Economic sociology has not yet found its Robert Merton who in *Social Theory and Social Structure* consolidated and strengthened the foundation of sociology by closely following what was happening in the field and by relating new studies and insights to earlier research findings and concepts.

It is also clear that a few different perspectives exist within the tradition of economic sociology. In contemporary economic sociology there is, for example, the embeddedness perspective of Granovetter as well as the economic field perspective of Bourdieu. In classical economic sociology one can find a fully developed perspective in Weber, and in the period after World War II, in Polanyi as well as in Parsons and Smelser. Many important ideas, which can be enlarged upon and developed into full-scale theoretical perspectives, can also be found in the works of Durkheim, Simmel, Pareto, and Veblen.

As for the concept of interest, it has been shown in this and the earlier chapter that *all* of the major thinkers in economic sociology made use of this concept—but that they did not assign it an explicit role in their theoretical schemes. The scope that those authors have assigned to the concept of interest within economic sociology has also varied quite a bit. On the one hand, there is the minimalist position of someone like Durkheim, who argues that unless individual interests are subordinated to the general interest, they will harm society—even if they are crucial to the economy. On the other hand, there is the maximalist position of someone like James Coleman, who argues that the concept of interest should constitute the foundation of all of sociology. Weber, Simmel, Bourdieu, and many others fall somewhere in between these two positions. What they argue—and my own position is close to theirs—is that it is essential for sociology to use the concept of interest properly to understand the economy as well as other spheres of society; but also that there is quite a bit more to sociology than interests.

A plethora of suggestive ideas for how to use the concept of interest can be found in the works that make up the tradition of economic sociology. Weber suggests that there are material interests as well as ideal interests; Granovetter that economic actions are driven by a mixture of economic and social interests; and Bourdieu that every field has its own set of interests. With the help of these and some other ideas on interests, I will try to show in the following chapters that it is possible further to advance economic sociology.

III

Economic Organization

THE term "economic organization" is often used as more or less synonymous with the "firm," especially in modern organization theory. But the term economic organization can also be understood in a different and more general sense—as *the organization of whole economies*; and it is in this sense that it will be used in this chapter (firms will be discussed in chapter 4). This second sense of the term economic organization is related to the concept of "social organization," which was popular in early sociology and refers to the general organization of society. Economists have sometimes conceived of the economy in terms of social organization. In *The Economic Organization* (1933) Frank Knight writes, for example, that

> economics deals with the *social organization* of economic activity. In practice its scope is much narrower still; there are many ways in which economic activity may be socially organized, but the predominant method in modern nations is the price system, or free enterprise ([1933] 1967:5–6; cf. Arrow 1974:33).

Economic sociology, I argue, should deal with the wider definition of the social organization that Knight refers to, and not only discuss the market economy or "the price system," as Knight calls it. It should also try to conceptualize the social organization of the economy in a different manner than standard economics, namely by consistently and systematically introducing a social dimension into the analysis.

By conceiving of economic organization in the two different senses that I have just outlined, it becomes easier to integrate the analysis of firms into a general analysis of the economy. Another advantage of proceeding in this manner is that one can start the analysis by simultaneously referring to actors with their interests *and* to the social structure that these actors have to take into account when they try to realize their interests. It should be emphasized that not only are individuals actors in the economy but so are organizations—or at least they are thought to be so by the individual actors (see Weber [1922] 1978:14 for this last point). Further complexity is added to this statement by the fact that firms are created to realize the economic interests of their founding members, but soon develop interests of their own. According to Coleman, "this new set of interests consists primarily of interests towards freeing the corporate actors from the shackles imposed by the sovereigns [that is, by its members]" (Coleman 1974:44).

Reflecting the argument about the two different meanings of the term economic organization, this chapter is devoted to economic organization in the broad sense, while the next chapter is devoted to economic organization in the narrow sense, that is, to the modern firm. An effort has been made in both of these chapters to relate the discussion of economic organization to the concept of interest. In so far as the modern firm is concerned, there already exist a few attempts to introduce this concept into the analysis, as seen in agency theory, James Coleman's theory of economic organizations, and James March's view of the corporation as a coalition of different interests. Similar attempts to include interests in the analysis of economic organization in a broad sense also exist but are less common.

One general way to remedy this, I suggest, would be to conceptualize the totality of the economy as an enormous web of economic and other interests, connected in different ways through social interaction and social structures. Institutions constitute crucial knots in this network of interests and social relations—knots that are especially hard to undo. What is connected, it should be added, may be just as important as what is *not* connected. Indeed, much of what we think of as distinct social organizations are patterns of social interactions and interests that are disconnected at crucial points. Depending on the structure of the social relations, interests may reinforce one another, block one another, and so on.

Though this conceptualization of economic organization is simplistic, in the sense that it starts out with a much too sharp division between interests and social relations, it can still give a sense of how to proceed. This way of conceptualizing economic organization in a broad sense, it can be added, also needs to be made much more specific to be of use. A first step in this direction would be to map out what is undoubtedly the most important form of economic organization in today's society, namely capitalism. This will be done in the next section, which also covers two other forms of economic organization in the broad sense, namely industrial districts and globalization.

On the Social Organization of the Economy

It seems clear that economic sociology should set capitalism at the very center of its analysis since this is *the* dominant way of organizing the economy—legally, politically, and socially—in today's world. Before entering into a discussion of capitalism, however, a few more words need to be said about economic organization in a broad sense. The scope of economic organization in this sense is clearly enormous and includes in principle everything from a collection of firms to the global organization of the economy. Markets can also be seen as a form of economic organization—as can cities, regional economies, national economies, and trade blocks. Several of these examples show that the line between the two meanings of economic organization is fluid and can be drawn at different points, depending on the purpose at hand.

Some of the topics that fall under the category of economic organization in the sense of a whole economy have a close relationship to the environment—to physical reality and space. The social science branch that has paid the most attention to this topic is economic geography, and it is clear to me that economic sociology can learn quite a bit from this type of analysis. There exists not only a tradition of important works going back to the beginnings of economic geography, but economic geography is also currently going through something of a revival (for a useful introduction to this field, see Clark, Feldman, and Gertler 2000).

A few words about economic geography need to be added at this point since this field has been totally neglected in economic sociology. Economic sociology, one could argue, is not very different from mainstream economics in this respect. During the last few years, however, economists have begun to pay attention to economic geography and developed what is known as a "new economic geography" (Malecki 2001). In 1995, for example, Paul Krugman published *Development, Geography, and Economic Theory*, which represents an important attempt by a well-known economist to stake out a general position on this issue. Krugman advocates an integration of economic geography into economic theory in forceful terms, but also criticizes most of what has been produced in economic geography. The main flaw of economic geography, Krugman states, is its lack of analytical rigor and well-crafted models.

Krugman's way of approaching economic geography, however, does not seem very fruitful for economic sociology, since what is primarily interesting with this type of analysis is precisely its attempts to deal empirically with the fact that economic activities are grounded in material and spatial reality. As a contrast to Krugman's stance, one can cite the work of Jeffrey Sachs, also an economist and an advocate of economic geography. Sachs's own contribution to economic geography is to have drawn attention to the extreme economic difficulties of countries of situated in the tropical zone: such countries operate under a series of geographical conditions that tend to impede their economic growth (Gallup and Sachs 1999; Sachs 2000; Sachs, Mellinger, and Gallup 2001). Sachs does not argue that geography determines a country's economic fate; social institutions and culture are also decisive. Still, geography must be included in the picture.

Countries that are situated in the tropics tend, according to Sachs, to have weak soils, high soil erosion, and many infectious diseases. The only countries that are situated in this geographic zone and that have done well economically, he points out, are Singapore and Hong Kong—two small economies that have not been dependent on agriculture for their success. In an essay entitled "Notes on a New Sociology of Economic Development" Sachs sums up the relationship between economic success and geography in the following way:

> The adoption of capitalist institutions is strongly favored by certain geographical conditions:
>> coastal states rather than hinterland states,
>>
>> states proximate to other capitalist societies,
>>
>> states on major international trade routes,
>>
>> regions with fertile agriculture, which in turn supports a high level of urbanization (2000:36–37).

Capitalism

"Capitalism," to return to the social dimension of the economy, is a term that dates to the nineteenth century and that over the years has acquired a number of partly overlapping as well as contradictory meanings (Braudel [1979] 1985c:231–39; cf. Block 2000). Economists, for example, have avoided the term till a few decades ago. The most common definition of capitalism incorporates some variation of the theme that it constitutes an organization of economic interests that allows for the "the pursuit of profit, and forever *renewed* profit" (Weber [1904–05] 1958:17). Marx expresses the same idea in *Capital* in his famous formula M-C-M', where M stands for money, C for commodity, and M' for money plus an increment (Marx [1867] 1906:163–96). To this should be added that private property is a precondition for capitalism, or, to phrase this last condition in a more sociological way, that capitalism can only exist if the individual has a legal right to exclude others from using some object or person (cf. Weber [1922] 1978:44).

The opposite of capitalism is an economy that is centered around *the satisfaction of needs* and not around *the accumulation of profit—*

where *"householding"* and not *"profit-making"* is what matters (Weber [1922] 1978:86–100). Examples of this would be the huge estate in antiquity, the communal economy, and planned economies of the socialist type. Property can be private as well as collective in this type of economy; and when it comes to the latter, it is important to distinguish between formal ownership and the actual right to dispose of a property.

This distinction between householding and an economic organization that is centered around profit is closely related to Marx's distinction between "use value" and "exchange value," and ultimately has its roots in Aristotle's famous pair of concepts "the art of household management" (*oekonomia*) and "the art of acquisition" (*chrematistica*; cf. Marx [1867] 1906:42–43; Aristotle 1946:18–38). The origin of the word economics is conventionally traced to the Greek word for the management of a household or a manor (Finley [1973] 1985:17). Capitalism is primarily related to exchange and *chrematistica*, while use value and *oekonomia* are characteristic of noncapitalist forms of the economy.

A different strategy for approaching the general nature of capitalism that I advocate would be to use the economists' traditional definition of the economy as consisting of *production, distribution*, and *exchange* (e.g., Samuelson 1970:4). From this perspective, the economic process starts with production and is then followed by distribution and consumption. The key to the different ways of organizing the economy, according to this perspective, is primarily found in the organization of *distribution*. According to Polanyi, as noted earlier, distribution can take one of the following three forms: redistribution, reciprocity, or exchange (cf. chap. 2). Redistribution is typically used in an economy dominated by the state, such as socialism or that of ancient Egypt, and what drives production is the need for consumption. Reciprocity is common in a family-based economy or in an economy where kinship is of primary importance; and here, too, what drives the production is the need for consumption. Exchange, finally, is directly related to the existence of a market; and it alone can lead to capitalism. The reason is that production in a capitalist economy is driven not only by the need for consumption but also by the desire for *profit*.

The way in which profit is related to exchange, and why actors want to engage in an exchange, can be illustrated by a reference to the so-called Kaldor-Hicks concept of efficiency (Posner 1998:14–15). According to this concept, an exchange is efficient when it benefits both of the actors with an amount that exceeds the possible damage to a third party. The social profit, in brief, has to exceed the social loss.

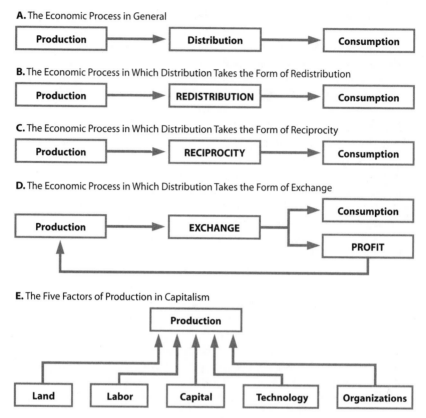

A. The Economic Process in General

Production ⟶ Distribution ⟶ Consumption

B. The Economic Process in Which Distribution Takes the Form of Redistribution

Production ⟶ REDISTRIBUTION ⟶ Consumption

C. The Economic Process in Which Distribution Takes the Form of Reciprocity

Production ⟶ RECIPROCITY ⟶ Consumption

D. The Economic Process in Which Distribution Takes the Form of Exchange

Production ⟶ EXCHANGE ⟶ Consumption / PROFIT

E. The Five Factors of Production in Capitalism

Production ← Land, Labor, Capital, Technology, Organizations

Figure 3.1. Capitalism and Alternative Ways of Organizing the Economic Process and Economic Interests.

Note: All economies involve production, distribution, and consumption. What distinguishes capitalism from other economic systems is primarily the way in which distribution is organized: as exchange in the market and not as reciprocity or redistribution. The continuous reinvestment of profit into production is also central. Production depends on five factors: land, labor, capital, technology, and organization (Marshall).

One example of this would be when actor A, who owns a bike worth $100, sells it to actor B for $150, with no damage to actors C, D, and so on. This example shows clearly why two actors want to engage in an exchange: both gain from it.

What makes capitalism so unique is that it is driven not only by the need for consumption but also by the desire for profit. This profit has also to be continuously reinvested in new production for new profit to become possible (see figure 3.1). It is precisely this feedback loop from profit to production that turns capitalism into such a dynamic economic system, forever revolutionizing the economy as well as society. Capitalism, to cite *The Communist Manifesto*, leads to "constant revolutionizing of production, uninterrupted disturbance of all social conditions, everlasting uncertainty and agitation" (Marx and Engels [1848] 1978:476). Redistribution and reciprocity, in contrast, lack this search for profit and the feedback loop of investment, and essentially constitute static forms of economic organization. The state and the family/kin group typically channel some of the surplus into new production, in order to ensure reproduction, but this is very different from a dynamic profit-oriented system where change is constant.

What has just been presented is a basic model of capitalism that needs to be made more complex in order to be useful in economic sociology. One way to would be to take a closer look at its four key components and analyze each of these with the help of sociology. This would give us a sociology of production, distribution, consumption, and profit. Production, for example, can be further subdivided into land, labor, capital, technology, and "organization" (Marshall). In addition—and of crucial importance—culture as well as political institutions (including the legal system) must be taken into account. Each of these factors may either *facilitate the process of profit-making, slow it down*, or *block it*. To study capitalism along these lines, I argue, would provide economic sociology with an agenda for a long time ahead (see Swedberg forthcoming b).

There exist other theories of capitalism that are useful to keep in mind. The one that is perhaps the most congenial to today's economic sociology is, in my opinion, that of Max Weber. First, Weber does not speak of capitalism (in singular), but of capitalisms (in plural), which is also the way that the term is increasingly used in contemporary social science. It has, for example, recently been argued that "capitalism as a construct is only analytically interesting in plural: *capitalisms* must be defined and compared *vis-à-vis* each other" (Stark 1996:1017; cf. Swedberg forthcoming c). Second, Weber tried to develop a concept of capitalisms centered around social action, as opposed to seeing capitalism as some kind of system with its own laws, along the lines of Marx. And finally, Weber's typology of capitalisms is deeply historical in nature, with each type growing out of intense historical research.

In Weber's work as a whole one can find a plethora of different types of capitalism, akin to the notion of capital in Bourdieu's work. Some of these are highly evocative, such as adventurer's capitalism, rentier capitalism, and pariah capitalism. In his theoretical economic sociology, however, Weber takes a more restrictive stance, and here he only talks of three main types of capitalism: *rational (or modern) capitalism, political capitalism,* and what can be termed *traditional commercial capitalism* ([1922] 1972:164–66). Instead of defining these, however, Weber simply uses them as labels for six different "principal modes of capitalistic orientation of profit-making." Weber defines profit-making as constituting a form of economic action that is oriented to "opportunities for seeking new power of control over goods on a single occasion, repeatedly or continuously" (90).

The act of profit-making with a capitalistic orientation can take a number of qualitatively different forms, each of which constitutes "a definite [sociological] type." Four of these have been around for thousands of years, Weber says, while the remaining two can be found only in the West and in modern times. The latter two are examples of rational or modern capitalism and basically consist of advanced finance, continuous production, and permanent buying and selling in a free market. Of the four other forms of profit-making, political capitalism ("politically oriented capitalism") includes the cases where profit is made through the state, via contacts with the state or under the direct physical protection of the state. Traditional commercial capitalism consists of small-scale acts of trade in goods and money (see figure 3.2).

Weber's tendency to dissolve the different types of capitalism into various kinds of social action is probably due to his desire to ground the notion of capitalism in the everyday activities of the economy, and to get away from the tendency to see capitalism as a system far beyond the individual actor. On this last point, incidentally, Weber's reasoning is close to that of Hayek, who argues that to portray capitalism as a system represents a form of "objectivism" and creates the illusion that capitalism has its own set of laws (Hayek 1943:41; cf. Hayek 1942:286).

It would be wrong, however, to leave the reader with the impression that Weber's conception of capitalism consists only of interactions among individuals and that institutions play no role. As mentioned in the account of Weber's theoretical economic sociology in chapter 1, the economic actor orients her behavior not only toward other actors but also toward "orders," which consist of prescribed sets of social action that are enforced in different ways. These orders are sometimes instituions; and the central economic institution in modern capitalism is the rational enterprise, led by an entrepreneur and with a work force that is separated from the means of production. The economic order of private property is similarly defended and upheld in a predictable and reliable manner by the state and its administrative agencies. The legal system is part of the rational state and is sim-

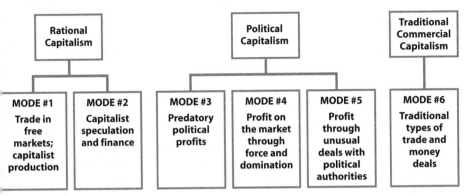

Figure 3.2. The Different Types of Capitalism, according to Weber.
Note:
#1. Continuous buying and selling in free markets, continuous production of goods in capitalist enterprises.
#2. Speculation in standardized commodities or securities, continuous financial operations of political organizations, promotional financing of new enterprises by selling securities, speculative financing of new enterprises and other economic organizations to gain power or a profitable regulation of the market.
#3. Predatory profit can come, e.g., from the financing of wars, revolutions, and party leaders.
#4. Continuous business activity thanks to force or domination, e.g., tax and office farming, colonial profits (plantations, monopolistic, and compulsory trade).
#5. No more information on this type of political capitalism can be found in chapter 2 of *Economy and Society.*
#6. Trade and speculations in currencies, professional and credit extension, creation of means of payment, the taking over of payment functions.
According to Weber, there exist different types of capitalism—not just one type, as Marx had argued. In *Economy and Society* Weber suggests the following three: *rational capitalism, political capitalism,* and *traditional commercial capitalism.*
Source: Richard Swedberg, *Max Weber and the Idea of Economic Sociology* (Princton: Princeton University Press, 1998), 47.

ilarly reliable and trustworthy. Huge investments in industry can be profitable only if the state authorities and the legal authorities are predictable in their decisions. Modern capitalism, Weber concludes in a famous passage, is *not* the same as unleashed greed:

> It should be taught in the kindergarten of cultural history that this naïve idea of [modern] capitalism must be given up once and for all. Unlimited greed for gain is not the least identical with capitalism, and is still less its

spirit. Capitalism *may* even be identical with the restraint, or at least a rational tempering, of this irrational impulse. But capitalism is identical with pursuit of profit, and forever *renewed* profit, by means of continuous, rational, capitalistic enterprise ([1904–05] 1958:17).

Weber's view of capitalism is deeply historical in nature and based on comparative research on several different civilizations as well as on primary research on capitalism in the West. The aspect that interested Weber the most was the origin of modern, or rational, capitalism, and it is clear that this theme occupied him from his earliest research as a doctoral student until his death some thirty years later. "*Why solely* in the Occident has a rational capitalism based upon profitability developed? . . . Somebody has to explore this question," as Weber wrote in a letter a few weeks before his death (cited in Hennis 1991:29).

Just as Weber emphasizes that capitalism must not be seen exclusively as an economic phenomenon, he also takes political, legal, and cultural factors into account when he traces the history of modern capitalism ([1922] 1978, [1923] 1981). Unlike today's economic historians, who typically view the industrial revolution as the decisive event in the history of modern capitalism, Weber traces its origins much further back and partly to other factors. One particularly important event took place in the 1500s and the 1600s with the rise of ascetic Protestantism, which made it possible to break the hold of religion over economic life and to energize people in their work, including profit-making (see Marshall 1982 for the debate of Weber's thesis).

But many important events also took place *before* the Reformation, according to Weber, such as the invention of certain key economic institutions, including money and the family firm. The rational state has its origins in the political community of the medieval city—and so does modern commercial law with its rules about bankruptcy, bills of exchange, and the like. Several key events also took place *after* the rise of ascetic Protestantism, such as the emergence of mass demand for consumption and the use of science in industry. At one point in the 1700s Western capitalism nearly stalled for good, before some crucial discoveries in metallurgy got it going again. All in all, one can say that according to Weber, modern, or rational, capitalism, emerged through an evolution that lasted for several centuries and that was largely accidental in nature. Weber was also quite worried that the modern type of capitalism, which is extremely dynamic in nature, would soon be replaced by a different kind of capitalism, characterized by bureaucratic stagnation and oppression (cf. Mommsen 1974).

Today's economic sociologists have often taken capitalism for granted and have failed to develop a sociology of capitalism. On the whole, they have preferred to deal with middle-range phenomena, such as firms and networks of various kinds (but see Block 1996, Nee and Swedberg forthcoming). Since the mid-1990s, however, a growing body of work on different types of capitalism has emerged (e.g., Hollingsworth, Schmitter, and Streeck 1994; Berger and Dore 1995; Crouch and Streeck 1997; Hollingsworth and Boyer 1997; Hall and Soskice 2001; in its modern version the genre dates back to Shonfield 1965). These studies mainly draw on the tradition of political economy and have only recently begun to show some interest in economic sociology. Their focus has typically been on presenting and comparing different national forms of capitalism, especially in Western Europe, the United States, and Japan. A concern with flexible specialization in industrial districts and the impact of globalization on the national state is also common.

Studies in the tradition of political economy are strongly critical of the idea of convergence to one universal type of economic organization, an idea that is still popular among economists; and as an alternative they have tried to map out the different combinations of governance mechanisms that can be found in the different types of national capitalism. One research result from this agenda is that no single form of governance—including the market—is responsible for the way that a national economy works; a number of governance forms are typically involved (Schmitter 1997). Another research result is that once a certain combination of governance forms has been established, it tends to persist over time (path dependency). One issue that is currently being debated is whether European countries are characterized by a special configuration of governance mechanisms beyond the state and the market, which include not only employers' associations but also trade unions (Hollingsworth and Boyer 1997). Other issues under discussion include the possible convergence of Europeans states within the European Union and the consequences for the countries in Eastern Europe of having capitalism and democracy introduced simultaneously (Stark and Bruszt 1998).

As an example of an analysis that draws not only on political economy but also on new economic sociology, one can take Roger Hollingsworth's essay "The Institutional Embeddedness of American Capitalism" (1997). According to the author, the social system of production in the United States has been profoundly influenced by the absence of an aristocracy and consequently of a need for a democratic revolution of the type that occurred in many European countries. Already by the mid-1800s the organization of industry, known as the

"American system of manufacturing," was in place, characterized by the norms of individualism and entrepreneurship. The strength of this cultural heritage, which was related to American Puritanism, also helps to explain why a strong native labor movement failed to emerge.

By the end of the nineteenth century, Hollingsworth continues, mass production, with its emphasis on hierarchy and repetitive jobs, had begun to dominate industry ("Fordism"); and this situation would last until the 1950s and the 1960s. By that time, however, other countries with more efficient systems of production started to challenge U.S. firms. For a variety of reasons American firms are weakly embedded in existing social relations, and this has made it hard for them to produce high-quality merchandise. Today's manufacturing industry, for example, has difficulty competing with countries such as Japan and Germany, where the firms are more embedded in the social structure and the workers get better training. The traditional dependence of American firms on the capital market for financing has also encouraged a certain "short-termism."

This very lack of embeddedness has, on the other hand, made it easy for American corporations to respond quickly to new demands and put together new businesses. Areas such as computers and semiconductors are, for example, flourishing in the United States, in response to rapidly changing demands and conditions. Looking to the future of the American economy, Hollingsworth concludes that the lack of a welfare state, in combination with a weak civil society, makes for difficult prospects for all but a minority of the population (see Campbell, Hollingsworth, and Lindberg 1991 for a detailed study of the U.S. economy, and, more generally, see Lipset 1996 on U.S. exceptionalism).

By way of concluding this section about the organization of the economy in the form of capitalism, it is useful to refer once more to the model in figure 3.1. What, according to this model, makes rational capitalism so dynamic is the feedback loop from profit to reinvestment in production. Weber's theory of the three different types of capitalism shows an awareness of this mechanism; and one of Weber's main points about political capitalism and traditional commercial capitalism is precisely that these two types of capitalism have never succeeded in developing a well-functioning feedback loop of this type.

When it comes to the discussion of capitalism among contemporary sociologists, in contrast, the situation is somewhat different. Here the desire to show that social relations and institutions matter is often so strong that the key mechanism in capitalism—the generation of profit and its reinvestment in production—is hardly ever mentioned, and rarely theorized. This leads to a flawed view of capitalism, and a failure to understand its dynamics as well as its capacity to mobilize people and resources for its purposes.

Industrial Districts

Another type of social organization of the economy that has attracted much attention during the past decade or so is that of industrial districts. This phenomenon was first studied by Alfred Marshall, who also coined the term. As opposed to national forms of capitalism, industrial districts are defined by geographic and social boundaries, not by political boundaries. In terms of the basic model of capitalism industrial districts represent ways of organizing production on the basis of exchange and with competitors as well as related firms in close geographic proximity.

Research on industrial districts was ignited a few decades ago by Italian scholars through a series of studies of the middle and northeastern regions of Italy. It soon turned out that industrial districts could also be found in many other countries, inside as well as outside of Europe, and also during the early stages of industrialization. Today the discussion of industrial districts has merged with a more general debate about the importance of economic regions. It has also been extended to include huge corporations, not only small and medium-sized firms.

Alfred Marshall addresses the issue of industrial districts in both of his two major works, *Principles of Economics* ([1920] 1961, 1:271–73) and *Industry and Trade* (1919:283–88; cf. Bellandi 1989). He notes the advantages for an industry to be located in the vicinity of other industries: "The owner of an isolated factory, even if he has access to a plentiful supply of general labour, is often put to great shifts for want of some special skilled labour; and a skilled workman, when thrown out of employment in it, he has no easy refuge" ([1920] 1961, 1:271–72). Apart from the fact that in an industrial district workers with specialized skills will more easily find employment, and employers who need workers with specialized skills will more easily find these workers, Marshall also points to the "great advantages [for industrial districts], that not are to be found elsewhere; and an atmosphere [that] cannot easily be moved" (1919:284). "The mysteries of the trade become no mysteries; but are, as it were, in the air, and children learn many of them unconsciously" ([1920] 1961, 1:271). Sheffield in England and Solingen in Germany are mentioned as typical examples of industrial districts. Marshall also states that if many small firms are situated close to each other, they may be able to use more expensive and specialized machinery than if they were isolated.

In the mid-1970s Italian scholars started to develop similar ideas as those of Marshall, in studies of middle and northeast Italy. Arnaldo Bagnasco, in particular, pointed out that in the "Third Italy" the economy is neither organized by the state (as in southern Italy) nor dominated by huge industrial corporations (as in northwest Italy). Instead it relies on small and medium-sized firms (Bagnasco 1977; cf. Trigilia 1995; Barbera 2002). The type of products that are produced in this part of Italy are fairly traditional, such as tiles, textiles, and leather goods.

Some time later Charles Sabel and his collaborators introduced a historical perspective into the debate (Piore and Sabel 1984; Sabel and Zeitlin 1985). They also raised it to a more general level by suggesting that small and medium-sized firms were much better at "flexible specialization" (as they termed it) than the old-fashioned "Fordist" industry, with its need for hierarchical organization and huge, stable markets. Flexible specialization was also held up as an ideal for the future, since it could handle markets that undergo sharp and unpredictable swings, which are common in modern capitalism.

Many interesting empirical studies have been made of industrial districts in Europe, from the Third Italy to, say, Baden-Württemberg in Germany and Gnosjö in Sweden (e.g., Semlinger 1995, Sjöstrand forthcoming). The English-speaking reader can get a flavor of what an Italian industrial district is like by reading Mark Lazerson's studies of Modena in Emilia Romagna (1993). Here a number of interconnected small firms cooperate in the production of knitwear. One firm does the weaving, another the cutting, a third adds the buttonholes and the buttons, and so on.

But today there also exists a type of industrial district different from the ones that were initially studied in Europe, with their small and medium-sized firms. This new type consists of firms at the very cutting edge of modern technology; and mixed in with the small and medium-sized firms are also huge firms. Silicon Valley represents the archetype of this kind of industrial district, where the value of what is being produced is truly enormous and where venture capital is heavily invested.

One of the best sociological studies of the computer industry in Silicon Valley, which also draws heavily on the literature on industrial districts, is AnnaLee Saxenian's *Regional Advantage: Culture and Competition in Silicon Valley and Route 128* (1994). The key thesis of this work is clear from its title: what matters is not so much the individual entrepreneur or the single firm, but rather the structure of the regional economy or the industrial district. Saxenian's study, it should also be noted, focuses on two such districts, an approach that allows her to distinguish between factors that make for a well-functioning and effective district, and those that do not.

Both the Route 128 area in Boston and Silicon Valley in Northern California have their origin in the support of the U.S. government for war-related research during World War II. At first there only existed a link between the government and the university (MIT in Boston and Stanford University in California). Later, however, a third, crucial partner was added: business. Initially Route 128 was doing much better than Silicon Valley, but since the late 1980s it has fallen sharply behind. The main reason for this, according to Saxenian, is that from early on the two regions had very different social structures. Route 128 was what she calls an "independent firm-based [industrial] system" and Silicon Valley a "decentralized regional network-based [industrial] district" (1994:8). Along Route 128 the firms were typically located far from each other. They wanted to be independent of one another and they had traditional hierarchies. Financing came from banks; bankruptcy meant personal failure; and employees who changed employers risked being sued.

In Silicon Valley, on the other hand, firms were located close to one another; hierarchy was avoided as much as possible; and the employees often socialized after work. Capital came through a new type of financier: venture capitalists, who often were ex-entrepreneurs themselves and wanted a stake in the business. Employees changed jobs so often that there was no point in suing them; and entrepreneurs often failed in their businesses once or twice before they succeeded ("repeat entrepreneurs"). A major reason for the success of Silicon Valley, Saxenian concludes, is to be found in the role that informal networks play in the region.

Since 1999 there also exists a large sociological project on Silicon Valley, led by Mark Granovetter and entitled "Networks of Silicon Valley" (Granovetter 1999b). The main idea is that despite the fact that everybody talks about the crucial role of networks in Silicon Valley, no one has actually studied them empirically and over time. The general point of doing so, Granovetter and his collaborators argue in an early publication from this project, is that this will lead to a much more precise and rich sense of the social structure of Silicon Valley (Castilla et al. 2000). It is also suggested that the key to success in Silicon Valley is not so much to be found by researching (and copying) single successful firms, as in understanding the distinct constellations of networks that are made up by the actors from several different sectors, such as firms, venture capitalists, law firms, educational institutions, political authorities, and so on.

To illustrate the fruitfulness of using a systematic network analysis, Granovetter and his collaborators have carried out a few sample analyses (Castilla et al. 2000). One of these deals with the creation of firms in the semiconductor industry in Silicon Valley, more precisely with the spin-off process set off in 1957 by the departure of several employees from William Shockley's corporation (the "Traitorous Eight"). If a tie represents a situation in which a person has been active in the founding of two corporations, the results from an analysis of 1947–86 indicate that a small number of well-known people each had more than ten of these ties. The analysis, however, shows as well that a number of considerably less-known actors have also been very active in setting up companies. The result, in other words, indicates the need to go beyond popular accounts of entrepreneurship to get the history straight.

A study by Granovetter and colleagues of venture capital firms, which have been active on the West coast between 1958 and 1983, reveals a very different kind of network (Castilla et al. 2000). Instead of a relatively evenly connected network, as in the spin-off process in the semiconductor industry, there is, first of all, a cluster of firms with many ties to one another. This means that these firms have all been founded by people who were also involved in the founding of other venture capital firms. But, as it turns out, there are also a number of firms that are *not* connected to one another, raising the question whether they have been founded in some alternative fashion.

The third and last networks analysis provided by Granovetter and his collaborators represents an attempt to study the interaction among different sectors in Silicon Valley. Data on California firms of a certain type, involved in initial public offerings in 1999, indicate that there exists a distinct pattern of interaction among law firms, investment banks, and accounting firms (see figure 3.3). A small number of high-prestige firms from each of these categories are involved in many deals. The law firms, however, surprisingly turn out to be local rather than national. If the results would be the same with a better sample is hard to know, according to the authors. Still, the general point is clear: namely that actors from several sectors cooperate in the information retrieval services industry in California—and that Granovetter and his colleagues may well be correct in their guess that it is ultimately this fact that accounts for the success of the region.

Globalization

The kind of economic sociology that has emerged since the mid-1980s in the United States has not been very international in nature. It has

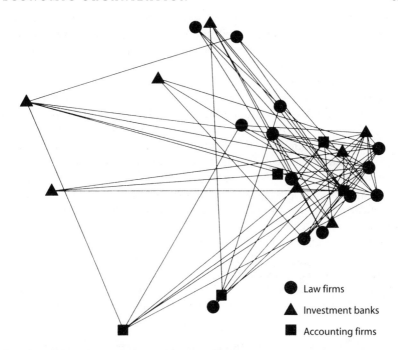

Figure 3.3. Social Networks in Silicon Valley.

Note: This figure shows the network made up of initial public offerings in the "information retrieval services industry" (SIC 7375) in 1999 in California. Among these nineteen IPOs, fourteen law firms were involved, nine lead investment banks, and six accounting firms. A line in the figure indicates two firms who participated in one of these IPOs. The length of a line is inversely proportional to the number of coparticipations. "The longer the tie, the weaker the relationship" (Castilla et al. 2000: 243).

Source: Emilio Castilla et al., "Social Networks in Silicon Valley" in *The Silicon Valley Edge, A Habitat for Innovation and Entrepreneurship,* edited by Chong-Moon Lee et al. (Stanford University Press, 2000), 243. © 2000 by the Board of Trustees of the Leland Stanford Jr. University, by permission of Stanford University Press.

also shown little interest in connecting up to other research traditions that study the international economy, such as international political economy, world systems theory, and development economics (for exceptions, see, e.g., Gereffi 1994; Evans 1995; Orrù, Biggart, and Hamilton 1997; Riain and Evans 2000; Guillén 2001a,b). This trend represents a weakness in contemporary economic sociology, as does its absence from the debate on globalization.

From an economic viewpoint, globalization is the term used these days to denote the spread of modern capitalism throughout the world. Exactly how far this process has gone, however, is hotly contested. While production, distribution, and consumption used to take place in one and the same country (minus import/export), globalization means that national boundaries are increasingly less important for the operation of capitalism. This weakening of the boundaries between countries expresses itself in many ways. Production, for example, often involves several countries these days; and consumption may take place in yet another country. The reinvestment of profit in production also often ignores national boundaries. In brief, the whole capitalist machinery—production, distribution, consumption, and reinvestment of profit—is to some extent already operating globally, often with full support from the political authorities.

Concern with globalization began around 1990 and is interdisciplinary in nature, with several high-profile sociologists from specialties other than economic sociology participating. One of the key figures and advocates of the idea that the world is becoming global is urban sociologist Manuel Castells, author of *The Information Age: Economy, Society and Culture* (1996–98). According to Castells, a "new economy" has emerged, driven by new technologies (1996:66). This economy is *global* in nature, not just international:

> A global economy is a historically new reality, distinct from a world economy. A world economy, that is an economy in which capital accumulation proceeds throughout the world, has existed in the West at least since the sixteenth century, as Fernand Braudel and Immanuel Wallerstein have taught us. *A global economy is something different: it is an economy with the capacity to work as a unit in real time on a planetary scale* (92; emphasis in original).

What characterizes the global economy, according to Castells, is first and foremost that it is based on a new kind of infrastructure technology—information processing devices and information processing itself. The use of this technology and other factors have led to an increase in trade, foreign investments, and the creation of international financial markets in which the turnover is enormous, especially in currency. Capital markets in different parts of the world are all connected to one another and capital is managed around the clock. Markets for goods and services are becoming increasingly internationalized (much less so, however, the labor market). The dominant firms are all active in the world market and are also in the process of being transformed from multinational corporations into transnational corporations. The latter are organized in a horizontal manner and can best be characterized as networks ("networks enterprises"; Castells 1996:151–200).

Castells's view that the world economy has gone through a fundamental change and become "global" has been challenged by a number of social scientists, including economic sociologists. Neil Fligstein, for example, has pointed out that world trade has not expanded very much in relative terms during the past few decades, that information technology and telecommunications only constitute a small part of world trade and world GDP, and that the basic structure of firms has not changed because of information technology (1996, 2001:191–222). Other social scientists have also challenged the view that globalization has led to substantial changes in the economy (see, e.g., Held and McGraw 2000).

But even if a major shift of the type that Castells and some other globalization theorists talk about may not have occurred, sociologists have nonetheless recorded a number of interesting changes at the international level. One of these is the emergence of what Saskia Sassen calls "legal regimes," which regulate firms that operate transnationally (2000; cf. Dezalay and Garth 1996). For an example of a legal regime Sassen points to the many international arbitration centers that have recently come into being; she also calls attention to the Americanization of international commercial legislation.

Another sociological contribution to the understanding of the global economy has been made by John Meyer and his associates in their analyses of the global culture (see Meyer 2000 for an overview). Their general argument is that distinct models for how politics, education, and the economy should be organized are currently being produced in the West, then copied and diffused throughout the world. According to one of these models, a modern nation state should be concerned primarily with economic development. Other models can be described as scripts for accounting, for organizational training programs, for describing what a successful firm should be like, and so on. Of crucial importance in all of these models, it is argued, is the idea or myth of the rational actor—be it in the form of the nation-state, the modern organization, or the individual. Meyer explains how these actors are viewed in modern society:

> Actors are entities with rights or interests *and* with the assigned right and capacity to represent these interests. Actors, thus, are assigned agency—derived mainly from the moral universe: it is in this sense that they are small gods (2000:239).

Much work at the international or global level clearly remains to be done in economic sociology. In particular it seems important for economic sociology to find its own way of analyzing topics at this level, instead of simply taking over the approach of world-systems theory,

"I totally agree with you about capitalism, neo-colonialism, and
globalization, but you really come down too hard on shopping."

for example. One way to proceed might be to make better use of
network analysis, organizational theory, and cultural sociology—
three approaches that have all worked very well on middle-range
economic phenomena. Another way would be to emphasize the importance of certain interests in driving this whole process. To enumerate topics that need to be researched is probably futile since there are
so many. Nonetheless, solid sociological studies of the international
financial agencies (such as IMF, IBRD, and WTO) are definitely
needed, as are studies of economic regions and countries outside of
the usual OECD countries that sociologists tend to write about. It is
also important to keep in mind that the key objective of capitalism is
profit; and that culture, organization, and networks will all be used by
the key actors in their hunt for profit.

Summary

There exist certain advantages to using the concept of economic organization in a conventional sense as well as in a broad sense, that is, as synonymous with the general organization of the economy. By proceeding in this way, as I will show in the next chapter, it also becomes easier to get a handle on what is distinctive about firms and how these are connected to one another, as well as to the political system, society as a whole, and so on. It also becomes clear that firms are in one sense very similar to other forms of economic organization, such as industrial districts, globalization, and capitalism. All social life, including the economy, can be conceptualized in terms of interests, connections and disconnections.

Of all the types of economic organization in a broad sense, capitalism is by far the most important and also the natural point of departure for economic sociology. Capitalism can be understood as a form of social and economic organization, which is characterized by the fact that it has profit as one of its goals, not only consumption; and that the profit has to be continuously reinvested in new production. Profit has first to be generated and then fed back into production through a feedback loop. This is precisely what makes capitalism such a dynamic form of economic organization, leading to constant "creative destruction" (Schumpeter). Of early attempts to conceptualize capitalism, that of Weber deserves to be singled out, with its useful typology of rational capitalism, political capitalism and traditional commercial capitalism. The modern discussion of capitalism, which emphasizes on varieties of capitalism, is also of much interest.

Industrial districts and the process of globalization are examples of economic organization in the broad sense. The literature on industrial districts—from Alfred Marshall on England to AnnaLee Saxenian on Silicon Valley—is of great interest to economic sociology. Much of what has been written on globalization consists no doubt of exaggerations and hype. Nonetheless, an economic sociology of globalization is much needed, and some attempts in this direction have already been made. That firms play a key role in modern capitalism—on a local, national and global level—constitutes the topic of the next chapter.

IV

Firms

NEXT to capitalism and its underlying market mechanism, the modern corporation represents the most important type of economic organization in today's world, and this is also why it is important for economic sociology to prioritize the development of a sociology of firms. My own opinion for how this can be done includes three suggestions. First, economic sociologists should decisively break with the tendency in much of organization theory to treat firms as if they were similar to all other kinds of organizations. Second, it has to be realized that firms can take many different forms, each with its own sociological profile: partnerships, family firms, joint-stock corporations, and so on. And third, economic sociologists should attempt to introduce the concept of interest into the analysis of firms. Organization theory is built on the assumption that all organizations are at some basic level identical, and this blurs an important concern to economic sociology, namely that there exist differences between organizations that have profit-making as their goal and those that do not.

There are general advantages of looking at firms in interest terms: it allows the strength or the power of the actors to be better taken into account; it helps to explain why one type of action rather than another is chosen; and it helps to understand how a number of actions can add up to a powerful dynamic. Exactly how to conceptualize firms with the help of a sociological interest theory is, however, something that still needs to be worked out and discussed. Different ways of accomplishing this goal are possible—and probably also necessary since many different types of firms exist (small firms, family firms, share-holding firms, transnational firms, and so on). Firms, of course, also constitute institutions—and as such they can be described as distinct constellations of interests and social relations, which are backed up by the legal machinery.

One way to start reasoning about the firm as a specific institution as well as in interest terms might be as follows. On a general level, the modern share-holding firm represents a special way of mobilizing and organizing a number of different economic interests. It can also be said to constitute a legitimate economic order, which assigns to a number of individuals the collective task of producing for the market.

This order is centered around profit-making, and it is legally as well as socially seen as an individual actor. The people who work for a firm have their own interests for doing so, and it is essentially by appealing to these interests that a firm can produce what it sells. In pursuing their own economic interests as well as those of the firm, the actors inside the firm also tend to develop group interests, which may or may not be of help in producing profit. The modern firm takes many different forms and must not be automatically identified with the giant joint-stock corporation controlled by a huge number of owners. In particular, family firms are much more common than is usually thought and have been much neglected in economic sociology.

Economic Theories of the Firm

Both economists and sociologists have made contributions to the analysis of the firm that are of much value for the sociology of this organization. Their approaches to this topic, however, have been quite different. While economists, still working in the tradition of the theory of the firm, typically look at the single firm, sociologists study firms in plural and also consider their environments. Sociologists draw on organization theory and, as noted earlier, prefer to talk about organizations in general, rather than economic organizations per se. Economists, in contrast, look exclusively at economic organizations, especially the firm. Economists also single out the role of interests in their analyses, something that sociologists rarely do. On the other hand, economists have little to say about the social relations of the firm, unlike sociologists. Finally, while economists assume the existence of a few stylized actors inside a unitary type of firm, sociologists distinguish among a number of different groups inside a number of different types of firms.

The theory of the firm is traditionally seen as originating in the work of Cournot during the 1830s (Blaug 1980:175). Cournot essentially conceptualized the firm as maximizing profit, subject to the constraints of technology and demand. A standard tool for analyzing the firm in twentieth-century economics has been the so-called production function, which is typically defined as "the technical relationship telling the maximum amount of output capable of being produced by each and every set of specified inputs (or factors of production); it is defined for a given set of technical knowledge" (Samuelson 1970:516). Also much of the information that the firm needs from its surroundings is conveyed through prices, according to modern economics, and not through contacts and social relations (Hayek 1945).

During the past few decades the conventional theory of the firm, however, has met with harsh criticism for its failure to deal with the internal structure of the firm. One author writes that "in standard price theory, the firm is itself a primitive atom of the economy, an unindividuated, single-minded agent interacting with similarly unindividuated consumers and factor suppliers in the market economy" (Putterman 1986:5). A different way of phrasing this criticism would be to say that even though a few stylized actors are assumed to exist in the firm, its internal structure (as well as its environment) is basically treated as a black box.

When economists today discuss the firm, they refer primarily to one or several of the theories that make up "organizational economics" or they attempt to analyze the structure of the firm with the help of microeconomics. This approach has more or less replaced what once used to be known as the theory of the firm. Before we turn to organizational economics, however, we should consider some other attempts by economists to develop a richer analysis of the firm's internal structure, as well as its environment, than can be found in the traditional theory of the firm. These works display, among other things, a great sensitivity to the way in which the different interests in the firm are structured and what effects this has on the way that business is conducted. The interests they look at include those of the owners, managers, and employees.

One of these alternative analyses can be found in *The Wealth of Nations*. Adam Smith notes, for example, that in a "private copartnery" you are liable with all of your fortune, but in a "joint stock company" you are only liable with the sum you invested; and that this leads to considerably more risk-taking in the latter case than in the former ([1776] 1976:741). He also points out that people are not as careful with "other people's money" as with their own; and that this makes the interest of the owners of a joint-stock company diverge from that of its manager:

> The directors of such companies, however, being the managers rather of other people's money than of their own, it cannot well be expected that they should watch over it with the same anxious vigilance with which the partners in a private copartnery frequently watch over their own. . . . Negligence and profusion, therefore, must always prevail, more or less, in the management of the affairs of such a company (741).

Another alternative analysis of the firm by an economist can be found in the work of Alfred Marshall. According to a well-known statement by Marshall, economics should not only deal with land, labor, and capital but also with a fourth factor of production: "*organi-*

zation" (Marshall [1920] 1961, 1:138–39, 240–313; 1919:178–394). The "organization" of the economy exists at different levels, one of which is the firm or the joint stock company; and Marshall devotes much energy to an analysis of its internal structure as well as its external relations. His most important contribution to the study of the external relations of the firm is found in his theory of the industrial district, which was presented in chapter 3 of this book. As to the internal organization of the firm, Marshall points out, among other things, that a joint stock company that is headed by a (salaried) manager has a tendency to shy away from innovation:

> The owner of a business, when contemplating any change, is led by his own interest to weigh the whole gain that it would probably bring to the business, against the whole loss. But the private interest of the salaried manager, or official, often draws him in another direction: the path of least resistance, of greatest comfort and least risk to himself, is generally that of not striving very energetically for improvement; and of finding plausible excuses for not trying an improvement suggested by others, until its success is established beyond question (Marshall 1919:324).

Marshall also discusses the place of loyalty in a corporation and how it makes the employees take pleasure in its success and in its good reputation, a bit like people who love their country. "This loyalty," he adds, "is being furthered by a multitude of movements, designed to give the employees a direct interest in the prosperity of the business for which they work" (Marshall 1919:327).

The rich empirical knowledge of firms and industries that characterizes Marshall's work in general, as well as his *Industry and Trade* (1919) in particular, disappeared from mainstream economics till it was revived in the 1940s by economists in the field of industrial organization. This field has recently been taken over by game theorists, something that has greatly increased its analytical strength—and also ended the tradition of producing empirical studies. The reader may get a sense of this development by comparing the long-time standard textbook by F. M. Scherer to its foremost competitor these days, Jean Tirole's *The Theory of Industrial Organization* (Scherer and Ross 1990; Tirole 1988; cf. Bourdieu 2000c:243).

It is often pointed out that a lack of analytical sharpness was characteristic of the older approach to industrial organization, which helps explain why this field yielded so quickly to game theory. This charge, however, cannot be leveled at the three creators of the theory of the behavioral firm: Richard Cyert, James March, and Herbert Simon. The relevance of their ideas to economic sociology is clear enough but has not been fully realized; and at the most one can find an occasional reference to their works. A natural place for economic sociologists to start would be the discussion of conflicts of interest within the firm, as discussed in Cyert and March's *A Behavioral Theory of the Firm* (1963). The authors here note that the conventional way to address how a firm's goal is decided upon is either to identify a common goal or assume that the goal of the firm is identical to that of the entrepreneur. This, however, leads to a contradiction: "neoclassical theories of the firm recognized the principle that economic actors are self-interested, but conflicts of interest internal to the firm were ignored or assumed to be resolved through a prior contract by which employees agreed to pursue the interest of the entrepreneur" (Cyert and March [1963] 1992:215). It was also pointed out by Cyert and March that "the existence of unresolved conflict is a conspicuous feature of organizations" (1963:28).

In "The Business Firm as a Political Coalition" James March elaborates on some of the ideas in *A Behavioral Theory of the Firm*, especially that actors with an interest in the firm try to put together a coalition to realize their interests (1962; Cyert and March 1963). The range of actors that March discusses goes well beyond the ones mentioned by Adam Smith and Alfred Marshall, and includes suppliers, customers, governmental agencies, trade associations, trade unions, different types of employees, and so on. The similarities between March's ideas and so-called stakeholder theory are obvious (Donaldson and Preston 1995; Jensen 2001).

Some suggestive additions to the theory of conflicts of interests inside the firm can be found in Herbert Simon's writings on the role of organizations in the economy. In one of these writings Simon discusses the loyalty of employees and notes that it represents a pervasive and important phenomenon in its own right (Simon 1997; cf. Simon 1991). He adds to Marshall's analysis of loyalty by emphasizing its quality as an economic emotion. Loyalty, to Simon, is more than just a way for the employees to identify with the interests of the firm; it also represents a powerful source of aggression. "In many cases where there are conflicts of interest or supposed conflicts of interest between the group we call 'we' and the group we call 'they', we not only are willing to be very protective of the 'we', but we are also willing to be very aggressive against 'they'" (Simon 1997:54).

Organizational Economics

What goes under the name of organizational economics (or the economics of organization) is part of new institutional economics, which was born in the 1970s and more or less joined mainstream economics a decade or two later (Barnes and Ouchi 1986; Milgrom and Roberts 1992; Gibbons forthcoming; for a brief overview, see Douma and Schreuder 1998). Organizational economics consists of several distinct types of analyses, of which transaction cost analysis and agency theory are the best known. Attempts to analyze the firm from the viewpoint of game theory, evolutionary theory, and law and economics also exist. Analyses in organizational economics typically draw on a mixture of these theories.

What unites the different theories that make up organizational economics is that they all begin with the individual and her economic self-interest. As opposed to, say, historians, organizational economists do not begin by studying their topics historically and then develop an analytical model. Instead they construct their theories primarily through analytical reasoning. And as opposed to sociologists, organizational economists do not start from the premise that social relations are crucial to the economy and that you need to ground these empirically. Instead they typically begin with individual self-interest and introduce social relations or institutions at a later stage, perhaps to explain why it is efficient to use an institution or how an interest can be realized through the creation of certain social relations. A logical argument is usually enough, and empirical data is often absent.

But even if the sociology of firms differs on some key points from organizational economics—especially when it comes to the importance that is attached to social relations for the realization of interests—it is also clear that this latter type of analysis represents a great advance in economic theory, and that economic sociology has much to learn from it. The tendency to overemphasize the element of economic self-interest, at the expense of social relations, is at times offset by a sensitivity to history (as in the work of Douglass North), by the introduction of a long-term perspective (as in evolutionary approaches), or by the idea that there exists a contradiction between rational behavior that is cooperative and rational behavior that is noncooperative (as in prisoner's dilemma). The end result, as we soon shall see, is in many cases a flexible and innovative kind of interest analysis that adds new and important insights to the general tradition of interest analysis that was briefly discussed in chapter 1.

Transaction Cost Analysis

The origin of transaction cost analysis goes back to "The Nature of the Firm" (1937), which R. H. Coase wrote when he was in his twenties and knew little economics (Coase 1991). This article was crucial in winning Coase the Nobel Prize in 1991, and it can be described as an analytical exercise, which starts out from conventional price theory and then tries to introduce some realism into it. "The Nature of the Firm" was not much read until the 1970s, when it was realized that it not only contains a fresh approach to the firm but also to economic analysis in general. What was especially appreciated was that Coase's approach fit so well into the effort that was then under way to apply the economic model to noneconomic phenomena—what economists like to refer to as "economic imperialism" (cf. Udehn 1991). From then on, the interest in Coase's article has been enormous.

Coase begins "The Nature of the Firm" by noting that in standard economic theory everything in the economy works by itself and in a voluntary fashion. When prices change, individuals and firms adjust to this fact on their own accord because it is in their self-interest to do so. But this description of the economy is not all there is to the story, according to Coase, and the reason is that the individual does *not* act in a voluntary manner inside the firm. A worker is told what to do and acts accordingly. From this fact Coase concludes that there exist *two* different ways of organizing an economy: through the market and through a firm. Markets and firms represent "alternative methods of co-ordinating production" ([1937] 1988:36).

But if there exist two ways of getting things done in the economy, when is one rather than the other to be used? And, more generally, why do firms exist if there are markets that can handle everything? Coase's answer to these questions is that there is a cost for using the market, and if this cost exceeds the cost for using a firm, a firm will in principle be used. "The main reason why it is profitable to establish a firm would seem to be that there is a cost of using the price mechanism," to cite the single most important sentence in "The Nature of the Firm" ([1937] 1988:38). Coase does not use the term "transaction cost" in his article, but the idea is there. The cost of using the market, he says, covers such items as the cost to acquire information, to draw up a contract, and so on. Coase concludes that his theory of the firm is both "[analytically] manageable" and "realistic" (54).

If Coase was the person who invented the idea of transaction cost, it was Oliver Williamson who popularized it and made it widely known in economics as well as in neighboring sciences. This was done through a steady stream of books and articles in the 1970s and 1980s, the most important of which is *Markets and Hierarchies* (1975; see also Williamson 1985, 1986). The key idea of *Markets and Hierarchies* (1975) is nicely captured by its title and dramatizes Coase's insight from 1937, namely that markets and firms constitute alternative methods of coordinating production (or, in Williamson's terminology, that they constitute different "governance structures"). In the 1970s, when Williamson's book appeared, organization theory had also come into its own, unlike the 1930s, when Coase published his article; and Williamson felt very strongly that economists had made a great mistake when they let the study of organizations slip away and become a separate discipline of its own. According to Williamson,

> The study of economic organization commonly proceeds as though market and administrative modes of organization were disjunct. Market organization is the province of economists. Internal organization is the concern of organization theory specialists. And never the twain shall meet (1975:ix).

Even though Williamson's main inspiration for transaction cost analysis came from Coase, he also put his own mark on it. The term "transaction cost" was also popularized by Williamson, who defines it in the following way:

> The ex ante costs of drafting, negotiating and *safeguarding* an agreement and, more especially, the ex post costs of maladaptation and adjustment that arise when contract execution is misaligned as a result of gaps, errors, omissions, and unanticipated disturbances; the costs of running the economic system (Williamson 1991:103).

While Coase had spoken only of two governance structures—markets and firms—Williamson, under the pressure of criticism, soon added a third: the "hybrid" or an autonomous form of organization, based on long-term contractual relations (Williamson 1991:102). Very importantly, Williamson also attempted to operationalize Coase's insights and to state under exactly which circumstances the market rather than a firm is likely to be used. The general answer to this question, he argues, is that a firm will be used when transactions are frequent; when they are uncertain; and when special investments are necessary (so-called asset specificity). The market, in other words, will be used when no asset specificity is involved, when transactions are straightforward, or only occur once.

Both Coase and Williamson typically operate with a fairly simple version of interest analysis: whether a firm or a market will be used depends exclusively on which is the cheapest. If this argument is used to explain the historical emergence of the modern firm, it is not convincing. As the history of the firm shows, its emergence has been slow and difficult—well beyond the grasp of a simplistic interest analysis in terms of costs and profits (cf. Weber [1923] 1981:225–29, 279–82). But when the transaction cost approach is used to explain what will happen when someone chooses between using the market or a firm, when the latter is easily available, the theory has considerably more plausibility (but still remains a proposition to be empirically tested).

Transaction cost analysis in Coase's and Williamson's versions has, however, led to an innovation in interest theory, partly due to its argument about the cost of using contracts. In standard economic theory during most of the twentieth century it was typically assumed that all actors obey the law, which means that there was not much point in discussing the price for policing the economic system or referring in some other way to the legal system. Transaction cost analysis, on the other hand, does *not* make the assumption of lawful behavior but assumes instead that the actor is opportunistic and will break the law if she can get away with it. According to Williamson, who is responsible for this innovation, "opportunism is a variety of self-interest" (1975:7). He explains his position in the following manner:

> the consequences of opportunism are incompletely developed in conventional economic models of firms and markets. As Diamond has noted, standard "economic models . . . [treat] individuals as playing a game with fixed rules which they obey. They do not buy more than they know they can pay for, they do not embezzle funds, they do not rob banks." But, whereas behavior of these kinds is disallowed under conventional assumptions, opportunism, in a rich variety of forms, is made to play a central role in the analysis of markets and hierarchies herein (Williamson 1975:7).

Another novel angle on the concept of interest in transaction cost analysis can be found in the work of economic historian Douglass North, who regards himself as belonging to a different branch of transaction cost analysis than Williamson—"the University of Washington approach" (North 1990:27). In general, North has been very interested in the task of introducing different types of transaction costs into economic history, such as measurement costs, protection costs, and so on. Combined with his early emphasis on price differences as the motor of economic development, this makes for a realistic and innovative type of analysis (e.g., North and Thomas 1973; Nee forthcoming).

In *Institutions, Institutional Change and Economic Performance* (1990) North adds to this analysis by suggesting that institutions can be defined as rules, and that organizations can be seen as players of games that are based on these rules. All organizations play to win, according to North, presumably because of their self-interest (the reader may recall Bourdieu's argument about interest as *illusio*, or that the game is worth playing, versus *ataraxia* or indifference toward the game, as presented in chapter 2). All players, however, cannot win, and there is consequently a high probability that the attempt to realize one's self-interest will end in failure. And the organizations that do win, North argues, mainly do so through their skill in playing the game, which they have acquired over time. In other words, while a concern with costs and profit is central to North's analysis of the firm, he also makes it more complex by opening it up to the possibility that firms may err in realizing their self-interest, that these attempts may end in failure, and that the firms need to develop a skill in realizing their self-interest.

Agency Theory

While the concept of agency is still somewhat new to mainstream economics, where it was introduced a few decades ago, it has held a central place for many centuries in Western legal doctrine (Müller–Freienfels 1978). The so-called law of agency governs the relationship between a person (the agent), who acts on behalf of another person (the principal), vis-à-vis still another person (the third party). The key idea is that the agent can act in a legally binding way for the principal, in relation to a third party. The law of agency is of much importance to economic life, where it is applicable to the position of the manager, the broker, the salesperson, and so on.

The notion of agency is used in a somewhat different way in economics than in law. Economists mainly look at the relationship between the principal and the agent (the so-called internal contract), while they are less interested in the capacity of the agent to bind the principal and a third party (e.g., Pratt and Zeckhauser 1985; Clifford Smith 1987). The real innovation in economics, however, is to have recast the principal-agent relationship in pure interest terms and then apply it to the internal organization of the firm. The principal (e.g., the owner) uses the agent (e.g., the CEO) to realize her interest—but this is complicated by the fact that the agent also has her own interest to take care of, and that these two interests often clash. To cite a typical sentence: "if both parties to the relationship are utility maximizers there is good reason to believe that the agent will not always act in the best interest of the principal" (Jensen and Meckling 1976:308). Various ways exist, however, to align the interests of the two parties, for example, through supervision (monitoring) or through the help of economic incentives. Both of these ways cost money; there is also the additional problem of "who will monitor the monitor?" (Alchian and Demsetz 1972:782).

Economists tend to use agency theory primarily to study the ways in which those who invest in corporations can assure themselves of a

"On the one hand, eliminating the middleman would result
in lower costs, increased sales, and greater consumer satisfaction;
on the other hand, we're the middleman."

return (see e.g., Schleifer and Vishny 1997). The best-known study in
this genre is Michael Jensen and William Meckling's "Theory of the
Firm: Managerial Behavior, Agency Costs, and Ownership Structure"
(1976; cf. Fama and Jensen 1983, Jensen 1998). The authors here note
that if the manager owns less than 100 percent of the firm, she will
have less of an incentive than the owner to work to increase its profit.
To counter this, the owner may try to supervise the manager (leading
to so-called monitoring costs) and/or give her an economic incentive
to act in the interest of the owner (leading to so-called bonding costs).
If the capital markets are efficient, the authors argue, these two
types of costs plus the residual loss (together making up agency
costs) will be carried by the manager.

A few sociologists have tried to make use of the economists' version of agency theory in their own work, while changing it on certain
points to better fit their purposes. One is Harrison White, who argues
that the concept of agency goes very well with sociology: "it is intensely social in its mechanisms, since it gets one person to do something for another vis-à-vis a third person but only with heavy reliance
on the lay of the social landscape" (1985:187). In *Identity and Control*
White also argues that agency is very interesting since it helps to initi-

ate an action and controls this action at the same time (1992:245–54). In doing so, it also introduces flexibility and counters hierarchy. Agency is furthermore crucial to the identity of the agent in various ways.

Another sociologist who draws on agency theory in his work is James Coleman, especially in *Foundations of Social Theory*. Like Harrison White, Coleman emphasizes that agency theory lends itself very well to sociology: "Once a transaction has been made, in which the principal satisfies interests of the agent (for example, through a monetary payment) in return for the agent's using his actions to pursue the principal's interests, a social system has been created" (1990:152). As opposed to the economists, however, Coleman argues that not only managers but also workers have their own distinct interests, and that these may run counter to the interests of the corporation.

Coleman introduces another novelty into interest analysis by suggesting that an agent may identify very sharply with a principal and make the interest of the principal her own (1990:157–62). An affine agent (as this type of actor is called) can in this way identify with an employer, a nation, a community, and so on. Coleman adds that this type of identification is never total; and the reason for this is that "interests are not arbitrary, to be shaped at the will of the individual, but are held in place by constraints, some of which are physiological" (161).

Other Perspectives in Organizational Economics

Besides analyses based on agency and on transaction cost, economists have also used game theory, evolutionary theory, and law and economics in analyzing firms. As mentioned earlier, economists often use a mixture of these perspectives. In their essay from 1976 Jensen and Meckling, for example, make the argument that the firm can be seen as a collection of contracts, where the contracting parties include employees, customers, creditors, and so on. The notion of the firm, Jensen and Meckling conclude, is "a legal fiction," and a better way to describe the firm is as a "nexus of a set of contracting relationships" (311). Many other economists have also found this a useful perspective (e.g., Hart 1995).

While the economists' idea of the agency contract introduces realism into the analysis of the firm, to conceive of the whole firm as a collection of contracts may have exactly the opposite effect. As an example one can cite a well-known article by Armen Alchian and Harold Demsetz, "Production, Information Costs, and Economic Organization" (1972). These two authors argue that the firm has no power whatsoever since all of its relationships are contractual or voluntary:

> The firm . . . has no power of fiat, no authority, no disciplinary action any different in the slightest degree from ordinary market contracting between only two people. . . . Telling an employee to type this letter rather than to file that document is like my telling a grocer to sell me this brand of tuna rather than that brand of bread (1972:777).

Another perspective that has been used by economists to analyze organizations is that of game theory, which has become especially important in industrial organization (Tirole 1988). The type of problems that are dealt with in this type of analysis include collusion, barriers to entry, and monopolistic competition. The main strength of game theory in analyzing firms, as well as other phenomena, is its emphasis on strategic behavior whereby an actor takes the possible actions of another actor into account when deciding upon her own action (for a discussion of the relationship of game theory and sociology, see Swedberg 2001).

From an interest point of view, the most innovative contribution of game theory to organizational economics is perhaps to be found in the notion of prisoner's dilemma or the fact that when each of several actors follows her individual interest in a rational manner, they all will end up in a worse situation than if they had cooperated. Robert Axelrod and other game theoreticians argue that the disjunction between individual and collective rationality can be overcome under certain circumstances, especially if the game is played a large number of times (1984). How realistic Axelrod's ideas are on this particular point is difficult to judge. What is clear, however, is that the idea of evolution goes well with a social approach to the firm (see e.g., Nelson and Winter 1982; Nelson 1994).

Reactions by Sociologists to Organizational Economics

There currently does not exist a major attempt in sociology, including economic sociology, to discuss organizational economics and evaluate its various strengths and weaknesses. In general, one can say that it is possible to find praise as well as critique and indifference among members of these fields. As already mentioned, James Coleman and Harrison White have found parts of agency theory very helpful. One also senses that many sociologists are positive to the reintroduction of institutions into mainstream economics and have followed the efforts on this particular point by Williamson and his colleagues with distinct sympathy. The sociological analysis of organizations has been vital-ized simply by being in contact with another social science and its approach.

A few sociologists have been very negative toward organizational economics and have rejected it outright. A case in point is Charles Perrow, who argues in *Complex Organizations* that agency theory is potentially "a dangerous explanation" (1987:235–36; for a general cri-tique of the rational choice approach in organizational economics, see Zey 1998). The reason for this danger, we are told, is that agency theory assumes that the actor is opportunistic, and this view may spread to society at large with negative consequences. Moreover Per-row, one senses, finds it distasteful that economists so easily assume that workers will loaf off if they are not closely supervised.

While it is correct that mainstream economists (minus labor econo-mists) have not shown much interest in workers and their problems, this type of critique nonetheless seems much too broad and also mis-taken. For one thing, the analytical power of agency theory does not depend on the assumption that the actor is opportunistic. A worker-owned firm, for example, will have agency problems, just as a firm owned by traditional capitalists—be they opportunistic or not. It is also a mistake, as I see it, to think that an interest analysis entails a suspicious and condescending view of human beings, and that oppor-tunism must be central to it. Surely the use of interest theory that one can find in the works of Weber, Mill, and Tocqueville would indicate the opposite.

A more useful critique of organizational economics can be found in Mark Granovetter's article on embeddedness from 1985. Granovetter essentially argues that economists are not sophisticated when it comes to analyzing social relations, which causes their analyses to suffer badly. The reason for this is that they are new at this game and have no training; they are "sociological babes in the wood" (Gra-novetter 1985b:502). Oliver Williamson, for example, assumes that markets and organizations belong to two different worlds that have little in common. And Kenneth Arrow handles morality in a non-sociological manner by assuming that all actors behave in accordance with some general morality. Reality, according to Granovetter, is much more complex; and the decision whether to trust someone or not depends, for example, on whether we know the person in ques-tion, if other people whom we know trust this person, and so on. Granovetter also criticizes the economists for their tendency to as-sume that all economic organizations that exist are by this very fact efficient; since otherwise they would have disappeared. This is a clas-sical functionalist error, Granovetter says, which sociologists left behind a long time ago (for a similar argument, see Roy 1990). The end result of the type of analysis that Williamson and his colleagues engage in, he adds, is to "discourage a detailed analysis of social structure" (Granovetter 1985b:505).

Apart from Granovetter's critique in his embeddedness article, a mention should also be made of Oberschall and Leifer's related attempt to criticize organizational economics on the basis that it uses efficiency as an explanation for everything it analyzes (1986). This argument is similar to that of Granovetter, but the authors proceed in a different way to make their point. Oberschall and Leifer note, for example, that power is typically ignored in efficiency explanations; that goal ambiguity is ignored; and that a much more complex notion of choice than the one that is used in economics is needed. In a subtle aside, they also note that in mainstream economics "the economic actor is never disappointed or surprised" (249).

Two final points should be added. First, the critiques of Granovetter and of Oberschall and Leifer cover only developments up until the mid-1980s; and much has happened since then. Secondly, a number of social scientists have also challenged organizational economics on the grounds that its predictions have not been confirmed in empirical tests. David and Han, for example, cite Williamson's statement that transaction cost analysis "is an empirical success story"—but note that around half of all empirical tests have come out negatively (1998; see also Williamson 1996b:55). A similar assessment of agency theory does not exist, as far as I know, but is clearly needed (for some empirical impressions, see e.g., Arrow 1985).

Sociological Theories of Firms

Sociologists, as opposed to economists, have tried from early on to analyze firms as social institutions or social organizations, and there exists today a long tradition of sophisticated sociological analysis of this type. This tradition starts with Max Weber around the turn of the twentieth century; it was then continued in the new field of industrial sociology; and it is today mainly carried on within the sociology of organizations. Industrial sociology and the related field of sociology of work are still alive, but the former especially has lost much of its original vigor.

If sociologists have always been interested in the social structure of firms and other organizations, they have, on the other hand, paid little attention to the role of economic interests in these. In organization theory it is of little consequence if a firm is worth one billion dollars or one hundred billion dollars. While Weber and Marx tried to combine an analysis of economic interests with an analysis of social structure, as part of their attempts to understand capitalism, this way of proceeding is rarely found in twentieth-century sociology. Much of industrial sociology and the sociology of organizations seem, for example, to have consciously stayed away from the economic dimension (that is, from the role of economic interests), perhaps better to lay bare the role of social relations. When interests have reemerged in this type of analysis, as they were bound to do, it has typically been in a modified form. It is, for example, common with references in organization theory and industrial sociology to speak of the "resources" of the firm, the "incentives" of the workers, and the like. To theorize about these elements and to study their impact, however, has been left mostly to the economists. An important task for contemporary economic sociology is therefore to reintroduce economic interests into the sociological analysis of firms, while drawing on the insights of sociology into the social structure of organizations.

Max Weber

What Max Weber has to say about economic organizations is much less known than is commonly thought, and there are several reasons for this. One of them has to do with the general lack of interest that sociologists have shown for his economic sociology. But there has also been the tendency of organizational sociologists to ignore Weber's view of the firm and pay attention only to one part of his analysis of organizations, namely his theory of bureaucracy. This tendency has much to do with the reluctance of sociologists who work in organization theory to address what is specific about economic organizations; their ambition is instead to add to the knowledge of organizations in general.

The text by Weber that is typically cited in organization theory is an excerpt entitled "Bureaucracy" from Hans Gerth and C. Wright Mills's influential anthology *From Max Weber* (Gerth and Mills 1946: 196–244; cf. Weber [1922] 1978:956–1005). A full account of Weber's analysis of economic organizations would, however, have to include quite a bit more than his theory of bureaucracy, even if the theory represents the most spectacular part of his work on organizations. The account would also have to show how economic organizations are treated (1) in his theoretical sociology, (2) in his historical sociology, and, more generally, (3) in his analysis of Western capitalism. To illustrate what such a full account might look like, I shall use Weber's analysis of the firm as an example.

In the early theoretical chapters of *Economy and Society* Weber carefully lays the foundation for how to conceptualize the firm from a social action perspective (see especially Weber [1922] 1978:48–56, 74–5). Social actions that are oriented to one another constitute social relationships; and when these exist over time they may turn into a so-called order (see my earlier discussion in chap. 1). An organization is defined by Weber as a closed or restricted social relationship, which has become an order and which is enforced by an individual or a staff. Relationships are formed because people either feel that they belong together (communal relationships) or that they have interests in common (associative relationships). Economic organizations are associative in nature and often voluntary. Some are only partially involved in the economy, while others may regulate parts of the economy (such as trade unions) or be in charge of maintaining the general economic order (such as the state). Some economic organizations, however, deal primarily with the economy—and the firm is one of these.

The firm in a capitalist society is oriented toward profit-making, as opposed to householding and consumption. The modern rational firm makes use of capital accounting, which represents a way of establishing exactly how much profit has been made during a specific time period. It is headed by an entrepreneur, and its employees typically include obedient and efficient bureaucrats as well as disciplined workers. The modern firm appropriates profit opportunities in a rational manner and can operate effectively only if it is backed by a rational state and a rational legal system, since it demands a large measure of predictability to operate efficiently.

Along with this theoretical analysis of the modern firm in social action terms, Weber's work contains an account in broad strokes of its historical emergence (see especially Weber [1923] 1981:225–29, 279–82). "It must not be forgotten," Weber says, "that forms of establishment and of the firm must be 'invented,' like technical products" ([1922] 1978:200). Some of these institutional inventions have taken place in several different civilizations, such as the use of the family as a permanent trading unit and the commenda for single trading operations.

A commenda, it should be added, can be described as an economic relationship between two merchants—one who stayed at home while the other went abroad and was in charge of the selling. If the partner who stayed at home had invested all the money in the enterprise, he would typically be entitled to three quarters of the revenue; and if he had invested half, he would get one third. A very important feature of the commenda was that its investment structure necessitated an early form of capital accounting, since it was necessary to figure out the value of the whole enterprise before as well as after the goods had been sold.

Some institutional features of the firm, however, have appeared only in the West or much earlier in this part of the world than elsewhere. Extending the trading unit beyond the circle of the family, for example, first became common in the West. Another important institutional innovation was joint responsibility or the capacity of a family member to make agreements which were binding also for the other members. The separation between property that belongs to the individual, on the one hand, and property that belongs to the firm, on the other hand, took place in medieval Italy, more precisely in fourteenth-century Florence. "Out of the property of the firm, for which we find the designation *corpo della compagnia*," Weber notes, "evolved the capital concept" ([1923] 1981:228). Around the same time a very important legal concept was also invented: the notion of juristic personality or the idea that an organization, from a legal perspective, can be treated as an individual with a capacity to enter contracts, own property, and so on (Weber [1922] 1978:705–31).

But the Western firm, as it existed in the Italian city states during the Middle Ages, was still a far cry from the modern firm. During the Reformation, Weber notes, a new and much more methodical attitude to business was introduced into the firm, which deeply affected its operations. Firms now tightened up their activities and became much more active and competitive; entrepreneurs and workers changed attitude and became energized. The idea of investing via shares also slowly evolved, first within the political sphere and later in the giant colonial corporations, such as the Dutch and English East India companies. It would take quite a bit more time, however, until shares would be freely traded and the modern shareholding corporation could become a common feature in economic life.

Ralf Dahrendorf argues that Weber should be regarded as the founder of industrial sociology, and it may well be true that he was among the first to analyze the situation of the workers at their workplace with the help of sociology (Dahrendorf 1956:24). But it should also be noted that this type of analysis formed an integral part of Weber's general analysis of the firm and the rise of rational capitalism. Weber distinguishes among three main categories of people inside the firm: the entrepreneur, the bureaucrat, and the worker. It is the transformation of these into the *methodical* entrepreneur, the *dutiful* bureaucrat, and the worker *with a vocation*, to which modern capitalism owes much of its power as well as its historical breakthrough.

The entrepreneur has a very different mentality from that of the bureaucrat: he is independent in judgment, eager to make a profit, and in general "the leading spirit" of the firm (Weber [1922] 1978: 1403). On a number of accounts, he is the opposite of the bureaucrat. The bureaucrats are specially trained for what they do; they have delimited areas of responsibility; and they are imbued with a sense of duty and status honor. The workers, finally, have no property and are totally dependent on employment to support themselves and their families. The modern factory has also made it imperative that the work force is methodical and disciplined. The workers, however, are not only shaped by industry but can also influence it (Weber [1908–09] 1988). If a worker, for example, works harder than her peers, and thereby threatens to lower the piece rate, she is often forced by the other workers to reduce her efforts (Weber [1908] 1980:133).

When Weber's analysis of firms has been referred to by sociologists, it has been treated exclusively as part of his theory of bureaucracy. By "bureaucracy" Weber means not only the management and the clerical workers, but also the general structure of the firm. Huge corporations, according to Weber, are likely to be organized as bureaucracies, the main reason being that bureaucracies are efficient. They work as a "machine"—that is, with precision and speed (Weber [1922] 1978:973).

In Weber's view there has also been a general tendency in modern capitalism to merge with the bureaucratic tradition (which has a different origin than the firm), and this movement has resulted in a "bureaucratization of capitalism" (Weber [1922] 1978:999). A balance between profit-making and bureaucracy is what characterizes Western capitalism. If bureaucracy some time in the future will win out over the profit motive and tip the balance in its favor, modern capitalism will soon loose its "revolutionary" character, suffocate, and eventually be replaced by a nondynamic totalitarian system, reminiscent of Ancient Egypt (Weber [1922] 1978:202; see also Mommsen 1974, Swedberg 1998:51–52). Bureaucracy, in brief, did not simply mean "efficiency" to Weber.

Weber's view of bureaucracy as a rational way to organize the world, which had joined forces with capitalist interests, has largely been ignored in the sociology of organizations, where scholars have preferred to view Weber's theory as a description of how organizations in general are constructed and work. Robert Merton (1952), for example, has pointed out that the methodical and objective stance of the bureaucrat may unintendedly result in the opposite kind of behavior; Alvin Gouldner (1954) that power and knowledge in an organization do not necessarily go together; and Arthur Stinchcombe (1959) that there exist other ways of organizing production than through a "Weberian" bureaucracy. There also exists quite a bit of research showing that the half dozen features that together characterize a bureaucracy, according to Weber, do not necessarily coexist in empirical reality (e.g., Albrow 1970:50–66; Scott 1998:42–49).

While it is clear that studies of this type have pointed to a number of errors and inconsistencies in Weber's analysis (and also have added many valuable insights of their own), it is less obvious that they have successfully addressed Weber's main concerns in his analysis of the firm. What Weber was especially concerned with in studying the firm was a series of issues intimately related to the Western type of capitalism and its mixture of exploitation, domination, and efficiency.

In interest terms, one can perhaps express it in the following way. Weber was primarily trying to figure out the exact constellation of interests and social relations that characterizes the modern firm, and also how the individual reacts to it. One of his answers in *Economy and Society* to this latter type of question is as follows:

> All economic activity in a market economy is undertaken and carried through by individuals acting to provide for their own ideal or material interests. This is naturally just as true when economic activity is oriented to patterns of order of organizations, whether they themselves are partly engaged in economic activity [such as a state], are primarily economic in character [such as a firm], or merely regulate economic activity [such as a trade union]. Strangely enough, this fact is often not taken account of ([1922] 1978:202).

Industrial Sociology and the Sociology of Work

Weber's vision of a broad economic sociology that not only includes a discussion of the basic economic institutions of capitalism, but also accounts for the general organization of work, was never realized, neither in Europe nor in the United States. Instead the sociological study of the economy fragmented into a number of subfields; and the topics of factory life and work were taken over by a field called industrial sociology (including the sociology of work), which came into being in the 1930s in the United States. By 1970 many of the concerns of industrial sociology had been absorbed by organizational sociology since it was felt that industrial sociology had failed to renew itself and had a much-too-narrow focus on the firm ("plant sociology"; see Hirsch 1975). The idea that it would be helpful to have an area called the sociology of work, however, remained intact, and such a field still exists.

As I see it, economic sociology would definitely benefit from including many of the topics that industrial sociology and the sociology of work have traditionally been concerned with. Today's economic sociology, however, has failed on this account and on the whole has paid little attention to workers, trade unions, and everyday life in offices and factories. Today's economic sociology—including the sociology of firms—would also benefit from becoming better acquainted with what has been accomplished over the years in the traditions of industrial sociology and the sociology of work. To this can be added that these two fields have kept alive the practice of participant observation in studying the economy, which is rarely used in economic sociology (for an exception, see Abolafia 1998).

During its hayday industrial sociology was an extremely vibrant area that produced several classical studies. Whoever takes on the task of going through this field in an attempt to sort out its contributions to economic sociology will have an exciting time because industrial sociology is rich in insights as well as in ethnographic data about working life. Among the classics produced by American sociologists are *Human Relations in the Restaurant Industry* (1948) by William Foote Whyte, *Men Who Manage* (1959) by Melville Dalton, and *The Sociological Eye* (1971) by Everett C. Hughes. Equally masterful studies from Europe include *Marienthal: The Sociolgraphy of an Unemployed Community* (1933) by Marie Jahoda, Paul Lazarsfeld, and Hans Zeisel, *The Anatomy of Work* (1950) by Georges Friedmann, and *The Bureaucratic Phenomenon* (1964) by Michel Crozier.

Three areas to which industrial sociology has made particularly valuable contributions are work and the professions, informal relations at the workplace, and work-related conflicts. People in modern society, according to Everett C. Hughes, get much of their identity through work; and they will often try to upgrade what they do for a living into a profession. How mistakes at work are covered up and who does the "dirty work" are two other important issues (Hughes [1931] 1979, 1971). Classical industrial sociology also points to the important role of informal relations at the work place, showing that people in factories and offices tend to form small work groups and that these groups influence many important issues, such as racial discrimination, productivity, and people's self-esteem. Boredom as well as conflicts at work have also been studied in industrial sociology. And so have many of the everyday dramas of the workplace, as exemplified by Donald Roy's famous "'Banana Time'" (1958).

"There, there it is again—the invisible hand
of the marketplace giving us the finger."

Critics often charged that industrial sociologists treated the factory
as a closed social system, which was isolated from the rest of what
was happening in the economy. There was also a tendency to let the
economists handle all the "economic" topics, such as markets, prices,
and the like. Moreover, industrial sociology saw itself as part of a
more general paradigm in the social sciences, according to which
modern society can best be characterized as an industrial society. In
this type of society there was an essential harmony of interest between workers and management; it was also argued that all industrial
societies tend to converge.

Despite these shortcomings, it is nonetheless possible to find many
excellent insights about the role that interests play in working life in
studies by the industrial sociologists. Strikes and piecework systems
were, for example, studied from a highly realistic perspective (e.g.,
Gouldner 1954; Roy 1952). How incentive systems operate at the factory level was another popular topic, as suggested by the many
studies of this type that are summarized in *Money and Motivation*
(Whyte et al. 1955). One of the interesting results, which are reported

in this work, is that individual workers tend to respond very differently to individual incentives. Some people are totally unaffected by them and just keep working. Others respond to the incentives but stop at the level prescribed by the group norm. A few persons, finally, ignore the group norm and go beyond it—these are the so-called rate busters. While those who see it as their task to maintain the group norm are very social ("restricters"), rate busters tend to be isolated, inside as well as outside of the factory.

Another fascinating picture of the interaction between interests and social relations can be found in *Men Who Manage* by Melville Dalton. To make a business run smoothly, Dalton argues, many other qualities and resources are needed than those that are officially recognized. When problems emerge in the gray area between what is legal and illegal, employees are often asked in secrecy if they are willing to help out (against compensation), even if this means that they will have to brake the law or some moral code. They usually say 'yes'; interests, in brief, override morality in this type of situation. Or, in Dalton's words, "the active seeking nature of man, his ancient and obvious tendency to twist the world to his interests and to select as well as to respond to parts of his environment, erodes [in cases such as these] the preaching of parents and superiors" (Dalton 1959:265).

While industrial sociology has more or less died away and been absorbed by organizational sociology, the sociology of work is still alive in the sense that courses in this topic are taught, journals are being published, and so forth. Much of this material is relevant to the sociology of firms. An early example is Michael Burawoy's *Manufacturing Consent* (1979), a study of a factory in Chicago. This work continues in the best tradition of industrial sociology with its ethnographic account of everyday life on the factory floor. The author's main thesis is that the workers devise various ways to make the time pass, so that they can put up with the monotony of work. "Making out," as this practice is known, is in other words the product of two different interests: the worker's interest in being paid (which means that she has to do what she is paid for) and her interest in finding something challenging to do. A study that is similarly important to the sociology of firms, as well to economic sociology in general, is Andrew Abbott's *The System of Professions: An Essay on the Division of Expert Labor* (1988). This study contains a fascinating historical and comparative account of several major professions, including law and psychiatry. The key to an understanding of professions, Abbott argues, is to analyze how certain groups succeed in controlling certain types of work by producing abstract knowledge about it—and also by keeping other groups out.

One of the most important novelties in the sociology of work since the 1970s is the attention paid to gender. It has gradually been realized that gender plays a major role in determining who does what and with what pay in the firm. An exemplary early study in this genre is Rosabeth Moss Kanter's *Men and Women of the Corporation* (1977) with its discussion of secretaries, executives' wives, and women who try to make a career at work. When women are very few in a position, they are often seen as representatives of "women" rather than as individuals ("tokens," in Kanter's terminology).

By focusing on gender it is also possible to trace some novel ways in which firms are connected to their surroundings. It seems, for example, that many of the difficulties that women encounter at work have to do with the low status of women in society at large (Miller 1988). Sexual harassment is a case in point, since this type of behavior is related to the general power position of males in society and to the way that their sexual interests are allowed to be expressed. The position of women at work is also connected to their position at home, especially to their disproportionate responsibility for household work and children (for a more detailed discussion of these issues, see chap. 11).

Another novel topic on the agenda for today's sociology of work is whistle-blowing or what happens when an employee decides to expose her employer for unlawful or unethical behavior (e.g., Miceli and Near 1991; Miethe and Rothschild 1994; Alford 2001). Loyalty to the firm, which is usually seen as something positive, is in cases like this turned around and unleashed with brutal force against the whistle-blower, whose life may be destroyed in the process (Haglunds forthcoming). To analyze this type of event in terms of ideal and material interests may throw some new light on it, since the violence of the reaction to the whistle-blower as well as her courage to speak out indicate that powerful and deep-seated forces are involved. It can also be noted that the U.S. government uses material incentives to encourage whistle-blowing under certain circumstances. A whistle-blower who helps the government to recover money because of Medicare fraud, defense fraud, and the like is, for example, according to law, entitled to a certain percentage (usually 15–25 percent).

It would similarly be very useful—both for the sociology of work and for economic sociology—if more research was done on people who make their living by handling other people's money, such as people who work in banks, stock exchanges, and brokerage firms (e.g., Lockwood 1958; Eccles and Crane 1988; Abolafia 1998). Buying and selling more generally is another topic where the sociology of work and economic sociology could find some common ground.

Organizational Theories and the Sociology of Firms

It is clear that of all the work that is currently being carried out in sociology, organizational sociology has the most potential for being useful in the project of further developing a sociology of firms (for an overview, see Scott 1998). The four perspectives in contemporary organizational sociology that seem most promising in this context are resource dependency, population ecology, network analysis, and new institutionalism. Given the important contribution that organizational sociology can make, we must, however, keep in mind that organizational sociology does not single out firms as a special category with its own distinct profile, but rather tries to cover the entire spectrum of organizations and develop general theories of organizations. While the beginnings of a sociology of firms does exist, much remains to be done (Bernoux 1995; cf. Stinchcombe 1960).

Nonetheless, firms *do* differ on several accounts from other organizations, and it is these differences that constitute the justification for a sociology of firms and that also help to explain why this type of analysis reaches its own distinct results. First of all, firms have as their main goal to make a profit, and this influences the structure of their organization as well as their behavior. Firm are started for this reason, and they will also be closed down if they fail to deliver a profit. Second, firms are treated differently from other organizations in law. There are special legal procedures that have to be followed when a firm is started as well as when it is dissolved; some of its everyday activities are also covered by legislation and enforced by special courts. Third, firms have their own institutional features, and these have a different history from those that characterize other types of organizations. And last, many different kinds of economic interests play a crucial role in firms and deeply influence their behavior. More employees are dependent for their livelihood on firms than on any other type of employer; investors are dependent on firms for profit; and firms control more economic resources that they can decide what to do with than any other type of organization. The struggle over who will control economic organizations is also much sharper than the struggle for control in many other organizations.

As already noted, sociologists pay more sustained attention to the social dimension of organizations than economists do, including those who are currently spearheading organizational economics. But there also exists a second point on which sociologists who study organizations differ from economists: they do not focus so much on the single firm but rather study a number of firms. This shift from the single firm to a collective of firms, represents, according to Granovetter, just as much of a qualitative leap as the shift from the individual to the firm (1994:453). This move takes the following expressions: sociologists often refer to "the organizational field"; they analyze how an organization is dependent on other organizations (as in resource dependency); they look at a large number of organizations of a special type (as in population ecology); and they have developed the concept of a business group to study certain groups of firms. Sociologists have also pioneered networks as a way of analyzing the interconnections of firms. We will next consider how all of these efforts to focus on firms in the plural are relevant for the sociology of firms.

The idea of a *field* has been independently developed by sociologists in the United States and Europe, and it has been given its most elaborate theoretical expression by one of its founders, Pierre Bourdieu (see e.g., DiMaggio 1986; DiMaggio and Powell 1991:64–65; Bourdieu and Wacquant 1992:94–115; cf. chap. 2 of this book). "In analytical terms," Bourdieu states, "a field may be defined as a network, or a configuration, of objective relations between positions" (Bourdieu and Wacquant 1992:97). A field is also characterized by the fact that it has a distinct history and that the behavior of the actors is partly shaped by their past behavior (habitus). A constant struggle goes on in the field, and the actors have different forms of capital at their disposal (financial capital, social capital, and so on). The economy constitutes a special kind of field, as does an industry and the individual firm. In a recent study, for example, Bourdieu analyzes the construction industry of private homes as a field, and outlines how important the French state has been in shaping this market through various forms of regulation and special types of loans (Bourdieu 2000c). More generally, Bourdieu's idea of a field with a distinct power structure, where interest, or *illusio*, drives the individual actor, lends itself very nicely to the project of a sociology of firms.

The theory of *resource dependency* emerged in the 1970s in organizational sociology and basically states that to survive, an organization needs resources from its environment—that is, from other organizations (Pfeffer and Salancik 1978; for a general introduction, see chap. 2). An organization will therefore always be dependent on its environment, and its leadership will typically try to develop strategies for how to cope with external constraints. The idea of resource dependency can very easily be used to analyze the behavior of firms, and it has also inspired a large number of such studies (for a review, see Davis and Powell 1992). Criticism, however, has also been directed at this type of approach, among other reasons because it neglects the fact that U.S. firms increasingly get their financial resources from sources other than organizations (banks), namely from financial markets (Davis and McAdam 2000:203–6). The importance of using interlocks for coopting other firms has also declined in the United States.

In *population ecology* the relevant unit of study is not the individual firm but the population of firms of the same type (Hannan and Freeman 1989, Hannan and Carroll 1992; see also chap. 2). These populations develop over time as a result of two forces: *legitimation* (the more organizations of a certain type there are, the more legitimation they have) and *competition* (the fewer organizations there are, the more resources there will be for each of them). On the negative side, population ecology does not distinguish between economic and noneconomic organizations, nor does it take into account types of social structures other than organizations (Davis and McAdam 2000:206–8). Still, it is clear that the emphasis on populations of organizations of a specific type can add substantially to the present knowledge of specific industries—especially if factors other than the number of organizations are taken into account (see, e.g., the studies in Carroll and Hannan 1995). Proper attention to interests might also help in further developing the "demography of corporations and industries" that Carroll and Hannan (2000) have initiated.

The concept of the *business group* was given theoretical stature in the early 1990s by Mark Granovetter, who defines this type of organization as a collection of legally separate firms that are bound together in some formal and/or informal ways (Granovetter 1994:454; cf. Granovetter 1995a, forthcoming a). According to Granovetter, it is important for sociologists to study the kind of organizational configurations that can be found midway between the individual firm and macroeconomic phenomena. Business groups are in his opinion characterized by variation along six dimensions: ownership relations, principles of solidarity, authority structure, moral economy, finance, and relations to the state. Well-known examples include *keiretsu* in Japan and *chaebol* in South Korea. Also in such important countries as India, China, and Taiwan, business groups are major economic players. In Taiwan, for example, the top one hundred business groups accounted for 45 percent of the GNP in 1996 (Granovetter forthcoming a). What the situation is in the United States is not known—even if business groups are presumably weaker than in the countries just mentioned, primarily because of legal obstacles to their existence.

Sociologists have also made a key contribution to the study of economic organizations, including firms, by drawing on *network theory* (for an overview, see, e.g., Powell and Smith-Doerr 1994, forthcoming). As an analytical method, the network approach is very flexible and can be used to trace relations among as well as within firms (Uzzi 1996). There also exists a school of European thought which argues that artifacts—not only individuals and organizations, in other words—can be seen as nodes in a network (Callon 1997). The way in which an artifact is constructed—say, an instrument—will affect the behavior of the person who uses the artifact. This way of approaching things can lead to novel and interesting conceptualizations of firms (e.g., Sverrisson 1994).

A common network exercise has also been to investigate the patterns created by individuals who are members of several boards. By proceeding in this way a distinct pattern of how firms are connected to each other through so-called interlocks can be traced (Mintz and Schwartz 1985; for an overview, see Mizruchi 1996). The idea of networks has also been used to trace economic configurations of firms other than interlocks, such as industrial districts, interorganizational forms of cooperation, and "network organizations" (e.g., Powell 1990; Baker 1992; Saxenian 1994; Ebers 1997; Podolny and Page 1998; Knoke 2001).

The use of network analysis to understand the behavior of firms has, however, also undergone some criticism. One very broad type of criticism is that the network approach is part of the ideology of neoliberalism, as are flexibility and downsizing (Boltanski and Chiapello 1999). Network analysts, in brief, are more political than they may think. It has also been pointed out that sociologists who study interlocks do not know very much about the information that travels through the ties between the firms (Hirsch 1982; Stinchcombe 1990; cf. White 1992:65). This last type of criticism is close to that of "broken ties," or the idea that if interlocks are as important as they are claimed to be, they should be reconstituted if for some reason they are broken off accidentally (board members may die, retire, and so on). Research shows, however, that replacements are only made in a small number of cases (for a presentation of the literature on broken ties as well as a rebuttal of this argument, see Stearns and Mizruchi 1986). Finally, there exists a tendency in many network analyses to focus exclusively on social relationships and to ignore the role of interests—something that tends to make them less realistic than they could be.

The key ideas of *new institutionalism* are often traced to an article from 1977 by John Meyer and Brian Rowan, which deals with organizations in contemporary society but which is also very suggestive for the sociology of firms (Meyer and Rowan 1977; see DiMaggio and Powell 1991 for more recent work along these lines). The basic idea is that modern organizations, including firms, cannot be adequately understood in terms of efficiency and instrumental action (cf. chap. 2). Instead there exist two contradictory demands on the modern organization: to get things done and to incorporate features from its surroundings that will endow it with legitimacy. The problem is that doing the latter will make it harder to get things done. One solution to this problem, it is argued, is for organizations to adopt a formal structure that is legitimate, while everyday activities are allowed to continue as before, independent of the formal structure (decoupling). The idea that organizations snugly fit their environments for structural reasons (contingency theory) is consequently challenged. Meyer and Rowan propose that organizations can best be understood as "social constructions," and that modern society is filled with rational myths about the way that things should be done.

The perspective of new institutionalism partly emerged as a reaction to the idea that organizations can best be explained with the help of economic and technological variables; and this may also account for some of its reluctance to study economic organizations and instead concentrate on public organizations such as schools and universities. Nonetheless, some important studies of firms have emerged from new institutionalism, such as Neil Fligstein's *The Transformation of Corporate Control* (1990). Fligstein's study can be characterized as an attempt to explain the evolution of the huge American firm since 1880 that challenges Alfred Chandler's standard account (Chandler 1962, 1977; see also the critique of Chandler in Freeland 1996, 2001). While Chandler sees the emergence and the structure of the modern huge firm as a response to new advances in technology and the creation of a national market around the turn of the twentieth century, Fligstein highlights other factors. He especially stresses the role of the state, including its attempts to put a stop to monopolies through legislation; how leading managers view the industry in which they are active (conceptions of control); and the role that isomorphism has played in the diffusion of the huge firm (Fligstein 1985).

Just as network analysis has its advocates who reject the idea that interests should play a role in their studies, so does new institutionalism. It has, for example, recently been claimed by two of its key theoreticians that "elaborate interest-based theories" fail to realize that actors have much less power than is commonly thought in the social sciences. Western culture tends to glorify actors and to ascribe everything that happens to their actions; they are treated as if they were "small gods" (Meyer 2000:239, Meyer and Jepperson 2000:100). In my opinion, this critique of the actor is interesting—but much too radical, especially when it means that the role of interests in economic life is neglected (cf. DiMaggio 1988 for a similar but more positive view).

Summary

There exist a number of important approaches that can be used to analyze modern firms in economics as well as in sociology; and these were presented and discussed in this chapter. In economics, there is the theory of the firm and organizational economics (mainly agency theory and transaction cost analysis). In sociology, there is resource dependency, population ecology, and new institutionalism. I also argued that Weber's analysis of the firm as well as many of the insights of industrial sociology and the sociology of work should be taken into account. Network analysis and the concept of business groups are also important tools.

To further develop a realistic and sophisticated sociology of firms it is absolutely crucial to strengthen economic sociology in several ways. At the moment this would entail work along the following lines: First of all, economic sociology has to break with the current tendency in organization theory to equate the firm with all other organizations. Much better historical knowledge is needed about the emergence of the different types of firms, not least family firms, which have been unduly neglected in economic sociology. Much more attention should also be paid to the role of work on an everyday basis inside the firms; and on this point the industrial sociology of the 1950s could be a model to emulate. The focus of study, it can be added, should be on firms in plural, not on the single or representative firm as in mainstream economics. And finally the analysis has to be interest-oriented in order to be realistic.

There exist a few attempts to decouple the analysis of the firm from general organization theory, but this process needs to be accelerated. Parts of the history of the emergence of the firm are already available, in economic history and business history; and economic sociologists need to be better acquainted with this material, especially when it comes to family firms. Other parts of this history, driven by the special needs of economic sociology, still remain to be researched. As for the importance of work, it is clear from various studies in industrial sociology and in the sociology of work that people in modern society get much of their identity from their jobs, and also that most people spend large chunks of their lives in the workplace. For a number of reasons, a sociology of firms that does not pay proper attention to work would be seriously flawed. The sociology of firms should also continue to study firms in plural since this has turned out to be a profitable research strategy. That economic interests should always be taken into account, when economic organizations such as firms are analyzed, would seem obvious.

V

Economic and Sociological Approaches to Markets

THIS and the following chapter are devoted to markets. There are several reasons for having two chapters on this topic. One has to do with the centrality of markets to the capitalist economy. What differentiates the capitalist economy from the socialist economy and also from the communal/familial type of economy, has to do with the way that *distribution* is structured—as exchange, and not as redistribution or reciprocity (cf. chap. 3). Another reason for devoting so much space to markets is that the knowledge of markets is still fairly rudimentary in economic sociology. There exist a few attempts to develop general theories of markets, but none of these has been very successful.

How can this situation be improved? My attempt to answer this question will be given in two steps. In this chapter I will present where we stand today and what we can learn from economics; what the current state of the sociological study of markets is and what can be added to it from the work of the economists. I will begin with Adam Smith and end with new institutional economics, addressing along the way attempts by sociologists to develop theories of the market. In the following chapter, I will shift gears and try to advance the sociological understanding of markets by introducing some historical material. I will also attempt to show how the concept of interest can be used in analyzing markets.

Economists on the Market—From a Sociological Perspective

Sociologists are sometimes very critical of what economists have to say about markets, on the grounds that economists are only interested in price formation and not in the market as an institution in its own right. To a certain extent they are right. A few decades ago, for example, George Stigler noted that "economic theory is concerned with markets [and] it is, therefore, a source of embarrassment that so little attention has been paid to the theory of markets" (1967:291). Ten years later Douglass North pointed out that "it is a peculiar fact that the literature on economics . . . contains so little discussion of the central institution that underlies neoclassical economics—the market" (North 1977:710; cf. Barber 1977:30 for the same point). A little more than a decade ago, finally, R. H. Coase stated that "although economists claim to study the market, in modern economic theory the market itself has an even more shadowy existence than the firm" (Coase 1988:7). All that interests the economists, according to Coase, is "the determination of market prices" (7).

But even if economics has considerably more to say on price formation than on the institutional dimension of markets, I will argue that it would be a serious mistake for economic sociology to ignore what the economists have to say about markets. There exist, as I see it, a number of suggestive insights into the operation of markets in economic theory that would benefit economic sociology very much. There is also the fact that the existing literature is considerably more diverse than sociologists often think and that economists have become increasingly interested in the institutional dimension of markets during the past few decades.

The Market in Classical Political Economy
(from Adam Smith to Marx)

There exist many differences between the concept of the market in classical political economy and the one that was to emerge around the end of the nineteenth century through the marginalist revolution. First, classical economists saw the market as synonymous with either a marketplace or a distinct geographical area. In their eyes the market was something concrete, as opposed to the abstract market of latter-day economists. Second, the main emphasis in classical political economy was on production, not on exchange. What decided the price was essentially the amount of labor that it took to produce a commodity. And third, the market was a place where interests met and came to an agreement. These interests were sometimes linked to other interests, such as political interests, the general interest of society, and so on. This type of theorizing about the market in terms of different types of interests, and which drew on the tradition of interest analysis, would later disappear.

Of the more than thirty chapters in *The Wealth of Nations* only two have the word "market" in the title: "That the Division of Labour is Limited by the Extent of the Market" (Book I, Chap. III) and "Of the Natural and Market Price of Commodities" (Book I, Chap. VII). From this it might seem that the market mechanism was peripheral to Adam Smith. This, however, was not at all the case, even if he approached this topic from a different angle than what is common today. What first and foremost mattered to Smith was not so much how prices are formed in the market but that people only want to exchange goods with one another if they can get something else than what they themselves are producing—that is, if there is a division of labor. The more advanced the division of labor is, the more interest people will have in exchanging goods with one another—and the more "wealth" there will be. Since small markets cannot sustain an advanced division of labor, large markets are crucial.

Adam Smith was fascinated by the capacity of human beings to enter into exchange with one another. The "propensity to truck, barter, and exchange," he said, was something that human beings were endowed with by nature and that could not be found in animals. "Nobody ever saw one animal by its gestures and natural cries signify to another, this is mine, that yours; I am willing to give this for that" ([1776] 1976:25–6). What drives two people to engage in exchange with one another, according to Smith, is that this is a way of interacting that will satisfy *both* parties: "Give me that which I want, and you shall have this which you want" (26). A manufacturer will in principle enter into an exchange, Smith specifies, when he has an "interest" to do so—and this is the case when it repays his expenses for material and wages plus adds a profit (65–66).

Smith was also interested in trying to understand the price that would emerge in the market. His basic suggestion was that there are two types of prices: a "natural price" and a "market price." The natural price is based on the amount of labor that it takes to produce something and tends to establish itself in the long run. The market price, on the other hand, will oscillate around the natural price and settle below or above it, due to accidental causes. Through various measures a market price, which exceeds the natural price, can be artificially maintained, for example, through monopoly, legislation, and secrecy. There are, however, limits to how long this can go on.

As already mentioned, Adam Smith had a tendency to see the evolution of the market throughout history as the result of a natural progression. He basically ignored the fact that markets have very different structures and that markets are anything but natural. Still, Adam Smith paid quite a bit of attention to institutions, and throughout *The Wealth of Nations* one can find sharp-eyed observations about the size and location of markets, the role that laws and regulations play in them, and the like. He was also well aware of the qualitative difference between the labor market and other types of markets, as the following quote makes clear:

What are the common wages of labour depends every where upon the contract usually made between those two parties, whose interests are by no means the same. The workmen desire to get as much, the masters to give as little as possible. The former are disposed to combine in order to raise, the latter in order to lower the wages of labour.

It is not, however, difficult to foresee which of the parties must, upon all ordinary occasions, have the advantage in the dispute, and force the other into a compliance with their terms. The masters, being fewer in number, can combine much more easily; and the law, besides, authorises, or at least does not prohibit their combinations, while it prohibits those of the workmen ([1776] 1976:83–84).

Through the works of David Ricardo and John Stuart Mill, political economy became considerably more abstract, losing much of its interest in concrete economic institutions, including markets. The general thrust of their analyses was still that production determined the correct or the natural price, while the market price tended to be the result of accidental factors. Ricardo's *Principles of Political Economy and Taxation* (1817) contains, for example, a chapter to this effect, entitled "On Natural and Market Price"; and in *Principles of Political Economy* (1848) Mill assigns scientific priority to "the laws of Production" over "Distribution of Wealth." Both Ricardo and Mill, however, also created a certain room in their analyses for a demand-and-supply type of analysis. This is especially true of Mill, who, according to some commentaries, may have sensed that changes on this score were ahead.

Something similar can be said about the role of interest in the analyses of Ricardo and Mill. Both used the notion of "interest" and drew on the tradition of interest analysis; they also shifted the meaning of interest, however, in the direction of being exclusively economic and synonymous with economic analysis in general. Ricardo, for example, argued that in "a system of perfectly free commerce" the ways in which the individual nations will conduct themselves "binds together, by one common tie of interest and intercause, the universal society of nations throughout the civilized world" ([1817] 1973:81). Similarly John Stuart Mill borrowed his terminology from the interest tradition when he made his famous argument that economic theory can be a science only if the role of custom in the economy is disregarded and perfect competition is assumed to exist. In ordinary markets, he noted, people often pay different amounts for the same item, fail to locate the lowest price due to "indolence or carelessness," and so on—but all of this must be disregarded by the economist ([1848] 1987:242–48, 411). Economics could only become a true science "supposing all parties to take care of their own interest" (411).

Like the other classical political economists, Karl Marx was of the opinion that production was more important than the market when it came to deciding the price of a commodity. Nonetheless, throughout

Marx's work one can also find a number of interesting observations on the market or "the sphere of circulation," as he preferred to call it. First, Marx emphasized that the market essentially consists of social relationships. "It is plain," he notes sarcastically in *Capital*, "that commodities cannot go to market and make exchanges of their own account" ([1867] 1906:96). "Value" is not inherent in a commodity, but rather constitutes "a relation between people expressed as a relation between things" (85). The way that economists in Marx's time spoke about prices simply fed the illusion that values were not created by people but somehow constituted qualities of the objects themselves. A peculiar "fetichism of commodities" was the result, according to Marx, in which people projected life onto objects because they did not understand that they themselves had created these values through their work (81–96).

Marx also emphasized that all markets have a distinct history and that this history often included oppression and exploitation. One example of this would be colonial markets. The modern capitalist system began with the eviction of English peasants from their lands by the lords, from the 1500s onward, thereby creating people in need of paid work. "The so-called primitive accumulation . . . is nothing else than the historical process of divorcing the producer from the means of production" ([1867] 1906:786). Historical information of this type, however, was according to Marx hidden from people through bad history writing and an ideology according to which everything that takes place in the market is voluntary and peaceful. Marx also argued that the secret key to the workings of the capitalist economy was not to be found in the market but in production. It was in "the hidden abode of production" that surplus was created and not in the market—"this noisy sphere where everything takes place on the surface" (195–96).

The Marginalist Revolution: The Creation of the Modern Concept of the Market

Toward the end of the nineteenth century the concept of the market that can be found in economic theory underwent a major change through the works of Walras, Jevons, Menger, and others. The difference between the new concept of the market and that of the classical political economists was large. From having been depicted in a fairly concrete and realistic manner, the market now became something abstract and acquired tremendous analytical interest as a price-making and resource-allocating mechanism. Historical and social approaches in general were firmly rejected during this period through the Battle of Methods (*Methodenstreit*), which originated in Germany-Austria and soon spread to England and the United States. The concept of the market was thinned out to such a degree that John Neville Keynes, Sr., spoke of "the hypothetical market," ([1891] 1955:247–49), and W. Stanley Jevons simply equated the analysis of the market with a "theory of exchange" (Jevons 1911:74). This, however, was a price worth paying, according to the marginalist thinkers, since many difficult theoretical problems that had haunted the early economists could now be solved. In particular, it became possible to conceptualize and model the whole economy as a system of markets.

To approach the new concept of the market, it is convenient to start with two defining statements that were often cited around the turn of the century and that are still referred to in the economics literature. The first of these is by Cournot: "It is well understood that by *market* economists mean, not a certain place where purchases and sales are carried on, but the entire territory of which the parts are so united by the relations of unrestricted commerce that prices there take the same level throughout, with ease and rapidity" (Cournot 1838, as cited in Marshall [1920] 1961, 1:325). The second quote says roughly the same: "The more nearly perfect a market is, the stronger is the tendency for the same price to be paid for the same thing at the same time in all the parts of the market" (Marshall [1920] 1961, 1:324).

These two statements show, first of all, that economists around the turn of the twentieth century thought that the term "market" should be extended from simply meaning marketplace to any area where buyers and sellers of a particular commodity are located. As we know from the social history of the term "market," this suggestion mirrored the everyday use of the term (Oxford English Dictionary 1989). What represented an innovation, however, was the addition of a novel meaning to the word "market." This new meaning does not come out very clearly in the statements by Cournot and Marshall, but is hinted at by the latter's use of the word "perfect." In all brevity, a "perfect market" was a very abstract market, characterized by perfect competition and perfect information (Knight [1921] 1985:76–79; Stigler 1968). Harold Demsetz has described the change that took place in economic theory:

> Markets became empirically empty conceptualizations of the forums in which exchange costlessly took place. The legal system and the government were relegated to the distant background (Demsetz 1982:6).

Even though criticism can be directed at the new interpretation of the concept of the market that was ushered in by the marginalist revolution, it must also be acknowledged that one of its great accomplishments is to have conceived of the market as the central mechanism of allocation in the economy. This idea no doubt reflected the change that had gradually come about in the West: the economy *was* increasingly centered around markets, and these *did* allocate an increasing amount of essential goods. The new concept of the market also implied that all markets in an economy are interconnected, and that a change in one of them would lead to a change in the others. Léon Walras, in particular, is credited with having pioneered general equilibrium analysis. According to Walras ([1874] 1954:84), "the whole world may be looked upon as a vast general market made up of diverse special markets where social wealth is bought and sold." Production, it may be noted, played little role in Walras's vision, which was also exceedingly abstract.

Of the major economists from this period, Alfred Marshall paid the most attention to the market as an empirical phenomenon in its own right. He also added some analytical innovations that were to become part of mainstream economics. It is, for example, in Marshall's *Principles of Economics* (1890) that the famous demand-supply curve was introduced for the first time to a general audience ([1920] 1961, 1:346). The key idea in Marshall's definition of the market, to repeat, was that whenever local prices for the same product converged, the products became part of the same market. In the chapter on the market in *Principles of Economics* Marshall also drew up a very ambitious program for how to study "the organization of markets" ([1920] 1961, 1:324). According to this program, one would have to take money, credit, and foreign trade—as well as trade unions, employers' organizations, and the movements of the business cycle—into account when analyzing special markets.

Some of these issues were eventually discussed in *Industry and Trade* (1919) and in *Money, Credit and Commerce* (1923), but Marshall never found the time to tackle the market according to his original plan. Pulling together Marshall's thoughts from his various writings, we find that Marshall's thinking about markets changed quite a bit over the years. While in *Principles of Economics* markets were predominantly seen in terms of demand and supply, some thirty years later he emphasized their social dimension. In *Industry and Trade*, for example, Marshall defined the market in the following manner: "In all its various significations, a 'market' refers to a group or groups of people, some of whom desire to obtain certain things, and some of whom are in a position to supply what the others want" (1919:182).

Marshall's work indicates his belief that the following five factors were important for an understanding of markets: space, time, formal regulation, informal regulation, and familiarity between the buyer and the seller. The analysis of markets in *Principles of Economics* focuses on the first two of these five factors, while the latter three are discussed more fully in *Industry and Trade*. In relation to space, a market could be either "wide" or "narrow" (Marshall [1920] 1961, 1:325–26). The market area could also grow or shrink, depending on the circumstances. The extent to which time was taken into account would also affect the market—whether the period in question was "short" (meaning that supply was limited to what was at hand in the market), "longer" (meaning that supply was influenced by the cost of producing the commodity), or "very long" (meaning that the supply was influenced by the price of labor and other material needed to produce the item in question; see Marshall [1920] 1961, 1:330).

A market could also be "organized" or not; and by this Marshall (1919:256–57) meant that its proceedings were either formally regulated or not. The stock market was an example of an organized market (1923:88–97). In fact, Marshall—like many other economists from this period—saw the stock market as the most highly developed form of the market. Markets could also be either "general" or "particular" (1919:82). By a particular market Marshall meant a market in which there existed some social bond between the buyer and the seller that facilitated the transaction, while a general market was in principle anonymous. Depending on the degree of informal regulation, a market was finally either "open" or "monopolistic" (1919:395–99). In Marshall's opinion, competition usually differed depending on the type of market that was involved. The "fiercest and cruelest" form of competition was, for example, to be found in markets that were about to become monopolistic (1919:395–96).

The Austrian School: The Market as a Process

Neo-Austrian economics has its roots in the work of Carl Menger, who viewed the market as the spontaneous and unintended result of slow, historical development ([1883] 1985:139–59). The two main figures in the neo-Austrian School are Ludwig von Mises and his student Friedrich von Hayek; and many of their key ideas were developed during the interwar period. The intellectual interests of both Mises and Hayek were uncommonly broad and included social theory in general as well as economics. Mises, for example, knew Max Weber and was a member of the German Sociological Association. Both Hayek and Mises also made significant contributions to the debate about the economic nature of socialism, mainly by arguing that it was impossible to have a rational economy without price-making markets (see the articles by Mises and Hayek in Hayek 1935; for a history of the debate, see Udehn 1981; Brus and Laski 1989). During the past few decades the works of Mises and Hayek have become part of the neoliberal wave, and have gone from being rarely read to frequently cited today.

The centerpiece of neo-Austrian economics is its theory of the market as a process (Mises 1961, [1966] 1990; Hayek 1976; Shand 1984). "The market is not a place, a thing or a collective entity," as Mises (1949:258) puts it, "[it] is a process, actuated by the interplay of the actions of various individuals cooperating under the division of labor." According to the neo-Austrians, the market emerges spontaneously; it is the result of "human action," not of "human design." A market is by its nature decentralized and primarily constituted through local knowledge about how much something costs and where opportunities are to be found (see especially Hayek 1945, [1946] 1948). According to a famous argument by Hayek, most of the information that the actor needs to make a decision is transmitted through the prices of various items; all she has to take into account is whether the prices are going up or down, not why this happens to be the case (Hayek 1945). What would otherwise be an extremely complicated decision has in this way become a relatively simple one.

As opposed to what mainstream economists call an economy, Hayek argues, the market has no center but consists of "a network of many interlaced economies" (1976:108). This vision of the market is radically different from the neoclassical one, of which Mises and Hayek were both very critical. As they saw it, all of economics should be centered around the concept of the market, and the term "economics" should be replaced by "catallactics," or the science of exchange (Kirzner 1976:72).

Keynes's Critique of the Mainstream View of Markets

While the neo-Austrian theory of the market at first had little impact in the real world, it was very different with John Maynard Keynes's ideas. For several decades after World War II politicians in many countries tried to implement Keynes's suggestions, especially his idea that the state should actively intervene in the economy to soften the business cycle and create an acceptable level of employment (Hall 1989). "We are all keynesians now," as Nixon said in 1971—just a few years before Keynesianism started to decline.

Keynes's point of departure in *General Theory* (1936) is to be found in his observation that earlier economic theory had made an error in taking Say's Law of Markets for granted, namely that supply creates its own demand or that "the economic system is always working at full capacity" ([1943] 1954:69). If one looks at the way that markets operate in reality, Keynes argues, it becomes clear that disturbing gaps and imbalances exist between markets as well as between demand and supply inside individual markets. One result of these gaps and imbalances is that unemployment tends to be constant in modern society and the economy sluggish in general. Keynes's solution to the problem of how to match demand and supply, and thereby ensure that markets work properly, was to make use of the state. The state should, in particular, be responsible for adjusting consumption and investment.

Keynes's lack of faith in the idea that markets through their own working can ensure a high level of productivity and general well-being in society is evident from his analyses of the labor market and the stock market. As to the labor market, Keynes noted that according to classical and neoclassical economics, all markets eventually clear and consequently "unemployment . . . cannot occur" (1936:16). Since unemployment *does* exist, however, this analysis was obviously wrong and a new theoretical approach to labor markets was needed. In his analysis of the stock market Keynes similarly claimed that what was happening in reality was quite different from what should have been happening, according to economic theory. On the modern stock market, Keynes said, most of the efforts were directed at "anticipating what average opinion expects average opinion to be" (156). This effort to guess what the price of a share would be in the future—rather than make a sound investment in a productive enterprise—led to a number of problems, in Keynes's mind. Again, the solution he advocated was for the state to intervene and regulate the economy.

Industrial Organization and the Concept of Market Structure

The theory of industrial organization was to emphasize a specific type of market—the market of an industry—and also to introduce a strongly empirical approach to this type of market. Like Keynes's ideas, the field of industrial organization emerged from the troubled interwar period. And also like Keynes, the theoreticians of industrial organization wanted both to rebel against the neoclassical tradition and remain within it. The new approach had its roots in Marshall's *Industry and Trade*, but the catalyzing event for the emergence of the field of industrial organization was the publication in 1933 of Edward

Chamberlin's *Theory of Monopolistic Competition*. Chamberlin was very critical of the theory of perfect competition, which he felt suffered from a number of weaknesses. In particular, the theory of perfect competition considered only one of the two key elements in competition, namely the number of market actors. The differentiation of products, on the other hand, was completely ignored.

In reality, Chamberlin argued, monopolistic and competitive elements nearly always appear together—hence the term "monopolistic competition." Product differentiation, he continued, could be produced in a number of ways, for example through patents, trademarks, and advertisements. Purely social factors could also make products differ from one another, such as the "the reputation" of the seller, "personal links" between buyers and sellers, and "the general tone or character of his establishment" (Chamberlin 1933:56, 63). Chamberlin's view of differentiated products naturally implied a new perspective on markets: "Under pure competition, the market of each seller is perfectly merged with those of his rivals; now it is to be recognized that each is in some measure isolated, so that the whole is not a single market of many sellers, but a network of related markets, one for each seller" (1933:69). As a consequence of this argument, the boundaries among markets now became even more difficult to determine.

The next step in the evolution of the field of industrial organization came a few years later in an important article by Chamberlin's colleague at Harvard, Edward Mason (1939). According to Mason, it was imperative to study the price policies of corporations and to introduce more empirical content into neoclassical price theory. Mason suggested that this could be done through a classification of empirical material in terms of "market structures." Mason was somewhat unclear in his terminology, but in principle he claimed that "the market, and market structure, must be defined with reference to the position of a single seller or buyer; [and that] the structure of a seller's market . . . includes all those considerations which he takes into account in determining his business policies and practices" (1939:69). Once the market structure was known, Mason continued, it would be possible to determine how prices were set and, from there, what the impact would be on the economy as a whole.

Mason's ideas quickly generated a huge amount of empirical research and were soon referred to as the Structure-Conduct-Performance paradigm. According to this approach, the market was essentially seen as identical to an industry. "Market structure" was usually understood to mean such things as barriers to entry and concentration of sellers; "market conduct" meant policies aimed at rivals and price-setting policies; and "market performance" referred to more evaluative-political questions, such as whether something was equitable or not (Caves 1964). The most popular textbook in industrial organization still refers to the Structure-Conduct-Performance paradigm, even if it was understood early on that the causality involved was more complicated than what Mason had originally believed (Scherer and Ross 1990:5). The popularity of game theory in recent research on industrial organization has also tended to displace interest from Mason's paradigm (Schmalensee and Willig 1989; Tirole 1988). Most of this research, as noted in chapter 4, however, has been highly theoretical in nature and still awaits to be confronted with empirical material.

Postwar Developments in the Research on Markets

Since World War II many interesting developments have taken place in economic theory that have added to the understanding of markets as price-making mechanisms. This is true both for research on markets in general and for research within the various specialties of economics such as labor markets, financial markets, and so on. General equilibrium theory has, for example, successfully tackled and solved many of the difficult theoretical problems involved in analyzing a large number of interconnected markets (Arrow 1968). There is game theory, which has pioneered the introduction of intersubjectivity into mainstream economics by proposing a type of formal analysis in which each actor takes the decisions of the other actors into account (Kreps 1990, Gibbons 1992). The Chicago School has argued for a much more central role for the market in economic theory as well as in policy questions. And finally there have been a number of interesting advances in the economics of information. The emphasis on the role of knowledge in the working of markets has led to studies of "markets for lemons," "market signaling," and so on (Akerlof 1970; Spence 1974).

From the viewpoint of economic sociology, however, some of this more recent research is less relevant. The abstract model of the market that can be found in general equilibrium theory is, for example, unsuitable for economic sociology for a number of reasons, including the inability of this type of analysis handle unemployment, historical time, or significant economies of scale (Davidson 1981, Hahn 1981). Most studies in game theory are likewise very artificial and usually fail to make more than a symbolic connection to the real world (Swedberg 2001; for exceptions, see Greif 1993, 1994). The Chicago

"Oh, if only it were so simple."

economists have, on one hand, made a number of important advances by studying "implicit markets" (Becker 1981) and examining how the legal system can make the market work better (Posner 1981), what inspires public regulation of the market (Stigler 1971), and how freedom and the market are interrelated (Friedman 1962). On the negative side, the Chicago School tends to assume that the market is good a priori and to equate economic life in general with the market.

Nonetheless, quite a bit of current research in economic theory is suggestive to economic sociologists who are interested in markets. One example is Alan Blinder's attempt to test the validity of various theories of price stickiness through survey research. According to his results, prices do not increase more easily than they decrease; furthermore, managers do not seem to practice anticipatory pricing (Blinder 1998). There also exist a number of works that look at the role that community standards of fairness play in the market. The most important insight of these studies is that people's sense of what is fair affects the workings of the market. Evidence indicates, for example, that it is not considered fair to exploit shifts in demand to lower wages or increase prices, but that this is permitted when profits are threatened (Kahneman, Knetsch, and Thaler 1986). In general, the approach of behavioral economics is refreshingly empirical and in many ways close to economic sociology (Dawes and Weber forthcoming).

Dennis Carlton's work on market-clearing mechanisms (1989) represents another example of research on markets that is of interest to economic sociology. He argues that a variety of mechanisms exist through which markets can clear. Some markets clear through price, but these "auction markets" are expensive to create and often fail. Many markets, Carlton argues, only clear through price in combination with some other mechanism. This latter mechanism can be social in nature, such as the length of a buyer-seller relationship or the seller's knowledge of a buyer's need. In some cases, Carlton notes, no organized markets are possible at all; one has instead to rely on some other solution, such as salespeople. Depending on the business cycle, markets may also clear at different prices.

The work that is known as new institutional economics is also very useful to a sociological theory of markets. This approach, it should be emphasized, has attracted scholars from several adjacent fields, such as economic history and law. The three leading scholars in this field have already been referred to in this book—Ronald Coase, Oliver Williamson, and Douglass North—and so have the field's key concepts, such as transaction costs, property rights, and so on. These concepts have all been developed either with the market exclusively in mind (such as search costs and measurement costs), or they are applicable not only to the market but also to other economic institutions (such as transaction costs and property rights).

New institutional economics has also directed some attention to the market as a distinct social institution. This is especially the case with North and Coase. In *Institutions, Institutional Change and Economic Performance* (1990), North sketches the main steps in the development of the market, using the tools of new institutional economics. He also breaks with the common tendency to equate the market with efficiency and points out that some economic institutions—including the market—may actually entail *higher* rather than lower transaction costs. North concludes that the market "is a mixed bag of institutions; some increase efficiency and some decrease efficiency" (1990:69).

The thrust of Coase's work is similar to that of North, but displays some crucial differences. In an article from the late 1980s Coase produced a text that is more or less a programmatic statement for a theory of the market as an institution (1988). According to this article, economists have too often equated the market with the determination of the market price, something that has led to a situation in which "the discussion of the market itself has entirely disappeared" (7). He

also attacks the notion of market structure, arguing that much research on market structure looks at such factors as the number of
firms and product differentiation but that it fails to notice the market
in its own right. As a way to remedy this neglect, Coase suggests that
research should be directed at the market as a "social institution
which facilitates exchange" (8). The physical structure of a market, as
well as its rules and regulations, exists primarily to reduce the costs of
exchange, according to Coase. In a highly organized market, such as
the stock market, enforcement of the rules can typically be left to its
members. When, on the other hand, a market is scattered over a wide
area, Coase suggests, the state may have to intervene and regulate
buying and selling if there is to be a market at all.

Sociologists on Markets

The lack of communication between economists and sociologists that
characterized the twentieth century has led to a situation well captured by Schumpeter's quip that economists have had to create their
own "primitive sociology," and sociologists their own "primitive economics" (Schumpeter 1954:21). But there is more to the story than
this; and just as it is possible to find many sophisticated observations
in the economics literature on the social dimension of markets, one
can also find some interesting attempts by sociologists to understand
the general way that markets operate. Since the sociological literature
on markets is so much smaller than the economics literature, it is
considerably easier to present the contribution by the sociologists and
judge its value.

In what follows I have singled out what I consider to be the most
important and helpful attempts by sociologists to explain the workings of markets. These are Weber's approach, Harrison White's W(y)
model, and works addressing what I call "markets as networks" and
"markets as parts of fields." Other possible candidates would include
the efforts by Parsons and Smelser in *Economy and Society* to provide
some "starting-points for a systematic development of a sociology of
markets" (1956:143–75) Karl Polanyi's analysis of markets, ([1944]
1957, [1947] 1971, [1957] 1971) and the attempt to view markets from
a cultural-sociological perspective (Zelizer 1979; Abolafia 1998).

All of these approaches have contributed to the sociological analysis of markets in various ways. Parsons and Smelser, for example,
show very clearly how markets are part of the larger social system,
and so do the sociologists who draw on a cultural approach. Karl
Polanyi's argument that one should not use the modern theory of the

market to analyze markets in precapitalist societies is also important (for the heated debate in economic anthropology over the status of economic analysis in early societies, see Orlove 1986). A number of valuable studies focus on some special aspect of markets without necessarily suggesting a full theory of markets. There exist, for example, interesting analyses of the role of status in markets, the way that market identities are formed, and much more (Abolafia 1984; Garcia 1986; Collins 1990; Lie 1992; Podolny 1992; Aspers 2001c, d).

Weber on Markets

Of the early sociologists Weber was the one who was by far most interested in markets, and especially during his last years he tried to develop what he termed a "sociology of 'the market'" ([1922] 1978:81). But even during his presociological period, Weber paid quite a bit of attention to markets. As a young scholar and professor of economics, Weber, for example, wrote voluminously on the stock exchange (1999, [1894–96] 2000; see also Lestition 2000). These writings demonstrate Weber's belief that stock exchanges fill a crucial role in the modern capitalist machinery and that they can be organized in very different ways, depending on the stance of the state, experience of the businessmen in operating on stock exchanges, and so on. Weber emphasized the legal and ethical dimension of the dealings in the modern stock exchange, but was also fascinated by its political role—its role as *"a means to power"* in the economic struggle among nations ([1894–96] 2000:369).

This emphasis on struggle is evident in Weber's lectures a few years later as a professor of economics. In the 1890s Weber lectured on economic theory in Freiburg and Heidelberg, and he followed primarily Menger's thinking when it came to markets. Weber, however, also added his own distinct touch to these lectures by arguing that "the price on the market is a result of economic struggle (price struggle)" ([1898] 1990:45). The struggle over prices, he explained, has two aspects that must be separated. On the one hand, there is a "struggle of competition" between those who are potentially interested in an exchange; and on the other hand there is an "interest struggle" between the two parties who end up in an exchange. Weber also argued that when "the empirical price" has to be determined in an analysis, as opposed to "the theoretical price," several new factors have to be taken into account, such as the fact that the actors lack perfect information.

When Weber started to define himself as a sociologist about a decade later, he reworked his analysis of the market from the viewpoint of social action. Some early results of this effort can be found in *The Protestant Ethic and the Spirit of Capitalism*, which will be discussed in the next chapter. The most systematic expression of Weber's attempt to develop a sociological approach to markets can, however, be found in *Economy and Society*, where one of the key passages on the market reads as follows:

> A market may be said to exist wherever there is competition, even if only unilateral, for opportunities of exchange among a plurality of potential parties. Their physical assemblage in one place, as in the local market square, the fair (the "long distance market"), or the exchange (the merchants' market), only constitutes the most consistent kind of market formation. It is, however, only this physical assemblage which allows the full emergence of the market's most distinctive feature, viz. dickering ([1922] 1978:635).

As in his earlier lectures on economic theory, Weber now made a conceptual distinction between exchange and competition. Social action in the market begins, according to Weber, with competition but ends up in exchange. In phase one, "the potential partners are guided in their offers by the potential action of an indeterminate large group of real or imaginary competitors rather than by their own actions alone" ([1922] 1978:636). Here, in other words, there is orientation to others rather than direct social interaction. Phase two, or the final phase, is however, structured differently; and here the only actors involved are the two parties who end up making the exchange (635). As Weber saw it, exchange in the market was also exceptional in that it represented the most instrumental and calculating type of social action that is possible between two human beings. In this sense, he said, exchange represents "the archetype of all rational social action" and constitutes "an abomination to every system of fraternal ethics" (635, 637). While classes thrive on markets, these represent a threat to status groups.

Weber also emphasized the element of struggle or conflict in his sociology of markets. He used such terms as "market struggle," and he spoke of "the battle of man against man in the market" ([1922] 1978:93, 108). Competition, for example, is defined as "a 'peaceful' conflict . . . insofar as it consists in a formally peaceful attempt to attain control over opportunities and advantages which are also desired by others." Exchange, on the other hand, is defined as "a compromise of interests on the part of the parties in the course of which goods or other advantages are passed as reciprocal compensation" (38, 72).

Weber was furthermore very interested in the interaction between the market and the rest of society. Weber's thinking on this point can be approached through his analysis of the role that regulation (including legal regulation) plays in the market. A market, Weber explains in *Economy and Society*, can be free or regulated ([1922] 1978:82–85). In precapitalistic societies there typically exists quite a bit of "traditional regulation" of the market. The more rational a market is, however, the less it is formally regulated. The highest degree of "market freedom" or "market rationality" is reached in capitalistic society, where most irrational elements have been eliminated. In order for the market to be this rational and predictable, Weber notes, several conditions have to be fulfilled, including the expropriation of the workers from the means of production, the existence of calculable law, and so on (161–62). Capitalist markets, in other words, are the result of a long historical process. How Weber envisioned the historical evolution of the market can be gleaned from *Economy and Society* as well as from *General Economic History*.

Harrison White on the Market: The W(y) Model

Since the mid-1980s sociologists have become more interested in the market than ever before, and if one person deserves the credit for having helped to ignite this interest it is Harrison White (see especially 1981b; for an introduction to White's ideas on the market, see White and Eccles 1987; Aspers 2001d; Azarian forthcoming). White's research on markets, which began in the mid-1970s, represents a bold attempt to create a totally new and a totally sociological theory of markets—the so-called W(y) model. To some extent this theory has been shaped by White's deep dissatisfaction with neoclassical economics. Contemporary economics, according to White, has no interest in concrete markets and is mainly preoccupied with exchange market, as opposed to production ones (or markets where the actors produce goods). As a result, White says, "there does not exist a neoclassical theory of the market—[only] a pure theory of exchange"(1990:3).

But even if White wants a total break with the economists' theory of the market, it is also clear that he has been deeply influenced by the work of a few select economists. He refers, for example, repeatedly to the analyses of Marshall and Chamberlin, and he makes extensive use of Michael Spence's theory of signaling (White 1976, 1990; cf. Spence 1974). Spence clearly influenced a key feature of White's theory of markets, namely the notion that markets consist of social structures that are partly produced and reproduced through signaling among the participants. In a production market, the firms constantly check what the other firms are up to and adjust their actions accordingly.

The typical market that White describes is a production market;

and the reason for this is that production markets, as opposed to exchange markets, are characteristic of industrial economies. This type of market, according to White, consists of about a dozen firms that have come to view each other as constituting a market, and are also perceived as such by the buyers. The central mechanism in the social construction of a market is its "market schedule," operationalized by White as $W(y)$, where "W" stands for revenue and "y" for volume. This schedule, according to White, is considerably more realistic than the economists' demand-supply analysis. Businesspeople know what it costs to produce something and try to maximize their income by determining a certain volume for their product. On the other hand, they do *not* know how the consumers view their product—all they know is what items sell in what volumes and at what prices.

If businesspeople are correct in their calculations, they will be able to locate a niche in the market for their products, which their customers acknowledge by buying a certain volume at a certain price. Depending on its structure, a market can be one of the following four types: "paradox," "grind," "crowded," and "explosive" (White 1981b). Each of these is modeled by White and can exist only under certain specified conditions. The statement closest to a definition of a (production) market that can be found in White's work is the following:

> Markets are tangible cliques of producers watching each other. Pressure from the buyer side creates a mirror in which the producers see themselves, not consumers (1981b:543).

After having devoted several years of work exclusively to markets, White shifted to other concerns in the late 1980s and early 1990s. In *Identity and Control* (1992), for example, he presents a general theory of action. In so far as markets are concerned, this work is primarily interesting in that his earlier research on markets is here integrated into a larger theoretical whole. Production markets are seen as an example of what White calls "interfaces," which are defined as a certain way of achieving control in a "social molecule" (1992:41–43). In the interface, the individual identities of the actors (such as firms) come into being through continuous production. But control can also be achieved in a different manner; in the so-called "arena" it comes about via the creation of a different and much more general type of identity that is essentially interchangeable. Exchange markets are typical examples of what White terms "arena markets" (1992:51–52).

In a recent work entitled *Markets from Networks* White further develops his theory of production markets and also broadens its scope. Instead of focusing exclusively on individual production markets, White here attempts to see how they fit into the larger whole of an industrial economy. Three different "layers of action" are distinguished: "up-stream," "producers," and "downstream" (White 2001). The up-stream firms basically supply the input to producers whose output goes to the down-stream firms. There also exists a dynamic relationship between markets with goods that can substitute for each other (White 2002).

Markets as Networks

Using networks to analyze markets appears to be more popular than any other perspective in current economic sociology (see, e.g., the studies cited in Powell and Smith-Doerr 1994 and in Lie 1997). The main reason for this is probably that network analysis is a very flexible method, which allows the researcher both to keep close to empirical reality and to theorize. On the negative side, the network approach does not come with a full theory of what a market is, but rather constitutes a general method for tracing social relations. Why people engage in an exchange, and under what circumstances a market can be established, are not part of the theory but something that has to be added—and rarely is. Harrison White's W(y) model can be used as a contrast to markets as networks, with its explicit focus on terms of trade that decide whether a market can exist, and under what conditions some actor can become part of a market. As indicated by its title, White's *Markets from Networks* includes a network approach. This part of the analysis, however, is complementary to his general theory of production markets.

Mark Granovetter's *Getting A Job* (1974) can be described as so far the most successful network study of a market. More generally, it constitutes an exemplary study in economic sociology: it is theoretically innovative, meticulously researched, and analytically sharp. It may also be the most cited book in today's economic sociology, just as Granovetter's article on embeddedness is the most cited article (1985b). Although *Getting A Job* was written in the 1970s, its author has claimed it for "new economic sociology" with the following motivation:

> In retrospect, [*Getting A Job*] was one of the first exemplars of what I have called the "new economic sociology," which differed from older work in its attention to a core rather than a peripheral aspect of the economy, and in its willingness to challenge the adequacy of neoclassical economic theory in one of its core domains (1995c:vii).

Getting A Job represents an attempt to analyze the social mechanisms through which people find employment, which is based on a study of professional, technical and managerial workers in Newton, a small suburb of Boston. A random sample was taken: some 280 people filled out a questionnaire, of which 100 were interviewed. The questions especially tried to establish from whom did they receive information that led to a new job. Granovetter wanted to know, for example, if the economists were correct in seeing the labor market as a place where information about jobs reached all the participants. In particular, was it true that the person who got a new job could best be understood as someone who engages in a job search, according to utility-maximizing principles?

Granovetter's conclusion was that "perfect labor markets exist only in textbooks" and that the idea of a rational job search does not capture what happens when people find jobs (1974:25). Some people do indeed engage in a job search—but not all of those who get a job. There exists, for example, a sizeable number of people who will apply for a job only if they are approached by someone with a concrete proposal ("quasi-searchers"; about 20 percent). Furthermore, those who actively look for a job are not the ones who are likely to end up with the best jobs. What the job search theory of the economists also misses is one crucial fact, namely that "much labor-market information actually is transmitted as a byproduct of other social processes" (52). What matters in many cases is *contacts*—so much so, the author concludes, that "regardless of competence or merit, those without the right contacts are penalized" (100).

What Granovetter's research showed is the following: almost 56 percent of the respondents got their jobs through contacts, 18.8 percent through direct application, 18.8 percent through formal means (half of which through advertisements), and the rest through miscellaneous means. The economists' assumption that information about new jobs spreads evenly through the labor market was clearly invalidated (39.1 percent got information directly from the employer, 45.3 percent got it via one contact, 12.5 percent through two contacts, and only 3.1 percent through more than two contacts). Of special importance to Granovetter was that in the great majority of the cases, the person who got the job only associated "rarely" or "occasionally" with the person who supplied the information (27.8 percent "rarely," 55.6 percent "occasionally," and 16.7 percent "often"). This situation was theorized by Granovetter in the following way: people who you know intimately ("strong ties") all tend to share the same limited information and are therefore rarely able to help you. People you know casually ("weak ties"), on the other hand, have access to very different information—and may therefore be of more help to someone looking for a job (for a full presentation of the strength-of-weak-ties thesis, see Granovetter 1973). People who stay very long in one job,

Granovetter also noted, have much more difficulty in finding a new job, than those who change jobs often.

Granovetter's analysis of the labor market differs quite a bit from that of his thesis adviser, Harrison White, in *Chains of Opportunity* (1970). White's argument in this work is that when someone gets a new job, another opening is created that has to be filled—which results in yet another new vacancy that has to be filled, and so on. When a person gets a new job, in brief, a movement is set off that traverses the labor market. Tested against Granovetter's results in *Getting A Job*, it is clear that White's ideas about "vacancy chains" do capture quite a bit of the dynamics in the labor market—but by no means all. In 44.9 percent of the cases, the person who got a new job was replacing a particular person; in 35.3 percent, on the other hand, the position was totally new; and in 19.9 percent the job was new but of a type that had existed before.

In 1995, when Granovetter's study was reissued, the author noted that new evidence confirmed his assessment from 1974 that it was common to find a job through information supplied by a network (in the United States, 45 percent, in Japan, 70–75 percent; cf. Granovetter 1995c:139–41). He also noted that economists during the past few decades continued to ignore this fact and stuck to their theory of the rational job search.

Of the early network studies of markets there is also one by Wayne Baker that deserves to be singled out. In his doctoral dissertation, "Markets as Networks" (1981), Baker presented both a general theoretical argument for a sociological theory of markets and an empirical analysis. Economists, according to Baker, have developed an implicit rather than an explicit analysis of markets: "Since 'market' is typically assumed—not studied—most economic analyses implicitly characterize 'market' as a 'featureless plane'" (1981:211). In reality, however, markets are not homogeneous but socially constructed in various ways. Analyzing this structure constitutes the main task for "a middle-range theory of 'markets-as-networks'" (183).

How this can be done with the help of networks analysis is clear from the empirical part of Baker's thesis, which has also been published separately (Baker 1984; see Baker and Iyer 1992 for a mathematical rendition). Using empirical material from a national securities market, Baker showed that at least two different types of market networks could be distinguished: a small, rather dense network and a larger, more differentiated, and looser one. On this ground Baker argued that the standard economic view of the market as an undifferentiated whole was misleading. But Baker also wanted to show that the social structure of a market has an impact on the way that the market operates; and to do this he looked at volatility in option prices. He found that the fragmented, larger type of network caused much more volatility than the smaller, more intense ones. "Social structural patterns," he concluded, "dramatically influenced the direction and the magnitude of price volatility" (1984:803).

A third important network study of the way that a market operates can be found in Brian Uzzi's "Social Structure and Competition in Interfirm Networks: The Paradox of Embeddedness" (1997; cf. Uzzi 1996). Drawing on an ethnographic study of some twenty firms in the apparal industry in New York, the author found that the firms tended to divide their market interactions into what they call "market relationships" and "close or special relationships" (1997:41). According to the author, the former more or less match the kind of relationships that can be found in standard economic analysis, while the latter reflect Granovetter's notion of embeddedness. Market relationships tended to be not only more common than close or special relationships but also considerably less important. Embedded relationships were especially useful in the following situations: when trust was important, when fine-grained information had to be passed to the other party, and when certain types of joint problem-solving were on the agenda.

Uzzi interpreted his results as follows. For a business to operate successfully you cannot rely exclusively on market ties (as the economists claim), nor exclusively on embedded ties (as some sociologists claim)—you need a mixture of the two. The ideal is a balance between market ties and embedded ties or an "integrated network." Too many market ties make for an "underembedded network," and too many embedded ties for an "overembedded network." A firm with an overembedded network would, for example, have difficulty in picking up new information.

Uzzi's interpretation of his findings, in terms of interest analysis, is that the actors in his firms were neither selfish nor altruistic; they rather switched forward and backward between self-interest and cooperation. "[S]tringent assumptions about individuals being either innately self-interested or cooperative are too simplistic, because the same individuals simultaneously acted 'selfishly' and cooperatively with different actors in their network" (1997:42). The author adds complexity to his analysis by arguing that cooperative behavior can sometimes be a way of satisfying interests that are difficult to satisfy in arm's-length deals: "multiplex links among actors enable assets and interests that are not easily communicated across market ties to enter negotiations" (1997:50).

Markets as Parts of Fields (Bourdieu and Others)

One theory of how markets operate that has not received proper recognition is that of Pierre Bourdieu, most succinctly outlined in his programmatic statement entitled "Principles of Economic Anthropology" (2000a, forthcoming; cf. 1997). Bourdieu starts out from the idea that economic life is largely the result of the encounter between actors with special dispositions (habitus) in the economic field; and that the market is deeply influenced by the field of which it is an integral part (cf. chap. 2 of this book). The economic field can be an industry, a country, the whole world, and so on. Its structure, if we use an industry as our example, consists of the power relations among the firms, which are maintained through capital in various combinations (financial, technological, social, and so on). There are dominant ones, as well as dominated firms, and a constant struggle goes on between them. What happens outside the field, especially on the state level, also plays an important role in the struggles within an industry.

The market, to repeat, is conceptualized as part of a field and dominated by its dynamics. Prices, for example, are determined by the structure of the field, and not the other way around. "The whole is not the result of prices; it is the whole that decides the prices" (Bourdieu 2000a:240). Mark Granovetter's and Harrison White's theories of the market are mistaken, according to Bourdieu, because they ignore the impact of the structure of the field on the market; they express an "interactionist vision," as opposed to a "structural vision." Bourdieu's own view of the market is best captured by the following statement from "Principles of Economic Anthropology":

> What one calls the market is therefore the totality of exchange relations between actors who compete with one another. These interactions depend, as Simmel says, on an "indirect conflict," that is, on the structure [of the field] that has been socially constructed through power relations. The actors in the field contribute in different degrees to these power relations, through the modifications of these that they can muster, especially by controlling and directing the power of the state (2000a:250; my trans.).

In "Principles of Economic Anthropology" Bourdieu refers to the work of Neil Fligstein, and it is clear that there exist significant parallels between their views. At one point in "Markets as Politics"—Fligstein's most important theoretical statement on markets—he says, for example, that "my view of markets is roughly consistent with the idea of organizational fields, in that a market consists of firms who orient their actions toward one another" (1996b:663; cf. 2001:67–78).

Fligstein also agrees with Bourdieu that the attempt to use networks analysis to analyze markets is unsatisfactory since it focuses exclusively on social interaction. Networks analysis fails in his opinion to consider the role of politics, the view of the actors, and what characterizes markets as social institutions.

According to Fligstein, markets can be characterized as social situations in which goods are exchanged for a monetary price; and these situations can come into being only if the following three elements are present: "property rights," "governance structures," and "rules of exchange." Property rights are defined as social relations that determine who is entitled to the profit of a firm. Governance structures consist of rules for how to organize a firm as well as competition and cooperation. And rules of exchange determine under what conditions exchange can take place and who can participate in it.

As do Bourdieu and Weber, Fligstein emphasizes the role of conflict and struggle in the market. But Fligstein also adds to this type of analysis by proposing that what drives the individual firms and what characterizes modern production markets are, primarily attempts to *eliminate competition*—"attempts to mitigate the effects of competition with other firms" (1996b:657). "Markets as Politics" contains a number of propositions for empirical verification, all related to this idea. According to one, the state typically tries to help to stabilize markets and eliminate competition. According to another proposition, a market crisis will ensue when the largest firms in a field fail to reproduce themselves, with interorganizational power struggles as a result. Existing markets, Fligstein suggests, can also be transformed through exogenous factors, such as economic crises and invasions by other firms.

The theories of Bourdieu and Fligstein may seem somewhat schematic and dry as presented here; and it should therefore be emphasized that both of these authors have made empirical studies of concrete markets. Bourdieu, for example, has analyzed the markets for individual homes and literary products in France (1995, 2000c). In both of these studies, the relevant field is presented in rich empirical detail, which makes Bourdieu's scheme come alive while showing how it can be used to analyze markets. And Fligstein has shown the importance of looking at markets in terms of property rights, governance structures, and rules of exchange, by using the Single Market of the European Union as a case study (Fligstein and Mara-Drita 1996; cf. Fligstein and Sweet 2001). How firms try to control competition, and how the state in different ways can shape the market, also comes out with great force in Fligstein's study of the evolution of the huge firm during the twentieth century in the United States (1990).

Prices and Price Formation

There also exist some crucial aspects of markets that have been little explored by economic sociologists. Two of the topics I have in mind are how prices are set and the role of law in the market. The second of these topics will be explored in chapter 8, but it deserves a mention in this chapter too. No exchange can take place without a contract, and law plays an important role in markets in many other important ways as well.

As to prices and their determination, it is clear that economic sociologists have on the whole paid little attention to this problem. The classic writings pretty much ignored it, and so have the current generation of economic sociologists. As always, however, there are some instructive exceptions. Among the classic authors, Weber notes, for example, that the introduction of the fixed price represented a revolution in economic ethics, and that it was pioneered by the Baptists and the Quakers ([1920] 1946:312; cf. Kent 1983). Weber also points out that the Puritans helped to make the competitive price popular in the Anglo-Saxon countries and to counter the idea of "just" and traditional prices ([1922] 1978:872–73). One can finally also find the following programmatic statement about prices in *Economy and Society*: "money prices are the product of conflicts of interest and of compromises; they thus result from power constellations" (108). Weber adds that prices result from "struggle" and that prices "are instruments of calculations only as estimated quantifications of relative chances in this struggle of interests" (108).

One contemporary attempt to draw on these ideas can be found in a study of price-setting in the American electrical utility industry in the nineteenth century (Yakubovich and Granovetter 2001). Weber's suggestion that prices are the result of power constellations and struggle is fleshed out in an interesting manner in this study, which also draws attention in this context to the few empirical studies of this topic by economists (Blinder 1998; see also the important debate between Machlup and Lester in Machlup 1946, 1947; Lester 1947).

Granovetter has also used the embeddedness approach to explain the "stickiness" of prices (Granovetter and Swedberg 2001:13–14). Economic sociologists have in addition studied price-fixing, how status affects price, and how prices are determined in different types of auctions (Smith 1989; Podolny 1992; Baker and Faulkner 1993; Uzzi and Lancaster forthcoming). It has furthermore been noted that for a long time the following simple rule of thumb was used to determine prices in the U.S. computer industry: three times the manufacturing cost (MacKenzie 1996:53). Economic sociologists, in all brevity, have started to look at the issue of price formation—but few general insights have been formulated and most of the work still remains to be done.

Summary

Sociologists primarily view markets as institutions, while economists focus on the issue of price formation, mainly by constructing models. But even if mainstream economics has not paid much attention to markets as institutions or as empirical phenomena, I tried to show that many useful ideas on this topic can be found in the economics literature. This was illustrated by a discussion of the works by a number of economists, from Adam Smith till today. A special attempt was made to highlight the ideas of Alfred Marshall, the neo-Austrians, Keynes, and a few other economists who are particularly suggestive on this account. In Marshall we found, for example, a whole program for how to study markets in a realistic fashion; the neo-Austrians suggest that the market should be seen as a process; and so on.

Sociologists have paid considerably less attention to markets than the economists. Nonetheless, several theories of markets have been produced, such as Weber's idea of markets as competition into exchange, the W(y) model of Harrison White, markets as networks, and the idea that markets can be conceptualized as part of a field. Some ideas about the way that prices can be determined and analyzed from a sociological perspective were discussed, from Weber on the role of power in deciding prices to Fligstein's idea that corporations try to avoid competition and want stable prices. Much work, however, remains to be done before there exists a satisfying body of sociological literature on markets, including the formation of prices. Some suggestions for how to advance will be presented in the next chapter.

VI

Markets in History

MANY economic sociologists feel discontent with the current state of knowledge about markets, in economics as well as in economic sociology. While they realize that some good insights into the workings of markets have indeed been produced, they also sense that much—or most—of the work remains to be done (e.g., Krippner 2001). Given the various theoretical approaches in economic sociology that have been used to analyze markets, we should in principle be able to push ahead in several different directions—by using network theory, the concept of field, and the W(y) model.

One step in the right direction could be taken by drawing more upon historical material about markets than has been done up till now. The concept of interest also needs to be explicitly introduced into the analysis of the market. Historical material has not been used much by economic sociologists in analyzing markets, but can be very instructive, especially for an understanding of the interaction between markets and society at large. The concept of interest, as I will try to show, can add to the realism of the analysis—for example, by drawing attention to the way that economic and political power grow out of markets and how these in turn influence the structure of markets. The concept of interest can also be used to show the degree of dependence on the market that characterizes different groups of people.

Drawing upon the terminology that was introduced in chapter 3, we can see that markets constitute distinct forms of economic organization, as do firms and industrial districts. Labeling a market an economic organization has, among other things, the healthy effect of countering a notion that one sometimes encounters in political discussions, namely that markets are primarily created by tearing down other social structures—and that they then spring up spontaneously, like mushrooms after rain. Simple forms of markets may appear by themselves in many situations, but the major types of markets that exist in modern society constitute elaborate social structures. Once you decide that a market can be seen as a form of economic organization, it also seems natural to try to determine exactly what type of a social organization a market is, what sets it apart from its surroundings, and how it is connected to them.

In analyzing the links between a market and its surroundings, mainstream economic theory is not of much help since it starts out from the assumption that markets can be analyzed as if they constitute more-or-less self-contained systems. "By economic theory, we [economists] mean that in some sense, markets are the central institution in which individual actions interact and that other institutions are of negligible importance" (Arrow 1998:94). But if mainstream economic theory is handicapped by its assumption that the market is a self-contained system, it has, in comparison to economic sociology, the advantage of better understanding the role of economic interests in the market. It is self-interest, according to economic theory, that makes the actors engage in exchange until an equilibrium has been established in the market.

The economic theory of the market is, however, very narrow in focus and only covers a small part of what markets actually do. More precisely, in mainstream economics the theory of the market is more or less synonymous with abstract price theory. Social relations within the market are typically left out, as can be illustrated by the following description by Kenneth Arrow of how the market is viewed in economic theory:

> The theoretical picture of a market is one of impersonal exchange. I confine myself to the competitive case. At a given price (or, more precisely, given all prices), individual agents choose how much to supply and how much to demand. These supplies and demands are simply added up; when the prices are such that total supply equals total demand in each market, equilibrium prevails. There is no particular relation between a supplier and a demander; that is, a supplier is indifferent about supplying one demander or another, and vice versa (1998:94).

One strength of economic sociology, when it comes to the analysis of markets, is that sociologists are skillful at uncovering the social structure of a phenomenon. As was shown in the preceding chapter, sociologists have also developed several theories of markets, which all assign a central place to social structures. But as the work on a sociological theory of markets has advanced, new problems have also emerged. This is especially true of the attempt to view the market *exclusively* in social terms ("markets as social structures"). While it is possible to find references in this type of analysis to resources and profits, little sustained attention is paid to these. That interests play a central role in the functioning of markets is not much discussed nor theorized.

While I think that it represents a serious error not to deal with interests in developing a sociological analysis of markets, it is also clear that this can be done in a number of different ways. My own suggestion for how to proceed is outlined in the following five propositions:

- What gives the market its unique strength is that the actors use it *voluntarily*, the reason being that it offers both parties in an exchange the possibility of getting something better than what they had before (cf. chap. 3).
- The degree of interest that an actor has in a market depends on her degree of dependence on it.
- The type of interest that an actor has in the market depends largely on whether she defines her interest as economic, political, and so on.
- Economic power represents the likelihood that an actor can make other actors *voluntarily* devote their energies to some task, through the offer of money (in contrast to other forms of power that operate by authority, that is, by order or coercion).
- The interest that political actors have in a market depends on the amount of resources that pass through the market, and how dependent society as a whole is on the market.

The way in which these propositions can be used to illuminate how markets operate will be shown in the rest of this chapter, which is devoted to a presentation of some important types of markets that can be found throughout history.

The Starting Point: Real Markets in History

In their attempt to develop further the theory of markets, economic sociologists should, in my opinion, take concrete markets as their point of departure—how these work in real life and what their consequences are for the economy as well as for society at large. This is not the only way to proceed, but it helps to break with the artificiality that has come to characterize the concept of the market in mainstream economic theory as well as in public discourse. It may also help to inspire novel conceptualizations of markets, which is precisely what is needed today.

Sociologists should not only study contemporary markets but also markets of the past, since this supplies added information on the role that markets play in different types of societies and economies. Much of the relevant material for analyses of this type will naturally come from historians, who over the years have produced a wealth of studies on markets. An excellent introduction to this type of historical material can be found in the second volume of Fernand Braudel's giant work *Civilization and Capitalism, 15th–18th Century*, which represents one of the few attempts to write a history of markets and to survey the existing literature ([1979] 1985b:25–137).

I will present a few general types of markets from different historical periods in order to indicate what kind of issues a sociology of markets needs to work with today. I will start with markets at the dawn of history and then move on to markets for merchants, national markets, and so on. In each case, I shall try to show how different economic interests have been cast in different social configurations—and how this has resulted in markets that operate in different ways. The impact on society of these different types of markets will also be analyzed.

External Markets

Trade is generally thought to go far back in human history, even if it is impossible to set an approximate date for its original appearance (e.g., Weber [1923] 1981; Curtin 1984; Clarke 1987). One reason that people engaged in trade so early is that resources are unevenly distributed in the world—such as salt, minerals, and obsidian (a form of black volcanic glass that is ideal for making tools with sharp edges). Communities living on an ecological boundary have also tended to trade with one another. A nomadic tribe in a desert, for example, would trade with a sedentary tribe living in the area next to the desert.

According to Weber, the earliest type of market had a very distinct sociological structure: "in the beginning commerce is an affair between ethnic groups; it does not take place between members of the same tribe or of the same community but is in the oldest social communities an external phenomenon, being directed only toward foreign tribes" ([1923] 1981:195). That trade could be entered into only with members other than those from one's own local community in these *external markets* (as I shall call them) is highly significant from a sociological point of view. Weber writes,

> We find everywhere a primitive, strictly integrated internal economy such that there is no question of any freedom of economic action between members of the same tribe or clan, associated with absolute freedom of trade externally. Internal and external [economic] ethics are distinguished, and in connection with the latter there is complete ruthlessness in financial procedure ([1923] 1981:312–13).

The level of trust in this type of market was probably low, but it is also possible that stable norms for how to conduct exchange developed after some time—we simply do not know (Simmel [1907] 1978: 94–97; Benet [1957] 1971). The earliest form of trade was barter; and it took some time before money was used as payment to people living *outside* one's own community ("external money" as opposed to "internal money") (Weber [1923] 1981:237–39).

In interest terms, it is likely that the value of the items exchanged in external markets was fairly insignificant and that society was not dependent on this type of trade, either for survival or for the generation of wealth. No group devoted itself exclusively to trade; and trade was primarily engaged in because of use value, not profit. As specialization grew, however, so did trade. Longer distances were covered and the range of traded objects increased. Certain tribes began to specialize in trade; riches were made; and groups of merchants began to emerge. As markets grew in wealth, they also began to attract the interest of political rulers. For a long time to come, however, rulers would show disdain for the merchants; it was considered much more honorable to use violence to acquire wealth than to haggle in the market (Brown 1947).

Internal Markets

As my example of an internal market I will use the Athenian agora, which is one of the best researched markets in antiquity (e.g. Thompson and Wycherley 1972; Camp 1986). This market will also serve to illustrate a more general point, namely that markets soon came to acquire a very complex social structure and were heavily regulated. Internal markets, as opposed to an external market, are first and foremost characterized by their situation *inside* the community. Another defining feature is that community members trade with one another, not only with foreigners. This represents an important change in economic ethic, even if fixed prices were still far away. Money was extensively used at this stage of development, which facilitated the trade and dramatically increased the scope of items that could be traded.

All Greek city-states had an agora or a public area at their center, where trade, politics, worshipping, and socializing took place. The agora is often called the living heart of the Greek city and essentially consisted of an open square, marked off from the rest of the city through boundary stones. Typical buildings included market booths, public buildings, and a stoa, that is, an open collonade that could be used for different purposes. Temples and religious statues could be found all over the area. Some of the economic features of the agora come out in the following description:

Marketing 'when the agora was full,' i.e., in the morning, must have been a
noisy and nerve-racking business, with much haggling. The fishmongers
have a particularly bad reputation: according to the comic poets they used
the Greek equivalent of 'Billingsgate' [a famous fish market in London],
glared at their customers like Gorgons, asked exorbitant prices with a take-
it-or-leave-it air, and faked rotten fish. Most cities had officials called *agoranomoi* to exercise control and ensure fair dealing. Athens had, in addition,
corn-inspectors for a particularly vital trade and inspectors of weights and
measures. We read in inscriptions of the agoranomoi seeing that agora and
streets are kept clean and tidy and watching relations between employers
and employed (Wycherley 1976:66).

From this quote it is clear that the Athenian agora was one of the
most advanced among the Greek city states. Its main physical features
can be seen by looking at figure 6.1, which represents a reconstruction
of the agora around 400 B.C. A quick inspection shows that a number
of commercial, political, social, and religious activities took place in
the agora. The Athenian senate and its executive committee used two
of the buildings along the western boundary (the bouleuterion and
tholos). At the center one can see the area for the spectators of various
contests and similar amusements (the orchestra). In general the Athe-
nians enjoyed going to the agora, like people today take pleasure in
going downtown or to a shopping mall. Of the religious statues and
shrines in the agora, some were devoted to Hermes, the god of the
market.

Commercial activities went on all over the agora—in the temporary
booths, in the shops, and at the tables where money changers and
bankers could be found. The south Stoa at the southern boundary
appears to have been a commercial center; and close to it one can find
the mint, where the bronze coins of the city were produced. The political authorities checked the weights and the measures that were used
in the market as well as the quality of the coins. From various inscriptions it is also possible to find out what happened if someone used
false weights or coins of too low quality: the coins were destroyed or
confiscated. Crimes, including breaches of the market law, were handled by the many courts in the agora.

Even if the citizens of Athens were dependent on the market for
their economic survival to some extent, they basically relied on farming. The impact of the market on the social relations of the local community was nonetheless very important, as the presence of wealthy
merchants and bankers indicates. The Athenian market also played a
crucial role in financing the city-state and its foreign policy. The merchants and bankers had made their money mainly through trade, not

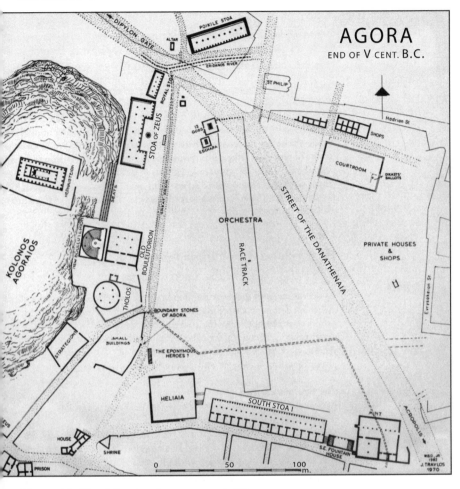

Figure 6.1. The Athenian Agora around 400 B.C.

Note: The Athenian market had a complex social structure—as its courts, market booths, boundary stones, and so on indicate.

Source: John Camp, *The Athenian Agora: Excavations in the Heart of Classical Athens* (London: Thames and Hudson, 1986), 89.

through manufacture; and the predominant economic ideal was still the independent farm. Many of the citizens looked down on the merchants and the haggling in the market, including Aristotle, whose hostility to money-making is well known. Hermes, according to Greek mythology, not only protected the market but was also the patron god of the thieves—something that indicates how the big landowners and many other people in the community looked at the merchants (Brown 1947).

Markets for Merchants (The European Fair)

Internal markets were essentially local markets in the sense that they supplied people with items from their immediate surroundings. At a very early stage in history, however, long-distance trade also appeared. The Athenian agora, for example, got much of its economic vitality from contacts with other markets in the Mediterranean. While the difference between local trade and long-distance trade may at first seem to be one of geographic distance, their social structure was very different. Long-distance trade could be extremely profitable, as opposed to local trade; hence the actors differed as well as the level of investment. While a peasant might just walk over to the local market and buy or sell a few items, this was obviously not possible with distant markets. Once the merchant left his community, the risk for attacks also increased and special protection was needed. The interaction with foreign buyers and sellers typically took place in an area under foreign rule, which lead to various complications. If the merchant decided to stay abroad, special arrangements had to be made for his living, which usually meant physical segregation from the native population. Markets for long-distance trade were often organized as external markets.

One very special type of market that involved long-distance trade and was also an external market was the *fair*, which played a key role in Europe during the eleventh to the fourteenth centuries (e.g., Huvelin 1897; Verlinden 1963; Lopez 1976). The fair is often defined as a marketplace where merchants from a whole region met at periodic intervals. Weber specifies that "the first form of trade between merchant and merchant is met at the fairs" ([1923] 1981:220). The name "fair," it can be added, comes from "feria," meaning "feast" or "holiday," and is a reminder that the merchants were not the only participants in this type of market: it was also open to common people. Fairs constituted huge and festive occasions—"fairs meant noise, tumult, music, popular rejoicing, the world turned upside down, disorder and sometimes disturbances" (Braudel [1979] 1985b:85).

Most of the European fairs were situated in the area between Italy and Flanders, and they basically helped to exchange goods from the South, including spices from Asia, with goods from the North, especially wool products from England and Flanders. The fairs were also extremely important money markets, especially the ones in Champagne. A fair typically took place on the land of a feudal lord, in a specially designated area where stalls were erected and tents pitched. The lord guaranteed the safe conduct of the merchants and would typically provide an escort for them, once they arrived to his land with their merchandise, for this service a fee was charged. Fairs also presented many other opportunities for the lord to make money. He could mint new coins, grant the right to gamble, and give permission to trade without regard to the prohibition of usury. Inside the market area the international law of the merchants (the *lex mercatoria* or the Law Merchant) was valid, and the merchants had their own court with their own elected judges. Many ordinary people came to the fairs to enjoy themselves, to drink and to gamble. Order was upheld by special guards.

New financial instruments were both used and perfected at the fairs. Soon bills of exchange could, for example, be discounted and pass more easily from hand to hand. These bills, it should be emphasized, represented a form of credit that had been specially tailored to the needs of merchants. Similarly, the *lex mercatoria* consisted of legal rules adopted to the needs of the merchants. Of special importance was the introduction of *bona fides* in the Law Merchant, which meant that an item that had been bought in good faith could not be reclaimed by the original owner. It has also often been noted that the merchants lacked a coercive apparatus to enforce their legal decisions. To compensate for this they tried to screen which merchants were allowed to participate in the fairs and admit only those in good standing. If someone broke the law, the main recourse that the judges had was to let it be known that the merchant in question was dishonest. In recent scholarship this is referred to as an attempt to enforce the rules of the market with the help of "the reputation mechanism" (Milgrom, North, and Weingast 1990; Barzel 2002; see also the section on the *lex mercatoria* in chap. 8).

The most important of all the fairs were the ones that took place during the twelfth to the fourteenth centuries in the province of Champagne. Here the merchants met in four small cities at six fairs, which each lasted fifty days. By far the most important business was the trade in money and credit. While other fairs typically covered a region, the fairs in Champagne covered all of Western Europe. Their importance in financial matters was enormous, and they essentially operated as a clearinghouse for much of Europe.

After the fourteenth century the fairs in Champagne and elsewhere started to decline, due to a number of reasons. The expansion of trade in Europe made it necessary to have permanent as opposed to temporary markets. The Italians had by now begun to sail straight to Flanders, which made them less dependent on the inland fairs. The fairs in Champagne also got incorporated into the Kingdom of France and became heavily taxed. Finally, a new type of market for merchants had emerged at the end of the Middle Ages, which soon took over some of the functions of the fair—the exchange (*bourse*). This institution differed on especially two points from the fair: it was continuous, and the merchants did not have to bring their goods to the market, just samples.

The fair of the Middle Ages represents a much more powerful type of market than the internal or local market of the type that we met in Athens. The reason for this does not so much have to do with the dependence of ordinary people on the goods that were traded at the fairs; common people still lived mainly off of agriculture, and what was sold at the market were basically agricultural products and what the artisans produced. Manufacture, which would revolutionize everyday life for ordinary people, had not yet become dominant.

What gave the fairs a great deal of power, however, was the concentration of money that came with the trade among the merchants. By this time in Western history, the merchants had established themselves as a distinct group with their own identity, and they also started to develop their own financial instruments as well as their own type of commercial law. The feudal lords were well aware of this and tried to control and tap into this new economic power as best as they could. One way to do so was by imposing taxes and fees on the fairs; another to borrow money from the merchants and the bankers or simply confiscate their resources (e.g., Coser 1972). The constant need of the feudal lords to finance wars against their neighboors made them dependent on the merchants and the bankers.

National Markets

If one takes a quick look at the early history of markets, one may get a sense that there is a natural progression from small and simple markets to large and complex ones, and that the key to this whole development is in the activities of the merchants. One popular version of this view can be found in *The Wealth of Nations* with its argument about "the natural propensity" of people to engage in trade (cf. chap. 5). Another version of this view can be found in the works of some economists, who have argued that the development of markets is primarily due to economic causes, especially the activities of the merchants (Sombart 1902–27; Hicks 1969). Creating national markets was, however, anything but automatic; it could only be done, with the help of political actors, especially the state (e.g., Braudel [1979] 1985a:277–385).

The obstacles to a development of huge markets were enormous in Europe during the Middle Ages. To travel along roads and rivers you constantly had to pay tolls. In the 1400s there were, for example, more than sixty different customs along the Rhine (Heckscher [1931] 1994: 57). To participate in a city market, you had to pay a fee unless you lived there. The city population forbade the peasants to trade any-where but inside the city, at prices the city dwellers decided on. Guilds closely controlled who was allowed to produce a large range of products. The only huge markets that existed during this period—the fairs—did not challenge this situation so much as adapt to it. The fairs were not permanent, and they often took place in the country-side, far away from the cities.

One of the forces that helped to counter this fragmentation and bring about national markets was the emergence of the mercantilist statesmen. The view that mercantilism was nothing but a fetter on the economy and blocked all economic development was popularized by Adam Smith in *The Wealth of Nations*. Historians, however, soon de-veloped a different view, initiated by Gustav Schmoller. According to Schmoller, mercantilism was primarily to be understood as a way of the ruler to counter medieval localism and construct a modern state, including a national economy. According to Schmoller,

> What was at stake was the creation of real *political* economies as unified organisms, the center of which should be, not merely a state policy reach-ing out in all directions, but rather the living heartbeat of unified sentiment. Only he who thus conceives of mercantilism will understand it; in its inner-most kernel it is nothing but state making—not state making in a narrow sense, but state making and national-economy making at the same time; state making in the modern sense, which creates out of the political com-munity an economic community, and so gives it a heightened meaning ([1884] 1897:150–1).

Today Schmoller's argument is more or less accepted by historians. Alexander Gerschenkron, for example, similarly notes in his critique of *A Theory of Economic History* (1969) by John Hicks that the author exclusively talks about the role of the merchant in the creation of markets and ignores the fact that "mercantilist statesmen from Col-bert to Peter the Great were first of all the great unifiers . . . it was at least just as much the policies of the state as the activities of the mer-chants that laid the ground both for subsequent great spurts of indus-trial development (metaphorically described as revolutions) and for the advent of *laissez-faire* policies" (Gerschenkron 1971:665).

The types of measures carried out by the mercantilist rulers to com-bat medieval localism can be exemplified by the case of France (e.g., Schmoller [1884] 1897; Heckscher [1931] 1994). Louis XI (1461–83) fought against various local interests and tried to unify weights and measures in his kingdom. In the early 1500s freedom of trade in corn was introduced, and Richelieu tried to launch the idea of a large national market through various measures. First and foremost, however, it was during the administration of Colbert (1662–83) that a concerted effort was made to bring about a uniform market in France. Colbert developed efficient roads and canals; he reformed the river tolls; and, most important of all, in 1664 he succeeded in eliminating the customs in about half of France.

But much more was needed to create national markets than what the mercantilist rulers could accomplish by themselves. Through the great political revolutions in the seventeenth and eighteenth centuries, free trade as well as freedom of movement and settlement were introduced, which both advanced the creation of national markets (Hintze [1929] 1975). In the United States it was especially the second revolution of 1787 and the Constitution that helped to bring about a unified American market for the first time (Hurst 1956). Interstate trade, for example, was assigned to the jurisdiction of the Congress of the Union, not to the individual states. The founders of the Constitution, many of whom were big landowners and merchants, also advanced things in other ways. Otto Hintze concludes, "[I]n sum: the rise of the great national markets . . . were brought about not only by economic developments but also by political actions intimately tied to the great revolutions in England, America, and France" ([1929] 1975:442).

The establishment of true national markets would not be complete until much later, when various means of communication—such as the telegraph, the telephone, and the railroad—would tie together even the most distant localities. In the United States, for example, the modern national market came into being around the turn of the twentieth century (e.g., Chandler 1977). Nonetheless, the foundations of the national markets were laid much earlier; and to understand fully the evolution of this type of markets, it is essential to take political as well as economic interests into account. The situation in the Middle Ages, which preceeded the creation of national markets, was essentially one where local interests in the cities had succeeded in getting the upper hand and held the countryside in an iron grip. In Schmoller's words,

> [W]hat, then, we have before our eyes in the Middle Ages are municipal and local economic centers whose whole economic life rests upon this— that the various local interests have, for the time, worked their way into agreement, that uniform feelings and ideas have risen out of common local interests, and that the town authorities stand forward to represent these feelings with a complete array of protective measures (Schmoller [1884] 1897:11–12).

No economic power could break this hold of the local interests on the economy; only political force could accomplish this. The success of various political powers in this situation does not, however, mean that the actions of the mercantilist state were invariably beneficial to the creation of the national market. Adam Smith has much to say on this point and notes, for example, how the bureaucratic mentality of someone like Colbert made it impossible for him to conceive of a truly free market ([1776] 1976:663–64). Part of the mercantilist project was also to create colonies, and all independent economic development was effectively stifled in these since manufacture was allowed to develop only in the home country.

Early Rational Markets

According to Max Weber, mercantilism made several important contributions to the creation of the rational state, including a pioneer attempt to develop a national economic policy ([1923] 1981:343–44). It did not, however, assist in the creation of the famous "spirit of capitalism," which Weber saw as absolutely central to the creation of modern, or rational, capitalism. For this, mercantilism was far too "despotic" and "authoritarian" in character; it demanded conformity, not independence and initiative from the population ([1904–05] 1958:152).

Weber's ideas on the emergence of a new spirit of capitalism are, of course, much debated and have been challenged on a number of points. The reason why they nonetheless deserve to be mentioned in this context, in connection with what I call "early rational markets," is that they do raise the important issue of the role played by the market actors' *mentality* in the creation of new types of markets. Weber's ideas constitute, from this viewpoint, a complement to what has already been said about the role of more conventional economic, social, and political factors, such as legal rules, money, weights and measures, and so on.

For those who find it hard to accept Weber's key thesis in *The Protestant Ethic*, it should also be emphasized that what is being discussed here is not the impact of Protestantism on capitalism, but something different, namely the existence of a new spirit of capitalism, *whatever its causes may have been*. Weber's essential claim (minus its religious part, in other words) is that a new spirit came to infuse Western capitalism some time after the sixteenth century, and that it was now that "modern economic man" came into being—and with him a general rationalization of economic life, including markets ([1904–05] 1958:174).

In *The Protestant Ethic and the Spirit of Capitalism* (1st ed. 1904–05; 2nd ed. 1920) Weber illustrates the difference between traditional capitalism and modern capitalism by using the continental textile industry as his example. Weber was very familiar with this type of industry since textile mills were owned in his family; and in 1908–09 he would also publish a detailed empirical study of work in textile mills ([1908–09] 1984). Weber was careful to stress that his example from the textile industry should be understood as an "ideal type," by which he meant that he was deliberately trying to capture what was characteristic about its social structure and not present an average empirical type (cf. [1904] 1949).

Until the mid-nineteenth century, Weber says, business in many parts of the continental textile industry was still carried out in a traditional manner ([1904–05] 1958:66–69). The merchant supplied the peasants with material to weave; and when the peasants were ready with the weaving, they delivered the cloth and were paid the customary price. The merchant was then approached by middlemen, who bought cloth from his warehouse. They also placed new orders, which were passed on to the peasants. The merchant worked about five to six hours a day and made a small but respectable profit. His relationship to competitors was friendly, and all agreed on the way that business should be done.

Weber emphasizes that the merchant's business was capitalist in nature. The merchant made his money exclusively through business; it was essential for him to have capital; and he kept a close watch on how much he earned with the help of accounting. Nonetheless, Weber emphasizes, this was definitely not a business that belonged to the modern type of capitalism:

> It was traditionalistic business, if one considers the spirit which animated the entrepreneur: the traditional manner of life, the traditional rate of profit, the traditional amount of work, the traditional manner of regulating the relationships with labor, and the essentialy traditional circle of customers and the manner of attracting new ones. All these dominated the conduct of the business, were at the basis, one may say, of the *ethos* of this group of businessmen ([1904–05] 1958:67).

What changed the way of doing business in the continental textile industry into modern capitalism, Weber says, was *not* a change in the way that it was organized—caused, for example, by the introduction of new machinery or the factory form ([1904–05] 1958:67–69). Something different was involved. At some point in time, Weber argues, a young merchant started to conduct his business in a very methodical and goal-oriented way. He chose his peasant weavers with much care;

he supervised them more closely; and he basically transformed them from peasants into workers. He also would market his merchandise in a different way than was the tradition, sometimes approaching the final consumer himself. Customers were personally solicited and the merchant carefully listened to what they wanted. The principle of low prices and a large turnover was introduced. Profits were reinvested, not consumed. As a result of all these changes in how to do business, a bitter struggle soon broke out in the industry, and the only ones who survived were those who could assimilate the new way of doing business.

As part of this whole process, according to Weber, many types of traditional markets changed and became more rational. One of these was the labor market, and a new type of worker now came into being who saw her work as a vocation or a *Beruf* (Weber [1904–05] 1958:59–63). Traditional workers, according to Weber, reacted to higher piece-rates by working *less*; they had traditional needs, and once these had been fulfilled, they saw no reason to continue working. But there also existed small groups of workers who had a very different attitude to their work, and they belonged to the Protestant sects. From his own empirical research in a textile factory, Weber knew that young Pietist women worked extra hard and in a very methodical manner. He was also aware that Methodist workers in the eighteenth century had often been attacked by their fellow workers because they worked so hard and regarded work as a goal in itself. And just as hardworking entrepreneurs soon drove out traditional entrepreneurs, hardworking workers soon drove out traditional workers.

The rational market can be described as a market wherever renewed profit is at the center and where substantive regulation is kept at a minimum. Since a rational market is more predictable, it is also easier to analyze it with the help of economic theory. Work, including profit-making, has a value of its own and is methodical in nature. Since Weber's arguments in *The Protestant Ethic* have often been misunderstood, two final points need to be emphasized. First, Weber is not arguing that the new type of market that came into being with Protestantism was exclusively the product of the novel spirit of capitalism. A capital market, for example, already existed with a full institutional setup, including law and market rules; all that was added was *a new mentality*. And what started out as a new mentality originating in religion soon translated into a series of secular institutions, which made it necessary for workers and entrepreneurs to develop a rational and methodical mentality.

The second point, to repeat, is that there are two parts to Weber's famous argument in *The Protestant Ethic*—an economic part and a religious part. Only the first of these needs to concern us here, this being that a change occurred in the mentality toward profit-making and work, some time after the 1500s in the West. What ultimately caused this change in mentality, and what role religion played in its diffusion, is a different question. The empirical issue to be decided, from this point of view, is not whether Protestantism caused the appearance of a rational attitude toward markets from the 1500s onward or not, but if such a rational attitude did indeed develop.

Modern Mass Markets

The industrial revolution, which first occurred in England (ca. 1760–1830), also initiated a new and crucial stage in the history of markets. The industrial revolution is conventionally defined in terms of changes in production: a series of key inventions were made; the modern factory was introduced; and new types of fuel, especially fossil fuel, began to be used. All of these changes, however, occurred in a capitalist society, which means that the role of markets in the economy was dramatically changed. According to a famous statement by the historian who popularized the term "industrial revolution," "the essence of the Industrial Revolution is the substitution of competition for the medieval regulations which had previously controlled the production and distribution of wealth" (Toynbee [1884] 1969:58).

Another way of stating what happened would be to say that from now on markets began to channel most of production and most of consumption. For this to be possible, not only new production and consumption markets had to be developed but also new financial markets and new markets in distribution. In addition, all of these markets had to be coordinated and connected to each other. The industrial revolution, according to Karl Polanyi in *The Great Transformation*, set off a development that meant that the traditional economy was replaced by a radically new type:

> A market economy is an economic system controlled, regulated, and directed by markets alone; order in the production and distribution of goods is entrusted to this self-regulating mechanism. . . . Self-regulation implies that all production is for sale on the market and that all incomes derive from such sales. Accordingly, there are markets for all elements of industry, not only for goods (including services) but also for labor, land, and money (Polanyi [1944] 1957:68–69).

Before the industrial revolution markets were typically defined in terms of a specific place; a market took place in a clearly delineated area—say in a special city square or on a designated piece of land belonging to a lord. Now, however, markets were no longer confined to distinct areas but spread out geographically, a change that is also reflected in the definitions of markets that we find in the nineteenth century. and later—for example, in the definitions by Cournot and Marshall (see chap. 5).

The "market economy" that now began to emerge was centered on the modern mass market. First of all, there was the mass market in consumption, which eventually was to provide the great majority of people with what they needed in their everyday lives. There also existed mass markets in production, distribution, and finance. A prerequisite for all of these markets to function smoothly, Weber notes, was stability and order in society. Large amounts of capital were needed for this type of economy to operate, and the capitalists had to be able to count on a steady demand as well as predictable behavior by the state and the legal system (Weber [1923] 1981:161, 276–77). From a Weberian perspective, in other words, the modern mass market represents a further development of the rational market, initially created under the impact of ascetic Protestantism.

At the center of this new system of markets was the modern consumer market, whose beginnings are usually traced to England in the second half of the eighteenth century. Its full appearance, however, came roughly a century later, as part of what Douglass North has called "the second economic revolution" (1981:171–86). The role of consumption in eighteenth-century England has been much debated in recent economic history (e.g., McKendrick 1982; Mokyr 1993; Brewer and Porter 1993). What has mainly been discussed, however, is whether the industrial revolution was primarily caused by consumption (demand) or by technological and related factors (supply). This is a somewhat academic question since demand and supply are closely connected. Nonetheless, a growing amount of empirical material has become available through this debate; and it is today possible to say something about early mass consumption—what items were consumed, by which kind of people, and how they were distributed. Information about the financial side of this whole development— minor borrowing, credit, and the like—is considerably less known.

A common channel of distribution during this period was via single stores—an institution that has its origins in eleventh-century cities (for the history of the store, see Braudel [1979] 1985b:60–75). By the eighteenth century the first shop windows of glass had begun to be installed in London, to the amazement of foreign visitors; and a crude and early form of advertisement had also come into being, which supplemented the information on shop signs and the traditional crying of goods.

The two social groups that primarily sustained the emerging mass market were the middle strata and the laboring poor; the rich preferred items that were made by hand and were in any case too few to matter in this context (Fine and Leopold 1990; Styles 1993). The laboring poor bought such items as cotton gowns, breeches, earthenware teapots, and watches. They also consumed an increasing amount of coal. The middle strata bought household items such as clothes, prints, cutlery, and window curtains. Ready-made clothing was marginal, and the great majority of clothes were still made by hand. The level of standardization was low and far from modern standards:

> In a purely numerical sense, none the less, there was in the eighteenth century a kind of mass market. Hundred of thousands of humble consumers bought a wide range of goods from distant producers with some regularity. But caution needs to be exercised regarding the implications of a mass market in this limited sense for product design and particularly product differentiation (Styles 1993:540).

The first real mass markets came into being in the second half of the nineteenth century. This development took place more-or-less simultaneously in several countries, including the United States. The system of distribution also changed around this time, and new institutions for mass consumption emerged. Single stores, that were supplied by wholesalers, from now on had to compete with chain stores and department stores. It was during this period that Macy's was founded in New York and Bon Marché in Paris—two of the world's first department stores (Miller 1981). Advertising greatly advanced, and brand names began to appear for the first time (Schudson 1984: 147–77). The shipping of goods was much quicker than during the eighteenth century, mainly due to railroads and steam ships. Customers also started to travel quite far in order to shop, using trams and later, automobiles. In the 1910s Henry Ford installed a moving assembly line in one of his Detroit factories; he also created the first truly standardized consumer item with the Model T automobile. Ready-to-wear clothing began to replace handmade clothing, a development that was set off by the invention of the sewing machine in the 1850s. Finally, science was increasingly being used in production, leading to the creation of many new products.

A novel type of firm emerged around the turn of the twentieth century—the so-called multidivisional firm—which had the administrative capacity to handle the production of enormous amounts of goods. In many cases these giant corporations also took care of the marketing of their goods, since it was difficult to move huge amounts of merchandise through the existing system of distribution. According to the main historian of the multidivisional firm, Alfred Chandler, it was especially hard to market machines that had been produced for the mass market:

> The mass marketing of new machines that were mass produced through the fabricating and assembling of interchangeable parts required a greater investment in personnel to provide the specialized marketing services than in product-specific plant and equipment. The mass distribution of sewing machines for households and for the production of apparel; typewriters, cash registers, adding machines, mimeograph machines, and other office equipment; harvesters, reapers, and other agricultural machines; and, after 1900, automobiles and the more complex electrical appliances all called for demonstration, after-sales service, and consumer credit. As these machines had been only recently invented, few existing distributors had the necessary training and experience to provide the services, or the financial resources to provide extensive consumer credit (1984:489–90).

Around 1900 modern mass markets had begun to dominate the economy totally in the United States. As part of this process people were also becoming increasingly dependent in their everyday life on this type of market. In 1790, for example, 80 percent of all clothing in the United States was made in the home, while a century later 90 percent was made outside the home (Boorstin 1974:97–99). The number of people deriving their livelihood from agriculture was also steadily declining during the same time. This naturally changed the food habits of people as well as the number of items that had to be bought. The canning of food and the use of refrigerated railroad cars, for example, made it possible to transport food from one part of the country to another.

All of this increased the dependence of the average American on getting a wage, that is, on working for an employer. The owners of the factories and their managers were at the same time also becoming more powerful through their control of ever larger amounts of capital. In this process they were helped not only by the emergence of national markets but also by the creation of new capital markets that allowed unprecedented amounts of capital to be concentrated. In the late 1890s U.S. manufacturers increasingly started to use the stock exchanges, and the aggregate value of stocks and bonds had by 1903 jumped from one billion dollars to seven billion dollars (Roy 1997:4–5).

International Markets

Like national markets, international markets have their own distinct social structure: a certain type of actor, of social control and regulation, and of financial order (e.g., Braudel [1979] 1985b; Curtin 1984;

Cameron 1993:275–302). They can also be the result of conscious political design, as in the case of national markets. The current international market, for example, illustrates this point, with many of its key institutions having their origin in the immediate post–World War II period (e.g., Bourdieu 2001:93–108; Fligstein 2001).

The embryo of international trade can be traced far back in time, more precisely to Mesopotamia circa 3,500 B.C., when surplus for agriculture allowed a small part of the population to devote themselves to something other than farming. The earliest forms of trade were local trade and long-distance trade. The latter was often carried out with the help of so-called trade diasporas or networks of traders who lived abroad and operated as brokers between two communities (Curtin 1984:1–3; cf. Greif 1989).

From 500 B.C. to the time of Christ, long-distance trade typically took place within large regions, such as the Hellenic world, India, or China. Soon, however, the area widened, and from around 200 B.C. the Mediterranean was connected to China, through trade on land as well as by sea. The earliest form of long-distance trade was in luxury goods, but from the thirteenth century onward the evolution of ship technology made it profitable also to transport bulk merchandise over long distances. A few centuries later, the so-called maritime revolution took place, which helped the European traders take over much of world trade through their superior knowledge of world wind patterns. The trade diasporas, which represented a peaceful form of trade, were now replaced by trading posts, backed up by force. A very different type of international market had come into being.

The industrial revolution led to an explosion in international trade and strengthened European domination. During 1780–1880 world trade increased by twenty times and by the mid-nineteenth century some people began to speak of the existing "world market" (Marx and Engels [1848] 1978:475; Kuznets 1966:306–7). Advances in weapons technology allowed Europeans to strengthen their hold on world trade, and the trading post system was now replaced by direct territorial control, made possible by new and superior means of communication. In the 1830s it took five to eight full months for a letter to reach London from India by ship. In the 1850s, in comparison, it took only forty-five days by train and steamer; and in the 1870s a message could be sent and received the same day, with the help of the telegraph (Curtin 1984:252). A free trade ideology was formulated in England in the early 1800s and quickly spread throughout Europe, even if protectionist sentiments were still strong. "By the beginning of the twentieth century," economic historian Rondo Cameron concludes, "it was possible to speak meaningfully of a world economy, in which virtually every inhabited portion participated at least minimally, though Europe was by far the most important" (1993:275).

It is often noted that the world market that existed around the turn of the nineteenth century did not find its equal until after World War II. The world economy started to disintegrate after World War I for a number of reasons, leading to the creation of different currency blocs as well as the introduction of autarchy by Nazi Germany. The Depression also hurt international trade and slowed it down considerably. After World War II the United States rebuilt world trade, with the help of such institutions as the International Monetary Fund, the World Bank, and GATT (e.g., Block 1977; Shoup and Minter 1977). In the 1950s national European currencies were strengthened and the foundations laid for the European Union. By the mid-1960s an international capital market began to emerge, thanks to the so-called Euromarkets, and soon it had grown enormously in size. The turnover in the global foreign exchange market was 1.5 trillion dollars per day in 1998, up from 36.4 billion in 1974 (Knorr-Cetina and Brügger 2002:905). According to some globalization theorists, the traditional world economy has been replaced by a so-called global economy (see chap. 3; for the traditional concept of the world economy, see Braudel [1979] 1985c:21–22).

What is characteristic of a fully developed international market is, first of all, that people in different countries are to a large extent dependent on what happens in the economies of other countries. This goes for consumer items—food, clothes, and so on—as well as for jobs and income. Already by the end of the nineteenth century, the exports of such countries as Great Britain, Germany, and France amounted to between fifteen and twenty per cent of the total national income for each of these countries (Cameron 1993:283). Transborder ownership has also grown rapidly during the twentieth century and led to new forms of economic and political dependencies. Local capitalist elites have been challenged and have had to adapt. The existence of a giant international market in currencies has tied the value of national currencies to forces outside the individual countries and decreased the power of central banks to intervene. International corporations are also beginning to operate outside the jurisdiction of national governments. In 1999 there existed some 63,000 transnational corporations with 690,000 foreign affiliates (Gordon and Meunier 2001:6).

Money and Capital Markets

I have so far tried to show that the different types of markets found throughout history have each had their own types of financial instruments and sometimes also their own type of money. At one point, however, separate markets in money and capital began to emerge with their own distinct dynamic (for the early history of money and banking, see Weber [1923] 1981:236–66; cf. Menger 1892). These markets are of special importance to the sociologist because of the enormous amount of money that circulate within them. It is also important to realize that money and capital markets are dependent on other markets for their existence, which explains their relatively late appearance in history. The first modern savings banks, for example, emerged during the industrial revolution, when an increasing number of people began to work for a wage (Smelser 1959:358–77). Fully developed banks that served merchants and political rulers already existed during the Middle Ages, as many examples from the Italian city-states testify to (e.g., De Roover 1963; McLean and Padgett 1997). Still, it was not till the 1800s that banks started to move into the very center of everyday economic life by shifting from trade in money to financing industry, with the Pereires brothers in France as the pioneers. Central banks, national currencies, and modern stock exchanges also became integral parts of the modern nation-state that emerged in the nineteenth century (Gilbert and Helleiner 1999; Weber [1894–96] 2000; for central banks, see Zysman 1983; Lebaron 2000b; Abolafia forthcoming).

A discussion of money and banking within the context of markets differs from the way in which these topics are usually treated in economic sociology. Money is often discussed apart from markets, as if it had an independent existence and origin. Sociologists may study the impact of money on society or the function of money at a very abstract level (e.g., Parsons 1963; Luhmann 1988:230–71; but see Baker 1987 for a market-oriented approach). Money has also been seen as some kind of homogeneous entity, which is essentially the same regardless of the social situation. This position has recently been challenged by Viviana Zelizer (1994), who argues that even if money may seem to be the same everywhere, people often "earmark" money and set aside different sums for different purposes. That this often happens in the household economy is clear—a certain sum may be set aside for rent, another for clothes for the children, and so on. Whether earmarking also takes place in firms and in the state has not been explored empirically, but may well be the case.

When sociologists study banks they tend to see them as organizations with links to other organizations (firms), rather than as profit-making actors in distinct markets. One example of the first view is *The Power Structure of American Business* by Beth Mintz and Michael Schwartz, in which the authors analyze networks between major American banks and corporations in the 1960s (1985). According to Mintz and Schwartz, banks have the power to coordinate firms and to intervene if something goes wrong ("financial hegemony," as opposed to "bank control," which implies a stronger form of control; see also Kotz 1978). Firms naturally resent being dependent on banks and

"Sure, it may be great for us, but it's hell on the markets."

try to free themselves through internal financing and by dealing with several banks, for example (e.g., Katona 1957; Stearns 1990).

According to a recent study of American investment banks, this type of institution lost much of its power during the twentieth century (Chernow 1997; for a networks study of investment banking, see Eccles and Crane 1988). "Relationship banking" of the kind that J. P. Morgan excelled in and that gave him such enormous power, has been replaced by "transactional banking," where banks compete on the basis of price in fairly anonymous markets. One reason for this development is that a variety of new financial instruments for procuring capital have been devised, making it possible for firms to bypass banks and put pressure on the latter to develop new products. It has, for example, become much easier for firms to raise capital in the market without resorting to intermediaries—by selling equity on the stock exchange, by borrowing directly from other firms, and so on. Furthermore, firms in countries where the dependence on banks by tradition is very high (such as in France, Germany, and Japan) have all begun to rely increasingly on the equity market for funds (e.g., Stearns and Mizruchi forthcoming).

It is not only investment banks that have lost power during the past few decades. Statistics on the assets of financial intermediaries during the period 1989–99 show that commercial banks and savings banks in the United States control about 10 percent less funds today, while pension funds and mutual funds have grown very quickly (Stearns and Mizruchi forthcoming). Institutional investors more generally, it can be added, have become key financial players and control many of the largest corporations in the world today.

Attempts during the past few decades to respond to this whole development by reshaping the banking industry have expanded the repertoire of the average bank and changed it into something very different from what it once was. "In these twenty years [from 1975–1995]," according to Martin Mayer, "banking has changed beyond recognition" (1997:17; cf. Davis and Mizruchi 1999). The old-fashioned, prudent deposit bank has more or less disappeared, just as the old type of bank teller has been replaced by automatic teller machines and banking on the internet. Economic organizations that are not banks have also started to deal in money in ways that once only banks were permitted to do:

> General Motors sells insurance, makes loans, and issues mortgages. General Electric Capital Corporation heads a growing life-insurance empire and is a major issuer of commercial paper. IBM is deeply involved in home-banking and electronic-payments system while AT&T issues credit cards. For five of the past six years, Ford Motor has actually made more money as a banker than as a car maker. The list could be expanded indefinitely (Chernow 1997:71).

In brief, the buying and selling of money and capital today goes on in number of markets that are very dynamic in nature (Mizruchi and Stearns 1994, forthcoming; MacKenzie and Millo 2001). The enormous sums involved—sometimes trillions of dollars on a daily basis—create a strong pressure for financial innovations, and also make it hard for political authorities to keep up with these markets and regulate them. There is also the fact that financial markets are always connected to other markets, which means that problems in one type of market typically spread to other markets. The collapse in 1998 of Long-Term Capital Management, for example, threatened to undo the whole financial system of the United States; and to avoid this disaster the New York Federal Reserve Bank orchestrated a savings operations that cost several billions of dollars (MacKenzie 2000). An added danger exists when it comes to the international financial markets that have come into being after World War II, since they often lack regulation and have no authorities in charge of them.

Labor Markets

Labor markets represent a distinct species of their own, when it comes to markets. According to Robert Solow, everybody except mainstream economists feel that "there is something special about labor as a commodity and therefore about the labor market too" (1990:3). That Marx viewed labor as different from other commodites is well known, as is his attempt to unlock the secrets of capitalism by analyzing the values created by "this peculiar commodity" ([1867] 1906:189). According to *Capital*, "the capitalist epoch . . . is characterized by this, that labor power takes in the eyes of the laborer himself the form of a commodity which is his property" (189).

The person who was perhaps the most incensed by the idea that labor had come to be seen as a commodity, to be bought and sold as any other object, was, however, Polanyi. *The Great Transformation* is filled with outrage over the attempt in nineteenth-century England to turn labor into a commodity. According to Polanyi, this attempt was all wrong since "labor is only another name for a human activity which goes with life itself, which in turn is not produced for sale but for entirely different reasons, nor can that activity be detached from the rest of life, be stored, or mobilized" ([1944] 1957:72).

The earliest labor markets appeared in the thirteenth and fourteenth centuries, when small groups of men would gather at some public place in a village or a city and offer their services for sale (Braudel [1979] 1985b:49–54; cf. Weber [1922] 1978:679). Labor markets, however, did not necessarily advance in tandem with capitalism since early capitalist production often took place in the homes of peasants and craftsmen. From the industrial revolution onward, however, the situation changed dramatically, and work was now transferred to the factories, where it could be better organized and monitored by the capitalists. The disorder and poverty that was initially created by this change have been classically described by Engels in *The Condition of the Working Class in England* (1845). It was during this period as well that the concept of unemployment emerged. During the twentieth century it became common not only to hire people from outside the corporation but also to promote those who already worked there (internal labor markets). Personnel departments began to emerge around the turn of the twentieth century, at which time it also became increasingly common to categorize workers into different occupations (Tilly and Tilly 1994).

In today's society some types of work are bought in labor markets and others are not. Voluntary work, work in the household, and some of the activities that take place in the so-called informal economy are typically unpaid (for household work, see chap. 11). Crafts and professions also have labor markets with distinct features of their own. Professions, for example, control the number of practitioners and often the price and quality of the services that they offer.

Buyers and sellers in ordinary labor markets typically locate each other with the help of advertisements, placement agencies, and connections. That networks play an important role in transmitting knowledge about vacancies is something that has been shown by sociologists (cf. the account of Granovetter's *Getting A Job* in chap. 5). Researchers also discern a common career pattern in which workers switch jobs frequently until they reach their mid-30s and then settle down. While some employers, such as the military and the church, rely exclusively on internal labor markets, most employers use the traditional labor market as well.

According to mainstream economics, it is the productivity of the worker that decides salaries as well as who gets hired and who gets promoted. Productivity, however, is notoriously hard to measure; and it is furthermore clear that many other factors play a role besides productivity, such as seniority, ethnicity, gender, and whether one works in an expanding or in a contracting firm (Granovetter 1986; Farkas and England 1988; Berg and Kalleberg 2001). The number of openings that exist in one part of the economy may also be affected by the number of openings in some other part, due to so-called vacancy chains, as mentioned earlier.

It is obvious that interests play a very special role in labor markets. The average person in modern society is totally dependent on her wage; and her status as well as her personality are deeply influenced by what she does at work. It is furthermore very difficult to understand such phenomena as unionization and strikes without the concepts of interest and interest struggle. Labor history is full of events that testify to the strength with which employers and employees have tried to defend and advance their interests (see also the discussion of free riding in Olson 1965 for a different approach to an interest analysis of trade unions).

Interest, in brief, is at the very heart of what makes labor markets so different from other markets, since these are the only markets in which the item that is sold is the activity of a human being. What is traded in labor markets differs from the ordinary inert objects that are exchanged in a market by having interests of their own, a distinct subjectivity, and links to other people. A person's perception of what is fair pay may also affect her productivity, and so may her links to other people.

Summary

This chapter begins with the observation that some economic sociologists feel that there currently does not exist a satisfactory theory of markets. To remedy this, I suggest, one should introduce the concept of interest into the analysis and also make better use of existing historical material on markets. When this is done, it soon becomes clear that the place of markets in human communities has varied quite a bit over time. Some markets have been located in a specific place, while others have covered a more diffuse area. The earliest markets were probably situated at the margin of a community, while later markets are to be found at its center. Whether located in a specific place or in a general area, order has to be kept in a market through norms and laws, and quite a bit of variation exists on this point as well. The act of exchange also has to be regulated through norms and laws.

What can be exchanged in the different types of markets has also varied quite a bit throughout history. Labor, for example, is a very special commodity and demands a very special type of market. As to nonhuman goods, these come in different kinds: luxury goods, everyday items, mass produced items, and so on. Political authorities may encourage markets and help to construct them—but they may also block them under certain circumstances since markets can upset the status quo or otherwise threaten established interests. As to the role of money—and I strongly advocate seeing money and its development as part of the evolution of markets—there are first of all markets where barter takes place and those where money is used. Money can be internal, external, local, national, or international, and a huge variety of credit instruments have gradually come into being. Interest, finally, highlights the importance of markets to individuals, political authorities, and society at large by emphasizing the extent to which all of these are dependent on markets for resources. The dependence of all of these actors on the market has gone from being very low to very high—and continues to grow even stronger. Interest also helps to elucidate the economic power that accumulates through markets and the economic resources that different types of actors can command.

It is no doubt true that several other market types can be added to the ones that have just been presented. By looking at what can be called electronic markets it would, for example, be possible to highlight the crucial role that communication and related technology play in the modern economy. It is also possible to question the usefulness of some of the markets that I have singled out. Whether Weber's rational markets answer to some meaningful empirical reality can be discussed. Nonetheless, two general points should be clear: that today's sociology of markets can learn quite a bit from existing historical material on markets, and that the concept of interest can be of help in understanding the way that markets work.

VII

Politics and the Economy

FIRMS and markets are central topics in economic sociology, and it is therefore natural to start a general book in this area with a discussion of them. But there also exist several noneconomic institutions without which no modern economy could exist, the most important being the political authorities and the legal system. It is clear that the very existence of modern economic actors and economic institutions presuppose, among other things, that the issue of violence has been solved and removed from the arena of the economy; that when conflicts emerge in the economy, solutions can be reached and enforced; and that decisions can be taken about the role of economic and noneconomic activities in society as a whole. All of these factors point to the crucial existence of separate political authorities, and to politics as a way to influence these authorities.

I should stress that the emergence of separate "political" and "economic" phenomena is the result of a long and difficult historical process. Norbert Elias describes it in *The Civilizing Process*:

> We are accustomed to distinguish two spheres, "economics" and "politics." By "economic" we mean the whole network of activities and institutions serving the creation and acquisition of means of consumption and production. But we also take it for granted, in thinking of "economics," that the production and, above all, the acquisition of these means normally takes place without threat or use of physical or military violence. Nothing is less self-evident. For all warrior societies with a barter economy—and not only for them—the sword is a frequent and indispensable instrument for acquiring means of production. Only when the division of functions is very far advanced; only when, as the result of long struggles, a specialized monopoly administration has formed that exercises the functions of rule as its social property; only when a centralized and public monopoly of force exists over large areas, can competition for means of consumption and production take its course largely without the intervention of physical violence; and only then do the kind of struggles exist that we are accustomed to designate by the terms "economy" and "competition" in a more specific sense (Elias [1939] 1994:380–81).

Apart from the process of monopolization that Elias is referring to, it is also possible to enumerate several other topics that an economic sociology of politics would want to deal with. One of these is the question of how economic and political interests are defined and assigned distinct roles in the constitution of society. This constitution also often decides how political and economic interests are to be balanced against each other; when one of them is to be given preference; and how conflicts between various interests are to be solved. Another set of topics involves interest groups: how these come into being and how they influence the political authorities—as well as how they influence the economy, via the political authorities. As the number of interests and interest groups grow in society and become officially recognized, the more likely it also is that there will be conflicts of interest as well as interest struggles more generally.

An important role in the economic sociology of politics would also have to be assigned to a series of topics that form their own semi-autonomous field, namely the economic sociology of law. The primary task of this type of analysis (to which the next chapter is devoted) would be to make a sociological analysis of the role of law in the economy, as well as to study how legal phenomena influence the economy and how economic phenomena influence the legal process. To political and economic interests should be added legal interests or the interests of those who administer the legal system.

An economic sociology of politics would in some respects be similar to political economy (Offe 1996). Its main focus would, for example, be on the link between economics and politics; it would also be interested in the extent to which the state can be used to steer the economy. On some points, however, an economic sociology of politics would differ from political economy (as this term is used in sociology). It would, for example, assign a much more important role to law, and it would draw on a different analytical tradition (cf. chaps. 1 and 2). It would also have a broader focus than the traditional economics-politics interface; and it would have less of an explicit political agenda.

By taking interests into account—economic, political, and legal interests—an economic sociology of politics would be assured of realism. It would also assign a key place to fiscal sociology—an approach that suggests that the financing and the expenditures of the state represent a privileged position from which to analyze the state. Similarly, an economic sociology of law would not primarily rely on legal facts for its explanations, but on social relations and various types of interests. Realism in the economic sociology of politics, including law, would increase if researchers took such factors into account as the identity of the actors, their emotions, and the social structure in which the actors are embedded (Hirschman 1982; Udehn 1996).

An alternative way of presenting the subject area of an economic sociology of politics would be to say that it is centered around the three central tasks of the state when it comes to the economy:

1. how the state generates and spends its economic resources (fiscal sociology);
2. how the state attempts to direct the economy; and
3. how the state establishes and polices many of the basic rules of the economy, including the legal rules.

That fiscal sociology is important is clear not only from the fact that the state itself has to be financed in order to function, but also that an increasingly large part of a country's GNP has recently come to be channeled through the state during the past. At the moment this figure is enormous—roughly between 30 and 50 percent of the GNP for OECD countries. The state's desire to intervene in the economy and steer it in various directions, however, goes much further back in history, even if it has changed quite a bit over time (Polanyi et al. [1957] 1971). The state finally plays a crucial role in establishing and policing many of the rules that govern the economy. Some of these rules are political in nature, while others can better be characterized as social or legal. If these rules are not upheld, the economy will soon have difficulty in functioning.

This chapter will cover some of the key topics in the economic sociology of politics. There will first be a brief introduction to the way in which sociologists and economists have tried to conceptualize the relationship between the state and the economy. This will be followed by a presentation of the tasks and accomplishments of fiscal sociology. The final section is devoted to various attempts by the state to direct the economy, either on its own accord or under the pressure from interest groups. The attempt by the state to police the basic rules of the economy will be discussed in the next chapter, which is devoted exclusively to law.

The State and Its Role in the Economy

The state and its relationship to the economy have been much discussed in the social sciences and also constitute an area that falls within the economic sociology of politics. It is a topic, however, that covers such a broad area that the discussion in this chapter will be restricted to the modern Western state. Analyses of the state-economy relationship often have a certain air of artificiality to them, with references to an entity called "the state," on the one hand, and to an entity called "the economy," on the other. One way to avoid this sharp distinction between the two would be to conceptualize the state as part of the general organization of the economy, as suggested in chapter 3. We would then focus on the state *in* the economy rather than discuss the state *and* the economy. The state is obviously connected in a multitude of ways to the economy. There are, for examples, economic flows from every corporation and every individual to the state in the form of taxes; every economic exchange is also a contract, which falls under the jurisdiction of the state. The state itself is furthermore only a label for a number of organizations, which are linked in various ways to the economy as well as to one another.

An additional way of breaking with some of the artificiality implicit in the expression "the state and the economy" is to assign a place in the analysis to *politics* or to the attempts to change the state and its policies. This would draw attention to topics such as the financing of political parties and social movements; under which economic conditions citizens tend to become active (or passive) in politics; how economic ideals can be translated into political action; and to what extent the existence of democracy depends on capitalism (for an attempt to introduce the notion of social movement into economic sociology, see Davis and McAdam 2000).

These and other topics in the literature on the state and the economy will be touched on in the section that follows, which is devoted to a presentation and discussion of some of the classical approaches to the relationship of the state to the economy. I will begin with Adam Smith and his well-known discussion of "the three duties of the sovereign." Public choice and new institutional economics will then be commented on from a sociological perspective. The way that sociologists have viewed the theme of the state and the economy will finally be covered, in two steps: first the classics (Marx, Weber, and Durkheim) and then new economic sociology.

The State in the Economy: The View of the Economists

The Wealth of Nations contains a famous discussion of what Adam Smith calls "the three duties of the sovereign" (Smith [1776] 1976:687–947). These ideas had an important impact on public finance in the nineteenth century. The reason for referring to them here, however, is that they can also serve as an introduction to the role of the state in the economy, from the perspective of economic sociology. Here, as elsewhere, the vitality of Smith's ideas is obvious.

Understanding the role of the state in the economy was very important to Smith: roughly one fourth of *The Wealth of Nations* is devoted to this topic—or more than one half, if one includes Smith's critique of mercantilism (Smith [1776] 1976:428–686, 687–947). Smith's view of mercantilism is also of great interest in this context since his ideas on the liberal state can be seen as an effort to avoid the regulatory excesses and general activism that were the hallmarks of the mercantilist state. According to Smith, the state should as a rule *not* interfere in the workings of the economy. "Innumerable delusions," he says, are to be expected if the state engages in "superintending the industry of private people, and of directing it towards the employments most suitable to the interests of the society" ([1776] 1976:687).

Smith's view of the state was based on a set of ideas that he refers to as "the system of natural liberty" and that can be characterized as a form of liberalism. Each individual should in all brevity be free to pursue her own interests in whatever way she wants, within the framework of the law. In Smith's words, "Every man, as long as he does not violate the laws of justice, is left perfectly free to pursue his own interest his own way, and to bring both his industry and capital into competition with those of any other man, or order of men" ([1776] 1976:687). Smith concludes that the state should not interfere with what is going on in the economy beyond its "three duties": *defense, justice,* and *the maintenance of a minimal infrastructure, including education.*

The first duty of the state, according to Smith, is to defend the country against invaders. As civilization advances, he says, societies tend to become less and less warlike. The reason for this has to do with the division of labor: the kind of work that exists in an advanced commercial society allows for less and less leisure time, and leisure time is absolutely necessary for martial exercises. While this argument may not seem very convincing to the modern reader, the next ones will. The richer a country is, according to Smith, the more likely it is to be attacked. Weapons also have a tendency to become increasingly expensive, as they become more sophisticated. In former times a society that was not as civilized and prosperous as another country would have the upper hand in a war, but this is not the case today. "In modern times the poor and barbarous find it difficult to defend themselves against the opulent and civilized" (Smith [1776] 1976:708).

The second duty of the state is to maintain justice or to prevent the inhabitants from oppressing one another. Influenced by various "passions," people want the property of their neighbor; the rich want it because of their "avarice" and "ambition," and the poor because of their "hatred of labour" and "love of present ease and enjoyment" (Smith [1776] 1976:709). If the state did not exist, Smith maintains, no person with property would be safe. According to *The Wealth of Nations,*

It is only under the shelter of the civil magistrate that the owner of that valuable property, which is acquired by the labour of many years, or perhaps of many successive generations, can sleep a single night in security. He is at all times surrounded by unknown enemies, whom, though he never provoked, he can never appease, and from whose injustice he can be protected only by the powerful arm of the civil magistrate continually held up to chastise it ([1776] 1976:710).

Like John Locke, Adam Smith regarded the defense of private property as one of the most important tasks of the state, and he approvingly cites Locke's statement that "government has no other end but the preservation of property" ([1776] 1976:674). Smith also points out that the upholding of justice invariably means inequality: "Civil government, so far as it is instituted for the security of property, is in reality instituted for the defense of the rich against the poor, or of those who have some property against those who have none at all" (715).

The third duty of the state is to maintain certain "public works" and to support some elementary types of education and religious instruction. For commerce to flourish, a country must have good roads, bridges, harbors, and the like. The state also has to finance certain types of education or these will not exist. Every person should, for example, be able to learn how to read and write for a small sum of money. The teaching of science needs similarly to be subsidized. Whenever the state has expenses, however, the state should pay only part of them, according to Smith. The rest should be paid by those who benefit the most from it.

Smith similarly draws on the concept of interest in his suggestions for how best to ensure that the duties of the state are carried out in an efficient manner. University teachers, to cite one of his examples, are not very likely to give good lectures unless their income is directly related to the quality of their teaching. Smith's view of university teachers and their tendency to slack off comes out very well in the following quote:

> It is the interest of every man to live as much at his ease as he can; and if his emoluments are to be precisely the same, whether he does, or does not perform some very laborious duty, it is certainly his interest, at least as interest is vulgarly understood, either to neglect it altogether, or, if he is subject to some authority which will not suffer him to do this, to perform it in as careless and slovenly a manner as that authority will permit. If he is naturally active and a lover of labour, it is his interest to employ that activity in any way, from which he can derive some advantage, rather than in the performance of his duty, from which he can derive none ([1776] 1976:760).

Smith also uses the concept of interest in his analysis of the clergy and here he reverses his recommendation. Since a passive clergy is preferable to one that is active, he says, one should *not* make the salaries of the clergy dependent on success in proselytizing.

THE THEME OF THE STATE AND THE ECONOMY IN PUBLIC CHOICE AND NEW INSTITUTIONAL ECONOMICS

According to a statement by Douglass North, economists have paid little attention to the state and its role in the economy (1981:20). To some extent this has been changed by recent attempts in economics to "endogenize" the state, even if much of mainstream economics has retained its traditional focus on pure market behavior. Of much more importance than these efforts to recast standard economics, however, is the attempt from the 1960s and onward—by economists as well as by political scientists—to apply the logic of economic theory to the analysis of political behavior in what has become known as public choice theory (for overviews, see Mueller 1989; Weingast 1996).

From a sociological point of view, however, the results of public choice are somewhat ambivalent. On the one hand, it is clear that a number of suggestive concepts and ideas have been generated. The notion that politicians and voters have their own distinct interests in political life is by now firmly established and has replaced more idealized notions of what influences political actors (cf. Schumpeter's analysis of democracy in [1942] 1994:250–83). This represents an important achievement for public choice or "politics without romance," as James Buchanan has called it (cited in Mueller 1998:180).

It is, on the other hand, hard to find empirical support for several of the key propositions of public choice. People do not consistently vote according to their wallets; bureaucrats do not always try to maximize the resources they control; and decision-making in political bodies cannot routinely be explained with the help of vote-trading or logrolling. Or, to put it differently, what drives political behavior is not exclusively self-interest; ideology and emotions are important as well, and so is the social structure in which the political actors are embedded (for surveys of studies that have attempted to test public choice ideas, see Lewin 1991 and Udehn 1996).

Many suggestive ideas and concepts have nonetheless emerged from public choice analysis, and some of these deserve more attention than they have yet received in economic sociology. One example is rent-seeking or the attempt by an actor to withdraw resources for her own disposal from the free market (for the original formulation, see Krueger 1974; for a discussion of its use in economics, see Tullock

1987). Very few attempts, however, have been made in sociology to use this concept (for an exception, see Sørensen 2000).

Another perspective in public choice that might be useful in economic sociology is that of constitutional economics, as developed by James Buchanan and others. The focus in this type of analysis is on the basic framework of the economy and not, as in traditional economics, on the way that the allocation of scarce resources takes place in a market economy (Buchanan 1987; Brennan and Hamlin 1998). While traditional economics analyzes "choices within constraints," constitutional economics analyzes "constitutions" or "choices among constraints" (Buchanan 1987:586). An early example of constitutional economics, *The Wealth of Nations* juxtaposes two very different types of economic systems: mercantilism and the market economy. Constitutional economics also draws heavily on the work of Knut Wicksell, who argued that one should study not only the effect of different rules of taxation but also how these rules are generated in the first place ([1896] 1959; for Wicksell's attempts to mix economic and noneconomic topics in an analytical manner, see Swedberg 2002).

In many cases, however, it is not clear what makes up the basic framework of constraints that constitutional economics refers to, and which is alternatively described as "legal," "institutional," or simply "constitutional." Nonetheless, the idea that what goes on in any economic system rests on several layer of rules, so to speak, does represent a valuable insight, which is also of potential interest to economic sociology (for an attempt to apply it to sociology, see Coleman 1990: 325–70). As opposed to traditional economics, it can be added, constitutional economics also lends itself in a natural way to a comparative approach. Finally, this type of analysis gives considerably more room for a normative discussion of economic matters than what conventional economics does, including concepts such as Pareto optimality and social choice.

In new institutionalist economics it is first and foremost Douglass North who has tried to develop a new theoretical approach to the state and its role in the economy. North differs from many economists by explicitly starting out from the premise that "the existence of a state is essential for economic growth" (1981:20). He has also made an interesting attempt to set property rights at the very center of the theory of the state and the economy. In *The Rise of the Western World* (1973) by North and Robert Thomas, it is assumed that rising prices will lead to more efficient institutions, including more efficient property rights.

This view, however, was later corrected by North in *Structure and Change in Economic History* (1981). In a chapter entitled "A Neoclassical Theory of the State," he still starts out from the premise that the ruler in principle is interested in encouraging economic growth, since this will lead to more revenue in the form of taxes. His constituents, it is also assumed, are willing to trade protection and order for taxes. Two circumstances, however, can make the ruler institute property rights that will *impede* economic growth, but nonetheless maximize his revenue. One is when the transaction costs for raising the kind of taxes that the ruler wants are so high that it is more profitable for him personally to settle for other taxes. There is also the case when the ruler fears some of his constituents, and adjusts the taxes accordingly.

One can find many other interesting ideas about the state and its relationship to the economy in North's work. One is the notion of credible commitment or the challenge for a capitalist state to convince its citizens that it is strong enough to guarantee the enforcement of contracts, but will not use this strength to confiscate property (North and Weingast 1989; North 1990:58–59). This has been called "the fundamental political problem of an economy" (North, Summerhill, and Weingast 2000:21).

North's theory of the state is innovative in its emphasis on property rights and how these are related to economic growth. Once this has been said, however, it should be noted that North does not adequately specify how property rights and taxation are related to one another. He also does not address the issue of other ways in which the state can steer the economy. North, in other words, does not present a full theory of the role of the state in the economy.

The State in the Economy: The View of the Classical Sociologists

The early sociologists—especially Marx, Weber, and Durkheim—have all added to the sociological analysis of the role of the state in the economy. Marx's major contribution is to have shown that the economy plays a decisive role in influencing the actions of the state. The modern state, contrary to Hegel's argument in *The Philosophy of Right*, does not represent the general interest of society but rather the general interests of the bourgeoisie. According to the well-known formulation of *The Communist Manifesto*, "The executive of the modern State is but a committee for managing the common affairs of the whole bourgeoisie" (Marx and Engels [1848] 1978:475). In Marx's later historical studies, especially *The Eighteenth Brumaire of Louis Bonaparte*, this instrumentalist view of the state was complemented by the notion that under certain conditions the bourgeois state may acquire a relative autonomy from bourgeois economic interests. The social classes may for example balance each other, and thereby make it possible for the state to chart an independent course (Marx [1852] 1950; cf. Miliband 1961).

The notion that the state is not simply an instrument for capitalists but an actor with interests of its own, became popular with the neo-Marxists in the 1970s (for an overview, see Van den Berg 1988). Fred Block attempted to add sociological flexibility to this proposition by introducing the notion of "business climate" into the analysis (1987). Block argues that "state managers" are basically concerned with maintaining a good "business climate," a concern that makes the state act in the general interest of capitalism. In trying to keep businessmen happy, he also adds, the state managers will commit errors and make concessions to the workers, as they "grope toward effective action as best they can within existing political constraints" (66).

While Durkheim had much less to say about the role of the state in the economy than either Marx or Weber, his ideas are nonetheless noteworthy since they address this theme from a different and original angle. To Durkheim, modern industrial society had emerged so rapidly that it had not yet acquired a stable social structure. The result was, on one hand, a very powerful state, and, on the other, a number of isolated individuals. What was missing in this situation—which to Durkheim represented "a veritable sociological monstrosity"—was a layer of intermediary economic groups ([1893] 1984:liv; cf. Tocqueville [1835–40] 1945, 2:109–13). Durkheim advocated that such intermediary groups take the form of corporations in every industry. These corporations would be coordinated at a regional as well as a national level, and eventually also at an international level. In Durkheim's view, the state had an important role to play in economic affairs, but it was not to dominate the economy along the lines of the modern welfare state (Giddens 1986).

As opposed to ordinary trade unions, these industrial corporations should not only represent the economic interests of their members, but also take care of their social needs. They should be true communities, in which their members could enjoy each other's company and in this way overcome the unrest and unhappiness caused by the prevailing "economic anomie." In the preface to the second edition of *The Division of Labor in Society*, which contains the fullest account of Durkheim's corporatist vision, he writes, "When individuals discover they have interests in common and come together, it is not only to defend those interests, but also so as to associate with one another and not feel isolated in the midst of their adversaries, so as to enjoy the pleasure of communicating with one another, to feel at one with several others, which in the end means to lead the same moral life together" ([1893] 1984:xliii–xliv).

The reference to "moral life" in the previous quotation is not accidental. According to Durkheim, society is first and foremost a moral entity, and to elevate the economy to the most important factor in society would not solve any of the problems that beset modern industrial society. What matters is ultimately "subordination of the particular to the general interest—[this] is the very well-spring of all moral activity" ([1893] 1984:xliii). According to Durkheim, to phrase it a bit differently, there has to be a proper balance between individual and general interests if society is to prosper.

Of all the classical sociologists, however, Weber can be of most help to the modern sociologist trying to analyze the role of the state in the economy. Weber was not committed either to the thesis that the economy should have primacy over society (Marx) or that society should have primacy over the economy (Durkheim). Weber approached the theme of the economy and the state in a more dispassionate manner, trying to outline the basic mechanisms involved.

Although Weber never got around to producing the sociology of the state, as he had planned, he often wrote about the state and its relationship to the economy. He made an important contribution to fiscal sociology, and he had much to say about the economic policy of the state. He also addressed the issue of the relationship of the state to the economy in more general terms, and it is to these reflections that we now shall turn. According to Weber, the state represents a special type of "[ruling] political organization," which is characterized by the following: it controls a territory; it is "more" than just an economic organization; and it is ready to resort to violence, or to the threat of violence, in order to defend its territory ([1922] 1978:54, 901–04). The state differs from other ruling political organizations on the last of these criteria, in that it does not only have control over its territory but also has a monopoly on the legitimate use of violence.

Using the expression that a ruling political organization is "more" than an economic organization, Weber introduces a theme that is central to his analysis of power, namely that relying exclusively on violence (or on economic interests) makes for an unstable power. Something more is needed to make the power difficult to challenge, and this "more" consists primarily of two items: that the ruling political organization does not only control economic affairs but also other activities in society, and that its value system extends beyond purely economic matters.

There have been times in history when no ruling political organization existed, and no one was in control of the territory. This was especially the case when the economy was undifferentiated, according to Weber. When a need for permanent provision was felt, the institution of village chieftain emerged, first in wartime and later also in peace.

The process of acquiring control over the use of violence was to be long and difficult. Weber notes that the merchants and the church often lent support to the pacification of society; and by the time that this process was completed, the ruling political organization had turned into a state with a monopoly on the legitimate use of violence. The use of violence is, according to Weber, as characteristic of politics as peacefulness is of the economy. On this, as on other issues, economics and politics follow "two different logics" (Weber 1923:1).

The idea that the ruling political organization has somehow to be "more" than the economy is also central to what constitutes Weber's most important contribution to political sociology: his typology of the different types of legitimate domination—traditional, charismatic, and legal (Weber [1922] 1978:212–301, 941–1211). These three types are all primarily political in nature and essentially ensure the continuous existence of the state. Without support of this type, the existing property structure would be threatened. Legitimate domination is also of crucial importance to the economic sphere more generally.

Each type of legitimate domination, according to Weber, is associated with some general organization of the economy. It also affects the economy in a distinct way. *Legal domination* is characterized by the subjects' willingness to follow their political leaders not because of the individual qualities that these possess, but because the leaders have been chosen according to accepted rules. This type of domination needs a bureaucracy to function properly. Legal domination has historically come to coexist with modern rational capitalism, which needs the kind of predictability and expertise that only a bureaucracy and the following of rules can ensure.

Charismatic domination is characterized by a leader's ability to attract followers through her extraordinary or supernatural powers. The spirit of a charismatic movement is violently opposed to the existing order, especially to the economy, which constitutes the backbone of everyday life. Soon, however, a certain routinization sets in, and a reconciliation between the charismatic movement and the existing state of affairs is gradually reached. The end result is typically an order with a traditional kind of economy, which does not encourage rational capitalism.

Traditional domination, finally, comes in two major forms—patrimonialism and feudalism—even if it is present, to some extent, in all regimes. In patrimonialism, obedience is due mainly to the sanctity of tradition; and in feudalism, to the contract between the lord and the vassal. Patrimonialism is positive to political capitalism since the ruler is eager to have more resources at his disposal; but negative to rational capitalism, due to its arbitrary elements (for Weber on the differ-

TABLE 7.1.

Type of Domination and Its Effect on the Rise of Rational Capitalism, according to Weber

	Legal Domination	Charismatic Domination	Traditional Domination: Patrimonialism	Traditional Domination Feudalism
Nature of Legitimation	obedience is to the law and to rules, not to individuals	obedience is inspired by the extraordinary character of the leader	obedience is due to the sanctity of tradition; there is a corresponding loyalty to the leader	contract of fealty between lord and vassal; a mixture of tradition and charismatic elements
Effects on the Economy, Especially on the Rise of Capitalism	indispensable to rational capitalism through its predictability; hostile to political capitalism	initially hostile to all forms of systematic economic activity; when routinized usually a conservative force	hostile to rational capitalism because of its arbitrary element; positive to economic traditionalism and to political capitalism	the ethos of feudalism goes against all types of capitalism; deeply conservative effect on the economy

Note: According to Weber, each of the main types of domination have all had an impact on the possibility for the rise of rational capitalism.

Source: Max Weber, *Economy and Society* (Berkeley: University of California Press, [1922] 1978), 212–301.

ent types of capitalism, see chap. 3). In a traditional society there typically exist areas where the ruler has to follow tradition—but also areas where he is free to do as he pleases, and this is where the arbitrary element comes in. Feudalism has an ethics that is deeply antimercantile in spirit, and it basically has a conservative impact on the economy (see table 7.1).

Weber also has much to say about the economic dimension of everyday political activity. His most important concepts in this context are "economical availability [to participate in politics]" and "living off politics [that is, being paid to participate in politics]" ([1917] 1994: 109–12, [1919] 1994:318). Certain categories of people, by virtue of the kind of work that they do, are free or available to participate in politics when they want. This, however, is not the case for other groups. Farmers and peasants, for example, could not simply leave their work and get involved in politics, while this was perfectly possible for, say, the patricians in the medieval city. The modern entrepreneur, according to Weber, is typically so engrossed in his work that it is hard for him to establish a proper distance to politics. Weber also emphasizes that unless those who do political work get paid for this, only the rich will be involved in politics: "Democracy has only the choice of being run cheaply by the rich, or of being run expensively by paid professional politicians" ([1918] 1994:276).

It should finally be added, apropos politics and money, that there exists no elective affinity whatsoever between capitalism and democracy, according to Weber ([1906] 1994:68–70, [1922] 1978:1415). Their coexistence in contemporary Western society is simply the result of a series of historical coincidences, and in the future capitalism may well come to exist without democracy. Capitalists, according to Weber, are not particularly democractic; and they typically prefer to deal behind the scenes with a single authority than to deal with a number of elected officials ([1906] 1994:68; for a different view of the relationship between democracy and capitalism, see Lipset 1960; Moore 1966; Diamond 1992; Rueschemeyer, Stephens, and Stephens 1992).

NEW ECONOMIC SOCIOLOGY ON THE STATE AND THE ECONOMY

Most of the recent work in sociology that has been devoted to the state comes from subfields other than economic sociology, mainly from political sociology but also from organizational sociology. These types of studies often touch on economic topics even if economics is usually not their main focus (e.g., Evans, Rueschemeyer, and Skocpol 1985; Laumann and Knoke 1987). One example would be *Capital, Coercion and European States, a.d. 990–1990*, where Charles Tilly discusses, among other things, the role that control over economic resources has played in the creation of the modern nation-state. Tilly's argument is that the search for efficient coercive means (which must be financed) has led to a crowding out of alternatives to the nation-state, such as city-states, empires, and urban federations (1990; see esp. pp. 84–91).

Work on the economic dimension of the welfare state has also been carried out primarily in political sociology (e.g., Weir, Orloff, and Skocpol 1988). The emphasis in this type of study has typically been on the redistribution of economic resources via the state, while less attention has been paid to the way that the income of the state is generated, what relationship the welfare state has to the business community,

TABLE 7.2.

Attitudes toward Various Forms of Government Activity in Some OECD Countries

	Percent of persons surveyed				
Agree Government Should . . .	United States	West Germany	Great Britain	Austria	Italy
control wages by legislation	23	28	32	58	72
reduce workweek to create more jobs	27	51	49	36	63
control prices	19	20	48	—	67
provide health care	40	57	85	—	88
finance job creation projects	70	73	83	—	84
spend more on old-age pension	47	53	81	—	80
reduce differences in income between those with high and low income	38	66	65	70	80

Note: The data in this table comes from various surveys carried out by different agencies during 1985–90. Research on the attitudes of economists to the role of the state in the economy show that these mirror the general attitudes in the countries from which the economists come (see Frey et al. 1984).

Source: S. M. Lipset, *American Exceptionalism: A Double-Edged Sword* (New York: Norton, 1996), 75.

and the like. A variety of studies also exist that have helped to map out the differences that exist among countries regarding people's attitudes toward state intervention in the economy (see table 7.2).

It is fair to say that the role of the state in the economy has not been very high on the agenda of new economic sociology, at least during its first years of existence. The only attempt by a key contender to develop a general theory of the relationship of the state to the economy can be found in the work of Neil Fligstein (1996; cf. 1990). A number of studies on special topics, which in one way or another involve the role of the state in the economy, have nonetheless been produced. Many of these will be discussed in the next section, which deals with the financing of the state; in the final section of this chapter, which examines how the state attempts to direct the economy; and in chapter 8 on the economic sociology of law.

Several other studies, however, should also be mentioned. These include studies of the role of national currencies in the formation of the modern state (Gilbert and Helleiner 1999), the tendency in American ideology to portray the state as a negative influence on the economy (Block 1996), the role of economists in governments (Markoff and Montecinas 1993; Babb 2001), and the role of money in U.S. political campaigns (Mizruchi 1992; Clawson, Neustadt, and Weller 1998). A special mention should also be made of Bruce Carruthers's attempt to compare two treasury departments during the interwar period. According to this study, the British Treasury in the 1930s was remarkably independent of the state and also held a very orthodox view of state spending, while just the opposite was true for the U.S. Treasury during the same period (Carruthers 1994).

The main novelty of Neil Fligstein's approach to the role of the state in the economy, as presented in his article "Markets as Politics: A Political-Cultural Approach to Market Institutions," is his argument about the intimate relationship between the state and the creation of markets (cf. chap. 5). The modern state and modern capitalist markets, he argues, are closely interrelated: "I view the formation of markets as part of state-formation" (1996:657). The state helps to construct markets in a variety of ways: by devising specific property rights, by introducing general rules for competition and cooperation, by setting the parameters for the way that corporations view the market, and by designing the rules of exchange. Of particular importance is the role of the state in insuring that markets are not competetive but stable—a policy that all corporations tend to support.

Fligstein also suggests a research agenda to test his theory of "state-building as market-building" (1996:660). A good working hypothesis, he says, is that firms will typically try to get the state to limit competition and thereby create stable markets. A variation of this theme is his suggestion that when capitalism begins to develop in a country, the state will develop property rights, governance structures and rules that will all stabilize the markets for the largest firms. Once in place, these structures will deeply influence the future economic development of the country. Since these rules also have the support of powerful firms, it will take a major crisis to change them—such as a war, a depression, or the collapse of the state.

Fiscal Sociology

One of the key topics of an economic sociology of politics would be fiscal sociology, or *Finanzsoziologie* as it was called when it was originally conceived in Germany, just after World War I. Fiscal sociology is a field that has attracted economists as well as sociologists; the term itself was invented by an economist, and during its first decades it was kept alive mainly by economists (e.g., Mann 1943; Musgrave 1980; Blomert 2001). A well-known quote from Jean Bodin could be its motto: "Financial means are the nerves of the state" (Bodin [1576] 1986, 6:35). The central issue of fiscal sociology, however, is broader and can be described in the following way: *how the generation of income and its expenditure by the state and other political authorities affect the political authorities themselves, the economy, and the rest of society.*

The two key elements in fiscal sociology, following from this definition, are on the one hand the generation of income and its expenditure and, on the other, the effect that these two processes have on the political authorities, the economy, and the rest of society. Income can be generated in different ways, of which the most important are taxes, tariffs, tributes, and debts. How this fund-generating process is organized will have an important impact on the political authorities, the economy, and the rest of society. Taxes can be of different kinds, each with its own sociological profile (income tax, corporate tax, inheritance tax, direct taxes, indirect taxes, and so on). The ability/inability of the state to raise income is also of much interest. The expenditures of the state can be used for different purposes—for war, welfare, and so on—and this will obviously have important effects. Political scientists and political sociologists will presumably prioritize studies in fiscal sociology that analyze the impact of income and expenditure on political authorities; while economists and economic sociologists will be more interested in studies that focus on how these impact the economy.

The Pioneer: Joseph Schumpeter's "The Crisis of the Tax State"

The concept of a fiscal sociology was introduced into the social sciences by Austrian economist Rudolf Goldscheid in *State Socialism or State Capitalism?* (1917). The study that popularized the field and gave it a firm sociological grounding, however, was "The Crisis of the Tax State" (1918) by Joseph Schumpeter. According to Schumpeter, fiscal sociology allows the analyst to penetrate deeply beneath the surface of the state and to approach a whole series of important social and economic phenomena "stripped of all phrases" ([1918] 1991:101). Interest analysis also plays a central part in Schumpeter's analysis of the crisis of the tax state, as it will soon become clear.

According to Schumpeter, fiscal events have deeply influenced the course of human history and have often been the cause of war. A country's general history and culture, he argues, cannot be properly understood without taking its fiscal history into account. The same is true for its social structure and important aspects of the economy, such as the evolution of industry and the economic policy of the state. Generally, "we may surely speak of a special set of facts, a special set of problems, and of a special approach—in short of a special field: fiscal sociology, of which much may be expected" (Schumpeter [1918] 1991:101).

The main part of Schumpeter's essay is devoted to the situation in Austria just after World War I, when the country's finances were so run down that many people felt that the Austrian state might collapse. Schumpeter thought otherwise, and history has proven him right. What is interesting with his essay, however, is not so much its analysis of Austria as Schumpeter's attempt to generalize from this particular case and initiate a discussion of the conditions under which the state in capitalist society would be able to survive and under which this would not be possible. He also presents his own version of the birth of what he calls the tax state, or the kind of state whose resources mainly derive from taxation, as opposed to tributes, tariffs, and the like.

Referring exclusively to Austria and Germany, Schumpeter argues that the modern state was born somewhere between the fourteenth and sixteenth centuries. During this period the prince succeeded in conquering the state from the estates and in procuring for the state a general right to tax the population, something which it had never had before. What made the prince so eager to procure this right was his need for money, caused by a mismanagement of his affairs, a costly court life, and constant warfare. It was especially the wars that allowed the prince to present his own needs as a common exigency and to wrestle the right of taxation away from the estates.

According to Schumpeter, the coming of the tax state led to a deep transformation of the economy, which under feudalism had been communal in nature. The individual was gradually set free, as money and taxes became more common, and what increasingly motivated the individual from then on was self-interest. Such a strong reliance on self-interest meant that a new and dynamic force was introduced into the economy, but also that a crisis might ensue. Schumpeter writes,

> Here we have arrived at the fact which can become the leading principle for the theoretical understanding of the economic capacity of the tax state. In the bourgeois society everyone works and saves for himself and his family, and perhaps for some ends he has chosen himself. What is produced is produced for the purposes of the private economic subjects. The driving force is individual interest—understood in a very wide sense and by no means synonymous with hedonistic individual egotism. In this world the state lives as an economic parasite. It can withdraw from the private economy only as much as is consistent with the continued existence of this individual interest in every particular socio-psychological situation. In other words, the tax state must not demand from the people so much that they lose financial interest in production or at any rate cease to use their best energies for it ([1918] 1991:112).

A crisis in the tax state can, according to Schumpeter, come about for a number of reasons. One would be overtaxation, especially of the entrepreneur. While Schumpeter argues that it would be harmless to tax away monopoly profits and windfall profits, it would mean an end to economic growth if entrepreneurs were taxed too harshly. Similarly, if a progressive income tax was to be imposed on managers and other high-income groups, these would soon lose an interest in working hard. A third situation that would endanger the tax state and spell its end would be if people started to demand more and more from the state, at the same time as they began to question the legitimacy of private property and the capitalist way of life. If this were the case, Schumpeter says,

> then the tax state will have run its course and society will have to depend on other motive forces for its economy than self-interest. This limit, and with it the crisis which the tax state could not survive, can certainly be reached. Without doubt, the tax state *can* collapse ([1918] 1991:112).

Schumpeter's main concern in "The Crisis of the Tax State" is political in the sense that he discusses various scenarios that can lead to the disappearance of the tax state. His fiscal sociology is also limited to one specific period, capitalism, while the precapitalistic state is hardly discussed. Some critiques have also been directed at Schumpeter's article on the grounds that it exaggerates the role of fiscal factors in the creation of the modern state, while downplaying the role of political factors (Braun 1975). Moreover, Schumpeter often speaks as if the economic motives of individuals could be directly translated into collective actions without any mediation of social structures. This type of error especially mars Schumpeter's argument that the tax state is bound to decline once taxes are so high that people feel that it is no longer worthwhile to work hard.

Max Weber's Fiscal Sociology

While Weber did not use the term "fiscal sociology," he was nonetheless deeply interested in the various ways in which ruling political organizations have been financed throughout history and what effect this has had on economy and society. In his economic history of antiquity, for example, one can find the following dramatic account of the way that taxes were collected in ancient Egypt:

> We know how an Egyptian tax levy was made: the officials arrived unexpectedly, the women began to cry; and soon a general flight and hunt began; those liable for taxes were hunted down, beaten, and tortured into

paying what was demanded by the officials, who were themselves held responsible for quotas based on the official cadaster. This was the guise in which the state appeared to the peasants in the Near East, and as it appeared in modern times to Russian peasants ([1909] 1976:131).

In his course on economic and social history from 1919 to 1920, which was published under the title *General Economic History*, Weber also discusses the process through which government finances have been rationalized in the West. During the Middle Ages, for example, "the city, like the territorial lord, lived from week to week as is done today in a small household" (Weber [1923] 1981:283). A rational administration of taxation first appeared in the Italian cities during the Middle Ages, from where it spread to France, Germany, and elsewhere. Rational taxation is an integral part of the modern state and indispensable to the type of capitalism that came into being in the West.

Weber's main attempt to deal with questions of fiscal sociology is, however, to be found in *Economy and Society* (see especially Weber [1922] 1978:194–201, and also 212–338). It is here suggested that "the most direct connection" between noneconomic organizations, including the state, and the economy can be found in the way that these organizations are paid for (194). The "provision of corporate activity with economically scarce means" is termed "financing" (194). A state is most commonly financed through taxation or liturgies (obligations attached to privileges). The source of financing can be temporary or permanent; and the latter is clearly more important. The ways in which a state is financed will also influence its organizational structure and the economy at large.

Weber provides a typology for the three main ways in which states have been financed: through their own productive units, through liturgies, and through taxation. A state can own enterprises of very different types, from feudal domains to modern firms, all typically of a monopoly character. Liturgies, or obligations attached to privileges, are rare in modern capitalism but have played a major role throughout history. One example of this would be an obligation to serve in the army, coupled with freedom from certain taxes, which was common for the European aristocracy. Another would be the obligation of some strata in ancient Rome to pay for the defense of the city and its entertainment, as described by Paul Veyne in *Bread and Circuses* (Veyne 1990). When the state lacks enterprises of its own as well as liturgies, it is usually financed through monetary contributions, in the form of taxation. This is typical for the modern capitalist state, or, as Schumpeter calls it, the tax state.

Weber also notes that the way in which states finance their activities have "very important repercussions on the structure of private economic activity" ([1922] 1978:199). This is true for the three main forms of financing as well as for their manner of organization. Through tax farming, for example, the state can sell its right to taxation (as in Rome); certain individuals can be endowed with an income for life in exchange for services (benefices, as in China); and so on. All of these ways of raising money will have an impact on the economy at large, and Weber was especially interested in whether specific forms of finance had helped or if they had hindered the rise of modern rational capitalism. Rational taxation, he notes, constitutes the only way of financing the state that directly encourages the modern type of capitalism. Ways of financing the state such as tax farming, monopolistic profit-making enterprises, and liturgical obligations attached to property, on the other hand, have all hindered the rise of modern rational capitalism. These forms of financing the state can, however, easily coexist with political capitalism. Benefices, deliveries in kind, and compulsory services, finally, have had a negative impact on *all* types of capitalism.

Weber also introduces some of his fiscal sociology into his famous analysis of domination. Each form of domination, he argues, has to be financed in a special way and also has its own way of paying for its staff. The charismatic leader, for example, is followed by a small band of disciples or admirers who are typically "paid" with booty or donations on an irregular basis. As routinization takes place, however, a different and more traditionalistic way of payment emerges.

The traditionalistic leader, on the other hand, pays his people out of his own pocket and may also feed them. The division of labor between the various ministeries in the modern state has its origin here: the chamberlain deals with the treasury; the marshal, with the stables; the intendant, with clothing and armor; and so on. The traditional leader may also, as in feudalism, grant huge areas of land to his followers. This way of payment, however, often creates problems for the lord since the vassals are tied to the lord only through loyalty and are not under his physical control. Finally, legal domination is supported by a bureaucracy, where the civil servants have salaries and pensions that are paid for through taxation (see table 7.3).

Fiscal Sociology Today

After the contributions by Schumpeter and Weber, very little happened in fiscal sociology for the next fifty years, and it would be wrong to state that it represents a coherent and lively field of research

BLE 7.3.
 Relationship between Form of Domination, Type of Administration, and Means of
ment, according to Weber

	Legal Domination	Charismatic Domination	Traditional Domination: Patrimonialism	Traditional Domination: Feudalism
e of Administration	bureaucracy; the official is trained and has a career and a sense of duty	followers and disciples who later become more like normal officials as a result of routinization	from household staff to more advanced officials with mostly ad hoc and stereotyped tasks	small-scale administration, similar to patrimonial staff but with a distinct status element to it; the vassal has especially military duties
eans to pay the Administration and to Compensate Officials	taxation; the official gets a salary and possibly a pension	booty and donations pay for the needs of the "officials" before routinization leads to other forms of compensation	from the ruler's own resources or treasury; the official first eats at the ruler's table, then gets a benefice	tributes and services from the subjects; fiefs to the vassals, while the minor officials get paid as in patrimonialism

Note: A different type of administration answers to each of his three types of domination, and it
o has to be paid for in a special way.
Source: Max Weber, *Economy and Society* (Berkeley: University of California Press, [1922] 1978),
2–301.

today. What currently does exist is a large number of scattered contributions from different social sciences. Economics, for example, has a long tradition of looking at state finances, mainly in the field of public finance, and some of this research is also relevant for fiscal sociology (Musgrave and Musgrave 1989). Buchanan, for example, has revived the concept of "fiscal illusion," which covers the situation when a state conceals its expenses from the citizens by taking loans and resorting to inflation (Buchanan and Wagner 1970; cf. Mueller 1998:180). There also exists work in new institutional economics on the historical evolution of state debt and how the Glorious Revolution of 1688 led to a lower rate of interest in the English capital market (North and Weingast 1989).

Political scientists have made a series of important contributions to the area of fiscal sociology as well, drawing on traditional approaches in government studies and on public choice theory (e.g., Buchanan and Wagner 1977; Steinmo 1989, 1993; Webber and Wildavsky 1986). An interesting example of the more traditional approach is Daniel Tarschys's "Tributes, Tariffs, Taxes and Trade: The Changing Sources of Government Revenue" (1988). As the title indicates, there exist, according to the author, four major sources of government income (with "trade" denoting income from state-owned enterprises; debts are not included as source of revenue since they ultimately have to be repaid). Tarschys notes a clear trend in revenue-raising activities in the modern capitalist states away from tariffs, trade, and tributes, and toward taxation. In many developing countries, however, states still rely heavily on sources of revenue other than taxation.

Works by historians on state finances represent another untapped source for studies in fiscal sociology (Brewer 1989). For an example of what can be done with this type of material if one adds a sociological perspective, the reader is referred to an essay by Michael Mann that uses data on the finances of the English state during the period 1130–1815 (1988). Mann finds that most of the expenses of the precapitalist state were military in nature, and that this had a deep impact on the way that capitalism later was to be organized—in the form of national territories, rather than in some other form, shaped exclusively by market forces.

As already mentioned, practically no contributions to the field of fiscal sociology were made by sociologists for about half a century after Weber and Schumpeter. In the early 1970s, however, James O'Connor made an effort to recast fiscal sociology in Marxist terms in *The Fiscal Crisis of the State*. His main thesis was that there exists a dangerous contradiction in late capitalism between the two central tasks of the capitalist state— "accumulation" and "legitimation"—and that this ultimately would lead to a situation where the state simply cannot afford to insure that capital is accumulated and that the population is kept happy through social expenditures (O'Connor 1973:5–10). After a few years of debate, O'Connor's thesis fell into oblivion, since it was considered much too mechanical and undifferentiated (Bell 1976; Block 1981).

As opposed to O'Connor, John Campbell has during the past ten to fifteen years tried to lay the groundwork for a fiscal sociology that is more in tune with empirical realities than O'Connor's thesis, and that draws primarily on sociology for theoretical guidance (Campbell 1993,

1996, forthcoming; Campbell and Allen 1994; cf. Padgett 1981; Tilly 1990; Carruthers 1996; Hobson 1997). In an important attempt to pull the field together through a survey article in the early 1990s, Campbell suggests that the two key topics in modern fiscal sociology should be to establish what determines tax policy and to investigate what effects tax policies have (1993). Corporations, for example, often try to influence corporate tax policy, and different political parties often disagree when it comes to taxes.

While class has an important impact on tax policy, according to Campbell, it may be hard to specify precisely the ways in which this comes about. The structure of the state itself—especially its capacity to extract taxes from the population in an efficient manner—may also influence the way that taxes are decided upon. As to the effect of tax policies, these range all the way from political rebellions (including "tax rebellions") to the role of philanthropy in society. It is also clear that tax policy can be used either to encourage the growth of large corporations (as in Sweden) or to encourage the growth of small businesses (as in Italy). Much information about the effect of tax policies on various groups can also be found in studies of welfare, including their impact on the number of poor people in modern capitalist states. While modern capitalist societies produce a huge number of poor people, it is possible to reduce their number substantially through transfer payments (see table 7.4).

In one of his most recent contributions Campbell argues that the globalization theorists are wrong in their assertion that the tax rates in capitalist countries tend to converge downward (forthcoming). Drawing on a sample of OECD countries, Campbell shows that during the past three decades the general taxation rate has slowly gone up, to a mean of about 40 percent of GDP in 1998. Liberal states tend to fall below this mean (the United States, with 28.9 percent), while more collectivistic regimes are above it (Sweden, with 52.0 percent); and no convergence is in sight. There also exists quite a bit of variation among the various OECD countries when it comes to the relative importance of the three major sources of taxation (income and profit taxes, social security taxes, and taxes on goods and services). What globalization theorists also tend to forget, according to Campbell, is the general role that is played by the institutional structure of each country in determining taxes. If there is one strong party that dominates the political scene, for example, taxes tend to be lower than if there are several contending parties. The impact of political coalitions is more complex, but these can, under certain circumstances, lead to higher taxes than if there is one-party rule.

TABLE 7.4.

Percentage of People in Poverty in Various OECD Countries, Pre- and Post-transfer Payments

	Year	Pre-transfer Payments	Post-transfer Payments
U.S.	1991	20.9	12.6
Germany	1984	21.6	2.8
France	1984	26.4	4.5
Great Britain	1986	27.7	5.2
Canada	1991	19.2	6.6

Note: The United States does not use transfer payments as much as some other Western countries, and as a consequence many more of its people live in poverty.

Source: Smeeding et al. 1995, cited in Neil Fligstein, "Is Globalization the Cause of the Crises of the Welfare States?", unpublished paper, University of California at Berkeley, 1996a, p. 52.

The State Directing the Economy

A second task that should be central to an economic sociology of politics would be to analyze the various attempts by the state to direct the economy. This type of analysis would, for example, cover the creation of a conventional infrastructure (roads, harbors, electricity). But it would also include a wholly different set of state activities, which are *not* part of what Adam Smith referred to as the third duty of the sovereign—namely, efforts to encourage economic growth. After World War II many states have increasingly come to see it as part of their responsibility to guarantee healthy economic development, including a high level of employment. The success or failure of a government has increasingly come to depend on its success in accomplishing this goal. One may possibly call this the fourth duty of the sovereign.

The scope of activities that fall under the heading of "the state directing the economy" is very broad, and it is not difficult to think of many other cases than those just mentioned: to create an infrastructure and to guarantee the population a healthy economic development. There is, for example, the case of mercantilism, which was discussed in chapter 6 (cf. Weber [1919] 1924:347–51). There is also the phenomenon of imperialism, which has been extensively analyzed by Marxist thinkers (Weeks 1991)—and also by Joseph Schumpeter in a neglected essay called "The Sociology of Imperialisms" ([1919] 1991). Unlike the Marxists, Schumpeter did not think that there has existed only one type of imperialism, nor that imperialism is the creation of

"Your majesty, my voyage will not only forge a new route to the spices
of the East but also create over three thousand new jobs."

capitalism. At the heart of the imperialist phenomenon, according to
Schumpeter, is rather a warrior class or a warrior stratum that faces
the dilemma of either expanding or going under.

Many examples of the state directing the economy can also be
found in the period that preceded World War II as well as during the
war itself. Albert O. Hirschman, for example, has analyzed the way in
which Nazi Germany concentrated its foreign trade with a few countries to gain power over them (1945). The control of the state over the
economy was extremely strong during World War II, not only in the
fascist states and in the Soviet Union but also in the democratic states.
Little sociological work, however, has been carried out on the role of
the state in the economy during wars or during the transition to non-
war conditions (for an exception, see Milkman 1987).

More current examples—which also await sociological analysis—
would include studies of fiscal and monetary policy. To this should be
added the participation of many states in regional associations, such
as NAFTA and the EU, and in international financial bodies, such as
the IMF and the World Bank (e.g., Block 1977; Swedberg 1986; Wood
1986). The use of economic sanctions represents another interesting
topic in this context—as does inflation, to the extent that it is consciously encouraged by the state (for economic sanctions and other
forms of "economic warfare," see Wallensteen 1971; Naylor 1999; and

for sociological analyses of inflation, see Goldthorpe and Hirsch 1978; Lindberg and Maier 1985).

There exist two important studies in recent economic sociology that give a sense of how the state's attempt to direct the economy can be analyzed from a novel perspective: *Forging Industrial Policy: The United States, Britain, and France in the Railway Age* by Frank Dobbin (1994b) and *Embedded Autonomy: States and Industrial Transformation* by Peter Evans (1995) (cf. Dobbin 1993, Dobbin and Dowd 1997). Dobbin's work can be characterized as a comparative study of industrial policy on railroads during the nineteenth century (cf. chap. 2). If one looks at "the industrial policy paradigm" in a country—that is, at its general approach or *Gestalt* toward policy in any economic sector—one finds, according to Dobbin, that it closely follows the way in which political decisions are made in that country. "Political culture," in Dobbin's terminology, drives "industrial culture," the reason being that when politicians are confronted with economic problems, they tend to react in roughly the same way as when they confront political problems. This is also true for other actors who are involved in industrial policy, such as state officials, engineers, and so on.

The empirical material in *Forging Industrial Policy* comes from a historical study of the United States, France, and Britain during the years 1825–1900. In the United States the local communities were at first very active in promoting the railroads. Because of corruption, however, this industrial policy paradigm was replaced toward the end of the nineteenth century by one in which the local state and, even more so, the federal state became the guardians of competition. Britain also went through two industrial policy paradigms during 1825 to 1900: first, laissez-faire, and later a defense of entrepreneurial firms. Cartels, for example, were encouraged in Britain. France developed only one industrial policy paradigm, according to which the state should guide the railroad industry and protect it from the anarchy of the market.

Throughout his study, Dobbin vigorously argues against interest group theory and, more generally, against the idea that economic interests should be seen as the direct cause of industrial policy. Empirical evidence, Dobbin says, indicates that in situations that are similar, policymakers in the United States, France, and Britain have all reacted in very different ways when it comes to railroad policy. The main reason for this has to do with the national tradition (or political culture) of the policymakers in question. Dobbins firmly rejects the notion that there exists some kind of universal economic law that is applicable to all countries and situations. Interest groups, as he phrases it, are "subjective" and "constructed," not "objective" and "primordial" (1994b:219–20).

Peter Evans's *Embedded Autonomy* contains a sharp attack on neo-liberalism, especially the idea that interventions by the state are negative by definition. The real question, according to the author, is not "how much" a state is involved in the economy but "what kind" of involvement it is. Using the latter criteria, Evans suggests the following typology for states in developing countries: "developmental states" (e.g., Taiwan), "predatory states" (Zaire), and "intermediary states" (Brazil). Drawing on the work of such scholars as Albert O. Hirschman and Alexander Gerschenkron, Evans also argues that a state should not develop an industrial strategy based on the theory of comparative advantage, but rather try to "construct comparative advantage" (cf. Gerschenkron 1962; Hirschman 1963).

The empirical part of *Embedded Autonomy* is devoted to a study of the attempt in the 1970s and 1980s to develop a computer industry in India, Brazil, and South Korea. The most successful country in this respect was South Korea, where the state tried to assist both the emergence of entrepreneurial groups and their activities ("midwifery" and "husbandry" in Evans's terminology). India and Brazil relied much more on state regulation, such as protectionism, and on encouraging the state to enter production on its own. In these cases the state assumed two roles that Evans finds increasingly outdated for encouraging economic growth in developing countries—"custodian" and "demiurge." What accounts for the success of South Korea's strategy, and for modern industrial policy in general, according to Evans, is the existence of a reliable "Weberian" state bureaucracy and the fact that the state has not been captured by some special interest group. Together these two conditions make up what Evans calls "embedded autonomy."

While much of Evans's analysis is cast in interest terms, he firmly rejects the way in which the economists use the concept of interest. The economists, he argues, have developed a dogmatic and undialectical type of interest analysis, often centered around rent-seeking, when they discuss developing countries. Evans's own analysis in *Embedded Autonomy*, he says, points in a more complex direction, with interests appearing as well as disappearing as the economic process unfolds. According to neoliberalism, Evans writes,

[T]he state creates rental havens that speak to the interests of politically powerful clients; clients benefit economically from state action and respond with political support. Static symbiosis is the natural political result of static involvement.

The histories of these three informatics sectors [that is, in India, Brazil, and South Korea] reveal a political dynamic that is anything but a static symbiosis. Local entrepreneurial groups were at first indifferent bystanders, then tempted entrants, then supportive but difficult clients, and eventually ex-clients with other, more attractive options. As the process of industrial transformation unfolded, the power and interests of private entrepreneurial groups changed. Their relations with the state shifted accordingly. The state's success in fostering industrial change undermined the political constituency that its earlier efforts had fostered (1995:224).

But there also exist ways of understanding the process through which the state directs the economy other than those that are embodied in the works of Dobbin and Evans, that is, where the state on its own chooses to pursue some strategy. The state, in brief, may also be pushed by certain groups into pursuing some policy, and this is where *interest groups* come into the picture. The literature on interest groups in the social sciences is enormous and mainly authored by political scientists (e.g., Puhle 2001). It encompasses interest groups in a broad sense as well as in a narrow sense. Interest groups broadly defined would include all groups in society that have an interest they want to realize in political or other ways. Examples of these would include unions, employers' associations, and professional organizations such as the American Medical Association. But interest groups can also be understood in a narrow sense, as organizations that are officially regulated as interest groups, that is, lobbies.

The political science literature on interest groups is of considerable importance to economic sociology, but has not been much used. Arthur Bentley's *Process of Government* (1908) helped to launch the modern American literature on the topic. One of the fascinating qualities of this work is the author's attempt to ground political analysis in a pragmatic theory of interests, mainly inspired by Dewey. Interests can be studied only in action, according to Bentley, and have no independent existence whatsoever. In political life each group attempts to realize its own interests. As a result of these attempts, various pressures develop, and what happens in political life is the result of these pressures. Interest can never be understood in isolation; only in relation to other interests: "There is no way to get hold of one group interest except in terms of others" (Bentley [1908] 1967:214).

Most of the literature on interest groups sees as its main task to explain or illuminate some aspect of the political process. The existence of interest groups, it is argued, may give a voice to interests that would otherwise have been neglected in the political process; they may also threaten the democratic process by setting aside the general interest. The studies by economists typically differ from this approach in that they are often interested in the effect of interest groups on economic life, via the mediation of the state. An example would be George Stigler's well-known theory of economic regulation (1971). While economic regulation is often perceived as having been instituted to benefit the general public, Stigler says, regulatory policy is often the result of some actors' successful attempt to get the state to act on their behalf. To the debate whether regulatory agencies indeed capture the state for their own interests or not, another position can be added: that regulatory agencies often start out acting in the public interest, but end up being influenced by the industry they regulate, since they have to coexist with the industry on a daily basis (Friedman 1975:128).

Of related importance is Mancur Olson's theory of interest groups. Its foundation can be found in *The Logic of Collective Action*, where Olson argues that the interest of individuals can be effectively united into a group interest only under certain conditions, due to the free rider problem (1965). The only way in which organizations with many members can come into being is if the organization can coerce its members to participate or offer them special inducements. If this is not possible, it is far too easy for the individual to fall back into apathy and hope that others will do the work—with the result that no organization is formed.

In *The Rise and Decline of Nations* Olson uses these insights to develop a full theory of interest groups or special-interest organizations, as he calls them. The key idea is that an interest group can either further its economic interests by increasing economic production as a whole, and get its (minute) share of the proceeds—or try to capture an increasing part of the already existing production (Olson 1982:36–74). The latter is far easier and much more profitable; and as a result the overall economy of society suffers under the impact of interest groups. One of the reasons why the economies of Germany and Japan have been so successful after World War II, Olson also argues, is precisely that their interest groups were destroyed as a result of the war.

Since economic sociologists have not paid much attention to interest groups, much work remains to be done. On the one hand, there is the task of looking at the influence of various economic interest groups on the political process, especially unions, employers' organizations, and various professions (e.g., Berger 1981; Wright 1996; Streeck and Schmitter 1985). On the other hand, there is the challenge of trying to map out not only how interest groups influence the political process but also what effects these types of groups may have on economic life itself, via the state. Is it the case, for example, that competition is always limited by the actions of interest groups? What role does the legal system play in facilitating/obstructing interest groups?

Can interest groups speed up the economy or, as Olson suggests, only slow it down? Finally, closely connected to the issue of interest groups is that of conflicts of interest (e.g., Davis and Stark 2001; Swedberg 2003). These types of conflict, which can be described as situations in which a private interest threatens to overtake a public interest, are rife in political as well as economic life.

Summary

This chapter attempted to develop an economic sociology of politics. To lay a foundation for this type of analysis, two of its three central themes were discussed: how the state generates and spends its resources (fiscal sociology), and how the state attempts to direct economic life. The third theme—how the legal system is related to the economy—will be discussed in the next chapter. The economic sociology of politics is similar in its concerns to political economy in that it looks at the intersection of the economy and politics. It differs, however, from this approach by being less normative and also by drawing on a different intellectual tradition.

Much can be learned about the state's role in the economy from the economics as well as the sociological literature. As to the former, the following contributions have been singled out: Adam Smith's "three duties of the sovereign," James Buchanan's constitutional economics, and Douglass North's neoclassical theory of the state. In sociology there is especially Weber's theory of domination, but also some recent material, such as Neil Fligstein's ideas about the centrality of the state in economic life.

Fiscal sociology, from Schumpeter onward, was presented and commented upon, with the argument that this approach still constitutes a vantage point from which to analyze the actions of the state. These followed a discussion of the way in which the state attempts to steer the economy. Recent work by Peter Evans and Frank Dobbin illustrates what economic sociology can accomplish on this score. A few words were also said about how interest groups try to make use of the state for their own purposes.

Throughout this chapter the basic message was that economic life in modern society is not possible without the state. This is an insight that can be found in economics as well as in sociology, from Adam Smith to Max Weber and onward. The state, to use the terminology that was introduced in chapter 3, is part of the organization of the economy. The same is also true for the legal system—to which the next chapter is devoted.

VIII

Law and the Economy

THERE currently does not exist what in this book has been called an economic sociology of law—that is, a sociological analysis of the role of law in economic life. Before trying to outline what such an analysis would look like, it may be useful to address whether an economic sociology of law is needed in the first place. There does, after all, already exist a well-established field called law and economics among economists. Furthermore, sociologists of law (including its Marxist proponents) have for many decades analyzed the relationship between law and society, including the economy.

All of this is correct, but it can also be argued that none of these approaches have accomplished what an economic sociology of law would set out to do. The law and economics literature does not approach legal phenomena in an empirical and sociological manner, as the economic sociology of law would do. Instead it relies heavily on the logic of neoclassical economics in its analyses. It is also explicitly normative in nature and advocates how judges *should* behave and how legislation *should* be constructed—usually so that wealth is maximized (Posner). While the economic sociology of law is only concerned with the legal aspects of economic life, the law and economics approach argues that one should extend the logic of economics to the analysis of *all* types of law.

The sociology of law has also paid some attention to the economy and produced a few studies that are of much relevance to the economic sociology of law (e.g., Selznick 1969; Aubert 1983; Bourdieu 1987; Edelman and Suchman 1997; cf. Posner 1995). Still, its main interest is usually in law and society in general, and it has definitely not singled out economic topics. This is also, on the whole, true for the law and society movement in the United States (e.g., Abel 1995; Garth and Sterling 1998). Finally, Marxist sociologists of law have produced surprisingly few studies of concrete legal phenomena that are of relevance to the economy, and have mostly preferred to discuss general aspects of the impact of capitalism on the legal system (Spitzer 1983; cf. Phillips 1980; Renner [1904] 1949, Tigar 2000). Moreover, these sociologists are hampered by viewing the law as part of the superstructure (for an effort to overcome this view, see E. P. Thompson 1975; D. Thompson 2001; cf. Cole 2001).

Nonetheless, what would be the task of an economic sociology of law? Generally, it should produce careful empirical studies of the role that law plays in the economic sphere—drawing primarily (I myself would add) on an analysis that highlights not only social relations but also interests. To use the word "careful" in this context may seem odd, but the few studies that exist in this genre testify to such a degree of complexity in the interaction of law and economy that one would like to issue a general warning for studies that produce sweeping answers to the question of how legal institutions function in the economy, including the question of the overall role of law in the economy. To study *the role of law in the ongoing economy*, would be one way to describe what the main task of the economic sociology of law should be.

As with the sociology of law, tasks for the economic sociology of law would be to analyze the relationship of law and economy to other spheres of society, such as the political sphere or the private sphere of the family. As in the case of the Marxist sociology of law, the economic sociology of law would look at the way in which economic forces influence legal phenomena; but in addition it would also analyze how law affects the economy, again with reservations for the complexity involved. Finally, in an approach similar to that of law and economics the economic sociology of law would study the way in which the legal system helps to further economic growth, and perhaps also show how the spirit of a commercial society can come to pervade parts of the law other than those that directly have to do with the economy. To this should be added the task of studying how law can slow down and block economic growth—a task that is implied in the research program for law and economics but is rarely carried out.

It is possible to outline the kind of topics that an economic sociology of law should cover on a general level by drawing on a scheme that Weber introduces in his essay on objectivity from 1904, in which he describes the area of social economics (*Sozialökonomik*). This scheme can be called a society-centered scheme, meaning that the phenomenon to be analyzed (law) is seen as being dependent on society, rather than being independent (see figure 8.1). The goal, in all brevity, is to produce a type of analysis in which law is subordinate to the general development of society (including the economy), rather than one in which law and its evolution is seen as primary. The key point is that what happens in law is usually dependent on what goes on in society, including the economy.

The general idea of a society-centered analysis can be made more precise, and also applied to the relationship between law and the

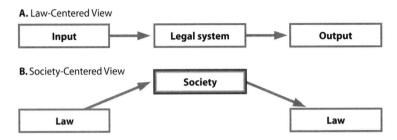

Figure 8.1. The Role of Law in Society: A Law-Centered View versus a Society-Centered View.

Note: It is common in the law and society literature to speak of an internal versus an external analysis of law. An internal analysis refers to an analysis that primarily looks at the legal system, while an external analysis refers to an analysis that studies the input into the legal system as well as the impact of the legal system on society (see A, which comes from an article by legal scholar David Gordon [1975]).

A different way of conceptualizing the relationship between law and society, however, has been proposed by Lawrence Friedman, a legal historian. Here society is central, not the law; and this means that the law is in principle dependent for its development on the general evolution of society. "Major legal change follows and depends on social change" (Friedman 1975:269).

Sources: For A, see David Gordon, "*Introduction*: J. Willard Hurst and the Common Law Tradition in American Legal History," *Law and Society Review* 10 (Fall 1975): 10. For B, see Lawrence Friedman, *The Legal System: A Social Science Perspective* (New York: Russell Sage Foundation, 1975).

economy; and this is where Weber's scheme for social economics comes into the picture. Social economics, Weber argues in his 1904 essay, should study three types of phenomena: "economic phenomena" (institutions and norms), "economically relevant phenomena" (noneconomic phenomena that influence economic phenomena), and "economically conditioned phenomena" (noneconomic phenomena that are partly influenced by economic phenomena; cf. chap. 1). Weber also introduces some qualifications into this scheme by arguing that economically relevant phenomena can never *totally* form economic phenomena, nor are economically conditioned phenomena ever more than *partly* influenced by the economy. These qualifications are important to keep in mind.

If instead of applying Weber's scheme to the relationship of the economy to society, we now apply it to the relationship of law to the economy, we get the following. There is first and foremost the economy *including* its legal dimension. This would include key economic

A. Weber's View of the Area to be Covered in Social Economics

B. Weber's Scheme Applied to the Relationship between Law and Economy

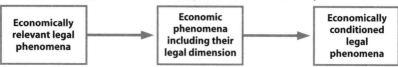

Figure 8.2. The Subject Area of the Economic Sociology of Law, according to Weber.

Note: In outlining the area of the economic sociology of law, one may draw upon Weber's scheme for economics (*Sozialökonomik*), as shown in the top row of this figure. When applied to law, this scheme yields the following result: economic phenomena, which are usually constituted by laws and regulations (*'economic phenomena including their legal dimension'*); legal phenomena that influence these economic phenomena (*'economically relevant legal phenomena'*); and legal phenomena that are influenced by economic phenomena (*'economically conditioned legal phenomena'*). In this scheme there is a primacy of the economy over the law.

Source: Max Weber, "'Objectivity' in Social Science and Social Policy," pp. 64–65 in *Essays in the Methodology of the Social Sciences* (New York: Free Press, 1949).

institutions and norms such as banks, corporations, and money. Law, in modern society, is *constitutive* for most economic phenomena, meaning by this that it is an indispensable as well as an organic part of them. Social scientists may separate the nonlegal part of economic phenomena from their legal part in their analyses. In reality, however, they are inseparable.

Besides the economy, including its legal dimension, there is also the (partial) impact of legal phenomena on economic phenomena, and the (partial) impact of economic phenomena on legal phenomena (see figure 8.2). Note that the economy is at the center of this scheme—and this is why we may call it an economic sociology of law rather than something like a sociology of law that specializes in economic legislation. There is a primacy of the economy and how it works, in other words, and not of law.

In its efforts to understand the role of law in economic life, the economic sociology of law should draw on the insights of economic sociology in general. It has, for example, been well established in contemporary economic sociology that economic actions take place in networks, and that these networks connect corporations to one another, corporations to banks, individuals to corporations, and so on. In all of these relationships law is present; and the concepts of networks and economic (social) action can therefore be used in an attempt to reach a better understanding of the role that law plays in the economy. This is similarly true for other concepts and approaches in economic sociology, such as the concept of the field and different kinds of capital.

But the economic sociology of law should also be able to make a contribution to economic sociology, as it currently exists. To introduce law into the picture typically means to add another factor, without which the picture would be incomplete. In mainstream economics before the 1950s, it was generally agreed that the legal system could safely be disregarded since it did not affect the typical course of events; and one sometimes gets the impression that this has also been the view in economic sociology: for example, law plays a marginal or nonexisting role in much of new economic sociology.

Law, however, is a factor that typically affects the economic actor, in the sense that she has to take law into consideration. If it can be disregarded in certain situations, this should be explicitly stated. The assumption that a decision by the state automatically translates into a law, and that this law is automatically followed, should not be made since there is no simple one-to-one causality involved. Law introduces, so to speak, an extra layer in the analysis; and it is *always* the case that what matters from a sociological perspective is the reaction of the actor to the law, not what the law (or legal doctrine) says.

To develop an economic sociology of law along these lines constitutes a huge challenge, since it demands knowledge of three different social sciences—law, economics, and sociology—as well as a capacity to wring something novel and sociological out of the combination. But there already exist some suggestive ideas for how to go about this task, as will be shown in the rest of this chapter. In the first section, some of these ideas will emerge in the discussion of the general relationship between law and economics. The work of Max Weber, it should be emphasized, is what comes closest to an already existing program for an economic sociology of law. Weber's work also contains some important analyses of the relationship between law and economics.

The section on the general relationship between law and economics will be followed by a discussion of the *lex mercatoria* and then by a discussion of a few legal institutions that are of particular importance to economic life, such as property (including intellectual property), inheritance, the contract and the concept of the firm as a legal personality. The fourth section covers some studies in contemporary economic sociology that are of relevance to the economic sociology of law. There are also some works relevant to our purpose that have been produced in the law and economics tradition. Due to the strong presence in contemporary legal scholarship of this latter type of approach, I indicate in the fifth section the points where the field of law and economics coincides, as well as where it differs, from the economic sociology of law.

On Law and the Economy

There exist a number of different approaches to the general nature of law, both in jurisprudence and in the sociology of law. It has, for example, been argued that law is a "command of the sovereign" (Austin) and that the essential nature of law is connected to the idea of "legality" (Selznick). There seems to be no reason, however, why the economic sociology of law should be closely connected to one of these approaches, as opposed to some other. With this in mind I will nonetheless argue that law, from a sociological viewpoint, is closely connected to the notion of *order*, and that order is crucial to society as well as to power elites. From this perspective, law can be seen as one of the many weapons in the arsenal of power, similar to physical coercion. Law and violence, of course, do not exclude one another; they are often mixed. Law imposes a distinct order on things by stating what should be done in specific situations. This goes both for when the ruler is directly challenged as well as for ordinary conflicts. Conflicts emerge continuously in society, and unless they are solved on a continuous basis, chaos will eventually ensue. It is also clear that economic activities thrive on order, and that there exists a close link between the two.

Weber's definition of law fits very well into this type of argument about the need for order in society, namely that law is present wherever there is a staff that has been specifically appointed to enforce a normative order. The exact definition is as follows: "An order will be called . . . *law* if it is externally guaranteed by the probability that physical or psychological coercion will be applied by a *staff* of people in order to bring about compliance or avenge violation" (Weber [1922] 1978:34; cf. 313–19). By "order" (*Ordnung*) Weber roughly means institution (cf. chap. 1).

Weber's definition of law has been criticized for downplaying the role of ideals. It can, however, be argued that the nature of the order that Weber talks about is not specified. The legal system of a perfectly

"Don't get me wrong. Legality has its place."

democratic society, for example, fits Weber's definition just as well as the legal system of the Nazis did. It should also be pointed out that law can also exist, according to Weber's definition, in situations where no physical violence whatsoever is used (or threatened) by the authorities; what is minimally needed is *psychological* coercion.

Duration in time is central to the concept of order, and according to Weber a political order is likely to last much longer if people find it legitimate and are not simply coerced to obey whomever is in power through the use of violence. "You can do anything with bayonettes," as Talleyrand is supposed to have said, "except for sitting on them." Weber does not address the issue of justice in his theory of legitimation, but it is clear that this is precisely where justice may come in, and that a regime based not only on legitimacy but also on justice would be very sturdy. As noted in chapter 7, there exist, according to Weber, several different types of domination, and each of these goes together with a certain type of law. Traditional domination rests primarily on customary law, charismatic domination on law established through inspiration, and legal authority on rational law.

Weber's argument about the important role of law in contemporary democratic society, where legal authority is the most common type of domination, does not mean that people always follow the legal rules, and that once we know what these rules are, we also know how people will act. Jurisprudence, as Weber is careful to point out, tells us what will happen under specific conditions, in the same way as the rules for a card game tell us how the game should be played ([1907] 1977:118–43). Sociology, however, has a very different approach to law: it tries to establish to what extent legal rules influence the behavior of people—to what extent they constitute *"actual determinants of human behavior"* (Weber [1922] 1978:312; emphasis added).

From a sociological perspective it is consequently obvious that many factors other than the law determine why people engage in the behavior prescribed by the law. The extent to which it is the law, rather than some other factor, that determines the behavior in question, has therefore to be decided in each particular case (Weber [1922] 1978:312). This can be termed the first principle of the sociology of law. In orienting her behavior to the legal order, it should be added, the actor may decide whether to obey the law or not. In the latter case, her behavior may still be influenced by the law. A thief, for example, will typically try to hide her action.

By introducing the notion of interest into the analysis of law and economy, I argue, it will grow in complexity as well as in realism. If economic interests are pitted against the law, we expect, for example, tension and possibly disobedience, crime, and corruption. If economic interests, on the other hand, encourage some behavior that is also prescribed by the law, it will be hard to stop this behavior. And economic interests that are not only protected by the law but also viewed as just and legitimate, would be even harder to stop. Note that some of these economic interests may lead to an increase in production, while others may slow it down or block it. Finally, one way to guarantee that laws are followed would be to make it in some people's interest to see to it that this is the case. A "regulatory interest" of this type can be created by paying some people to be judges, policemen and so on, but also in other ways (cf. Heckathorn 1988).

According to Vilhelm Aubert (1980:20), "the concept of interest has played an important role in law and jurisprudence." There also exists a school in legal philosophy called the Jurisprudence of Interests (for an introduction, see Schoch 1948). A well-known legal thinker such as Roscoe Pound, for example, assigned a key role to interests in his work. He defined rights as "interests to be secured," and saw society as evolving from "individual interests" to "social interests" (1920). Rudolf von Jhering viewed law as the result of struggle and argued that this struggle could be very violent since interest often stands against interest:

In the course of time, the interests of thousands of individuals, and of whole classes, have become bound up with the existing principles of law in such a manner that these cannot be done away with without doing the greatest injury to the former. To question the principle of law or the institution, means a declaration of war against all these interests, the tearing away of a polyp which resists the effort with a thousand arms (Jhering [1872] 1915:10–11).

David Hume's theory of law is similarly influenced by his general vision that interests influence human behavior ([1739–40] 1978:477–573; cf. Hayek 1968, Milgate and Stimson 1998). Justice is not so much an ideal, according to Hume, as a sense of right that people develop in relation to their interests. Law is instituted in society because people realize that it is in their "own and public interest" to have order in society. This way their property will be defended, trade will become possible, and so on (Hume [1739–40] 1978:496).

As two further examples of the way in which interests have been used in legal analysis, we have Vilhelm Aubert's argument about conflict resolution and Lawrence Friedman's theory of legal culture. According to Aubert, one can counterpose conflict resolution in the market to conflict resolution in the court. In markets it is often possible to reach a compromise, that is, to find a price that is acceptable to the buyer as well as to the seller. When people cannot negotiate a solution because they have different values or disagree about facts, however, a different way of solving the conflict than bargaining has to be resorted to—the court system (Aubert 1983; for a critique, see Friedman 1975:225–28).

According to Lawrence Friedman, individuals and groups have "interests" but these are not relevant to the legal system until they have been transformed into "demands" (1975:193–267; cf. 150–54). "Legal culture" is defined as that which converts interests into demands or permits this conversion. More generally, legal culture consists of "knowledge of and attitudes and behavior patterns toward the legal system" (193). Groups may, for example, feel that the legal system is unfair and does not translate their interests into demands. Legal professionals—lawyers, judges—have their own interests and also their own type of legal culture. As is clear from these two examples, values and customs are central to legal culture. Friedman sums up his view on legal culture, interests, and law-making, writing "We can rephrase the basic proposition about the making of law as follows: social force, i.e., power, influence, presses upon the legal system and evokes social acts, when legal culture converts interests into demands or permits this conversion" (193).

Something also needs to be said about the general relationship between law and the economy. To some extent this topic has already been touched upon in this book. In chapter 7, for example, a passage from *The Wealth of Nations* was cited according to which no person with property would be able to sleep without fear of being robbed unless her property was protected by the law. David Hume's interest theory of law was just referred to, and the three fundamental rules of justice that are mentioned in *A Treatise on Human Nature* are all related to the economy: "stability of possession," "the transferrence [of possession] by consent," and of "the performance of promises" (Hume [1739–40] 1978:526).

The thinker, however, who has made the most sustained attempt to establish the general relationships between law and the economy from a sociological perspective is Max Weber. In *Economy and Society* Weber suggests that it is possible to speak of six such relationships ([1922] 1978:333–37). The three most important of these all refer to interests in some way:

- "Law . . . guarantees by no means only economic interests but rather the most diverse interests ranging from the most elementary one of protection of personal security to such purely ideal goods as personal honor or the honor of the divine powers" (333).
- "Obviously, legal guaranties are directly at the service of economic interests to a very large extent. Even where this does not seem to be, or actually is not, the case, economic interests are among the strongest factors influencing the creation of law. For, any authority guaranteeing a legal order depends, in some way, upon the consensual action of the constitutive groups, and the formation of social groups depends, to a large extent, upon constellations of material interests" (334).
- When economic interests go counter to the law, "only a limited measure of success can be attained through the threat of coercion supporting the legal order" (334).

Weber also states that it is not necessary that just the state guarantees economic interests via the legal order—other authorities will do as well. The two last of Weber's general statements on law and the economy concern the situation in which there is a disjunction between what the law says and what actually goes on in the economy. Economic relationships may change, according to Weber, while the law remains the same; and an economic situation may be treated in different ways by the law, depending on what legal angle is involved.

The sweeping character of the six propositions is probably due to Weber's intent to make them fit many different societies, from all periods of history. One can, however, also find a few statements in Weber's work that are exclusively about capitalist society and its legal order, and that are more precise in nature. One of these is particularly interesting since it has to do with the capacity of law *to create new economic relationships*. The law, in brief, does not only consist of "mandatory and prohibitive [paragraphs]," when it comes to the economy, but also of *"empowering"* and *"enabling laws"* (Weber [1922] 1978:730; emphasis added). The key passage in Weber's sociology of law on this topic reads as follows:

> To the person who finds himself actually in possession of the power to control an object or a person the legal guaranty gives a specific certainty of the durability of such power. To the person to whom something has been promised the legal guaranty gives a higher degree of certainty that the promise will be kept. These are indeed the most elementary relationships between law and economic life. But they are not the only possible ones. *Law can also function in such a manner that, in sociological terms, the prevailing norms controlling the operation of the coercive apparatus have such a structure as to induce, in their turn, the emergence of certain economic relations* (667; emphasis added).

Weber adds that this type of law confers "privileges" of two distinct kinds: (1) they "[provide] protection against certain types of interference by third parties, especially state officials," and (2) they "grant to an individual autonomy to regulate his relations with others by his own transactions" ([1922] 1978:668). As examples of this second type—legal institutions that further economic relationships—Weber cites the modern contract, agency, negotiable instruments, and the conception of the firm as an individual actor. We have here something of a Weberian research agenda for the economic sociology of law, as I see it; and several of these institutions will be discussed later on in this chapter.

Legal historian Willard Hurst would later develop ideas that are parallel to those of Weber about the way in which the law enables economic actions and helps modern capitalism along. According to Hurst, American law played this role especially during the nineteenth century when it helped the economy to grow through "the release of energy," to cite Hurst's famous phrase (Hurst 1956, 1964; for an introduction to the work of Hurst, see Novak 2000). Hurst himself has characterized his work as "legal economic history" and "law and the economy"; and there do exist some interesting parallels between his approach and efforts by Posner and his followers (see esp. Hurst 1981:43–53; cf. Posner 1998). What separates Hurst from Posner and his coworkers, however, is his sociological and empirical approach: legal and economic phenomena are to Hurst's mind social in character and must be studied empirically, not through an exercise in abstract thinking.

Laying the Legal Foundation for Modern Capitalism:
The *Lex Mercatoria*

The innovations in commercial law that were made in Europe during the period of the late eleventh and twelfth centuries still constitute the foundation for capitalism. What happened in commercial law during this brief period can, to some extent, be compared to the technological innovations that ushered in the industrial revolution or the change in economic mentality that, according to Weber, came about with Protestantism. Given the enormous importance of *lex mercatoria*—which created *"all characteristic legal institutes of modern capitalism"* (Weber [1922] 1978:1464; emphasis added)—it seems natural that it should occupy an important place in the economic sociology of law. After a presentation of the *lex mercatoria* or the Law Merchant, as it is also known, the question of why such great legal creativity came to characterize just this period will be addressed (for commercial legislation in non-Western legal systems, see Weber as summarized in Swedberg 1998:90–98).

During the eleventh and twelfth centuries the Western economy experienced a very rapid growth in agricultural productivity and trade. New cities were founded and the number of merchants grew rapidly. Merchants crossed the sea as well as the countryside in search of profit, and they organized markets and fairs where these did not already exist. They also developed their own law, which soon came to coexist with canon, urban, and manorial law. Buying and selling, transporting goods and insuring them were all dealt with in the laws that now emerged from the merchants' communities. Together these made up a fairly coherent set of rules—the *lex mercatoria*—which was accepted all over Europe (for the actual *lex mercatoria*, see Goldschmidt [1891] 1957; Weber [1889] 1988; Berman 1983).

The merchants had their own courts at the markets and fairs that they organized, and they appointed fellow merchants as judges. Merchants also served as judges at guild courts and urban courts during the Middle Ages. The proceedings at the merchants' courts were typically very fast, and technical legal arguments were discouraged. Professional lawyers were not welcome and equity inspired the verdicts. The merchants controlled what went on in the markets and the fairs, but had no formal power outside of these when it came to enforcing the decisions of their courts.

What is truly remarkable about the *lex mercatoria* is that it created a series of institutions that still very much constitute the legal foundation for capitalism. In doing so, it helped to systematize and institutionalize a series of novel economic activities. A list of the most important achievements of the *lex mercatoria* includes

- protection of acquisition in good faith,
- patents and trade marks,
- the bond,
- the modern mortgage,
- the notion of the economic corporation as a legal entity,
- different kinds of transaction documents,
- symbolic delivery through contract replacing the actual transfer of goods,
- the bill of lading and other transportation documents.

(cf. Goldschmidt [1891] 1957; Weber [1922] 1978:1464, [1923] 1984:341–42; Berman 1983).

It is still somewhat unclear what accounts for the great legal creativity that could have produced the *lex mercatoria* in such a short period of time. In an aside, Weber has suggested that the emergence of the Law Merchant was facilitated by medieval society's allowance for the coexistence of different legal bodies, each of which "corresponded to the needs of concrete interest groups" (Weber [1922] 1978:688). Harold Berman, a historian of legal thought, has similarly argued that the merchants constituted a fairly coherent and autonomous group in medieval society, and that they created a law that reflected this fact (1983:334, 354). This was also a period of great economic expansion—what has been called "the commercial revolution of the middle ages" (Lopez 1976)—and merchants were quick to respond to the many opportunities that came in its wake.

A recent study of the *lex mercatoria* has drawn attention to the success of the merchants' courts at the Champagne Fairs in enforcing their verdicts, even though they had no state or similar political institution to back them up (Milgrom, North, and Weingast 1990). What to some extent compensated for not having access to a coercive machinery was the ability of the merchants' courts to destroy a merchant's reputation if he behaved in a dishonest manner. This sounds plausible, even if a systematic study of actual cases would be more convincing than the game theoretical exercises that have been marshaled as proof. It also seems that even if the merchants did not have recourse to the coercive apparatus of some state, political rulers often assisted them when called upon.

According to a number of legal authorities, a new type of the *lex mercatoria* has begun to emerge, from the 1960s onward, primarily in the West. Issues of international contracting, including international arbitration, is at the heart of this new legal phenomenon (K. P. Berger

1999). Some similarities between these developments and the medieval *lex mercatoria* do exist—both, for example, emerged outside of the state—even if these similarities should not be exaggerated (Volckart and Mangels 1999). A sociological study of international commercial arbitration was produced a few years ago, by a student of Bourdieu and by a U.S. legal scholar (Dezalay and Garth 1996). Based on a series of interviews, the authors of *Dealing in Virtue* argue that an important change has recently taken place in international commercial arbitration. While this type of arbitration used to be dominated by a small club of European legal scholars, it has increasingly been taken over by American law firms.

Key Legal Institutions

To discuss the legal institutions that make up the *lex mercatoria* and to follow their development over the centuries up until today constitutes an important task for the economic sociology of law, just as it is necessary to discuss the emergence of more recent legal innovations that are crucial to modern capitalism. In this section, however, only a few of the legal institutions that are central to the modern capitalist economy will be discussed. The first of these—*property*—is of fundamental importance to all economies and has, as a consequence, been heavily regulated in law with continuous enforcement. Class as well as status are crucially related to property. Marx paid less attention to the legal dimension of property than to its social meaning, and basically subsumed it under his concept of "relations of production." Durkheim lectured on the respect that people have had for property throughout history, and argued that the force behind this respect is ultimately derived from the moral authority of society ([1950] 1983: 110–70). Durkheim's analysis is intriguing and highly speculative in nature.

Max Weber wrote voluminously on property, in his sociological as well as in his legal and historical writings ([1889] 1988, [1923] 1981). It is also Weber who has so far made the most sustained attempt to conceptualize property from a sociological perspective and integrate the result into a broader framework of economic sociology (cf. Veblen 1898). Weber begins with the idea that property represents a distinct kind of social relationship, more precisely, it consists of a social relationship that allows for *appropriation* ([1922] 1978:44; cf. Parsons 1947:40–49). For property to exist, the relationship has to be closed—other people have to be excluded from it—and this allows the actor to monopolize the use of X for himself. This X can be an object, a person, and so on. When an actor has appropriated something for herself, she has what Weber terms a "right"; and when this right can be passed on through inheritance, there is "property." If the property in addition can be bought and sold, there is "free property."

One can find an enormous variation throughout history when it comes to dealing with property. We learn, for example, from Weber's early work on antiquity that land property in Rome had to go through several stages before it could be freely bought and sold on the market (Weber [1891] 1986). At first the land was owned by the community and could not be sold at all. At a later stage it could be sold by an individual, but only on condition that the community gave its permission. And finally, land became perfectly alienable; it could be bought and sold at will.

Just as land and objects have been appropriated throughout history, according to Weber, so have human beings. Weber's remarks on slaves as a form of property are well known, but less so is his observation that in many societies males have often had legal power over their wives and children, which is similar to that which slave owners have over their slaves:

This *dominium* [over wife and children in e.g., Roman Law] is absolute. . . . The power of the house father extends with ritualistic limitations to execution or sale of the wife, and to sale of the children or leasing them out to labor ([1923] 1981:48).

In *Economy and Society* Weber attempts to enumerate the most important sociological types of property that have existed throughout history—in agriculture, industry, and so on ([1922] 1978:130–50). He also discusses what kind of property relations and forms of appropriation are most suitable for modern capitalism. When it comes to labor, his answer is identical to that of Marx: modern capitalism works best (for the owners, Weber specifies) if the workers do not own the means of production. When this is the case, the owner gets to choose which workers she wants to hire, and is furthermore in a position to impose discipline on them. Weber also stresses that modern capitalism will be more efficient (again, from the viewpoint of the owners) if the managers, as opposed to the owners, are allowed to run the corporations. While the original owner and creator of a business may have once been a skillful manager, his heirs are less likely to be so than a hand-picked manager.

Modern sociology has not devoted much attention to the concept of property (Gouldner 1970:304–13). Nonetheless, a nearly ontological grounding of individual property has been suggested by Erving Goffman in *Asylums*. People who are admitted to this type of institution are often not allowed to keep any private items, including those that are important for their personal appearance. This causes much grief:

> One set of the individual's possessions has a special relation to self. The individual ordinarily expects to exert some control over the guise in which he appears to others. For this he needs cosmetic and clothing supplies, tools for applying, arranging, and repairing these, and an accessible, secure place to store these supplies—in short, the individual will need an "identity kit" for the management of his personal front (Goffman 1961:20).

In recent economic sociology there also exist a few attempts to analyze property with the help of the concept of property rights. These studies have typically taken their inspiration from the law and economics literature and not from Weber. It has, for example, been argued that sociologists tend to forget that the state can change existing property rights and introduce new ones, and in this way influence the economy (Campbell and Lindberg 1990). In the United States, this happened for example when AT&T's monopoly over the telecommunications sector was challenged in the late 1950s and replaced by a competetive market.

The notion of property rights has also been used to get a better grip on the transition to capitalism in Eastern Europe and in China, and to theorize the "hybrid" type of property that has recently emerged, that is, property that is neither fully private nor fully public (Stark 1996; cf. Hanley, King and Toth forthcoming). Drawing on the work of Harold Demsetz, some experts on China have, for example, recently suggested that the social structure of the rural industry in this country differs depending on the structure of the property rights, of which there are four kinds: the right to ownership, the right to manage, the right to the income that is generated, and the right to enforce the existing order (Oi and Walder 1999; cf. Nee 1992; Walder 1992). The great variety of social arrangements, under which the rural industry in China currently operates, lends itself very well to a flexible notion of property of this type (see table 8.1).

A topic that has not been much explored in the sociology of property is that of intellectual property rights, which covers such items as patents, copyright, trade secrets, and trademarks. The Statute of Monopolies from 1523 in England is often cited as the first patent law but also the American Constitution of 1787 includes a famous passage on patents and copyright. According to the Constitution, the U.S. Congress has the power "to promote the progress of science and useful arts, by securing for limited times to authors and inventors the exclusive right to their respective writings and discoveries." The basic idea, as Abraham Lincoln famously put it, was to use the patent system to "add the *fuel* of interest to the *fire* of genius" (Harmon 2001). The at-

TABLE 8.1.
Possible Variations in Property Rights: The Case of the Rural Industry in China

	Ownership	Management	Right to Income	Enforcement
State	X		X	X
Private person/ family		X	X	
Village community				

Note: In contemporary China, rural industry can neither be classified as fully capitalistic or fully socialistic, but is better characterized as a hybrid. This figure has been constructed with the help of the argument in Jean Oi and Andrew Walder, eds., *Property Rights and Economic Reform in China* (Stanford: Stanford University Press, 1999).

tempt to secure the rights of the "authors and inventors," however, was soon replaced by the use of intellectual property law to secure the rights of corporations (Friedman 1985: 255–56, 435–38). This took place in the nineteenth century when the first patent pools also were organized. Corporations, in other words, could from now on buy and sell patents from each other. The value of intellectual property to big corporations increased enormously during the twentieth century with the emergence of the music, drug, and computer industries—what are sometimes referred to as "the copyright and patent industries."

An interesting aspect of intellectual property law has been noted by Robert Merton, namely that the effort to encourage "the inventive interest" of the individual scientist was soon replaced by the internal reward system of scientists (1935, 1973, 2001). The scientist publishes her results and essentially is awarded the esteem of her colleagues. As science has become much more profitable, however, the applicability of this type of award system has shrunk considerably (Zuckerman 1988). This leads to the question if the current legal system still properly safeguards the interest of the inventor and encourages her activities.

Inheritance is closely related to the concept of property, as, for example, Weber's definition of property illustrates. This also means that it is part of the more general social mechanism of appropriation or of excluding other people from the opportunity to use a certain utility. While contemporary sociologists have paid little attention to inheritance, this is not the case with the classic sociologists (see, however, McNamee and Miller 1989; Beckert 2002b, forthcoming). In *Democracy in America*, for example, Tocqueville devotes several pages to inheritance, which he regarded as a legal institution of great social and political importance ([1835–40] 1945, 1:48–54, 380–81; 2:368–70). According to Tocqueville, primogeniture is associated with the aristocratic type of society, and the equal right to inheritance with the democratic type. What especially impressed Tocqueville was that once certain types of inheritance laws are in place, they will slowly but inexorably reshape society according to their logic:

> When the legislator has once regulated the law of inheritance, he may rest from his labor. The machine once put in motion will go on for ages, and advance, as if self-guided, towards a point indicated beforehand. When framed in a particular manner, this law unites, draws together, and vests property and power in a few hands; it causes an aristocracy, so to speak, to spring out of the ground. If formed on opposite principles, its action is still more rapid; it divides, distributes, and disperses both property and power ([1835–40] 1945, 1:50).

Tocqueville also draws a distinction between the "direct" and the "indirect" impact of inheritance. By the former he means the impact of inheritance on some material object, for example, when a landed property is divided into a certain number of plots. By indirect impact he refers to the fact that if landed property is divided, the division will also tend to dissolve the family's feeling for the property and the desire to keep it together (Tocqueville [1835–40] 1945, 1:50–1).

Durkheim and Weber both judged inheritance to be of much importance to economic life. According to Durkheim, inheritance in modern society represents the survival of an archaic and collective form of property, which leads to inequality. "It is obvious," he states in one of his lectures, "that inheritance, by creating inequalities amongst men from birth that are unrelated to merit or service, invalidates the whole contractual system at its very roots" (Durkheim [1950] 1983:213). In Durkheim's opinion, inheritance was incompatible with the spirit of individualism in modern society and should therefore be abolished; he also predicted its disappearance (Durkheim [1950] 1983:216–17; cf. Schwartz 1996).

Like Durkheim, Weber regarded the concept of inheritance as belonging to the legal past, since it deals with the actor in her capacity as a member of a family, and not in terms of what she has accomplished ([1922] 1978:669). The increasing freedom of testation in modern society Weber ascribed, among other things, to the need in families to adjust inheritance to the injustices of life. People "aim, in addition to munificense regarded as an obligation of decency, at the balancing of interests among family members in view of special economic needs" (670). Finally, Weber challenged the easy identification of primogeniture with aristocracy, by pointing out that equal division of land was the rule in France, before as well as after the creation of the famous Napoleonic Code ([1923] 1981:108).

When it comes to the *contract*, the most frequently cited work in sociology is without question *The Division of Labor in Society* by Durk-heim. In a rebuttal to Herbert Spencer, whose political ideal was a society that operated exclusively on the basis of individual contracts, Durkheim pointed out that a contract can work efficiently only if there already exists a social structure to support it. "Everything in the contract is not contractual. . . . Wherever a contract exists, it is sub-mitted to regulation which is the work of society and not that of indi-viduals" ([1893] 1933:211). When he lectured on the contract, Durk-heim also discussed its evolution throughout history. What especially fascinated him, as well as several of his students, was that once a contract has been entered into, it is respected by the actors as well as by society. That a contract in this way can acquire a truly "binding force" was the result, he suggested, of "a revolutionary innovation in law" and could be explained only with the help of sociology (Durk-heim [1950] 1983:178, 203; cf. Cotterell 1999:119–33).

To Weber, the law of contracts represents an "enabling law" par excellence since a contract allows the actors to engage in new types of behavior that they agree upon among themselves ([1978] 1922:666–752). Contracts were used very early in history, but not in the econ-omy; and at this early stage they also involved the whole person ("status contracts," in Weber's terminology). The modern type of con-tract, in contrast, is primarily used in the economic sphere and has a narrow scope ("purposive contracts"). For rational capitalism to oper-ate efficiently, it is absolutely essential that the transfer of property is stable and operates smoothly; and this is something that only the modern (purposive) contract can ensure.

Weber never got around to writing on the modern use of the pur-posive contract (or on the modern use of any of the other legal insti-tutions that are central to rational capitalism). He does, however, oc-casionally touch on the structure of the modern employment contract; and what he has to say on this point is reminiscent of Marx, namely that the asymmetry of power between the worker and the employer makes the freedom of contract largely illusory (Weber [1922] 1978: 729–30; cf. Marx [1867] 1906:195–96). Enabling laws, in other words, tend to promote formal freedom as opposed to substantive freedom:

> This type of rule [that is, enabling rule] does no more than create the frame-work for valid agreements which, under conditions of formal freedom, are officially available to all. Actually, however, they are accessible only to the owners of property and thus in effect support their very autonomy and power positions ([1922] 1978:730).

At one point in *Economy and Society* Weber notes that businessmen rarely go to court to settle their disputes over a contract ([1922]

1978:328). This insight is also central to an important article by legal scholar Stewart Macaulay, which deserves a special mention. In an article that appeared in 1963 in *The American Sociological Review*, and that is based on a study of businessmen in Wisconsin, the author argues that a common reason why businessmen hesitate to use the court system is that they feel that this is not the way to deal with business associates. Macaulay cites a businessman as saying the following:

> If something comes up, you get the other man on the telephone and deal with the problem. You don't read legalistic contract clauses at each other if you ever want to do business again. One doesn't run to lawyers if he wants to stay in business because one must behave decently (1963:61).

In a later study Macaulay has suggested that managers mainly avoid going to court because it is more expensive than settling a dispute through other means. In an interesting twist on this, he points out that money is also the reason why insurance companies do go to court in cases that involve huge claims in automobile accidents: "In such cases, the amount involved is so substantial that no official in the company wants to assume responsibility for writing the check; it seems safer to do this under the compulsion of a court order" (1977: 514).

While the innovative nature of Macaulay's research must be acknowledged, it should also be pointed out that it does *not* prove that businessmen always prefer to settle disputes about contracts between themselves. In a study from the 1990s Macaulay and other researchers found a dramatic increase in the number of contractual disputes that were brought to court (Macaulay, Friedman, and Stokey 1995:103). In the light of this later research, the "Macaulay Thesis" can perhaps be formulated in the following way: businessmen may prefer to settle contractual disputes between themselves, rather than go to court; exactly to what extent this is so, however, must be investigated in each particular case (for studies that follow up on Macaulay's intial article, see, e.g., Macaulay, Friedman, and Stokey 1995:103–4).

The sociological insight of Durkheim and others that the contract is embedded in society has been further developed in American legal thought under the heading of "relational contracting." Classical contract theory, it is argued in this type of literature, deals with an idealized and isolated part of what actually goes on. In real life everything from production to consumption is connected into one big whole of organically linked "relational contracts" (Macneil 1978, 1985). While there is some affinity between this type of argument and the way in which sociologists look at contracts, the notion of relational contracting has not attracted much interest from sociologists.

The reason for this neglect may well be related to the general lack of work done by modern sociologists on the contract in the first place. There do exist some exceptions, however, including a traditional concern with the labor contract (e.g., Streeck 1992). Oliver Williamson's argument that the contract is linked to the market, just as authority relations characterize the firm, has also led to some debate among sociologists, including the suggestion that things are considerably more complex in reality (e.g., Stinchcombe 1985). In Carol Heimer's study of insurance contracts, she investigates how risk is managed in this type of contract (1985). By trying to control for those parts of risk that have their origin in the observation that actors' behavior is interrelated ("reactive risk," in Heimer's terminology), the probabilities for loss are stabilized.

The legal evolution of the modern corporation is clearly of much interest to an economic sociology of law, and the notion of the firm as a *legal personality* is a particularly relevant topic. Most importantly, it is by virtue of this particular notion that the firm has been able to acquire full legal independence from individual persons. To cite Weber, "The most rational actualization of the idea of legal personality of organizations consists in the complete separation of the legal spheres of the members from the separately constituted legal sphere of the organization" ([1922] 1978:707). The notion of legal personality represents, in other words, a legal mechanism that allows individuals to act in novel ways. It is also an integral part of the structure of the modern Western firm.

Only two sociologists have paid more than cursory attention to the notion of legal personality, and this is Max Weber and James Coleman. According to Weber, this notion falls under the heading of "associational contracts" and can consequently be characterized as an enabling law ([1922] 1978:705–29). Weber unfortunately traces only the early history of the notion of legal personality and notes that it was used for certain political and religious organizations rather than for economic ones during the Middle Ages. He does mention, however, that the complementary notion of a firm owning property of its own, which is distinct from the personal property of individuals, started to emerge during the early fourteenth century in Florence ([1923] 1981:228). The notion of legal personality was eliminated from French law during the Revolution but was soon reintroduced to facilitate market transactions. No such interruption occurred in England, on the other hand, where the notion of legal personality was first used in the thirteenth century when charters were issued to towns. Still, it was not until the nineteenth century that the notions of limited liability and joint-stock corporation became common (for this development in the United States, see e.g., Horwitz 1992:65–108; in England, see Harris 2000).

While Weber discusses the notion of legal personality in his sociology of law, James Coleman assigns it a place in his general sociology (1974, 1982, 1993). According to Coleman, studying the notion of legal personality constitutes a way of tracking the evolution of a revolutionary innovation in human history, namely the discovery that people can create groups for their own specific purposes. People have always lived in groups, but it was first at a relatively late stage in history that they consciously began to create new ones. The conceptual breakthrough, according to Coleman, came in the thirteenth century when an Italian jurist called Sinibaldo de' Fieschi (later known as Pope Innocent IV), introduced the notion that a *"persona ficta"* or a *"fictitious person"* should have the same legal standing as an individual, even though it lacked a physical body (Coleman 1993:2). This also meant that organizations could have their own interests, something that has had enormous consequences for the development of society (Coleman 1982; 1993). Today we live in an "asymmetric society," in which the individual has next to no power, compared to that of the modern corporation (cf. Coleman 1990:145–74).

Current Research in Economic Sociology

While no effort has been made to develop a systematic and general analysis of the role that law plays in economic life—what has here been called an economic sociology of law—there do exist a number of studies that would naturally fall into such a field (cf. Stryker 2001b). In some studies, for example, economic sociologists have included a discussion of law in their analyses. One example of this is Neil Fligstein's analysis of the way in which antitrust legislation has influenced the strategies and the internal power structure of American firms during the twentieth century (Fligstein 1990; cf. Dobbin and Dowd 2000). Mark Granovetter has similarly noted that business groups can be defined as legally separate firms, and that antitrust legislation constitutes a serious osbtacle to the formation of business groups in the United States (Granovetter forthcoming).

There also exist a number of studies that draw on a combination of organizational sociology and the sociology of law, and that have produced valuable insights into the relationship of legal and economic forces (see the study of law firms in Silicon Valley, in Suchman 1985, 2000). In one study, the law and economics movement has been criticized for legitimizing gender inequality in the labor market (Nelson and Bridges 1999). Research on the informal economy also suggests that informal economic activities can be defined as activities that evade laws and regulations (e.g., Portes and Haller forthcoming).

But it is also possible to pick out some general themes of research that discuss certain aspects of the role that law plays in the economy. There exists, for example, an attempt in several studies to focus on the firm as a distinct legal actor. Several attempts have also been made to study the role of bankruptcy as well as what happens when a firm or some of its employees break the law. The most innovative of these three themes, insofar as the study of law in general is concerned, may well be the work on the firm as a legal actor. This type of research has grown out of new institutional analysis in organizational sociology and uses as its point of departure the idea that law is part of every firm's surroundings (e.g., Edelman 1990; Edelman and Suchman 1997). Through a series of studies of the 1964 Civil Rights Act and related legislation, it has been shown why certain firms rather than others have responded positively to this type of law and implemented a series of legal measures, such as formal grievance procedures for nonunion members and special offices for equal employment opportunity and affirmative action (Sutton, Dobbin, Meyer, and Scott 1994; Dobbin and Sutton 1998; Kelly and Dobbin 1999; Stryker 2001a; for a review, see Sutton 2001:185–220). Observers, however, have also noted that many of the measures that have created this "legalization of the workplace" serve mainly to legitimize the firm in the eyes of its surroundings; and that management is careful to see to it that these new legal measures do not interfere with important interests in the firm. In Edelman's formulation, "Organizations' structural responses to law mediate the impact of law on society by helping to construct the meaning of compliance in a way that accommodates managerial interests" (Edelman 1992:1567).

Some interesting sociological studies have also been carried out on corporate crime—when firms break the law as well as when their employees engage in criminal activities (for an introduction, see Simpson 2002). Policing the stock exchange constitutes an important and difficult task, given the enormous values that are at stake and the temptations that exist for the individual (Shapiro 1984; cf. Zey 1993; Abolafia 1996). While insider crimes and embezzlement constitute fairly straightforward phenomena from a conceptual viewpoint, this is much less the case with whistle-blowing and organizational crimes.

In whistle-blowing enormous pressure is put on the employee who accuses her firm for wrongdoing (chap 4).

As an example of organizational crime—that is, criminal behavior that benefits the firm, but not necessarily the individual—price-fixing is common in all industrial countries and involves enormous amounts of money. In a recent study of price-fixing, it has been shown that the social structure of this type of activity lends itself very well to network analysis (Baker and Faulkner 1993). Price-fixing of standard products (e.g., switchgear) typically leads to decentralized networks, since little direction is needed from above, while the opposite is true for more complex products (say turbines). The more links there are to an actor in a price-fixing network, the larger the risk that she will be found out.

One form of economic legislation that has been studied quite a bit by sociologists is bankruptcy. For more than a decade, research on personal bankruptcies has been conducted in the United States, and one of the findings is that during the 1977–1999 period these increased more than 400 percent and often involved middle-class people (see Sullivan, Warren, and Westbrook 1989, 2000). But there also exist a growing number of studies of corporate bankruptcies. The most important of these—*Rescuing Business* by Bruce Carruthers and Terence Halliday—is a comparative study of the 1978 U.S. Bankruptcy Code and the English Insolvency Act from 1986 (Carruthers and Halliday 1998; see also Delaney 1989; Carruthers and Halliday 2000). According to the authors, research on law and society has failed to understand that legal professionals play a role not only in interpreting the law, but also in shaping the way in which it is changed and reformed. They also argue that the legal system in the United States, unlike that in England, encourages the reorganization of a firm when it is in trouble, rather than liquidation.

Law and Economics

One of the most successful developments, not only in American legal thought but also internationally, is what is known as "law and economics," which traces its origins to the early 1960s in the United States (for an overview, see Mercuro and Medema 1997). During its early phase this type of analysis was quite radical and insisted that the logic of neoclassical economics could be used to solve a number of important legal problems, economic as well as noneconomic. Lately, however, law and economics has begun to include a number of institutional, psychological, and sociological approaches; and there

"From a purely business viewpoint, taking what doesn't
belong to you is usually the cheapest way to go."

seems to be no reason why one day the economic sociology of law
should not be part of it as well (e.g., Ellickson 1989; Macneil 2000;
Medema, Mercuro, and Samuels 2000).

The heart of the law and economics movement is sometimes referred to as "Chicago Law and Economics," and this is a reminder
that most of its founders were active at the University of Chicago. Of
these it is without doubt Richard Posner who has done the most to
turn law and economics into a general approach in jurisprudence. He
has, for example, produced the first and still very influential textbook—*Economic Analysis of Law* (1st ed. 1972, 5th ed. 1998)—and he
has also regularly tried to survey and pull together the field (1975,

1990). The basic idea in law and economics, according to Posner, is that the logic of economics can and should inform legal analysis as well as legislation. Every actor is driven by self-interest, be it a criminal, a legislator, or a lawyer. What especially informs judges and the legal system as a whole is "wealth maximization" (1990:356). A concern with justice, Posner says, is roughly the same as a concern with wealth. If you can rearrange the situation so that more social wealth is produced, you should do so. Judges, of course, also have to follow common law doctrines, but these often came into being during the nineteenth century when laissez-faire ideology was strong in American legal thought.

At the heart of Posner's reasoning is the so-called Kaldor-Hicks concept of efficiency (1998:14). According to the theorem of Pareto superiority, an exchange should be made only if at least one actor is better off and no one is worse off. The Kaldor-Hicks concept of efficiency is less demanding, and basically states that an exchange is efficient if there is an increase in social wealth—that is, if the change in wealth as a result of an exchange, minus any potential damage to a third party, is positive (see chap. 3 for an example).

Posner has lately started to define himself more as a pragmatist than as a strict law and economics person; and also when we look at the second key figure in the law and economics movement it is possible to perceive a similar drift away from a neoclassical stance. This is R. H. Coase, author of the most influential writing in this field, "The Problem of Social Cost" (1960). The standard interpretation of this article—the so-called Coase Theorem—can be summarized as follows (see also Medema and Zerbe 2000): On the assumption of zero transaction costs (i.e., that it does not cost anything to draw up a contract, go to court, and so on), it does not matter which of the two parties in a dispute about damages will be assigned the legal rights. The logic of the market will in both cases lead to the same result, namely, to the most efficient use of the resources.

The argument in Coase's article is difficult to follow, but has been explicated in an exemplary manner by Mitchell Polinsky (1989:11–14). Assume that the smoke from a factory causes damage to the laundry of some residents who live near by. The damage to the laundry is estimated at $75 per household; and there are five households, making the total damage $375. The damage can be eliminated in two ways. Either a smokescreen can be installed in the chimney of the factory, at a cost of $150, or each resident can be given an electric dryer, at a cost of $50 per resident. The efficient solution is clearly to choose the smokescreen, since this will cost only $150—considerably less than the total damage, which amounts to $375, or buying dryers for $250 (5 × $50).

Coase's argument, to repeat, is that if transaction costs are zero, the efficient solution will be the same, regardless of who is assigned the legal rights in the situation—be it the factory owner or the residents. This can be shown in the following way. Assume, to start out with, that the factory owner is assigned the legal rights (in this case: an entitlement to clean air). The residents will then have to decide if they want to suffer the full damage of $375, the cost for buying dryers for $250, or the cost of installing a smokescreen for $150. The last is the obvious efficient solution. Assume now that the legal rights are assigned to the residents. The owner of the factory can now choose between compensating the residents for the initial damage ($375), buying them dryers ($250), or installing a smokescreen ($150). Again— and this clinches the argument—the most efficient solution is to install a smokescreen.

To look at what represents the most efficient solution to various conflicts, followers of Coase have argued, allows them to approach many legal problems in a novel manner and to generate suggestions for judges to follow. One may also advance legal thought by gradually making Coase's argument more complex, for example, by introducing various types of transaction costs. This is done, for example, in *An Introduction to Law and Economics* by Mitchell Polinsky, where the Coase Theorem is applied to a number of issues, such as breach of contract, nuisance law, and pollution control (1989).

That law and economics contains more than strict logical reasoning can, however, be illustrated by Coase's own apparent tendency not to subscribe to the so-called Coase Theorem. The reason why he assumed zero transaction costs in his analysis, according to Coase himself, was to show that one should not automatically assume that the best way to solve cases involving damage is simply to let the guilty party pay for the whole damage. By introducing the idea of market forces, one can show that other—and more efficient—solutions are also possible. Coase has also pointed out that the main thrust of his argument in "The Problem of Social Cost" had to do with situations where transaction costs *are* involved:

> Because of this, the rights which individuals possess, with their duties and privileges, will be, to a large extent, what the law determines. As a result, the legal system will have a profound effect on the working of the economic system and may in certain respects be said to control it (1991:9).

Another well-known study that shows the breadth as well as the creativity of the law and economics approach is Robert Ellickson's *Order without Law*. Ellickson was an expert in law and economics and a believer in the Coase Theorem when he set out to test it through an empirical study in Shasta County, California (Ellickson 1991). The situation he chose to investigate was precisely the one discussed in Coase's article on the problem of social cost, namely when cattle belonging to landowner A strays onto the property of landowner B and causes some damage. According to the Coase Theorem, as we know, it should not matter in this situation if it is A or B who has the legal rights, given zero transaction costs. What Ellickson found in his study, however, was that people in Shasta county mostly chose to ignore the law because of the high transaction costs, or rather because it was so expensive to settle things according to the law. When damages of the type that Coase describes did occur, however, people tended to rely on local norms to settle their disputes. Ellickson also discovered that people were ignorant about the law. In brief, the Coase Theorem is of little use in analyzing reality.

Another insight of Coase that has received a neoclassical twist as well as a broader interpretation is that property rights are of great importance in the analysis of most economic phenomena. A major point in "The Problem of Social Cost," according to the author, was to make clear that "what are traded on the market are not, as is often supposed by economists, physical entities but the rights to perform certain actions, and the rights which individuals possess are established by the legal system" (Coase 1991:9). This idea has shown itself to be very productive, to judge from the enormous literature on property rights that has emerged since the 1960s (e.g., De Alessi 1980; Ostrom 2000). Once picked apart, it turns out that the concept of property covers a number of complex situations, as exemplified by the kind of property rights that are associated with such diverse economic institutions as land, capital, shareholding corporations, mutual savings institutions, and so on. The property rights perspective also invites a historical as well as a comparative perspective; and a number of studies along these lines have also been produced.

While it is obvious that many studies in the law and economics literature fail to single out and analyze the impact of social relations, it should also be clear from what has just been said that the law and economics movement is quite diverse and broad enough to encompass different types of analyses, including an economic sociology of law. This latter type of analysis may one day have quite a bit to offer the law and economics movement. In the meantime, however, law and economics has much that is of interest to the sociologist, both in terms of ideas and empirical research (cf. Davis and Useem 2000; Davis and Marquis forthcoming). When it comes to ideas, the notion of property rights is a case in point and has already been discussed. As to empirical research, there is much to choose from, including Rafael La Porta and his coauthors' attempt to compare the impact of common law on economic growth to that of civil law (1998). What these authors found was that the rights of minority shareholders as well as shareholders in general were much better protected in countries with legal systems that belong to the common law tradition than to the civil law tradition. Finally, it is time for sociologists to realize that law and economics is not a conservative or right-wing project (Rose-Ackerman 1992). It has practitioners who are liberals, social democrats, and the like. More importantly, many of its key ideas can be very helpful to economic sociology.

Summary

The legal system is part of the modern state, but not reducible to its actions. It is precisely this fact that makes it so important for economic sociology to start looking at the role of law in economic life. An attempt to develop an agenda for an economic sociology of law was made in this chapter. Weber's sociology of law, it was argued, can be used as the theoretical point of departure for such an enterprise. This is especially true for what Weber has to say about law as an enabling and empowerting device—which is similar to Willard Hurst's idea that law can sometimes operate as "a release of energy."

As an example of a law that has led to such a release of energy, the medieval *lex mercatoria* was discussed, and so was the following institutions: inheritance, property, the contract, and the corporation as a legal entity. Sociological research by the classic writers on these institutions was presented and discussed. What contemporary sociologists have added was also mentioned, especially work on the firm as a legal actor, bankruptcy law, and what happens when a firm and its employees break the law.

Most of the work in the economic sociology of law remains to be done; and in this process quite a bit can be learned from the sociology of law, the law and society literature, and what has been produced as part of the law and economics movement. The idea that law and economics is inherently conservative is rejected. The study of law and economics is in many respects ahead of the economic sociology of law, and can therefore—just as certain studies in law and society, and in the sociology of law—serve as a source of inspiration.

IX

Culture and Economic Development

FOR a full understanding of economic phenomena, it is not only necessary to pay attention to their political and legal dimension, but also to the role that is played by culture. In the classical studies in economic sociology this was done as a matter of course, which helps to account for their greatness. During most of the twentieth century, however, analyses in economic sociology have been less successful in this respect. As a result, rescue operations of the type "bringing x back in" have had to be carried out at regular intervals. One way to avoid this in the future would be to insist that any analysis in economic sociology routinely take political, legal, and *cultural* issues into account.

This chapter will begin with a section on the concept of culture, in early sociology as well as in contemporary sociology. The main section, however, is devoted to the theme of culture and economic development. A series of works that draw on the notion of economic culture—from Tocqueville and onward—will be presented and commented upon. The discussion of the relationship between culture and the economy continues in the next chapter, where the emphasis is on contributions in contemporary economic sociology.

The Concept of Culture and the Economy

Sociologists have used the concept of culture in a number of ways, including its everyday meaning as high culture. From an analytical viewpoint, however, the most common approach (following Weber) has been to see culture as involving *values*. From this perspective, a sociological analysis should always try to outline which values a certain social structure embodies (e.g., Lipset 1993; Harrison and Huntington 2000).

In the past decade or two, however, sociologists have begun to argue that there is more to the notion of culture than values, or, alternatively, that it is a mistake to center a sociological analysis around values in the first place (for an overview of the concept of culture, see e.g., Sewell 1999). The latter tendency can be exemplified by an often cited article by Ann Swidler in which it is suggested that culture should be seen as a "tool kit" of symbols, stories, rituals, and the like, which are used by the actors as "strategies of action" (1986). As cognitive psychology has become more advanced, it has also been suggested that its insights can be used to develop a new and more modern concept of culture (DiMaggio 1997). Finally, sociologists have also been influenced by the anthropological concept of culture, both in its classical sense as artifacts and in its modern sense as meaning structures (Geertz 1973). The end result of these developments is a mixture of the old and the new meanings of culture; values are typically still part of the analysis but not necessarily its central focus.

While there does exist some sociological literature on the relationship of the economy to culture, much still remains to be done (for a survey, see DiMaggio 1994). One concept that has not been much discussed, but that would seem central in this context, is that of *economic culture*. A nation, for example, is sometimes said to have its own economic culture, just as a region or a firm ("corporate culture"). The general idea is usually that economic values are seen as being related in some way to the overall values of the nation, region, and so on, or that a distinct constellation of values characterizes the economy. To what extent the notion of economic culture is compatible with more recent developments in the notion of culture remains, however, to be seen. It is, in any case, clear that while earlier economic sociologists were interested in analyzing the economic culture of whole countries or even whole continents, this type of analysis has largely fallen out of fashion in contemporary economic sociology.

Recent economic sociology has also not addressed the issue of interests in relation to culture. One reason for this, no doubt, has been the tendency in mainstream economics to separate radically the notion of self-interest from culture. While self-interest has been seen as the key to economic analysis, culture has been declared irrelevant. Some economic sociologists, it would appear, have responded by reversing the priorities and declaring culture as all-important, and self-interest as irrelevant. The position of this chapter, however, differs from that of the economists as well as from that of many economic sociologists. In brief, I will argue that culture and interests belong together, and that a discussion is needed to explore how they are related to each other.

One point of departure for such a discussion can be found in Weber's work, particularly in his discussion of ideal and material interests in his switchmen metaphor. Ideal interests—say interests in cultural values, such as art or religion—may have an underpinning force that easily equals or surpasses that of material interests. The notion that culture always represents some kind of disinterested action has to be rejected. The switchmen metaphor also points to an alternative way of conceptualizing the relationship between culture and interests. Weber, to recall, suggests that "very frequently 'world images' . . . have, like switchmen, determined the tracks along which action has been pushed by the dynamic of interests" ([1915] 1946b: 280). One way of interpreting this passage is to see interests as providing the force of action, or what drives action, while "culture" (or "values") determines its general direction. Recent approaches to culture can be brought in at this point to add complexity to the analysis. One can, for example, make use of the idea that people follow a certain script when they act or that their perceptions are structured by various cognitive mechanisms.

The Values Approach to Culture;
The Relationship of Values to Norms

In Ann Swidler's article "Culture in Action" (1986) the opening lines are devoted to a critique of what she terms "the values paradigm":

> The reigning model used to understand culture's effects on action is fundamentally misleading. It assumes that culture shapes action by supplying ultimate ends or values towards which action is directed, thus making values the central causal elements of culture (273).

A decade later Paul DiMaggio made a similar attack on the values approach to culture in a well-known article. Agreeing with Swidler that the values approach portrays culture as "unitary and internally coherent across groups and situations," he states,

> The view of culture as values that suffuse other aspects of belief, intention, and collective life has [today] succumbed to one of culture as complex rule-like structures that constitute resources that can be put to strategic use.
>   This shift makes culture much more complicated. Once we acknowledge that culture is inconsistent . . . it becomes crucial to identify units of cultural analysis and to focus attention upon the relations among them. In effect, our measures stop being indicators of a latent variable (culture) (1997:265).

What Swidler and DiMaggio argue, in brief, is that the values approach to culture represents an outmoded and unsophisticated view from which little, if anything, can be learned. This, however, represents a much too hasty conclusion, as I shall try to show in this and the next chapter. The values approach to culture may well have taken the form that Swidler, DiMaggio and others attribute to it in certain works—but this approach has also been put to sophisticated use in a series of studies of economic culture, from Tocqueville in the nineteenth century to Geertz in the twentieth. Values are not seen as the main causal variable in these works, nor is culture seen as something unitary, without contradictions and complexity. These works actually share quite a few traits with the approach to culture that is popular today among sociologists.

Before proceeding to a discussion of some works that draw on a sophisticated use of the values approach, a few words need to be said on the topic of *norms*, since these are often considered part of this approach. While norms and values are not identical in sociological analysis, it is often assumed that values do come to an expression in social life in the form of norms. A norm typically means a rule of behavior, departure from which is punished (Homans 1950:123; cf. Bendor and Swistak 2001:1494). A theoretically more elaborate and complex version can be found in Weber's definition of a convention: "An order (*Ordnung*) will be called *convention* so far as its validity is externally guaranteed by the probability that deviation from it within a given social group will result in a relatively general and practically significant reaction of disapproval" ([1922] 1978:34). An "order," it can be added, is a way of behavior that is regarded as valid by the actors.

That norms are ubiquitous in social life constitutes one of the earliest insights of sociology, and it was also soon discovered to be true for economic life. It was, for example, established in the famous Hawthorne studies that workers do not simply follow orders and rules but also develop their own informal norms (Roethlisberger and Dickson 1939). Some of these norms, as later research in industrial sociology was to confirm and elaborate upon, have to do with productivity. If someone in a work group produces above or below the norm, she will be punished by her coworkers (cf. chap. 4).

To analyze a situation with the help of norms constitutes a powerful weapon, and soon sociologists tried to explain practically everything with their help. By the 1960s, however, a reaction to this type of analysis set in. The basic stance among the critics was that sociologists had begun to assume that people's behavior is totally determined by norms, while in reality there is considerable room for independent action (Wrong 1961). In the 1980s a new and different type of critique made its appearance, mainly among sociologists who were interested in rational choice, but also among economists. These critics argued that sociologists tend to take norms for granted, rather than explain why they exist in the first place (Coleman 1990:241–44). Attempts to remedy this situation have involved propositions such as the following: norms are followed because of self-interest; norms promote self-interest; and norms promote common interests (Elster 1989; cf. Hechter and Opp 2001).

No consensus about these propositions concerning norms from a rational choice perspective has emerged, either among sociologists or economists. Some economists take the position that while most economic actions are guided by rationality, there also exist some that are exclusively guided by social norms. Other economists suggest that one can find a mixture of the two in any kind of economic action.

Some sociologists have proposed that there is an element to norms that make people follow them regardless of interest, while others insist that interest is always present. There is also disagreement among sociologists about the relationship between formal and informal norms. According to one position, formal norms are consciously portrayed as rational, simply to endow the organization with a certain legitimacy, while informal norms are more down to earth and help to get the work done (Meyer and Rowan 1977). According to another viewpoint, if the formal norms of an organization are weak, while the informal norms are strong, the latter may evolve into counteracting norms, or so-called "opposition norms," which may undo the efficiency of the organization (Nee 1998).

While it is much too early to try to settle the current debate about the nature of norms, further commentary is warranted on the relationship between interests and norms. While it would be reductionist not to acknowledge the existence of a vital noninterest element to norms—which are often followed simply because they are norms—this in no way means that one cannot illuminate the existence and structure of certain norms with the help of an interest perspective. When, for example, an organization is created for some specific economic purpose, this will lead to the emergence of norms that are deeply informed by the original economic purpose as well as by norms that have little to do with this purpose. Some of these latter norms may express a different interest, say that of a work group, while others will be more difficult to relate to any specific interest. There is always also the case that people—for interests of their own—orient themselves in different ways to formal and informal norms. They may decide to follow the norms or they may not. They may, for example, decide to be honest or they may decide to steal.

Culture and Economic Development

Economic sociology, as I shall try to show in this section, has a rich and important tradition to draw on when it comes to analyses of culture. What especially interested the early sociologists, I will argue, was the relationship between culture and economic development. This will be illustrated by Tocqueville's analysis of American economic culture in *Democracy in America*; by Weber's work in his sociology of religion; and by a series of works that grew out of post–World War II social science in the United States. Bourdieu's work on culture and economics will be discussed in the next chapter, as will the current attempt in modern economic sociology to reintroduce culture into its analysis.

American Economic Culture in the Early Nineteenth Century (Tocqueville)

Democracy in America contains a remarkable picture of the economic culture in the United States in the early 1800s. At this time there was plenty of opportunity for social mobility, few big fortunes had yet been amassed, and industrialization had hardly begun. In Tocqueville's terms, "democracy" and "equality"—as opposed to "aristocracy" and "inequality"—characterized the country. The "three great causes" that had shaped the United States were its geographic condition, its laws (including its political institutions), and what Tocqueville called its *moeurs* ([1835–40] 1945, 1:334). "*Moeurs*" are usually translated as "manners" and "customs," but can also be rendered as "culture" or, following Sumner, as "folkways" and "mores" (Sumner [1906] 1960:vi).

At one point in *Democracy in America* Tocqueville says that the mores (as I shall call them) of a country account for "the whole moral and intellectual conditions of a people" ([1835–40] 1945, 1:310). This and many other passages show that there is a clear evaluative element to Tocqueville's mores, which is also indicated by his term for the most important of these—what he calls "the habits of the heart" (*'les habitudes du coeur*; 1:310). Tocqueville argues that the laws (and the political institutions) have been more important than geography in shaping the United States, and that the mores have been more important than the laws and the political institutions. He also suggests that "it is the influence of the customs (*moeurs*) that produces . . . prosperity" (1:334).

The United States is characterized by Tocqueville as "a commercial nation," where there is "constant excitement" and where people are "restless" in their search for material riches ([1835–40] 1945, 2:45, 165, 212). "America is a land of wonders in which everything is in constant motion and every change seems an improvement" (1:443). The equality of conditions in the United States also makes it natural for people to use their own interest as a guide for how to behave, rather than just follow tradition as in an aristocracy:

> No power on earth can prevent the increasing equality of conditions from inclining the human mind to seek out what is useful or from leading every member of the community to be wrapped up in himself. *It must therefore be expected that personal interest will become more than ever the principal if not sole spring of man's actions* (2:132; emphasis added).

While work is not held in particularly high regard in an aristocracy, it is very different in a democracy. In the United States, Tocqueville says, "every honest calling is honorable" ([1835–40] 1945, 2:162). One reason for this is that there exists so little inherited wealth in a democracy that everybody has to work for a living and get paid. This norm is so strong in the United States, according to Tocqueville, that even the president gets a salary and also the rich feel compelled to work.

In the Southern states, with their slave culture, on the other hand, work is looked down upon, with the result that the economy suffers. While the North was full of life and energy, at the time of Tocqueville's visit, the South was lethargic and half asleep. In the North everybody worked, but in the South only the slaves worked (cf. ch. 1). Tocqueville also admired the fact that many of the Americans he met had had so many different jobs. He was well aware of the advantages of an advanced division of labor—he had carefully studied *The Wealth of Nations*—but he also observed that having many different jobs expanded the mind of the worker.

Trade and manufacture are very highly regarded by Americans, according to *Democracy in America*, because it is much easier to make a quick profit in these professions than in agriculture. Agriculture is also conducted in a different way in the United States than in Europe. In the former it has been turned into a business, while in the latter it is still part of aristocratic society where landed wealth rather than profit is the governing principle. As a result, there are no peasants in the United States, only people who "make agriculture itself a trade" (Tocqueville [1835–40] 1945, 2:166).

Americans are also superior in trade to the Europeans, according to Tocqueville, who uses transatlantic shipping as his example. Americans are invariably faster than the Europeans, even though they pay their sailors more and use the same kind of ships. What accounts for the difference is something that Tocqueville calls "heroism in their manner of trading"—the Americans, in brief, are bolder and take more risks than the Europeans ([1835–40] 1945, 1:442). Tocqueville sums up his argument as to why Americans are faster over the Atlantic in the following way: "I am of the opinion that the true cause of their superiority must not be sought in physical advantages, but that it is wholly attributable to moral and intellectual qualities" (1:441). Tocqueville's argument on this point, goes very well with the current tendency in the social sciences to emphasize the role of risk and risk-taking (e.g., Beck 1992; Baker and Simon 2002).

When it comes to consumption, Tocqueville notes, the Americans have a "love of well-being" and a "passion for physical gratification" ([1835–40] 1945, 2:136–37). They do not long for palaces and grandiose properties, as aristocrats do, but for "the little conveniences of life"—"to add a few yards of land to your field, to plant an orchard, to enlarge a dwelling, to be always making life more comfortable and convenient, to avoid trouble, and to satisfy the smallest wants without effort and almost without cost" (2:136).

This longing for the little conveniences of life is universal—the poor dream of them, the middle class loves them, and the rich live in constant fear of losing them. But having these objects does not necessarily make you happy, Tocqueville says; you always want more, and become restless in your search for new satisfactions. People who love "small objects" do not become corrupt or immoral through their possessions ([1835–40] 1945, 2:140). Still, valuing comfort and consumption has a tendency to "enervate the soul and noiselessly unbend its springs of action" (1945, 2:141).

Life in an egalitarian society such as the United States also affects the way that interest is seen and evaluated. In the Old World, Tocqueville notes, interest is viewed as something vulgar, as the opposite of selflessness and high moral values. "In Europe the principle of interest is much grosser than it is in America, but it is also less common and especially it is less avowed; among us, men still feign great abnegations which they do no longer feel" ([1835–40] 1945, 2:130).

In the United States interest is also less crude than in Europe since it has come to acquire a moral dimension, mainly through religion. The "principle of self-interest rightly understood" reigns in the United States, where people think that "it is in the interest of every man to be virtuous" (Tocqueville [1835–40] 1945, 2:130). In being virtuous in this way, Americans learn to say no to immediate gratification, something that teaches them discipline. The notion that "virtue is useful" may not represent the peak of human morality, according to Tocqueville, but it goes very well with a commercial society. He concludes, "I am not afraid to say that the principle of self-interest rightly understood appears to me the best suited of all philosophical theories to the wants of the men of our time, and I regard it as their chief remaining security against themselves" (2:131).

Culture, Religion, and Economic Ethic (Weber)

Max Weber uses the concept of culture in two different and partly overlapping ways: as meaning structures and as values. It is used in the former sense when Weber distinguishes "the cultural sciences" from "the natural sciences" on the basis that "understanding" (*Verstehen*) must be used in the *Kulturwissenschaften*, as opposed to the *Naturwissenschaften* ([1904] 1949:74). The concept of culture is used in a similar sense when Weber argues that " 'culture' is a finite segment of the meaningless infinity of the world process, a segment on which *human beings* confer meaning and significance" (81). One can say that when Weber speaks of culture as meaning structures, he often has sense-making in mind.

Weber is very careful to emphasize that economic actions and events can become "economic" only if they are invested with a particular meaning or sense. In one of his methodological essays he writes, for example, that "the 'essence' of what happens [in an exchange] is constituted by the 'meaning' which the two parties ascribe to their observable behavior" ([1907] 1977:109; cf. [1922] 1978:98). Weber also notes that the reason why actors choose one meaning rather than another has to do with their "cognitive interest" (cf. Habermas [1968] 1971). When we, for example, regard something as "economic" because it involves scarcity and the satisfaction of needs, Weber says, an interest of this particular type is involved:

> The quality of an event as a 'social-economic' event is not something which it possesses 'objectively.' It is rather conditioned by the orientation of our cognitive interest, as it arises from the specific cultural significance which we attribute to the particular event in the given case ([1904] 1949:64).

The second (and partly overlapping) sense in which Weber uses the concept of culture is as values. As the following quote makes clear, this meaning of the concept of culture is also a complex one:

> The concept of culture is a *value-concept*. Empirical reality becomes "culture" to us because and insofar as we relate it to value ideas. It includes those segments and only those segments of reality which have become significant to us because of this value-relevance. Only a small portion of existing concrete reality is colored by our value-conditioned interest and it alone is significant to us ([1904] 1949:76).

In the same essay from which this quote is taken Weber also refers to "value-conditioned interest" (76). This phrase shows that the concepts of interest and culture are by no means each other's opposites in Weber's work (as they often are in today's sociology of culture). The two go very well together, in the sense that interests are typically shaped by values (or culture). By this is meant, for example, that while an economic interest aims at utility, what is seen as utility differs quite a bit according to what values (or culture) are involved. While merchants, for example, hold trade in high esteem, aristocrats look down on trade and on those who buy and sell for a living.

According to Weber, there exist special clusters of values or "value spheres" in society. There is, for example, a "political sphere," an "economic sphere," an "erotic sphere," and so on ([1915] 1946a:331–58). Each of these spheres has a distinct autonomy (*Eigengesetzlichkeit*); and there exist conflicts in each sphere as well as between the spheres. As a metaphor for life in contemporary Western culture Weber uses the world of Greek mythology, where the plurality of values is represented by individual gods who are in constant conflict and competition with one another. Culture, in brief, also entails struggle and conflict for Weber.

In each sphere of their lives, Weber argues, human beings have to make a choice and decide what values to follow, that is, they have to develop an ethic. In the political sphere people will develop a political ethic, in the erotic sphere a sexual ethic—and in the economic sphere *an economic ethic*. Culture and economy are firmly united in Weber's concept of economic ethic, which plays a central role in his work during the 1910s. It was, in particular, during these years that he worked on his giant project entitled *The Economic Ethics of the World Religions*, which resulted in *Ancient Judaism*, *The Religion of China*, and *The Religion of India*. Besides these three volumes, Weber's project also included the second edition of *The Protestant Ethic* and a few essays. Some of these latter essays can be found in Gerth and Mills's anthology, such as "The Protestant Sects and the Spirit of Capitalism," "Religious Rejections of the World and Their Directions," and "The Social Psychology of World Religions."

The only place in Weber's work where you can find a discussion of the concept of economic ethic is in the last of these essays, "The Social Psychology of World Religions" (1915). This discussion is of particular interest because much of what Weber has to say on the role of culture in the economy can be found in his analyses of economic ethic (in the sense of values). Weber makes two major points about economic ethic—one that has to do with the level at which an economic ethic operates, and another that has to do with its social determination. It is of crucial importance, Weber argues, not to identify an economic ethic with theoretical advocacies of certain values in economic life, such as those that can be found in moral philosophy, theology, and the like.

An economic ethic always refers to what goes on in practical life and therefore constitutes a form of "practical ethics" (Weber [1915] 1946b: 268). In discussing the economic ethic of a religion, Weber notes, for example, that "the term 'economic ethic' points to the practical impulses for action which are founded in the psychological and pragmatic contexts of religions" (267).

As to the social forces that shape and determine an economic ethic, Weber's main message is that much complexity is involved. Different economic ethics may, for example, be found in similar economic organizations. "An economic ethic is not a simple 'function' of a form of economic organization; and just as little does the reverse hold, namely, that economic ethics unambiguously stamp the form of the economic organization" (Weber [1915] 1946b:268). An economic ethic is furthermore characterized by "a high measure of autonomy," and it cannot be "determined solely by, [for example], religion" (268). Despite the great number of different social forces that may be involved in the creation of an economic ethic, Weber notes that when it comes to the economic ethic of a religion, much importance must usually be attached to the social strata to which the carriers of a religion belong. For Hinduism, it was the hereditary caste of cultural literati; for Buddhism, contemplative and mendicant monks; and for Christianity, itinerant artisan journeymen.

The concept of economic ethic, as Weber constructs it, is in principle applicable to all types of economic activities since any form of economic action always entails evaluation. Examples are easy to find from the world of work to that of riches. Manual labor has usually been seen as inferior to nonmanual labor, just as trading with money has been regarded with suspicion all over the world. Women's work is usually devalued, compared to that of men. Warriors tend to have contempt for agriculture and aristocrats for business. During his travels in the 1830s Tocqueville discovered that working for a living had become a norm in democratic America. This, however, did not prevent Americans in the twentieth century—people from *all* strata—to devalue manual labor and other forms of "dirty work" (Merton 1968b:199; Hughes 1962).

Also wealth and luxury have been evaluated differently throughout history. From a religious point of view, riches can be viewed as a threat to salvation or as a sign that you are blessed. Luxury can be regarded as something to enjoy or as something that should be forbidden. Economic change and technology have also been evaluated in a number of different ways, sometimes positively, sometimes negatively. And so have the existence of poverty and the decision whether

"I love the middle class, with their values and everything."

to save or to spend—in brief, *all* economic activities are *always* evaluated.

The Economic Ethics of the World Religions can be characterized as a sociological study that attempts to investigate the impact of the major forms of religion on economic ethic, and what effects these ethics have had on the economy at large. It contains in particular an attempt to determine the role that economic ethic (or economic culture) has played in the creation of modern rational capitalism. Weber's work grew out of his analysis from 1904–05 in *The Protestant Ethic and the Spirit of Capitalism*, and it is therefore with this work that we shall begin (cf. chap. 5).

Two major types of economic ethics are discussed in *The Protestant Ethic*: one that answers to "traditional capitalism" and one that is integral to "modern capitalism." The latter type of economic ethic, however, did *not* grow out of the former; its main inspiration came from religion. The main social mechanism for how this came about is presented in *The Protestant Ethic*; and a supplementary one can be found in "The Protestant Sects and the Spirit of Capitalism."

The economic ethic of traditional capitalism—or "the spirit of traditional capitalism," to use Weber's terminology—is characterized by moderate profits, some competition, and a certain resistance to innovations. The capitalists do not work particularly hard, and the workers stop working once they have earned enough to satisfy their traditional needs. There is economic progress, but it is slow and held back by the negative stance of religion toward profit-making and work as the main goals in life.

The economic ethic of modern capitalism is radically different, especially when it comes to work. The workers as well as the capitalists in this type of economic culture view work as absolutely central to their lives; it constitutes a *vocation*. Not only do they work longer hours, but they also carry out their tasks in a more methodical and rational manner. A new set of economic values have come into being, which Weber illustrates with some quotes from the writings of Benjamin Franklin. "Remember, that *time* is money," "Remember, that *credit* is money," and "Remember, that money is of the prolific, generating nature. . . . He that kills a breeding-sow, destroys all her offspring to the thousandth generation. He that murders a crown, destroys all that it might have produced" (Weber [1904–05] 1958:49).

Franklin also says that one should be punctual in business and pay attention to one's behavior in public:

> The most trifling actions that affect a man's credit are to be regarded. The sound of your hammer at five in the morning, or eight at night, heard by the creditor, makes him easy six months longer; but if he sees you at a billiard-table, or hears your voice at a tavern, when you should be at work, he sends for his money the next day (Weber [1904–05] 1958:49).

The idea that work is a sacred duty for every human being comes from Martin Luther, according to Weber. That work should also be methodical and carried out in an energetic and nontraditionalistic manner comes, however, not from Luther but from the ascetic Protestant sects, such as the Calvinists, Pietists, Baptists, Methodists and Quakers. All of these sects, Weber argues, somehow made people change their attitude to economic issues in a procapitalistic manner. Exactly how this happened, however, is what needs to be explained. It was not so much a question of religious ideas or sermons influencing people, according to Weber, but that they felt that their innermost religious interests were at stake (the term that Weber uses is religious benefits or *Heilsgüter*). When this happens, people are ready and willing to change. The way that the people thought about religious issues

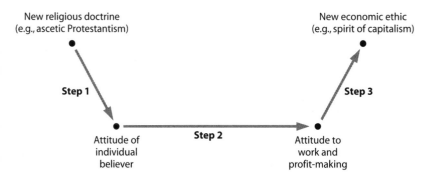

Figure 9.1. From Religious Ethic to Economic Ethic, or How to Make a Sociological Interest Analysis, according to *The Protestant Ethic*.

Note: In economic sociology you essentially try to move from the surface of things down to the level of interests and to study how these influence the individual actor. This figure shows how the individual believer, according to Weber, is first exposed to a new religious doctrine (ascetic Protestantism) and relates this to her religious interest (Step 1). She eventually also applies it to her economic interest (Step 2)—and when there are many people who do so, the end result is the creation of a new economic ethic (Step 3).

Source: David McLelland, *The Achieving Society* (Princeton: Van Nostrand, 1961), 47; James Coleman, "Social Theory, Social Research, and Theory of Action," *American Journal of Sociology* 91 (1986): 1322.

then spilled over into their economic activities, and soon these began to change as well.

In sociological terms, one can summarize Weber's argument in the following way, following David McLelland and James Coleman (see figure 9.1). The individual Protestant believer first assimilated the new ascetic doctrine to which she was exposed (Step 1). This doctrine then influenced her economic behavior (Step 2). When many of these ascetic Protestants interacted with one another, their economic behavior turned into a new economic lifestyle or a new economic ethic (Step 3).

Weber's suggestion for how the transition from the economic ethic of traditional capitalism to the economic ethic of modern capitalism came about has been much debated and often questioned. This book, however, is not the place for presenting the debate on *The Protestant Ethic*, which is far too sprawling and complex for thorough treatment here. For a balanced assessment, the reader should consult Gordon Marshall's *In Search of the Spirit of Capitalism: An Essay on Max Weber's Protestant Ethic Thesis* (cf. also Swedberg 1998:203–6). In all brevity, most contemporary historians and economic historians seem to think that Weber was wrong, although a few do find the argument in *The Protestant Ethic* convincing. According to David Landes, for example, "it is fair to say that most historians today would look upon the Weber thesis as implausible and unacceptable. It had its moment and it is gone" (2000:11–12; cf. 1998:174–81). Once having said this, however, Landes immediately adds,

> I do not agree [with this opinion]. Not on the empirical level, where records show that Protestant merchants and manufacturers played a leading role in trade, banking, and industry. Nor on the theoretical. The heart of the matter lay indeed in the making of a new man—rational, ordered, diligent, productive. These virtues, while not new, were hardly commonplace. Protestantism generalized them among its adherents, who judged one another by conformity to these standards (12).

Some time after the publication of *The Protestant Ethic*, Weber wrote an article on the economic ethic in the United States around the turn of the twentieth century (Weber [1920] 1946). Weber, who had toured the country in 1904, was especially impressed by the role that the Protestant sects had played during the nineteenth century in the United States, and noted that anyone who wanted to be successful in business had to join one of these. The reason for this was that the members of the sects were seen as absolutely trustworthy and honest—two qualities that greatly facilitated doing business in a huge country such as the United States.

In analyzing why the sect members had these high moral qualities, Weber noted that many sects had consciously cultivated honesty in commerce. The Methodists, for example, considered it forbidden

1. to make words when buying and selling ("haggling");
2. to trade with commodities before the custom tariff has been paid on them;
3. to charge rates of interest higher than the law of the country permits;
4. "to gather treasures on earth" (meaning the transformation of investment capital into "funded wealth");
5. to borrow without being sure of one's ability to pay back the debt; and
6. [to acquire] luxuries of all sorts (Weber [1920] 1946:313).

But it was not only that the Protestant sects valued honesty, used fixed prices, refused to bargain and so on, which made their members so unscrupulously honest; another mechanism was also involved. According to Weber, a sect can "breed" certain qualities into its members, because each member is constantly under the scrutiny of other members and wants to live up to their standard ([1920] 1946:320). In terms of figure 9.1, which summarizes the sociological argument in

The Protestant Ethic, Step 3—from the micro to the macro level—does not only depend on the formation of a new economic lifestyle (as Weber had argued in his main study), but also on the fact that the individual actor is a member of a sect, and as a consequence is closely watched by her peers.

Most of *The Economic Ethics of the World Religions* is devoted to a study of those parts of the world where the existing religions did *not* lead to a procapitalist stance in the economic ethic. In ancient Israel, as Weber shows in *Ancient Judaism,* the religious ethic did not hold economic activities in very high esteem, and covetous behavior was explicitly warned against. Widows, the poor, and the sick should be helped, and one should also treat animals with respect. The Sabbath, for example, included animals as well as humans. According to Weber, the ethic of ancient Judaism was, like most ethics, "double" or "dualistic" in the sense that while you had to treat the members of your own community with respect, this was not the case with foreigners. According to Deuteronomy 23:20, "You may exact interest on a loan to a foreigner but not on a loan to a fellow-countryman."

For historical reasons, including anti-Semitism, this dualistic tendency was later accentuated in Judaism, and led to the development of what Weber calls "pariah capitalism." This type of capitalism emerged as a response to the Jews being treated as "pariahs" by other ethnic groups, and it lacked the high moral qualities that would later characterize the economic dealings of the ascetic Protestants. As opposed to the arguments of Werner Sombart and others, Weber was of the opinion that the type of capitalism developed by the Jews, including its dualistic economic ethic, was to have little impact on the history of Western capitalism (Sombart [1911] 1982).

In *The Religion of China* Weber looks at the economic ethics of Taoism and Confucianism. Magic predominated in Taoism, which means that it strengthened economic traditionalism and led to an acceptance of the status quo. There was a strong belief in Taoism, for example, that the form of rocks and mountains could affect demons and spirits (geomancy). "Often detours of many miles were made because, from the geomantic viewpoint, the construction of a canal, road, or bridge was deemed dangerous" (Weber [1920] 1951:199). Mining was similarly thought to disturb the spirits in the ground—as were railroads and factory smoke.

Confucianism was popular among the mandarins and while it did not advocate the use of magic, the elite thought that magic was useful for controlling the masses. The ideal of Confucianism was the gentleman, who valued a long and peaceful life as well as material ease. *The Religion of China* ends with a famous section in which Weber compares Confucianism and ascetic Protestantism. While both shared a certain rationalism, according to Weber, they were miles apart on other issues. The ascetic Protestant did not accept the world as it is, but wanted to change it radically in accordance with her religious ideals. The Confucian gentleman, on the other hand, was a conformist and felt no particular urge to change anything. The ascetic Protestant saw hard and methodical work in her chosen vocation as a way of honoring God, while the Confucian had the somewhat detached and all-round gentleman as his ideal.

In *The Religion of India* Weber analyzes the economic ethics of Hinduism and Buddhism. In Hinduism the spirit of the caste system militates against any kind of economic change or innovation. Each person belongs to a caste, and to change one's trade or just one's working tools could lead to a disaster in the transmigration of the soul. You risked being reborn as a "worm in the intestine of a dog" (Weber [1921] 1958:122). What hinders innovations from being undertaken is consequently that the whole economic or occupational structure is anchored in "the individual's very personal interest in salvation" (123). Weber sums up the impact of the economic ethic of Hinduism: "A ritual law in which every change of occupation, every change in work technique, may result in ritual degradation is certainly not capable of giving birth to economic and technical revolutions from within itself, or even of facilitating the first germination of capitalism in its midst" (112).

Also Buddhism, according to Weber, would fail to develop a new type of economic ethic that could set off economic change on a large-scale manner, in the way that the economic ethic of the ascetic Protestants had done in the West. The kind of tranquility that comes with death is what is sought in Buddhism, not eternal life in salvation as in Christianity. Attachments to life on earth, including attachments to material objects and riches, are seen as imprisoning the soul, as are passions and desires. The true goal of a religious person is successfully to avoid the pain that comes with living life on earth, and in this way escape the wheel of rebirth. Finally, Buddhism, just like Hinduism, makes a strong separation between the religious elite and the masses. While the former often drew on a systematic and sophisticated religious vision, the latter were left with a view of the world as "an immense magical garden" (Weber [1921] 1958:255).

Economic Culture and Modernization

The works of Weber started to become available in English translation in the late 1940s and 1950s, and were received in a selective manner.

This, for example, was the case with the interpretation of Weber in much of the modernization literature, which became dominant in the social sciences in the 1950s and 1960s (e.g., Valenzuela and Valenzuela 1978; Chirot 1981). Weber's argument about the West in *The Protestant Ethic* was, for example, elevated into a universally valid model of "modernization," while all the nonindustrialized countries were lumped together as "traditional." Similarly, Weber's emphasis on the growth of Western rationalism throughout history was reinterpreted as a prescription for how to modernize the developing world. Western values and Western culture were seen not only as the end product of all development but also as the means for "becoming modern," to cite the title of a well-known study in this vein (Inkeles and Smith 1974).

Modernization theory has often been criticized for its simplistic approach and is seldom referred to today, except in disparaging terms. While this may be a positive development in some respects, it should not prevent a realization that a number of important insights were produced in the modernization literature. This is, for example, very much the case with the topic of economic culture, as I will try to show by a brief presentation of the following three works: Robert K. Merton's "Social Structure and Anomie" (1949), Clifford Geertz's, *Peddlers and Princes: Social Development and Economic Change in Two Indonesian Towns* (1963), and S. M. Lipset's, "Values and Entrepreneurship in the Americas" (1967). That this approach to culture and the economy is still alive, and still very useful, can also be illustrated by a reference to a recent volume on the role of values in economic development, with contributions by scholars such as S. M. Lipset, David Landes, Jeffrey Sachs, and many others (Harrison and Huntington 2000).

In discussing the impact of Weber's theory of culture as values on U.S. sociology, reference is often made to the early work of Talcott Parsons, especially to his suggestion that sociology should study the role of values in society, and economics the means for how to realize these ("the analytical factor view"; see Parsons 1935). A more faithful and interesting rendering of Weber's ideas can, however, be found in Robert Merton's work, where it is suggested that societies should study not only the values of society (its "cultural goals"), but also the norms that regulate the means that must be used to realize these values (its "regulatory norms") (1968b:187; cf. Merton 1968a). For Merton, values are "culturally defined goals, purposes and interests," and means are the ways of reaching goals that are considered legitimate in a society (1968b:186).

Merton uses American economic culture as an example to illustrate the usefulness of the distinction between cultural goals and institutional means. A dominant theme in this culture is that every American, regardless of social origin, can be successful and make plenty of

TABLE 9.1.
Reactions to the Pressure for Monetary Success in the United States

Modes of Adaptation	Culture Goals	Institutionalized Means
I. Conformity	+	+
II. Innovation	+	−
III. Ritualism	−	+
IV. Retreatism	−	−
IV. Rebellion	+/−	+/−

Note: According to Merton, all Americans share the ideology of monetary success—but are situated differently in the social structure and will therefore have different access to the legitimate means for pursuing this goal.

Source: Robert K. Merton, "Social Structure and Anomie," in *Social Theory and Social Structure* (New York: Free Press, 1968b), 194.

money—and must never give up. As Carnegie once put it, "Be a King in your dreams. Say to yourself, 'My place is at the top'" (cited in Merton 1968b:192). According to the American dream, you can also always make *more* money; and Merton cites a finding according to which everybody in the United States, regardless of income, wants to make about 25 percent more than they currently do. Since there is no stopping point, you always have to keep moving.

While all Americans tend to share the same economic goal, the legitimate means that can be used to reach this goal are distributed very unevenly in the social structure. At the bottom of the economic ladder, for example, there is little chance to find a good job or start a successful business; and since making lots of money is as much a sign of success to the poor as it is to the rich, the poor may be tempted to resort to illegitimate means. Merton calls this type of deviance an "innovation" (see table 9.1). The American dream is also hard on the lower-middle class since real success is likely to elude its members. One result of this, Merton suggests, is that lower-middle-class people may distance themselves from the goals of society but stick to its means. Examples of persons who adhere to this type of "ritualism" include the overzealous bureaucrat and the frightened employee.

Many people at the top of society also find it hard to live up to the American dream—and as a result they may come dangerously close to breaking the law or committing a crime. This represents an "innovation" as well in Merton's terminology. At this point of the argument—where the author for the second time establishes a direct link between thwarted economic ambitions and crime—he cites the following remark by Veblen: "It is not easy in any given case—indeed it is at times impossible until the courts have spoken—to say whether it is an instance of praiseworthy salesmanship or penitentiary offense" (Merton 1968b:195; for white-collar crime, see e.g., Aubert 1952; Shapiro 1984, 1990; Calavita, Tillman, and Pontell 1997). Two more ways to react to society's values and means are also possible, according to Merton's typology. First, people may decide that the current values in society should be replaced by new ones, even if it takes violence to accomplish this ("rebellion"). And second, people may simply withdraw from society, from its means as well as from its values ("retreatism"). The revolutionary would be an example of rebellion, and the hobo of the 1930s would be an example of retreatism.

The Weberian approach to culture as value or a practical ethic is also used with much skill by Clifford Geertz in *Peddlers and Princes* (1963), the next study to be discussed. The bulk of this work is devoted to an analysis of two small towns in Indonesia—Modjokuto in Java (population 24,000) and Tabanan in Bali (population 12,000). The need for economic growth, Geertz says, is felt very strongly in both of these towns; people's values and tastes have already started to change. But it is also very difficult to reorganize the economy better to fit the new times. What in particular is missing is the modern firm, as a way to organize economic activities, so that growth can happen.

In Modjokuto the bazaar is the main economic form, while in Tabanan the economy is based on the cooperative unit of a local kind. The bazaar economy, as Geertz calls it, is dominated by individual traders who spend much of their energy trying to outwit each other. These traders do not trust one another and rarely cooperate; the very idea of joining together in a collective enterprise such as the firm is alien to them. In Tabanan the economy is based on so-called *seka*, which can be described as egalitarian groups with a strong collectivistic spirit. While it is easy for authority figures such as the local aristocrats to mobilize these *seka* for various economic purposes, they also tend to discourage individual initiative and restrict self-interested behavior.

The main economic problem in both of these towns, Geertz concludes, is organizational as well as cultural. The modern firm is lacking—and so is a value system that makes it natural for individuals to cooperate in the form of a firm. The kind of value system that is essential for a "firm-type economy" must accomplish two interrelated tasks, he argues. On the one hand, it has to allow self-interest to dominate economic activities within certain moral bounds. And on the other hand, it has to assign a legitimate place to business in society's values at large.

In Modjokuto self-interest is hardly regulated at all and, as a consequence, the bazaar economy has had to be sharply segregated from the rest of society. In Tabanan, on the other hand, the line between the economy and the rest of society is not clear at all; and this makes it very difficult to assign a place to self-interested behavior in the economy. Geertz sums up his argument about the kind of culture that is needed in a modern capitalist economy:

> Economic development involves the establishment of a well-demarcated preserve within which economic rationality may operate independently of political, religious, familial and other interests, as well as a definition of the place and value of such businesslike behavior from the point of view of the total social system, the manner in which, even within its own preserve, it too must submit to regulation by the culture's general moral code. In modern society the range within which economic rationality is allowed to hold sway is generally wide and the control of more general normative concerns at least somewhat loose, but in any case the range has definite limits and the control is quite real (1963:138).

Before leaving *Peddlers and Princes* something must also be said about its analysis of the Chinese minority since the topic of ethnic minorities has come to play an important role in contemporary economic sociology (e.g., Bonacich 1980; Light and Karageorgis 1994; Granovetter 1995b; Light forthcoming). In Tabanan, Geertz says, most of the Chinese minority (826 of 12,000) are born in Indonesia and are fairly well integrated in the local Balinese culture. In Modjokuto, on the other hand, the Chinese are very successful and dynamic businessmen; they identify themselves as Chinese rather than as Indonesian; and they are discriminated against, by the local population as well as by the local authorities. A strong antagonism exists between the Chinese minority and the rest of society in Modjokuto. And as the old, integrated structure of this town is slowly being eroded and replaced by a more modern and open one, Geertz predicts, the antagonism between the Chinese businessmen and the rest of society is likely to increase.

Finally, in a number of studies S. M. Lipset has drawn on what he calls Weber's "value analysis" to analyze the economic cultures of the United States, Latin America, and Canada ([1967] 1988, 1989, 1993, 1996). According to Lipset, it is important to distinguish between the cultural values of a society and its social structure. Values play a major and independent role in society as a whole as well as in the economy, and they basically determine if a potential course of action will be taken or not. "Structural conditions make development possible; cultural factors determine whether the possibility will take place" ([1967] 1988:78). What role interests play in this process is not explicitly addressed; presumably they are embedded in the social structure but given direction by the culture.

In "Values and Entrepreneurship in the Americas" from (1967) Lipset argues that the values of Latin American society have been shaped by three centuries of colonial rule by Spain and Portugal. The elites in these two countries transmitted a disdain for labor, especially manual labor, to Latin America. Money-making and trade were also looked down upon by the Spanish and Portuguese elites and often assigned to some minority group, such as the Jews or the Muslims. A strong anti-bourgeois mentality coexisted with a tolerance for get-rich-quick schemes, such as those of the *conquistadores*. While the merchant had low status in Iberian culture, the soldier and the priest were held in high esteem.

Much of this heritage from Spain and Portugal is still very much part of Latin American culture, according to Lipset. The landowning class, with its *latifundias*, is still seen as an ideal, and the children of the elite prefer to study law and the humanities, over science or engineering. Firms are typically family firms and rarely become shareholding firms; outsiders are distrusted and kept at a distance. Latin American businessmen prefer not to take risks and are more interested in short-term schemes than in long-term projects. Bankruptcy is viewed as a disgrace.

If the values of Latin America are so anti-business, Lipset asks, why does it nonetheless have an important business sector? His answer is that in situations where the dominant values do not encourage business, minorities are in a position to take the lead. This fact, however, should not be seen as support for the theory that entrepreneurship represents some kind of deviant behavior—a position that was popular during the heydays of the modernization literature. Drawing upon Weber's argument in *The Protestant Ethic*, Lipset suggests that in countries where the dominant value system has been pro-business (as in the United States and in English-speaking Canada), most businesspeople have come from the dominant ethnic group. Where this has *not* been the case (as in Latin America), many businesspeople have come from minority groups.

Summary

This chapter began with a general discussion of the concept of culture in which it was pointed out that while economists pay attention to self-interest and disregard culture, some economic sociologists do precisely the opposite. Culture and interests, however, are not each other's opposites, but belong intimately together in the type of analysis that I argue economic sociology should be promoting. Different ways of theorizing how culture and interests belong together were presented, including the one that can be found in Weber's famous passage on the switchmen. According to this model, interests drive people's actions, while culture (say, in the form of religion) supplies them with a general direction.

Culture has been defined in different ways in sociology, but is typically seen as some kind of mixture of values and meaning structures. The suggestion of Swidler and others that the notion of culture as values represents an outmoded form of analysis, was rejected as resting on a misunderstanding of the way in which the concept of culture has been used by Weber and his followers. Several studies by sociologists of culture and economy were presented and discussed, such as Tocqueville's picture of American economic culture in the early 1800s, Weber's attempt to analyze the role of economic ethic in different civilizations, and the analysis of economic culture that can be found in the work of such scholars as Merton, Geertz, and Lipset.

Tocqueville's analysis is especially significant in this context, not the least because of its skillful interest analysis. At the core of American culture, according to Tocqueville, is "the principle of self-interest rightly understood"—that is, Americans feel that it is in their interest to be virtuous. Weber's work on economic ethic, or people's tendency to assign distinct values to all of their economic activities, is similarly important in this context. This last approach also informs much of American sociology just after World War II with its interest in the role that culture plays in economic development. Weber's influence is also very much evident in current contributions to culture and economy, which will be discussed in the next chapter.

X

Culture, Trust, and Consumption

WHAT differentiates much of contemporary work on culture and economy, from that which was carried out after World War II, is that it does not single out economic development. Instead it looks primarily at the role of culture in everyday economic life. What matters for contemporary economic sociologists is that all economic activities have a cultural dimension—they are embedded in culture, just as they are embedded in social structure.

The first section in this chapter is devoted to the work of Pierre Bourdieu, who has made the most original contribution to the understanding of the relationship between the economy and culture in contemporary sociology. This is followed by a discussion of the way that this theme, including trust, has been analyzed in new economic sociology. The reason for bringing up trust in this context, I argue, is that it represents a distinct value and therefore belongs to a discussion of culture. The third section is on consumption, as an instance of material culture or objects that people value.

Culture and the Economy in Modern Sociology

One of the most significant contributions to economic sociology since World War II has been made by Bourdieu, which includes his thinking on the theme of culture and the economy (cf. chap. 2). This theme appears in his early writings on Algeria and in his later works on France, and in his discussion of theoretical issues more generally. Several of the key concepts in Bourdieu's sociology—especially habitus and cultural capital—have shown themselves to be very helpful for understanding the relationship between culture and the economy. Another useful concept is on what he calls cultural fields, such as art and literature, and his thesis that interests play a disguised role in these.

Habitus or disposition can be roughly defined as the durable disposition of an actor to approach reality in a certain manner, as influenced by the past. Depending on her habitus, the actor will organize her practices and representations in different ways. *Homo economicus*, in contrast, has no past or a habitus; everything he does is eternally new. In *Algeria 1960* Bourdieu describes economic habitus as a "disposition [that] orients and organizes the economic practices of daily life—purchases, saving, and credit—and also political representations, whether resigned or revolutionary" (1979:vii–viii). The key theme in Bourdieu's work on Algeria is that the habitus of the local population is still precapitalist and out of joint with the capitalist reality that the colonizing powers have introduced. The result of this conflict has been extremely painful and disorganizing for the Algerians (for Bourdieu's major empirical studies of Algeria, see Bourdieu 1963; Bourdieu and Sayad 1964; for an English-language summary, see Bourdieu 1979).

The precapitalist habitus of the Algerians is portrayed by Bourdieu as qualitatively different from the capitalist habitus. In precapitalist Algeria the basic economic unit was the kinship group, not the nuclear family as in capitalism. Property was often owned collectively, and how much each individual contributed to the income of the household was not known. To meld into the group and not stand out was a norm, as in many peasant societies. In general, Bourdieu argues, much took place in this type of economy as if to *disguise* the fact that economic interests were at stake. The relationship of work to productivity was, for example, not known nor was it looked into. Gifts were common—and "gift exchange is an exchange in and by which the agents strive to conceal the objective truth of the exchange, i.e., the calculation that guarantees the equity of the exchange" (1979:22).

One important difference between the economic habitus of the Algerians and the rational habitus of people who live in a capitalist society, Bourdieu argues, has to do with the concept of time. One example involves attitudes toward work: and according to tradition in Algeria, a man with self-respect should always keep busy—"at least he can carve a spoon" (1979:24). Another example of the precapitalist attitude to time has to do with the relationship to money. Money is seen as something that is very abstract and inferior to what it can buy. According to an Algerian saying, "A product is worth more than its equivalent [in money]" (11). When the harvest has been good, Bourdieu also notes, the peasant will typically hoard the surplus for future consumption rather than invest it. As to credit, one lends only to friends or relatives; the time for repayment is left vague; and the idea of interest on a loan is not acknowledged (interest meaning that one must pay for the use of resources during so many time units, according to an exact scale).

One reason why it is so painful and difficult for the Algerians with their precapitalist habitus to adjust to the new, capitalist conditions has already been hinted at: capitalism did not develop organically in Algerian society, from within, but was instead imposed from the outside, by colonial powers. Another reason has to do with the economic conditions of the Algerian population; and at this point of his argument Bourdieu criticizes the tendency in social science to see cultural change in much too abstract terms and disregard that it is always anchored in economic reality.

If one looks, for example, at the economic situation of the Algerian population, it soon becomes clear that until the workers reach a certain limit of income, they are unable to think and calculate in rational terms, along the lines of people who live in a capitalist society. At a certain income level—when the Algerian workers feel secure and are able to take a calm and rational look at the future—they typically decide to have fewer children and develop a more realistic outlook. The Algerians who are poor, on the other hand, continue to have large families and are very unrealistic when it comes to the future. Their social and economic reality, Bourdieu says, push them into a "forced traditionalism" (1979:23).

Bourdieu's second major contribution to the analysis of the role of culture in the economy is his notion of cultural capital. This concept has its origin in research that Bourdieu and Jean-Claude Passeron carried out on the educational system in France in the 1960s ([1964] 1979, [1970] 1977). In trying to determine what role education plays in reproducing the class structure, Bourdieu and Passeron came to the conclusion that some crucial piece was missing in the analysis—and that it has to do with the cultural heritage that the students bring with them from their families. What is usually explained by referring to "ability" and "talent," they concluded, can much better be understood as the result of a cultural capacity that some students have been taught by their parents, as part of growing up in the "right" kind of family.

The notion of human capital, as developed in contemporary economics by Gary Becker and others, is criticized by Bourdieu on the ground that it fails to take into account what happens in the family. "From the very beginning, a definition of human capital, despite its humanistic connotations, does not move beyond economism and ignores, inter alia, the fact that the scholastic yield from educational action depends on the cultural capital previously invested by the family" (Bourdieu 1986:244). The fact that the role of cultural capital in the school system is not understood, Bourdieu emphasizes, only makes it so much more effective.

According to a typology introduced by Bourdieu some time after his studies on education, one can distinguish among three states of cultural capital: "the embodied state," "the objectified state," and "the institutionalized state" (Bourdieu 1986). The first of these states—the embodied state—is the one that was used by Bourdieu and Passeron in their research on education, and roughly covers culture in the sense of good upbringing and *Bildung*. No substitute for the years that it takes to develop a cultivated personality is possible, according to Bourdieu. It is like tanning—you just have to put in the time. This version of cultural capital, it can be added, has had a certain impact on stratification research, not least in the United States (for a discussion of how to operationalize cultural capital as well as the impact of this concept on U.S. sociology, see Lamont and Lareau 1988).

Cultural capital in its objectified state includes such items as paintings, sculptures, and monuments. While anyone with enough money can buy these types of objects, to "symbolically appropriate" them is a different matter, and for this cultural capital is necessary. Cultural capital in its institutionalized state refers mainly to academic degrees. While the autodidact may have as much knowledge as someone with an academic degree, she lacks a title or some other official sign of her knowledge. These signs are also used to determine salaries, a fact that leads to another theme in Bourdieu's theory of capitals, namely that different types of capital can often be converted into one another, including financial capital. This goes not only for cultural capital but also for social capital (connections) and symbolic capital (capital that does not acknowledge that it is capital; see later in this chapter).

Bourdieu has also made a number of studies of cultural fields, which all touch on the economy (1993a, 1995). What is most fascinating about these studies from the perspective of this chapter, however, is not so much what they have to say about the economic dimension of cultural phenomena. It is rather Bourdieu's thesis that what is distinctive about high culture is its ideology of being "disinterested," of portraying itself as an "anti-economy" (1993b:40; 1998). Art and literature tend to present themselves as utterly alien to such profane matters as money and profits, and as constituting their own separate realm of reality, which has little to do with the sordid struggles in society. The emphasis on the elevated value of art and literature is complemented by an ideology of the individual artist as the supreme creator—what Bourdieu refers to as a "'charismatic' ideology" (1993b:76).

In reality, however, the world of high culture is disinterested only in appearance. It is as much driven by interest and interest struggle as the rest of the social world, but what drives it primarily is *noneconomic interests* that are related to questions such as the following: What is to be regarded as literature? What literary genre is most admired? Who is the best author? The failure to see any interests in the world other than economic interests, Bourdieu notes, is something that we owe to the economists; and this way of looking at things may also lead to the corresponding error of trying to reduce the essence of art to economics, as in vulgar materialism.

The struggle over noneconomic interests, Bourdieu says, can be just as ferocious as the struggle over economic goods, sometimes even more so. There is also the fact that the "economic world reversed," as Bourdieu calls the world of high culture, does produce quite a bit of profit and income to certain actors—but only on condition that the anti-economic ideology is honored by the participants. Just as the pre-capitalist economy appears to be based on honor, generosity, and respect for kinship, high culture hides that its resources and profits are distributed in a predictable, structural, and exploitative manner. Again, in other words, we find ourselves in the strange world of symbolic capital, or capital that presents itself as a lack of interest in economic resources—and that distributes these resources precisely on the basis of a display of disinterest in economic matters (Bourdieu 1993a; Bourdieu and Wacquant 1993:119).

Culture and Trust in Contemporary Economic Sociology

Bourdieu's ideas on economy and culture have had little impact on new economic sociology in the United States. One reason is that mainstream new economic sociology has been deeply influenced by organization theory and the network approach; and these have either been indifferent to culture (organization theory) or openly hostile (network theory). Organization theory has typically disregarded the concept of culture except in the form of "corporate culture," which can be described as a mixture of hype and serious research (e.g., Deal and Kennedy 1982, 1999; Barley and Kunda 1992). Scholars studying networks have typically argued that the theory of culture is far too imprecise to be of much use in analyzing economic phenomena.

The critique of using a cultural perspective in new economic sociology has much to do with the identification of culture with the work of Talcott Parsons, but it has also spilled over into a general neglect of values, meaning structures, and the like among network analysts. A case in point is the influential work of Mark Granovetter, even though it should be mentioned that Granovetter has recently stated that he has become more interested in the cultural dimension of economic phenomena (Granovetter 1999a:11, 2000:2). He has, however, *not* withdrawn the main thrust of his critique, namely that the cultural perspective is so general that it is not of much use in producing precise explanations.

"I don't know how it started, either. All I know
is that it's part of our corporate culture."

It is inappropriate, according to Granovetter, to give "causal primacy to such abstract concepts as ideas, values, mental harmonies, and cognitive maps" (1999b). The cultural approach represents a form of the oversocialized concept of man type of analysis, and it is also close to being circular since beliefs are used to explain behavior, and the former are often derived from the latter (1992b:47–48). Compared to the exact mapping out of relational networks, cultural explanations are simply too imprecise (for a similar critique, see also Hamilton and Biggart 1988:S53, S69–S74, where it is pointed out that Confucianism cannot account for economic progress in Taiwan, South Korea, and Japan since these three countries all have very different industrial structures).

From early on, the position by the network analysts on culture has been criticized by Viviana Zelizer, who has argued that the neglect of culture may lead economic sociologists to miss a number of important economic topics and more generally to reproduce the kind of one-dimensional analysis that is characteristic of mainstream economics. Values and meaning structures are central to the very constitution of economic phenomena, Zelizer maintains. Taking culture into account, however, does not mean that the social structure can be ignored; and to reduce everything to culture would be a fatal mistake. What is needed, she says, is "to plot a theoretical middle course between cultural and social structural absolutism designed to capture the complex interplay between the economic, cultural and social structural forces" (Zelizer 1988:629; similarly Zelizer 2002).

Paul DiMaggio has also long opposed the position that tracing social structures, in the form of networks, is all that is needed for a full explanation in economic sociology. As opposed to Zelizer, however, he has been more positive to the mainstream vision in new economic sociology and has suggested various ways of improving upon it rather than abandoning it all together (DiMaggio 1994). Just as economic action is to be understood as embedded in networks, it must also be seen as embedded in culture ("cultural embeddedness"—DiMaggio 1990:113; Zukin and DiMaggio 1990:17–18). DiMaggio has also been much more interested than Zelizer in abandoning the view of culture as values, and in replacing it with a view that draws on recent developments in cognitive psychology.

What has been discussed up until now have primarily been theoretical positions on the role of culture in economic sociology, but there also exists a number of empirical studies of economy and culture that should be part of the discussion. Furthermore, something needs to be said about the concept of trust, which is closely related to that of culture. What one finds in the empirical studies are primarily an attempt to look at the role of values in various economic phenomena and, to a lesser extent, an attempt to take the view of the actor into account. Mitchell Abolafia has, for example, investigated the worldview of traders on various security markets (1998), and Zelizer has been able to show that people often earmark money, depending on the purpose for which they want to use it (1989, 1994).

In two other studies Zelizer has investigated the role of values in economic life—the changing attitude to life insurance and to children as economic assets. When life insurance was introduced in the nineteenth century to the United States, the initial resistance was very strong since it was felt that a human life should not be evaluated in monetary terms. There was also less of a need for something like life insurance, since neighbors and kin helped each other out in difficult times. What made it easier for life insurance to eventually become accepted, according to Zelizer, was that it surrounded itself with something of an aura of sacredness; it became part of the process that made it easier for the rest of the family to carry on, when one of its members had died. There was also the important fact that people no longer could rely on neighbors and kin in cases of hardship.

In a somewhat similar way, according to Zelizer, children in nineteenth-century America were evaluated in economic terms (1981, 1985). Increasingly, however, as time went on, children were excluded from the new, industrial economy. There was also an equivalent shift in attitude, from seeing children in economic terms to seeing them exclusively in emotional terms. Children had become "economically worthless but emotionally priceless" (1981:1052).

While Zelizer, DiMaggio, Granovetter, and some other of the leading figures in American economic sociology would all agree today that there should be a place for both social structure and culture in the analysis, this stance has recently been challenged by the so-called new institutionalists in organization theory, who are inspired by the work of John Meyer. According to this approach, the current notion of the state, the corporation, the actor, and so on are *all* to be understood as social constructions of a very specific type, namely Western culture. In economic sociology Frank Dobbin has explored this position in a theoretical paper (1994a) as well as in his study *Forging Industrial Policy* (1994b). The advantages of using such a broad concept of culture that it includes practically everything can no doubt be discussed. It is, however, also clear that Dobbin has been able to develop a number of interesting and important ideas by drawing on this perspective (for an account of *Forging Industrial Policy*, see chap. 7).

A few words need to be added at this point about the role of *trust* in economic life, since an argument can be made that trust belongs to a discussion of culture. Trust represents a distinct value, in the sense that it is highly valued by individuals, in economic life as well as elsewhere (for general discussions of trust, see e.g., Luhmann 1979; Gambetta 1990). People who cannot be trusted, and societies where mistrust prevails, are typically experienced in negative terms. The absence of trust, it has also been shown in a number of studies, has a negative impact on economic life (Fukuyama 1995).

As we know from chapter 1, Simmel pointed out that every money transaction builds on trust—the trust that someone else will accept the money that you have received as a payment ([1907] 1978:170). According to Weber, trust in a sib-dominated society, such as ancient China, tends to be personalistic and restricted in scope, while the trust of the ascetic Protestant is universal in scope and impersonal in nature (Weber [1920] 1951:237, 244–45; cf. Weber [1920] 1946). Durkheim has less to say on trust than either Simmel or Weber, but the concept of trust can be directly related to anomie. Where there are no regular links between people, they will tend to distrust each other.

Later scholars have also agreed that without widespread impersonal trust, it is hard to get economic growth going (e.g., Banfield

1958; Geertz 1963:126). It is clear that courts and institutions such as the Securities and Exchange Commission play a key role in upholding "economic trust," as Carruthers calls it (Shapiro 1984; cf. Carruthers forthcoming). There also exist a number of institutions that by supplying credit information, credit ratings, and the like, make it easier for businesspeople to trust one another—what is sometimes referred to as "impersonal trust" (Zucker 1986; Shapiro 1987; Carruthers forthcoming). Recent events in the United States show that accounting is to be seen as a trust-producing industry as well.

While economists often view trust in utilitarian terms—it functions as "an important lubricant of a social system" and has a price like any commodity (Arrow 1974:23)—sociologists, in contrast, emphasize that trust has an independent quality, which is irreducible to calculation and profit-making (Granovetter 1992b:38–47; cf. Williamson 1996a). Coleman's view of trust as a bet on the future falls somewhere in between these two positions (Coleman 1990:99; cf. chap. 2). It has finally been argued that trust and emotions are closely connected in economic life, especially in transactions that are geared to the future—as most financial transactions are (Pixley 2002).

Material Culture and Consumption

The step from culture to consumption is short (Zelizer forthcoming a). Before taking this step, however, it should be noted that the sociology of consumption has developed independently of economic sociology—and that this is something that needs to be changed if economic sociology is ever to cover all the major aspects of economic life (for an overview of the sociology of consumption, see Campbell 1995b). It can naturally be discussed from which angle economic sociology should try to approach and integrate consumption. It is, for example, possible to analyze consumption by focusing on its role in the economic process, following upon production and distribution (cf. chap. 3). According to this viewpoint, what drives consumption in capitalist society is not only the interest of the consumer to satisfy her needs, but also the interest of the capitalist to make a profit.

It is also possible to approach the phenomenon of consumption from the perspective of markets. One would then look at the emergence and evolution of consumer markets (see the discussion of mass markets in chap. 6). It must also be added that consumption typically has a political as well as a legal dimension (cf. chaps. 7–8). By applying import duties and taxes, for example, the state has often tried to steer consumption. Laws against luxury consumption (including so-called sumptuary laws) are similarly common in history (e.g., Sombart [1913] 1967; Hunt 1995, 1996).

But it is also possible to discuss consumption as part of culture or, more precisely, as part of the theme of "economy and culture." One reason for proceeding in this way is that the concept of culture can illuminate the fact that phenomena such as buying, selling, and consuming can be properly understood only if their *meaning* is taken into account. That this is actually done in much of today's sociology of consumption represents a positive development, which can be ascribed to the critique that some anthropologists have directed at sociologists (and economists) for viewing consumption in a one-dimensional manner (Douglas and Isherwood 1980; Appadurai 1986; for consumption in economic anthropology, see Miller 1995).

Once this has been said, however, it should be noted that there also exists a tendency in some contemporary studies of consumption to exaggerate the role of meaning, and to present consumption in a disembodied and disinterested manner. This is particularly the case among postmodernists, who argue that we live in a new type of society—a consumer society—where people consume signs and images rather than concrete objects (Baudrillard 1988; cf. Jameson 1983). While much of the postmodernist analysis should be credited with theoretical imagination, as well as a talent for capturing something of the *Zeitgeist*, this type of analysis nonetheless misses some crucial facts about consumption: that consumption is vitally linked to production; consumption is anchored in concrete social relations; and the driving force in consumption is individual interest, as encouraged and often shaped by profit interests. The opposite error of a "productionist" analysis, or the tendency to ignore consumption and look only at production, is no doubt the tendency to focus exclusively on consumption, in isolation from production (Glucksman 2000). It should be obvious that there can be no consumption without production.

Consumption is more than a semiotic game of meanings; it is sturdily anchored in a system of social relations, which does not only involve the buyer and the seller but often also the buyer's family, kin, peers, colleagues at work, as well as class relations more generally. That individual interest drives consumption is obvious enough since the human body cannot survive unless there is a certain nutritional intake. Historical studies of the consumption of food as well as contemporary studies of the same phenomenon should therefore be part of the sociology of consumption (e.g., Braudel [1979] 1985a:104–265; Fogel 1994; Dreze and Sen 1990–91). Not only material but also ideal interests drive the individual and make her consume different items.

That there exists a profit interest in consumption is equally obvious; and it helps to explain such phenomena as advertisement as well as the staging of consumption (Schudson 1984; Ritzer 1999). To this can be added that the attempt to analyze consumption in terms of interests has a long tradition. In *The Wealth of Nations* we find, for example, the following passage, which is still relevant today:

> Consumption is the sole end and purpose of all production; and the interest of the producer ought to be attended to, only so far as it may be necessary for promoting that of the consumer. The maxim is so perfectly self-evident, that it would be absurd to attempt to prove it. But in the mercantile system, the interest of the consumer is almost constantly sacrificed to that of the producer; and it seems to consider production, and not consumption, as the ultimate end and object of all industry and commerce (Smith [1776] 1976: 660).

The classic works in economic sociology have quite a bit to say about consumption, even though it would be wrong to argue that consumption was a topic that they were particularly interested in. Marx, for example, assigns a fairly marginal place to consumption in *Capital* (cf. Marx and Engels [1848] 1978; Marx [1844] 1978:101–6). Reference is made in this work to "the fetishism of commodities," an expression that roughly refers to the fact that people in capitalist society see no connection between the consumer goods in the stores and the exploitative process through which these are produced and in which they themselves participate ([1867] 1906:81–96). More to the point in this context, however, is Marx's suggestion that labor power as well as other commodities are consumed in the process of production, and that this type of consumption ("productive consumption") differs from the type of consumption that takes place once the worker has been paid for his work ("individual consumption") (626).

Weber operates with a somewhat different concept of class than Marx—one that is exclusively connected to "production," as opposed to the concept of status that according to a well-known passage in *Economy and Society* is connected to "consumption" and "style of life" ([1922] 1978:305–6, 926–39; cf. Weber 1989). People in a social class will typically try to limit competition and develop status groups; and if they are successful in this, "economically irrational consumption patterns" will emerge (Weber [1922] 1978:307).

Simmel touches on consumption in many places in his work, as in his article on the 1896 Berlin Trade Exhibition ([1896] 1991) and his analysis of the spendthrift in *The Philosophy of Money* ([1907] 1978: 247–51). His most cited study in this context, however, is "Fashion." According to Simmel, fashion is essentially "a product of class distinc-

CONSPICUOUS CONSUMPTION, 1993

tion" ([1904] 1957:544). It typically starts in the upper class and is then imitated by the lower classes, until it dies out—and then the whole cycle starts all over again. Simmel's light touch in this and other essays can be contrasted to the heavy hand of Thorstein Veblen in his great classic on consumption, *The Theory of the Leisure Class*. Veblen's thesis of "conspicuous consumption"—that the display of expensive items "becomes honorific," while "the failure to consume . . . becomes a mark of inferiority and demerit"—has, however, been much criticized and appears also to have largely fallen out of favor ([1899] 1973:64; e.g., Adorno 1967; Campbell 1995a).

Many studies of how families spend their income (on rent, food, clothes) were produced during the interwar period, but it was not until after World War II that studies of consumption started seriously to venture beyond this approach. One reason for this has to do with the expansion of consumption that took place after World War II, especially in the United States; another with the emergence of a series of new quantitative methods that now could be used to study consumption. That sociology of consumption as a distinct field still did not come into being during these years may have something to do with the ideological disdain for business that was common among

American sociologists in these days. In the opening line of an article in *The American Journal of Sociology* from 1959, entitled "Reflections on Business," Paul Lazarsfeld states that most American sociologists have "an ideological bias against business," and adds that this is the reason why the study of consumption is "largely undeveloped" (1959: 1–2).

Practically no articles on business can be found in *AJS* before 1950, according to Lazarsfeld, and little use had been made of the material in the files of various market-research organizations. For a contemporary reader of Lazarsfeld's article, the following quote gives a sense of the kind of research that could have been produced during these years, but for which there was no academic audience:

I prevailed upon a polling agency in 1957 to ask a national sample whether they approved or disapproved of continuous changes in car design. One-half disapproved. But, asked how these changes should be curtailed, only 10 per cent thought that consumers themselves could exercise the necessary discipline; 60 per cent wanted self-regulation on the part of the industry; and 30 per cent favored governmental intervention. Besides the astonishing lack of confidence people had in themselves and in one another, the most noticeable finding was a social difference: the lower-income groups were relatively more in favor of governmental regulation (1959:10).

But despite the ideological bias of many sociologists, some very important studies of consumption were produced during the 1950s and the 1960s in American sociology, especially but not exclusively at Columbia University (cf. Goffman 1951; Easton 2001). One of these led to the formulation of the theory of "the two-step flow of communication" or the idea that mass media do not influence people directly, but in an indirect way via so-called "opinion leaders" (cf. Katz 1960). In *Personal Influence* Elihu Katz and Lazarsfeld explored, among other things, how people decide what movie to go to and why they decide to pick a certain commodity or a certain fashion (1955). In all of these cases the authors found that personal contacts were more important than advertising.

When efforts were made at Columbia University to pinpoint the exact mechanism through which the two-step theory of communication operated, however, the whole thing tended to dissolve into new research questions and longer chains of influence than the initial two steps. Robert Merton succeeded, for example, in showing that opinion leaders not only process information from mass media but also actively seek it out from other sources (1968c:441–74). He also suggested that it can be useful to divide opinion leaders into different categories. While some opinion leaders are interested in what happens at a national level and in the world, and for this reason read national newspapers ("cosmopolitans"), others are much more interested in what happens in local affairs and prefer local newspapers ("locals").

Another classic work that was produced by sociologists, who had been trained at Columbia University, is *Medical Innovation: A Diffusion Study* by James Coleman, Elihu Katz, and Herbert Menzel (1966). This study analyzes the adoption by doctors in a number of small towns of a new drug, a tetracycline-based product called Achromycine. At first sight this study may not seem to be about consumption at all. It is, for example, true that doctors do not consume drugs—their patients do. Still, it is the doctors who make the decision which drugs their patients are to use, something that drug companies are well aware of. Doctors, in other words, can be said to consume on behalf of others—a bit like parents do for their children, like the army does for soldiers, and so on. Many studies of consumption all too often limit their examination to consumption by individuals, and forget about consumption by organizations. Advertisements, for example, are often addressed at organizations, not at private individuals.

The main result of *Medical Innovation* is well known, namely that the adoption of the new drug went considerably faster among doctors with many contacts to other doctors, than among doctors who were isolated. The reason for this, according to the authors, is that when people are unsure of how to behave (in this case: whether to prescribe the new drug or not), the impact of "information and reassurance" from other people is at a maximum (Coleman, Katz, and Menzel 1966:117). This finding in *Medical Innovation* is often cited in the network literature, and is generally held up as an early and important demonstration of what can be accomplished through this type of approach.

Whether this finding is all there is to the diffusion of new drugs and other commodities is, however, not clear. Throughout *Medical Innovation* the authors, for example, pay very little attention to the role of economic factors. This is obvious, not only from the questionnaire that was used, but also from the way that Coleman and his coauthors handled the information that they themselves had assembled about the activities of the salesmen who represented the drug company. These "detail men," as the salesmen were called, were, for example, singled out by the doctors themselves as *the* most important source in initially drawing their attention to the new drug (1966:58–60; cf. 179–81). A recent study in *The American Journal of Sociology* supplies further arguments that Coleman and his coauthors underestimated the importance of economic factors in their study. It is, for example, pointed out that the company that owned the new drug, Lederle, had launched a very aggressive campaign to establish it. Using new data on the role of advertisement, it is shown that the authors of *Medical Innovation* confound social contagion with marketing effects, and that when the latter is controlled for, the contagion effects disappear (Van den Bulte and Lilien 2001).

Consumer studies have accelerated and moved in different directions since the publication of *Medical Innovation*. The most spectacular study to date is Bourdieu's *Distinction: A Social Critique of the Judgment of Taste*, which appeared in 1979. Several qualities make this a landmark study (for its influence, see Longhurst and Savage 1996). One of these is its introduction of the concept of taste into the sociology of consumption. Similar to Kant, Bourdieu argues that the object of consumption is not a thing-in-itself; for there to be an object of consumption, you also have to take into account what the consumer herself brings to the object. According to *Distinction*, "objects, even industrial products, are not objective in the ordinary sense of the word, i.e., independent of the interest and tastes of those who perceive them, and they do not impose the self-evidence of universal, unanimously approved meaning" (Bourdieu [1979] 1986:100). Bourdieu's second major contribution in *Distinction* is to have moved beyond this viewpoint—a bit like the way in which Hegel and Marx moved beyond Kant's ahistorical idealism—with the help of the argument that you have to set the act of consumption in a wider social context, which includes production as well as social class, to properly explain it.

The conventional way of understanding taste, according to *Distinction*, is to view it as a capacity for aesthetic judgments in areas such as music, art, and literature. Though rarely made explicit, it is well understood that taste can be found only among the elite, and that the lower classes lack it. Bourdieu argues that it is imperative to break with this concept of taste and replace it with one that is sociological in nature. In order to do so, Bourdieu expands the concept of taste from including only "aesthetic consumption" to including "ordinary consumption," that is, the consumption of clothing, furniture, and food ([1979] 1986:100). He also extends the concept of taste to all social classes, and shows that what constitutes "good taste" is very much part of the struggle for domination in society. Taste has in Bourdieu's mind nothing to do with a disinterested view of life or disembodied values more generally. "The ultimate values, as they are called, are never anything other than the primary, primitive dispositions of the body, 'visceral' tastes and distastes, in which the group's most vital interests are embedded" (474).

In theoretical terms Bourdieu argues that taste (in its sociological sense) can be understood as one of the several social mechanisms through which a person's habitus operates. Unlike the economists, he insists that no consumer approaches commodities as if she encountered them for the first time. The consumer may make a free choice—but it will be informed by the past. More precisely, the theoretical scheme that Bourdieu operates with in *Distinction* can be described as follows. The habitus of every individual is on a general level shaped not only by the class to which the individual belongs, but also by the relationship of this class to other classes. An individual's habitus influences the way that an individual acts via two specific mechanisms: schemes of classification and taste. If many people consume the same item, a lifestyle emerges; and a lifestyle can therefore be described as a system of tastes (cf. Bourdieu [1979] 1986:171). Taste operates, according to Bourdieu, as an important and largely unconscious mechanism in the reproduction of class society, a bit like education.

Bourdieu describes *Distinction* as "very French," both in terms of its subject matter and its approach ([1979] 1986:xi–xiii). Still, the skill and imagination that inform this study make it unique from an international perspective as well. Few readers are likely to forget the most powerful parts of *Distinction*, such as the section on the food habits of the French working class. According to Bourdieu, French workers regard the male body as "a sort of power, big and strong, with imperative brutal needs"; and male workers prefer meat and sausages to "female" food, such as fish and vegetables (192). Why fish is seen as female is explained in the following way:

> In the working classes fish tends to be regarded as an unsuitable food for men, not only because it is a light food, insufficiently "filling," which would only be cooked for health reasons, i.e., for invalids and children . . .; but above all, it is because fish has to be eaten in a way which totally contradicts the masculine way of eating, that is, with restraint, in small mouthfuls, chewed gently, with the front of the mouth, on the tip of the teeth (because of the bones) (190).

During the past ten years or so the number of consumer studies has increased enormously and many new themes are currently being pursued. These include the role of lifestyles in consumption (as opposed to class-related behavior), the use of commercial credit (including credit cards), and the globalization of brand names (for general introductions with useful bibliographies, see Corrigan 1997; Slater 1997). There also exists a lively public debate about consumption—do people in the United States spend too much on useless items, for example (Schor 1998).

In economic sociology, in contrast, not much attention has been paid to consumption (see, however, Granovetter and Soong 1986; Biggart 1989; Frenzen, Hirsch, and Zerrillo 1994). One recent study, however, shows what a network approach can accomplish when applied to consumption: "Socially Embedded Consumer Transactions" by Paul DiMaggio and Hugh Louch (1998). According to the authors, it is often assumed in social science that people will use their networks to get information about potential transaction partners ("search embeddedness"), but it is much less common to find the argument that people acquire goods from *within* their own networks ("within-network exchange"). Drawing on a national survey in the United States from the mid-1990s, the authors are nonetheless able to show that in roughly one out of four cases, such items as a used car or a house were bought from someone who is a family member, a friend, a friend of a friend, or the like. Buyers were well aware of the advantages with buying from people in their own networks and especially attempted to do so when they were unlikely to buy anything else from the seller. The authors conclude that their study "demonstrates that economic sociology's view of markets as 'socially embedded' (Granovetter) is applicable to consumer markets" (DiMaggio and Louch 1998:634).

Consumer studies is a field that is very much alive today but that also sprawls in a number of different directions. Theories of consumer society, including postmodernism, view it, for example, as an autonomous field of study, reflecting the alleged autonomy of consumption in social life. From the viewpoint of economic sociology, on the other hand, consumption may have a certain autonomy—but it is also part of a much wider socioeconomic process; and as such it needs to be theoretically related not only to production and distribution but also to a series of other topics, such as savings and credit. The meaning that consumer items have for their buyers represents an indispensable part of their being and needs to be better understood than it is today. Cognitive psychology can possibly be of help in this process; at least this is what some economic sociologists currently think. The production and consumption of goods is, however, also a process that is driven by the interests of the actors—the interests of the consumers as well as the interests of the corporations that produce the products. The analysis of consumption, in brief, is incomplete if it does not address the issue of interests—including the meaning that these interests have for their actors.

Summary

This chapter continued the analysis of culture and economy from the preceding one. I argued that there was a shift during the past few decades in economic sociology, from primarily addressing the role of culture in economic development to investigating the role of culture in economic life more generally. The most significant contribution during the past few decades to this field of study has been made by Bourdieu, especially through his concept of cultural capital and his analysis of the seemingly disinterested nature of cultural fields, such as art and literature. The discussion of culture in new economic sociology has been much shaped by hostility to the Parsonian concept of culture, which then spilled over to culture in general.

As in much of contemporary sociology, economic sociology has also attempted to understand the role of trust—and with equally little success, one might add. One useful suggestion that has been made is that there exists a special type of trust in economic life, which can be called "economic trust" (Carruthers). It makes sense that trust would be more calculating in the area of the economy than, say, in the areas of love and friendship. According to this viewpoint, Coleman's notion of trust as a conscious bet fits better what goes on in an exchange between buyer and seller than what happens between wife and husband or between friends.

Consumption, just like trust, belongs to culture to the extent that it embodies something that people value. While the study of consumption for a long time has developed independently of economic sociology, it is time that an attempt be made to integrate it into economic sociology. This chapter contains an effort in this direction, and I tried especially to outline which of its contributions are of value to economic sociology. The most outstanding study of consumption in modern time, I argue, is *Distinction* by Bourdieu, with its imaginative attempt to develop a sociology of taste.

Gender and the Economy

DURING the past few decades, scholarship on the role of gender in the economy has advanced very rapidly, due to the attention that gender issues have received in academia and in society at large. This trend presents economic sociology with a unique opportunity to advance in an area of research where very little progress was made during most of the twentieth century. Innovative research has been made on a variety of topics that are of much relevance to economic sociology; and there is no doubt that gender and economy represents one of the most promising areas for the next few decades in economic sociology. It is a rich area and it will not be easily exhausted.

Up until now, however, economic sociology has on the whole failed to take advantage of this surge in research on gender and economy; economic sociology has also failed to make much of a contribution of its own to this area of research. There seems to be several reasons for this situation, and one of these may simply be the fact that most economic sociologists are male. Viviana Zelizer argues, for example, along these lines and adds that most male economic sociologists have a fairly conventional view of the economy, similar to the one that can be found in mainstream economics (Zelizer 2002).

In my own opinion, this fact may well explain why economic sociology, on the whole, has not made much of a contribution to the study of gender and economy. But there is also another reason why economic sociology has failed to assimilate much of the existing research, namely that research on gender and economy has been carried out in a number of different social science disciplines and is scattered throughout a large number of journals. No economic sociologist has been interested in trying to sift through this material and "bring back" what is relevant for economic sociology (for efforts in this direction, see Milkman and Townsley 1994; Zelizer 2002; England and Folbre forthcoming).

Sooner or later, however, this task has to be carried out if economic sociology is to be brought up to date on gender and economy. What no doubt would speed up this process would be a realization among scholars who are interested in this topic, and who do not currently identify themselves as economic sociologists, that economic sociology can provide a perspective that is helpful in generating new and important insights about gender and economy. My own view, very briefly, is that economic sociology does have a number of relevant concepts and perspectives—such as appropriation (Weber), embeddedness (Polanyi), and networks (White, Granovetter). There is also the more general fact that economic sociology has a much better understanding of the role of social relations than economics does. And as opposed to history (including economic history), economic sociology has more of an interest in generalizing its findings in the form of typologies and social mechanisms—which can also be of great help to the other social sciences.

The literature on a large number of topics that fall under the heading of economy and gender is, to repeat, scattered throughout the social sciences. The way I have chosen to deal with this situation here is to focus on what I perceive to be the two key topics, namely gender within the context of the household economy and women and work. I will start out by discussing the former topic, the reason being that an analysis of the household economy provides a structural perspective on gender and economy issues, from which it is possible to approach a series of other topics, such as work, consumption, savings, inheritance, and so on. Of these latter topics, the one that has easily attracted the most attention is work. The sections on "household, gender, and the economy" and "women, work and pay" will then be followed by a discussion of a topic that illustrates the creativity that a gender perspective can bring to economic sociology, namely emotions and the economy.

Would it be useful to introduce the concept of interest into the analysis of gender and economy? This has been argued by several feminist scholars, and I naturally agree (Folbre and Hartmann 1988; Jonasdottir 1988). There exists so much ideology about what is male and female, that it may be fruitful to start with the issue of interests. It is also clear that in order to make an effective interest analysis of gender, one has to go beyond the notion in mainstream economics that there only exists one type of interest, namely economic interest. This type of "economism," as Bourdieu calls it, is closely related to the idea that economic interest is associated with the male in the market, and altruism with the female in the family. Once inside the family, on the other hand, males are supposed to act out of altruism; and a joint utility function can therefore be used in the analysis of the family, according to mainstream economics.

But even if it is obvious that it would be much too restrictive to use only the notion of economic interests in analyses of gender and economy, does not the opposite danger also exist—that is, to introduce too many types of interests into the analysis? The candidates make a long list indeed: male interests, female interests, family interests, sexual interests, the interests of children, and emotional interests. One way to proceed in this situation would be to argue that parsimony is a virtue, and that one should try to cut down the number of interests as much as possible. Another strategy would be to argue that the tools of analysis should be decided upon depending on the type of analysis that one wants to carry out, and that there is really not much point in eliminating some interests ex ante. That all of the interests just mentioned can actually be quite useful will be illustrated by a brief discussion of each of them.

Unless biological determinism is accepted, the idea that there are male and female interests immediately raises the issue of how these two types of interest have come into being and what differentiates them. Whatever useful hints can be found in the voluminous literature on growing up as a boy versus growing up as a girl, could in my opinion be profitably merged with the emerging literature on the economic socialization of children—how children learn what property is, what money is, what it means to save, and so on (Lunt and Furnham 1996). This would introduce what is male and female into the analysis in a very natural way—and perhaps also provide some clues as to why young men and women often choose different jobs.

The existence of a general family interest, to which both male and female interests are subordinate and which is typically represented by the male, has been much criticized in the literature on gender. Already in a parliamentary debate in 1867 John Stuart Mill made the following ironic comment about males representing female interests in the name of the family:

> The interests of all women are safe in the hands of their fathers, husbands, and brothers, who have the same interest with them, and not only know, far better than they do, what is good for them, but care much more for them than they care for themselves. Sir, this is exactly what is said of the unrepresented classes. The operatives, for example: are they not virtually represented by the representation of their employers? Are not the interests of the employers and that of the employed, when properly understood, the same? . . . And, generally speaking, have not employers and employed a common interest against all outsiders, just as husband and wife have against all outside the family? And what is more, are not all employers good, kind, benevolent men, who love their workpeople, and always desire to do what is most for their good? All these assertions are as true, and as much to the purpose, as the corresponding assertions respecting men and women ([1867] 1988:150).

"I've called the family together to announce that, because
of inflation, I'm going to have to let two of you go."

But even if the oppression of women in the name of some overarching concept of family interest has been much criticized, the concept
itself can be of considerable help. This is particularly true for the period before the nineteenth century, as we soon shall see.

The idea that children have their own distinct interests may be useful in the sense that it can lead to a discussion of questions such as
the following: does an actor have to be aware of an interest for it to be
a legitimate interest; and under which conditions should a person be
allowed to represent somebody else's interest? As the total control
that parents have over their children is gradually released, there is
more room for the children to develop their own interests. It is also
clear that children very early develop their own economic interests,
and that these come to an expression in a variety of ways, in their
interactions with other children as well as with their parents (Zelizer
forthcoming a,b). That the concept of sexual interests can be helpful
in an analysis of gender and economy is obvious from the fact that
sexual attraction plays a role in heterosexual and homosexual rela-

tionships. This concept may also help to explain such phenomena as the use of sex in advertisement, the modern sex industry, and so on.

The concept of emotional interest, finally, may at first seem counterintuitive and superfluous. A reference to Viviana Zelizer's earlier cited research on children should, however, be enough to counter such a reaction. From originally having an economic as well as an emotional value, Zelizer argues, American children have come to have an exclusively emotional value for their parents (1981, 1985). In the key theoretical chapter in *Economy and Society* Weber also uses the term "emotional interest," as an example of what makes people enter into communal relationships ([1922] 1978:41).

Another helpful idea in this context from the tradition of interest analysis is Bourdieu's notion that there exist certain areas in society where "disinterested action" is the norm, such as high culture—and the family (1998b:88). Bourdieu's key argument—that disinterested actions mask as well as facilitate a certain type of interest (symbolic capital)—can also provide a useful point of departure for analyses of gender and economy. There is, for example, a division of resources that takes place in the family, often to the disadvantage of women. This does not only include money but also other resources, such as food. What the aggregate result of favoring boys over girls in this respect may look like can be read out of the title of Amartya Sen's well-known article "More Than 100 Million Women Are Missing" (1990).

Bourdieu's idea that people invest "disinterested acts" with symbolic value (since these decide whether resources will be forthcoming or not) might also be of help in explaining the tenacity of a number of traits that are typically associated with what it means to be a woman and a mother. These include warmth, care-taking, altruism, and a general lack of a competitive spirit—in brief, everything but a sharp and keen awareness of one's economic interests that is characteristic of *homo economicus*.

Household, Gender, and the Economy—
On the Family Interest

Any discussion of gender and economy will sooner or later come to the concept of household, which is indispensable to economic sociology for a number of reasons. One of these is that it helps to break with the common tendency to equate the concept of economy with that of the market and points in the direction of a much wider and more useful concept of the economy. Such a concept, I would suggest, should not only include the market and the household but also the informal economy, which is of much importance to issues of economy and gender.

It is true that one can also find a broad concept of the economy in the work of Karl Polanyi, as is clear from his argument about the three forms of integration (exchange in the market, redistribution through the state, and reciprocity among family or kin). I would, however, argue that the concept of household, when it is approached from a gender and economy perspective, may be more useful to economic sociology than Polanyi's forms of integration. One reason is that it does not start out from the idea that the family is characterized by reciprocity. There is also, of course, the convenient fact that the term "economics" comes from the Greek term for the management of a household. "The word 'economics,' Greek in origin, is compounded from *oikos*, a household, and the semantically complex root, *nem-*, here in its sense of 'regulate, administer, organize'" (Finley [1973] 1985:17).

Another advantage of using the concept of household in a discussion of gender and economy is that the species (and the labor force) is being reproduced in the household. Using the concept of the household allows one, in other words, to link up economic sociology to demography in a very natural way—something that is very important since demographic changes deeply influence the economy. The current growth of older people and decline of young people will, for example, have a huge impact on the economy in the near future (e.g., Drucker 2001).

The idea of reproduction of the species in the household also draws attention to the importance of the human body in the economy, and thereby helps to counter the exceedingly abstract nature of contemporary economics. From its original meaning as the analysis of "household management," and its later meaning as the analysis of the accumulation of "wealth," the term "economics" has evolved into something totally dematerialized (for a history of the different definitions of economics, see Kirzner 1976). Since the early twentieth century economics is primarily defined as a special perspective—as an analytical way of approaching a problem (Robbins 1932; Becker 1976). It is of course true that there are some good reasons for this way of looking at economics. Many abstract and nonmaterial items are, for example, part of the economy, from services to intellectual property. Many problems are also easier solved on the assumption that they are logical problems and that you can reason yourself to their solution. But there is also the fact that every economy is firmly anchored in the human body and its chances to survive in a material environment. Preparing food, feeding the children, cleaning the house—all of these are crucial parts of the household activities and the economy; and they should also constitute important subject matters in economic sociology. The field of household economics may not be accepted in mainstream economics but should be of much interest to economic sociology (e.g., Stage and Vincenti 1997).

For all of the reasons just mentioned, the household represents a good vantage point from which to approach an analysis of gender and economy. In the next few pages an attempt will therefore be made to trace the social structure of the household as well as its relationship to gender and economy. For the broad sweep I shall rely on Weber, who is one of the few scholars who has tried to use sociology to analyze systematically the relationship of the household to the economy, from the very beginnings of history and onward.

Weber carried out his analysis as part of an attempt in *Economy and Society* to analyze the relationship of *all* the major social groups to the economy throughout history ([1922] 1978:339–98). Since this work was produced in the 1910s the analysis obviously needs to be updated and added to, not least when it comes to the question of gender. But even with its various shortcomings, Weber's analysis represents a foundation from which to build. To show how Weber's analysis of the household can be deepened and improved upon in relation to gender and economy, I will primarily be drawing on work that covers the position of women in economic life during the period from 1700 till today.

The household represents a universal social group, according to *Economy and Society*, as do the kin group and the neighborhood (Weber [1922] 1978:356–80; cf. Weber [1923] 1981:26–27, 46–50, 225–29). In sociological terms, the household can be characterized as a closed social relationship, where the interactional pattern is centered around the sexual relationship between a man and a woman as well as the relationship between children and parents. The size of the household, and who should be included in it, has varied quite a bit throughout history. A household must nonetheless always have a certain stability, and it probably did not come into being, Weber suggests, until it was possible for humans to support themselves from agriculture. Residence in common is necessary for a household to exist. Much of the social structure of the household, Weber adds, can be described in terms of authority and loyalty. Authority gives power to the male over the female, to the parents over the children, and to the old over the young. Loyalty is very strong among all the members of a household, who also display solidarity vis-à-vis outsiders.

The primary purpose of the household is to enable human beings to survive, and it is described by Weber as "a unit of economic maintenance" ([1922] 1978:357). For this very reason the household is also "the most widespread economic group" in human society (358–59). Early in history "household communism" characterized its consumption as well as its production. The members of a household all contributed whatever they could and also took whatever they needed. The property of the household was used in common; and inheritance did not exist since the individual was subordinated to the group.

While Weber's analysis of the household and its relationship to the economy does not provide as much information about the role of gender, as one might wish today, the basic facts are noted. Inside the household one finds, for example, a "division of labor between the sexes," which constitutes "the oldest typical division of labor [in history]" ([1922] 1978:1009). Women, we are also told, are "the oldest agent of the basic economy, that is, the continuous provision of food through land cultivation and food processing" (1009). The property of the household is typically owned by the male and, as already mentioned, the male has authority over the female. Weber adds that "domestic authority and household are relatively independent of economic conditions, in spite of the latter's great importance, and appear 'irrational' from an economic point of view; in fact, they often shape economic relationships because of their historic structure" (377).

The household has evolved in different directions throughout history, according to Weber. On the one hand, it has helped to shape the economy by developing into new economic institutions; and, on the other hand, it has taken different forms in its capacity as the basic unit of economic maintenance for the individual. As an example of the former, one can point to the way that the original household developed into the large and autarchic estate that was common in antiquity as well as in the Middle Ages. Planned economies, including its socialist version, belong to this category as well. Satisfaction of needs is the main goal in this type of economy, not profit-making; in the same manner, it aims at the accumulation of wealth, not that of capital.

But the household has also developed in a market direction, first in the form of the family firm and later as the modern firm. "The family is everywhere the oldest unit supporting a continuous trading activity, in China and Babylonia, in India and in the early Middle Ages" (Weber [1923] 1981:225). One structural factor that has helped the modern firm to emerge from the household, according to Weber, is the solidarity that its members have always felt toward one another, especially in relation to outsiders. "This is the historic source," according to Weber, "of the joint liability of the owners of a private company for the debts incurred by the firm" (Weber [1922] 1978:359).

The household has varied quite a bit over time also as an economic unit of maintenance for the individual. While the male has typically had power over the female, his power has assumed different forms and different levels of intensity. In the large manorial household of antiquity, for example, patriarchy can be found in a pure form. According to Weber,

> the typical form of seigniorial development is the patriarchate. Its distinguishing characteristics are the vesting of property rights exclusively in an individual, the head of the household, from whom no one has the right to demand an accounting, and further the despotic position inherited and held for life by the patriarch. This despotism extends over wife, children, slaves, stock and implements, the *familia pecuniaque* of the Roman Law, which shows this type in its classical perfection. . . . The power of the house father extends with only ritualistic limitations to the execution, or sale of the wife, and to the sale of the children or to leasing them out to labor ([1923] 1981:47–8).

A precondition for pure patriarchy, according to Weber, is that the individual members of the household remain undifferentiated. Once there is public education, for example, this is no longer possible. The existence of a separate political authority also diminishes the need for physical protection by the patriarch. The development of money is another factor that helps to weaken patriarchy, by allowing the members of the household to calculate their exact contribution to the household. While a household that is based on property has a distinct stability, according to Weber, one that is exclusively based on work in common is unstable. In today's household you also typically live in one place and work in another. The modern household is primarily a unit for consumption in common and consists of mother, father, and children.

While *Economy and Society* does give a picture of the household from early history onward, it has considerably less to say about the role of the household in recent history. On this point Weber's work needs to be complemented and recent scholarship consulted. One work that is helpful in this is *Women, Work, and Family* by Louise Tilly and Joan Scott. This study analyzes the economic role of women from the popular classes in England and France during 1700–1950. Its focus is not so much on women as a separate category, but rather on women as part of the household and as affected by major demographic and economic trends.

For purposes of clarification it can be added that Tilly and Scott use the term family rather than household. What they mean by family, however, is roughly what Weber and others mean by household during this period, that is, "a conjugal kin group living in the same household" (Tilly and Scott 1989:7). Here as elsewhere, residence is the referent for the household, just as kinship is for the family (cf. Bender 1967).

Tilly and Scott argue that women and their relationship to work and family have changed quite a bit from 1700 to 1950 in England and France. At the beginning of this period, women were part of a "family economy," in which all work was carried out within the household. With the onset of industrialization, paid work, located outside the household, became more common, and a "family wage economy" came into being. Since the turn of the twentieth century the standard of living has increased among the working classes, and the family wage economy has been replaced by a "family consumer economy." For each of these three periods the authors analyze the social and economic role of children, unmarried daughters, married women, and widows. They also follow the evolution of what they call "the family interest," basically arguing that women as well as men during this period tried to subordinate their own individual interests to that of the family.

During the period of the *family economy* many households among the popular classes owned small plots of land in the countryside or a shop in the city. People worked and lived in the same place, and the family was primarily viewed as "an economic partnership" (Tilly and Scott 1989:43). The male as well as the female were both supposed to bring something substantial to this partnership when they married; the man either land or tools, for example, and the woman, a dowry (furniture, clothes, and the like). Inheritance was central to the transmission of the means of living; and the parents had power over the lives of their children through control of the family property.

A woman's life was burdensome at all of its different stages. As a daughter and a single woman, she would typically work in either her parents' home or as a servant in somebody else's home. Practically all women got married, since marriage represented the best chance to survive. The wife was in charge of managing the household economy, even if the husband had legal and physical power over her. The wife was, in all brevity, "the cornerstone of the family economy" (Tilly and Scott 1989:54). If the husband died, things would become very difficult since a widow could rarely remarry. Old age was hard in general, and widows could easily end up as beggars.

Women were also in charge of the children, although young ones rarely received much supervision at this stage in history. This arrangement, however, lasted only until they were old enough to work, which was at 4–5 years of age. At first the boys and the girls did similar things, but a few years later boys began to assist their fathers and girls their mothers. Tilly and Scott stress that all family members worked in the economic interest of the family, and that this interest informed most activities. If an unmarried daughter worked as a servant, for example, she was expected to hand over her salary to her family. One result of this emphasis on the family interest was that the individual always had to yield:

> In all cases, decisions were made in the interest of the group, not the individual. This is reflected in wills and marriage contracts which spelled out the obligation of siblings or elderly parents who were housed and fed on the family property, now owned by the oldest son. They must 'work to the best of their ability' for 'the prosperity of the family' and 'for the interest of the designated heir' (Tilly and Scott 1989:21).

With industrialization a new type of household economy started to come into being: *the family wage economy*. What characterized this economy was that the family had to live off wages rather than property. It was also now that the famous separation of work from home took place. Everybody in the family worked, and all of the wages were pooled to make it possible for the family to survive. The notion that most of the women began to work in factories during the industrial revolution is wrong, according to Tilly and Scott. While some women found employment in the factories, the majority did not. In brief, there was much continuity between the kind of work that women did in the early stages of industrialization and in preindustrial times.

The cycle of work that women went through during this period, which roughly lasted from the mid-eighteenth century to the end of the nineteenth century, was as follows: Young and unmarried women often worked in the textile factories. Sometimes they lived at home and sometimes not, but their wages were always handed over to the family. Being away from home and having wages of their own meant a certain independence from the family as well as a temptation to get away from the pressure of the family. Since the family and the kin provided protection, however, the vulnerability of young women also increased.

During the first few years of marriage, the economy of the household was relatively good since it was based on two full incomes. As soon as children began to arrive, however, the mother stayed at home and the family income became strained. Most of the income went to food. Married women preferred casual work and tasks that allowed them to manage the household at the same time. If the husband died or became unemployed, the wife had to leave the home and take a full-time job. Once the children left the family, some women returned

**Percent of women
in paid employment**

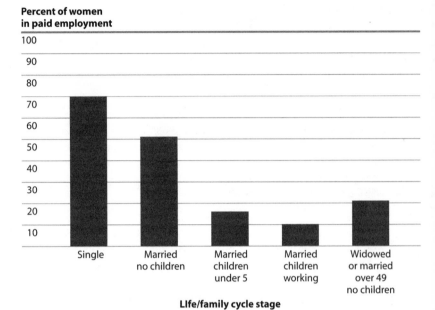

Life/family cycle stage

Figure 11.1. Schematic Diagram of Women in Paid Employment by Life/Family Cycle Stages. France and Britain, about 1850.

Note: This diagram shows the impact of industrialization and urbanization, as well as the separation of home from work, on women's work-force participation over the course of the family and life cycle.

Source: Louise Tilly and Joan Scott, *Women, Work, and Family* (New York: Holt, Rinehart and Winston, 1978), 127.

to the labor market. When women grew old their living conditions often deteriorated (see figure 11.1).

While married men were away from home during the workday, married women typically stayed at home and managed the family. The mother was responsible for the children and for everything else that had to be done in the household. She paid the bills and dealt with the landlord as well as with the pawnbroker and the local merchants. She also planned what to eat and did the cooking. "Families with mothers working away from home lived on soup and bread, or bought cooked food from itinerant street merchants until Sunday, when there was enough time to prepare a proper meal" (Tilly and Scott 1989:138). The mother was the emotional center of the family, and the children felt a deep sense of loyalty to her all their life.

Since the turn of the twentieth century onward, according to Tilly and Scott, a *family consumer economy* has emerged. What made this possible was increased productivity, primarily associated with the heavy industry that came into being around this time. Working-class families soon had some money beyond the bare necessities, and this extra money was spent on the children, on making the home look nice, and the like. "Small decorative items, pictures on the walls and flowers in the window, like a suit of good Sunday clothes, helped keep up appearances as well as make the house a more pleasant place" (Tilly and Scott 1989:208). More time had to be spent on shopping—again, by the women.

Jobs in the heavy industry were reserved for men and paid considerably more than the jobs that women could get. These latter were predominantly to be found in the many white-collar jobs that now appeared. Clerks, secretaries, teachers, shop girls, and so on were increasingly needed. Jobs in the textile industry declined, and nobody wanted to work as a servant. "[Working-class girls] preferred any kind of job in mill or factory, or even a place with rock bottom wages at Woolworth's and freedom . . . to the best that domestic service could offer" (Tilly and Scott 1989:182).

Men were paid substantially more than women during this period, and the differences between what men and women did at work also increased. Even if the incomes of the working class rose quite a bit, most of the family budget was still spent on food. In 1904, 33 percent of all English children were undernourished; and it was not until after World War I that malnutrition among children—and women—came to an end. Mothers often deprived themselves of food when times were bad. Food riots still took place and were typically led by women. A common reason for these riots was a rise in the price of bread, and women demanded a "just price" (cf. Thompson 1971).

After World War II the well-being of the working class further increased, as did the number of white-collar jobs for women. More married women than before began to work for pay. Women's income was not used for her own personal pleasure, however, but to increase the well-being of the family. It was spent on children, better food, a second-hand car, and the like. Men were still paid considerably more than women.

Throughout *Women, Work, and Family*, Tilly and Scott point to the central role of family interest. Today, as yesterday, what ultimately drives the behavior of many men and women, they argue, is family interest. Children's interests as well as those of the adults are subordinated to this more general interest. In 1989, when Tilly and Scott published the second edition of their work, they explained how they viewed their strong emphasis on the family interest in retrospect:

> As families devised strategies to cope with economic and demographic pressures, they seemed to act as coherent units. Our assumption in much of the book is that this was so, that a kind of collective ethos—a notion of shared interest—informed the behavior of individual family members. While we still think this is so, we also think our emphasis on the family as a strategic unit does not give sufficient attention to the process by which such strategies were implemented. That process involved contention, bargaining, negotiation and domination as well as consensus about what family interest was. Conflict erupted because of unequal power relationships in some instances—parents who controlled resources could force acquiescence by resistant children; husbands backed by legal codes that recognized their authority in family matters could extract compliance from their wives; men with access to better jobs demanded obedience commensurate with their status (Tilly and Scott 1989:9).

As an addendum to the study of Tilly and Scott, what they call the family consumer economy has also continued to develop very strongly after the 1950s, in France and England as well as in other OECD countries. The trend of married women entering the labor market has intensified and is one of the reasons for the growth in well-being. Another is the general rise in productivity. In many of these countries the welfare state has also helped to decrease the number of poor people (see table 7.4 in chap. 7).

As to the growing entry of women into the labor market during the post–World War II period, several studies indicate that this process has much to do with the possibility of getting childcare. This can be arranged either through the market—you hire someone to take care of the children while you are away at work—or by having the state subsidize childcare. The former option is only effective on a large scale in countries where the care-giver's wages are low, as in the United States. Some states therefore pursue the second option.

From the late 1960s onward a few welfare states, especially in the Nordic countries, have invested heavily in subsidized childcare, while other states have been reluctant to do so. The relationship between women in the labor force and assistance for childcare is straightforward: the more support there is from the welfare state, the more women there will be in the labor force (Esping-Andersen 1999:59–60; for the situation in the United States, see also Reskin and Padavic 1994:157). In some countries the household has also changed in another fundamental way during the past few decades, thanks to the welfare state. This has to do with taking care of the elderly. While this task formerly fell on the household (and particularly on women), some states have now begun to take it over—by helping the aged in their homes, by financing homes for the elderly, and so on.

Women, Work, and Pay—On Women's Interests

While the concept of family interest is useful for analyzing gender and economy within the setting of the household, once women enter the labor market you also need the concept of women's interests. Tilly and Scott have shown that when young women in the eighteenth century started to work for a wage, away from the home, their potential independence from the family household increased dramatically. More generally, it would seem that once women enter the labor market in large numbers, their individual interests become more accentuated and clear to themselves. This is naturally also the case for men; and clashes between the interests of men and women have increased during the past few centuries. The idea of an overarching family interest has by no means disappeared, but it has changed under the impact of the growing awareness by men and women of their individual interests.

One example of the increased awareness of women's interests involves the perception of the work that women do in the household. For a long time these activities were invisible, or, more precisely, they did not count as "work." They were not, for example, included in the measures for national income, which were developed in the 1930s which still are in use (Perlman 1987). Neither were cleaning, cooking, and so on perceived as "work" in public discourse.

Sociologists had a similar attitude and did not make use of the concepts that they had developed in industrial sociology and the sociology of work when they studied women's activities in the household. But as Ann Oakley has shown in *The Sociology of Housework*, these types of concepts—autonomy, monotony at work, and so on—also fit the activities of housewives (1974). In her study of London housewives, Oakley shows, for example, that what women like the most about being a housewife is that "you're your own boss"; and what they dislike the most is "housework" and the "monotony/repetitiousness/boredom" associated with being a housewife (1974:43).

Some time after Oakley's pioneering study, sociologists began to study women's work in the household with the help of time budgets. Today there exists a wealth of studies of this type, which compare the number of hours that women and men spend on work in the house-

TABLE 11.1.
Time Spent on Household and Tasks by Full-Time Workers in the United
States, Measured in Hours per Week, 1987

Household Tasks	Men	Women	Men as Percentage of Women
preparing meals	3.0	8.0	37.5
washing dishes	2.3	5.2	44.2
house cleaning	2.1	6.6	31.8
outdoor tasks	4.9	2.1	42.8*
shopping	1.7	2.9	58.6
washing, ironing	1.0	3.8	26.3
paying bills	1.6	2.0	80.0
auto maintenance	2.0	0.4	20.0*
driving	1.2	1.7	70.6

*Women as a percentage of men.
Note: Women do much more work in the home than men do. Two of the activities in this table—shopping and paying bills—are of special interest to economic sociology. While there exists quite a bit of information about the former, very little is known about the latter.
Source: Anne Shelton Beth, *Women, Men, and Time: Gender Differences in Paid Work, Housework and Leisure* (New York: Greenwood Press, 1992), 83.

hold. All of these show that women work much more, also when they have a full-time job with pay. They have, in a sense, a "second shift" waiting for them when they come home from work (Hochschild 1989). In 1998 in the United States, for example, women devoted 29 hours of work per week to the household, compared to 18 for men (England and Folbre forthcoming). It is true that men spend more hours than women in paid work (38 versus 30 hours per week in 1998). All in all, however, women work more hours than men (59 hours versus 56 hours per week 1998).

Another research result from this type of study is that the difference in hours that men and women devote to household tasks has changed very slowly over the past few decades; and that it is also reproduced in the amount of housework that daughters and sons do (Reskin and Padavic 1994:149–52). Furthermore, women and men do different things in the household. Men typically take care of outdoor tasks and the car, while women prepare the food, keep the house clean, and engage in "caring labor " (e.g., Folbre 2001). Shopping is another task that largely falls upon women (see table 11.1).

Just as work at home has gradually been reconceptualized as a result of women getting jobs in the labor market, so has the idea of an overriding family interest come to be replaced by the notion that several interests clash and contend with one another inside the family. As

one student of this issue has put it, "Instead of a unit of shared interests, it may be more appropriate to view the family as a bargaining
unit where negotiations can cover a wide range of decisions involving
the allocation of money, time and the division of market and domestic
work" (Hobson 1990:237).

One source of conflict that has been much discussed in recent
studies has to do with the economic resources of the family and who
decides over these: the husband, the wife, or the two of them jointly.
It has, for example, been suggested that it is possible to develop a
measure for married women's "economic dependency" on their husband (Sørensen and McLanahan 1987). Arguing that A's dependency
on B is the same as B's power over A, economic dependency has been
operationalized as the difference between the husband's and the
wife's relative contributions to their combined income. Using this
measure it can be shown that the number of women in the United
States who were 100% dependent on their husbands declined sharply
during the years 1940–1980 (from 83.7% to 30%, for women in white
couples; and from 68.5% to 27.1 %, for women in nonwhite couples).
About 50% of all married women are still economically dependent on
their husbands (10% to 100% dependence), while the same figure for
men is about 10%. It has also been shown that the overall relationship
in different countries between general level of inequality and economic dependency for women is relatively weak. While Germany, for
example, is relatively equal, German women are very dependent on
German men. The United States, on the other hand, is much more
unequal than Germany—but American women are less dependent on
American men (Hobson 1990).

In the concept of economic dependency it is assumed that married
people pool their resources and share them equally; and this assumption has recently been much criticized. It appears that in reality couples handle their economic resources in a number of different ways:
each partner may be in charge of his or her own resources; the couple
may pool some of their resources; or the two may pool all of their
resources (Pahl 1989). A difference must also be made between managing the family's income on an everyday basis and having the
power to make strategic economic decisions, since the two do not
always coincide. In a recent study of couples in England and Sweden,
for example, it was found that the wives are likely to be in charge of
the budget in a low-income household, where paying the bills and
making economic decisions is a chore, while the men tend to take
over when the income increases and becomes a source of power (Roman and Vogler 1999).

A large number of studies in the area of gender and economy are devoted to what happens to women outside of the household, once they enter the labor market. Three important themes for economic sociology in this type of research are the following: what women do at work; how they are promoted; and how they are paid. A number of interesting studies of women in economic professions—such as banking and real estate—exist as well (e.g., Strober and Arnold 1987; Bird 1990; Thomas and Reskin 1990).

It should also be noted that economists have suggested a number of theories to account for discrimination in the labor market, of women as well as of minorities. According to one of these, employers may choose to discriminate—but they have to pay for this since they will not be able to get the best employees (Becker 1957). According to another theory—the theory of statistical discrimination—employers judge the productivity of a potential employee on the basis of their perception of the group to which the worker belongs (Arrow 1972). A young woman may not be hired, for example, because the employer may think that young women tend to have children and be away from work. There is also the theory that employees get paid according to their education; and that women receive lower pay since they typically do not have as much education as men (for human capital theory, see Becker 1964). According to sociologists, these theories can explain some of the inequality of women in the labor market—but by no means as much as a sociological approach could (for overviews and critiques, see England 1994; England and Folbre forthcoming; Reskin and Padavic 1994:32–43, 110–20; see also Bielby and Bielby 1988).

Much research, to repeat, has recently been devoted to the theme of what kind of paid work women do. In *Women and Men at Work*, Barbara Reskin and Irene Padavic argue, for example, that the sexual division of labor goes far back in history and is still very strong. They also point out that there are several different ways in which one can approach the gender discrimination at work from a sociological perspective. One way would be to use the so-called index of segregation, whereby you look at the number of women or men who would have to change to another occupation, in which their sex is underrepresented, for there to be equality between the sexes. Between 1900 and 1970 in the United States, the index of segregation was between 65 and 69, and by 1990 it had fallen to 53 (Reskin and Padavic 1994:54, 61). By 2000 it appears that the figure was a few points lower (England and Folbre forthcoming).

The figure for sex segregation today is about twice that of race segregation, which means that twice as many women would have to move for all occupations to be integrated in terms of gender, than the number of women of color who would have to move for there to be racial integration. The actual segregation, it should also be added, is in reality higher than these figures indicate since census figures are used in estimating sex segregation, which means that segregation *within* occupations is not taken into account. To what extent the labor force is segregated at the firm level is another aspect of this issue that census figures do not capture.

The fact that women have been kept away from the better jobs and/or failed to find any job at all, has sometimes made women create their own economic organizations. A growing literature on female entrepreneurship is a sign of this phenomenon, even if it should be noted that this type of forced entrepreneurship has in many cases led to a very low income (Reskin and Padavic 1994:85; for female entrepreneurship more generally, see Allen and Truman 1993). A special mention should in this context be made of Nicole Woolsey Biggart's fascinating study of direct selling organizations, such as Tupperware, Amway, and so on. As she explains in *Charismatic Capitalism* (1989), these types of organizations have typically been founded by women, and the labor force is mainly female. Women who work for such organizations as Tupperware are often married women who want to supplement their income and who have husbands who do not want their wives "to work." These organizations have also realized that there exists a huge (and cheap) pool of skillful women, who are very eager to work but who lack formal qualifications and experience to get a good job.

As to the theme of women and promotion, it is clear that in all countries women tend to end up at the bottom of the ladder and men at the top—even in female-dominated professions. When women do get a foothold in a male-dominated profession and succeed in climbing upwards—say as bank tellers or clerks—it is usually because the men are in the process of leaving the profession. The difficulties that women have in advancing in the average corporation have been analyzed in a classic work in the gender and economics literature, *Men and Women of the Corporation* by Rosabeth Moss Kanter (1977). Kanter points out that the many obstacles to advancement encountered by women in the average corporation are structural in nature, not individual. Men prefer by tradition to see other men and similar men in the top positions ("homosocial reproduction," in Kanter's terminology). The few women who do succeed in making it high up in the corporation have also an extra heavy burden to carry since they are viewed as a representatives of all women rather than as an individuals ("tokenism"). Women low down in the corporation know that their opportunities to advance are minimal and adjust their aspirations accordingly. Secretaries and female clerical workers may also form groups that exert considerable pressure on the individual members *not* to move upward and leave the rest of the group behind. As to exploring the theme of women and pay, it is common to begin by looking at the earnings ratio between the sexes, that is, at women's earnings divided by men's pay. For several decades before 1998 the ratio was around 60 percent. During the 1980s, however, it changed to 70 percent, where it has roughly remained ever since (2000:73 percent; England and Folbre forthcoming). Several factors account for this huge difference. It was, for example, common during the mid to late twentieth century for women and men to be paid differently even if they did exactly the same thing—something that today is outlawed in many countries. What accounts now for most of the difference in income between men and women is in all likelihood, however, something else. It is sex segregation at the job level and a failure to pay women and men the same amount, even when they have jobs that are fully equivalent in terms of skill, difficulty, and so on ("comparable worth"—see England 1992).

In general, what seems to be at the bottom of this phenomenon is a very long-standing and more or less universal devaluation of women's work. This devaluation may come to a conscious expression in the actions of employers and male workers, but to a large extent it may also be unconscious—and therefore extra difficult to come to terms with. According to Barbara Reskin, recent advances in cognitive psychology may be of help in mapping out sexist behavior of the latter type. Experiments show, for example, that individuals automatically categorize people into in- and out-groups, and that they also systematically underestimate within-group differences and exaggerate between-group differences. When the members of a group are male, it is clear that men and women will tend to be treated differently—even if none of the men is aware of this and consciously intends to keep women out (Reskin 2002).

Emotions and the Economy

The literature on women and work shows that there exists a host of topics that economic sociology should start paying attention to. One of these, which has not been discussed so far, has to do with the role of emotions in economic life (see Berezin forthcoming a; Pixley forthcoming). What makes this topic so important is that ever since economics adopted the fiction of "rational economic man" in the nineteenth century, the role of the emotions in the economy has been pushed aside and essentially ignored. This stance is justified in modern economics on the ground that one can perfectly well understand the economy without taking emotions into account (for the role of emotions in economic theory, see Elster 1998).

How economic analysis has come to take this position can be explained in several ways. One would be to draw on Weber's analysis in *The Protestant Ethic* with its argument about the ascetic Protestant who tried to control his life, including his emotions, and act in a methodical manner. The notion of an emotional union with God, as in Lutheranism, was also utterly alien to the Calvinists. All of this stern discipline was later translated into the economic ethic of someone like Benjamin Franklin, who advocated "the earning of more and more money, combined with the strict avoidance of all spontaneous enjoyment of life" (Weber [1904–05] 1958:53; cf. Barbalet 2000).

Another attempt to explain how emotions came to be eliminated from economic theory can be found in *The Passions and the Interests* by Albert O. Hirschman (1977), which replaces an interest analysis of the Weberian type with a history of ideas approach. In this study he argues that a number of thinkers in the seventeenth and eighteenth centuries began to believe that "interests," in the form of trade and commerce, could be used to calm "the passions" of the feudal lord and princes, and thereby replace a war-torn society with a peaceful and prosperous one. From this time onward, Hirschman argues, it has been believed that emotions must be repressed when rational economic decisions are made—and also when these are analyzed.

The idea about the need to repress emotions in order to make the right economic decision is still part of the ruling economic ethic, as illustrated with a quote from recent ethnographic studies of the bond market in New York (Abolafia 1996, 1998). One of the goals of these traders is precisely "emotional control":

> The bond traders' ideal is the trader who is disciplined, cool-headed and focused. Traders engage in a continuous stream of fateful decisions involving millions of dollars. . . . As one explained, "I have a first rule of survival: not to become too personally involved in the market. Otherwise you can get caught up in fighting this thing and you can't win." Such expressions of emotional distance are made to confirm the traders' own sense of control as well as reflect it to whomever may be watching (1998:72–73).

The theme that emotions can erupt and destroy rational economic decisions is still the predominant one in economics, from Robert Shiller's analysis of the bull market in the 1990s to Paul Krugman's writings on "the fear economy" in the wake of the September 11 attack on the World Trade Center. While Shiller (2000) argues that investors with a high degree of optimism believe that the market will go up forever ("irrational exuberance"), Krugman points out that many Americans helped to push the economy downward after the September 11 attack, "feeling that having a good time was in bad taste" (2001a; cf. Krugman 2001b). That a similar approach to emotions also informs a sociological analysis of the spectacular crash in 1998 of Long-Term Capital Management is clear from its title: "Fear in the Markets" (MacKenzie 2000).

There does, however, exist a different way of looking at the role of emotions in economic life, as illustrated by the pioneer analysis in *The Managed Heart: Commercialization of Human Feeling* by Arlie Hochschild (1983). The major concern in this work is that many jobs in modern society have a strategic emotional component, and that this may be exploited by ruthless employers. Flight attendants and bill collectors, to use Hochschild's two main examples, do not only physical labor but also "emotional labor," that is, an important part of their job consists of inducing a special emotion in the customer: a sense of satisfaction in the airplane passenger and a sense of fear or shame in the debtor. By constantly having to psyche themselves up in order to induce these feelings in other people flight attendants and bill collectors run the risk, according to Hochschild, of disturbing their emotional life, especially their capacity to generate emotions in a spontaneous way. What is potentially dangerous for these people is constantly to perform what Hochschild calls "deep [emotional] acting," as exemplified by psyching oneself up, in contrast to mere "surface acting," like smiling when one has to.

Many more people than flight attendants and bill collectors do emotional labor as part of their jobs. This is, for example, the case with secretaries, sales people, social workers, ministers, and lawyers. Hochschild estimates that something like one third of the U.S. labor force does emotional labor; half of all employed women and one fourth of all men. Women typically specialize in the flight attendant type of work (that is, in pleasing and assisting others), while men specialize in the bill-collecting type (that is, in dominating and ordering others around). Since women typically lack material resources of their own, they often have to resort to emotions in order to get these. The low status of women in general also makes it much easier to take out one's anger on them; they lack what Hochschild calls "the status shield" of men. Passengers are typically more abusive to female flight attendants when things go wrong, than to male flight attendants.

What is new in Hochschild's analysis is that she does not see emotions as something that disturbs economic life, but as something that is an integral and organic part of it (cf. Lawler and Thye 1999). "We are all partly flight attendants," as she puts it (1983:11). This idea has its own ancestry in social theory: for example, in David Hume's notion that there are "calm passions" (as well as "violent passions"), and that interests and passions go together rather than oppose one another ([1739–40] 1978:417). Terms such as "interested affection," and "the passion of self-interest" are a reminder of this latter fact (492; cf. William James's notion of "the sentiments of rationality"— [1897] 1956).

The research agenda that is implicit in Hochschild's argument would then consist of exploring the role of emotions in everyday economic life—phenomena such as the fear of unemployment, the hope for economic success, the despair when one goes bankrupt or loses money through inflation or in other ways. Adam Smith pointed out in *The Theory of Moral Sentiments* that "the poor man . . . is ashamed of his poverty" ([1759] 1976:113). Proceeding along these lines would effectively counteract the current tendency to see the notion of interest as essentially nonemotional and highly rational/cognitive in nature. Emotions and interests, I would argue, often go together and are also similar in that both are deeply rooted in human nature and not easily suppressed.

Summary

Just as culture has often been ignored in economic sociology, so has gender. The literature on gender and economy, which has come into being during the past few decades, is little known in economic sociology. This presents a problem, especially since the relevant studies are scattered in several disciplines. In an attempt to help integrate some of this work into economic sociology, the following three topics were discussed in this chapter: the role of gender and economy in the household; the situation of women in the labor market; and the role of emotions in the economy.

For early developments in the history of the household the work of Weber is referred to. Much space and attention is also given to the analysis by Louise Tilly and Joan Scott of the situation of peasant and working-class women during 1700–1950 in France and England. These two authors emphasize the crucial role that the family interest played during this period to hold the household together and to integrate its members. During the past century women's role has increased in the labor market and the family interest has decreased in importance. Today's family can be characterized as the result of different and conflicting interests.

Women are treated differently on the job than men: women do different things and they are paid less, even when they do the same thing as men. Various theories have been advanced to explain these facts, by economists as well as sociologists. According to one of these, the discrimination of women that takes place in the labor market is largely unconscious; and this means that new ways to fight it have to be devised (Reskin 2002). In general, it appears that the discrimination of women is directly related to the devaluation of women in society, which is universal in nature.

The gender and economy perspective has led to many new and interesting insights into economic life. One of these has to do with the role of emotions in the economy—a topic that has been pioneered by Arlie Hochschild in *The Managed Heart*. As opposed to the conventional view that emotions always lead to a disturbance of the economy—people, for example, make bad economic decisions when they get "emotional"—Hochschild suggests that emotions constitute an organic part of many economic acts. This suggestion could be translated into an exciting research agenda for economic sociology—and help close the gap between "the passions and the interests."

XII

The Cat's Dilemma and Other Questions for Economic Sociologists

THIS concluding chapter is devoted to a series of issues that invite discussion rather than exposition and analysis as did the topics in the earlier chapters. The first issue on the agenda is what to do with the various topics that have been left out of economic sociology ("Issue # 1: The Question of Structural Holes in Economic Sociology"). Why have certain topics been ignored and how can this be remedied? This is followed by a section on the role of interests in economic sociology ("Issue # 2: The Concept of Interest and Its Role in Economic Sociology"). Since the main theoretical claim of this book is to have systematically introduced the concept of interest into economic sociology, what has been said on this topic in the earlier chapters needs to be summarized and discussed. One objection to using the concept of interest that has to be dealt with, for example, is the argument that if everything is due to interests, the notion of interest runs the risk of becoming redundant. Another is the argument that the concept of interest is reductionistic in nature.

A third issue that is important to touch on before this book comes to an end is the issue of objectivity and reflexivity, or the extent to which economic sociologists need to reflect on the conditions under which their own analyses have come into being and the extent to which they are reasonably objective ("Issue # 3: The Role of Objectivity and Reflexivity in Economic Sociology"). I will also argue that the discussion of reflexivity should be extended to include the production of economic knowledge in general, including economic theory, economic ideologies, and the role of economic news in the media.

The last issue on the agenda in this chapter is perhaps the most important of all: to what extent can economic sociology be used outside of academia, as a policy science ("Issue # 4: Should Economic Sociology be a Policy Science?"). This is the issue I had in mind when I decided to call this chapter "The Cat's Dilemma and Other Questions for Economic Sociologists." My viewpoint can perhaps best be summed up by the cartoon depicting a cat contemplating how to get a ball on a table. Should she first try to figure out exactly how this can be done theoretically and then get the ball? Or should she forget about the analysis and just go for the ball? There are a few other meanings that can be read into this cartoon as well if one looks at it with economic sociology in mind—but this I leave for the reader (see the cartoon on the next page).

Issue # 1: The Question of Structural Holes in Economic Sociology

Since its rebirth in the 1980s, economic sociology has devoted much effort to analyzing key topics in the economy, such as the role of corporations, banks, and networks. It has, however, failed to address a number of important topics, and as a result of this several "structural holes" have appeared (cf. Aspers 2001a). The metaphor of structural holes is useful in this context because it draws attention to the fact that these holes have not appeared in a random fashion, due simplt to the economic sociologist's inability to cover everything. On the contrary, there is a story behind each of these holes that it is important to know.

That this is the case can be illustrated by referring to some of the holes that this book has attempted to fill. That economic sociology has paid so little attention to the role of gender in the economy (chap. 11) is obviously related to the more general lack of interest for gender issues that is characteristic of all the social sciences and which is due to the devaluation of women. Why so little attention has been paid to law (chap. 8) is less easy to pinpoint. Perhaps it is because law and sociology are taught in different parts of the university and are also very different in nature. While professors of law essentially teach their students a practical skill that can be used in society, professors of sociology teach their students a certain way of analyzing problems— a skill for which there is little need outside of academia. Finally, consumption (chap. 10) is often disregarded by economic sociologists; and one reason is that this topic has a tradition of being studied by sociologists who specialize exclusively in consumption.

But why should economic sociology be so concerned with filling all of these structural holes? Is it not the case that economic sociology is a distinct perspective, and that it cannot possibly cover all of economic life in an encyclopaedic manner, especially since it is so young? This is true. Still, it would be odd if economic sociology did not discuss all the main topics in economic life. A student who takes a course in economic sociology, or who reads a general book in this field, should be able to get some sociological insight into all of the major areas of economic life.

This, however, is *not* the case today; and as examples of the many

structural holes that currently exist, the following can be mentioned:
entrepreneurship, stratification, and *the potential use of game theory in economic sociology.* Many others could be added, such as risk, technology, and the relationship between demography and economic sociology. The first three, however, will have to do for now since I want basically to illustrate the general issues involved.

It is, for example, clear that the existing literature on entrepreneurship, stratification, and game theory in the other social sciences can add substantively to economic sociology, both in terms of factual knowledge and in terms of theory. This is true not only for economics but also for economic history and economic anthropology, which are still largely untapped by economic sociologists. In some cases it is simply enough to highlight the sociological part of some insight in a neighboring social science, and downplay its nonsociological part, in order to turn it into economic sociology. This, for example, is the case with many of the studies of consumption that have been produced by social and economic historians. In many cases the difference between economic sociology and related social sciences is also terminological in nature.

If the minimum strategy for economic sociology, in handling structural holes, would be simply to "import" studies from outside of economic sociology without adding much of its own, the maximum strategy would be to produce innovative analyses by drawing on the tradition of economic sociology. The latter strategy is preferable for several reasons. For instance, if economic sociology would be able to develop an innovative approach to such topics as gender, law, consumption, and so on, students in the other social sciences would want to work in economic sociology. Economic sociology would also be freed from the burden of having to follow very closely what is going on in the other social sciences, instead of focusing on studies of its own.

While many economic sociologists agree on the existence of certain structural holes, this is by no means always the case. Economic sociology can be defined in different ways, and the ambitions for the field also vary. Of the three topics that I mentioned earlier, it seems fairly obvious that entrepreneurship should be part of the repertoire of economic sociology, and the sooner this happens the better. It is, however, more difficult to know how to deal with the other topics, and if they really constitute structural holes (stratification and game theory).

Entrepreneurship has been of little interest to social scientists during the twentieth century, including sociologists, but is today in the process of constituting itself as an interdisciplinary field, somewhat like organization theory after World War II. Economic sociologists, however, have been slow to realize that entrepreneurship plays a key role in the economy and will do so even more in the future (for some exceptions, see Thornton 1999; Swedberg 2000b; Aldrich forthcoming). In business schools all around the world, entrepreneurship is today being taught, just as courses in management have been taught for half a century; and the hope is clearly to turn entrepreneurship into a teachable and routinized skill.

The sociology of entrepreneurship would first of all have to break with the asocial individualism that pervades this field, from the attempt by psychologists to find the entrepreneurial personality to the focus on the entrepreneur as an actor who singlehandedly builds a fortune and an empire. One way to proceed would be to analyze entrepreneurship as a group activity, along the lines that Rosabeth Moss Kanter has suggested in *The Change Masters* (Kanter 1983; cf. Kanter 1988). The entrepreneur, from this perspective, is primarily a person who can motivate other people, coordinate their efforts, and weld them together into a group that can realize the goal that she has chosen. Another approach would be to analyze entrepreneurship with the help of network theory. Entrepreneurship, from this perspective, can, for example, be conceptualized as an attempt to string together resources with the help of a broker standing midway between different networks that are in need of each other (Burt 1992). The entrepreneur, in this scenario, essentially makes her profit by controlling the traffic between the networks.

Of much interest in recent studies of entrepreneurship is the issue of startups. Comparative studies of frequency rates in various countries have began to appear but still have some way to go (Aldrich 1999). Contrary to what was earlier believed, it has also been established that the initial vision of the entrepreneur has an important impact on the structure of the firm as well as on its performance (Baron and Hannan forthcoming). A firm where the employees have been handpicked because of their personal commitment tends, for example, to do better than a firm where the employees have been selected in a conventional manner. When a firm is started up, there is also a need for inputs of various kinds from other firms, such as law firms, venture capital firms, and the like; and the way that this is handled is very important for the development of the firm (Castilla et al. 2000).

It is also clear that sociologists can make use of the insights about entrepreneurship that have been produced in the neighboring social sciences, including economics. While economists on the whole have ignored entrepreneurship, there exist some outstanding exceptions. There is first and foremost the work of Joseph Schumpeter, who is the founder of the study of entrepreneurship and whose definition of entrepreneurship is still very useful: *the putting together of a novel combination of resources* (1912:chap. 2, 1934:chap. 2, forthcoming). There is also the work of the neo-Austrians on entrepreneurship as a form of arbitrage (Kirzner 1973, 1997). According to this approach, the entrepreneur is someone who is constantly on the outlook for opportunities to buy low and sell high. While Schumpeter's entrepreneur breaks an equilibrium, the activities of the neo-Austrian entrepreneur help to establish it. The work of William Baumol also contains many interesting ideas, one being that entrepreneurship can be destructive as well as constructive (1993). What differentiates the two is the social structure and social context within which entrepreneurship takes place.

The issue of *stratification* as a structural hole differs from that of entrepreneurship on several accounts. The most important of these is that stratification and economic sociology have been treated as two distinct subfields in sociology since its very beginnings; and this is something that is still seen as perfectly natural by most sociologists. Max Weber, for example, discusses economic sociology and stratification in two different parts of *Economy and Society* (1922); the former in chapter 2 ("Sociological Categories of Economic Action") and the latter in Chapter 4 ("Status Groups and Classes").

Little attempt has also been made by the leading experts on stratification to relate their work in some fundamental way to economic sociology—and vice versa for economic sociologists. Still, it is clear that the two fields do connect and also overlap at several points. Property, for example, is important to both of them, and so is consumption. One can also mention the topic of labor markets, since it involves conventional stratification issues as well as attempts to understand the way in which markets operate (e.g., Granovetter 1986; Reskin and Padavic 1994).

Property, it seems to me, is an example of a topic with much potential for further development in this context. Weber's analysis of situations in which actors are consciously excluded from some opportunity plays, for example, a key role in his concept of property as well as in his theory of stratification. While this has led to quite a bit of work on stratification, this is not the case with property (for "closure theory," see Parkin 1979; Murphy 1984, 1988).

It would also seem obvious that economic sociology and stratification theory would both be interested in the recent changes that have taken place in the property structure of industrial countries, from individuals being the main owners to institutions. Roughly 60 percent of the assets of the one thousand largest corporations in the United States are today owned by institutions, such as pension funds, mutual funds, and insurance companies (Davis and McAdam 2000:201). Also, while stratification theorists know much about income inequality, there has been little research on "wealth inequality" (Western 2001). What is very clear, however, is that the latter is much more unequal. While data from the beginning of the 1990s in the United States indicate that the top 1 percent received 16 percent of all income, the equivalent figure for wealth was 40 percent (Keister 2000b).

Similarly, economic sociology and stratification theory have both an interest in the topic of lifestyles and how these are related to the way in which the economy works. In economic sociology this interest grows out of its concern with consumption; and, as mentioned in Chapter 10, the concept of lifestyle has replaced class as the relevant unit of analysis in some contemporary studies of consumption. The concept of lifestyle has, on the other hand, always been important to stratification theory, or at least since Weber opposed class and production to status and consumption/lifestyle. Recently it has also been suggested by some experts on stratification that lifestyle and consumption have replaced class and production as the major source of differentiation in modern society (for an introduction to this literature as well as a rebuttal, see Grusky and Weeden 2001).

In my opinion there also exists another argument why economic sociology should try to incorporate some of the findings of stratification theory. As I see it, it would be very strange if economic sociology was *not* concerned with the end result of the economic process—or who gets what and how. Exactly how a substantial link between economic sociology and stratification theory can be forged is something that needs to be discussed. This type of enterprise would also help to counteract a certain tendency in today's economic sociology to deal only with the upper layer of the economy—with the corporations and their CEOs.

As to *game theory*—the last of my three examples—and its potential use in economic sociology, it should be noted that most economic sociologists are not interested in game theory and see little place for it in their field. The reason is that game theory uses a rational choice perspective; that it draws heavily on mathematics; and that it has strong links to standard economic theory. It is also difficult (if at all possible) to establish empirically what strategies of action are open to an actor and what their respective payoffs are. Moreover, it seems difficult to use game theory in quantitative research of the type that sociology specializes in. A well-known methodologist has, for example, stated that "unfortunately, it has turned out to be very difficult to do empirical work, using GT models" (Petersen 1994:501).

Some additional reasons why sociologists may find it hard to use game theory may be found in Erving Goffman's well-known essay on strategic interaction:

> Persons often don't know what game they are in or whom they are playing for until they have already played. Even when they know about their own position, they may be unclear as to whom, if anybody, they are playing against, and, if anyone, what his game is, let alone his framework of possible moves. Knowing their own possible moves, they may be quite unable to make any estimate of the likelihood of the various outcomes or the value to be placed on each of them. . . . Of course, these various difficulties can be dealt with by approximating the possible outcomes along with the value and likelihood of each, and casting the result in a game matrix; but while this is justified as an exercise, the approximations may have (and be felt to have), woefully little relation to the facts ([1961] 1972:149–50).

Much of this critique of game theory and its possible use in sociology may well be true, but it appears to me that game theory could still have a role to play in economic sociology. My own preference would be for game theory of a fairly elementary type, such as prisoners' dilemma and Thomas Schelling's work (for a fuller discussion of this and related issues, see Swedberg 2001). I also would argue that there do exist quite a number of situations in economic life where strategic thinking plays a crucial role—and game theory may be helpful in these.

Weighing all of the arguments together, it seems that we are currently far away from having the kind of game theory that we need in sociology. Phillip Bonacich, who has pioneered the use of game theory in sociology, may well be correct in his assessment:

> With respect to the future, my feeling is that sociologists don't know game theory and economists, who do, are hopelessly naïve about social structures. The best work remains to be done by those who have mastered both disciplines (Bonacich 2000).

Issue # 2: The Concept of Interest and Its Role in Economic Sociology

While the dominant approach in economic sociology emphasizes the importance of social relations for a proper understanding of the economy, I argue that while this is important, interests should be an equally integral part of the analysis. Institutions, for example, should be seen as distinct constellations of interests *and* social relations. An economic sociology that ignores the role of interests, I argue, runs the risk of becoming trivial because interests, much more so than social relations, is what drives economic action. This is by no means a novel insight, as the work of Weber and others show. It is, however, a position that has been forgotten in much of modern economic sociology.

Since this argument is obviously important for an economic sociology centered around the concept of interest, I will first quickly summarize the case for an economic sociology that assigns a key role to the concept of interest, and then indicate some issues that need to be addressed. These latter include how interest should be defined and how to go about an analysis that takes interests seriously. There are also the questions of circularity and reductionism. It is sometimes argued that an analysis that draws on interests runs the risk of being tautological. It tries to explain everything as the result of some interest, similar to the way one of the characters in a play by Molière explains the sleep-inducing effect of opium by its "dormative quality." Interest analysis, it is also argued, has a tendency to reduce everything in a mechanical way to some interest. Finally, we must consider the relationship between interest and motivation, its equivalent in psychology.

The idea that the concept of interest should be central to the analysis of social reality is common enough, as I have tried to show in this book. It stretches back to the very beginnings of social theory, and it can be found in the works of many of the classical social theorists as well as the founders of sociology. Among the former are David Hume, Adam Smith, and Alexis de Tocqueville; and among the latter Max Weber, Emile Durkheim, and Georg Simmel. Also some of the major sociologists of modern times have assigned an important part to the concept of interest in their analyses. This is especially the case with James Coleman and Pierre Bourdieu—two figures who usually end up in opposite corners.

Much more could have been said in this book about the general history of the concept of interest, but I have not had the ambition to improve on the works of Stephen Holmes and others in this regard, with one exception, however: I have wanted to show that there also exists *a sociological concept of interest*, which was developed around 1900. The basic idea of Weber, Simmel, and a few other thinkers is that interests can be realized only within the framework of society, and that the role of social relations always has to be taken into account in an analysis of interests.

As opposed to some writers on the concept of interest, I am favorably disposed to this concept and advocate its use. I think that it should be regarded as a major concept in the social sciences, and that it is absolutely indispensable to economic sociology. If sociologists use the concept of interest in their analyses, they tend to do so in a casual and unreflective manner, which differs from the way in which they usually deal with key concepts. "Throughout the tradition of sociological analysis [the concept of interest] is often referred to without further specification," as one commentator points out (Demeulenaere 2001:7715). Key concepts, in contrast, are typically discussed and defined in standard works; they are consciously improved upon; and they are taught to students in introductory courses and texts—all of which is currently *not* the case with the concept of interest in sociology. The concept of interest, in brief, constitutes a "proto-concept," in Robert Merton's terminology:

> "A *proto-concept* is an early, rudimentary, particularized, and largely unexplicated idea . . .; a *concept* [however] is a general idea which once having been defined, tagged, substantially generalized, and explicated can effectively guide inquiry into seemingly diverse phenomena" (1984:267; emphasis added).

I have also argued that a watershed took place in the history of the concept of interest when economists, toward the end of the nineteenth century, gave up on the more complex and many-faceted type of interest analysis that can be found in the work of such thinkers as Tocqueville and John Stuart Mill. It is from this point onward that the concept of interest began to be reduced to, and exclusively equated with, *economic self-interest*. It is also at this point that interests became the beginning, so to speak, as well as the end of the analysis. That is, instead of using interests *to suggest plausible hypotheses*, to be tested empirically, they were used to reason one's way to the solution of some problem.

This strategy may well have its advantages—but it has also impoverished the analysis of economic and other phenomena. It has, among other things, eliminated the concern with noneconomic interests and economic interests other than self-interest. However, this way of using the notion of interest cannot handle frequent situations in which people do not know what their interests are; nor can this approach necessarily address those situations in which people *do* know their interests, since they might not know what they should do in order to realize them (cf. Goffman's critique of game theory earlier in this chapter). When economic analysis is applied to noneconomic activities, it also tends to recast these exclusively in economic terms, such as competition, monopoly, trade, and so on. It furthermore fails to take social relations into account. This whole set of problems is what Bourdieu has in mind when he states that "the word *interest* . . . is also very dangerous because it is liable to suggest a utilitarianism that is the degree zero of sociology" (Bourdieu 1993:76).

Throughout this book I have tried to point out why interest, especially as it has been used by people such as Hume, Smith, Tocqueville, and Weber, is still a very useful concept. One reason why the concept of interest imparts a distinct dynamic to the analysis is that it is mainly interest which makes people take action. It supplies the force that makes people get up at dawn and work very hard throughout the day. Combined with the interests of others, it is a force that can move mountains and create new societies.

At the same time, an analysis of interest helps to explain conflict, which takes place when interests clash. This conflict can take place in a person's mind as well as among individuals, groups, and societies. But interests do not only clash and energize the actors; they can also block each other, reinforce each other, or immobilize an actor, for example, by making her back some religion or politics that supports tradition. The concept of interest, in brief, is a flexible tool of analysis.

Taking interests seriously also means shifting the center of the analysis from the surface of things to deep-seated forces that have an important impact on social action. In this respect, Weber's analysis in *The Protestant Ethic* is paradigmatic in that it attempts to analyze what made people change their behavior in such a fundamental way that a whole new rationalistic mentality was created. This aspect of *The Protestant Ethic* may in the long run prove as important as its well-known thesis about the importance of ascetic Protestantism for modern life.

Taking interests seriously can also help to give a balanced place to the role of subjectivity and culture in the analysis of economic behavior. These latter must indeed not be ignored—interests are to some extent always subjective as well as shaped by culture—but interests are also "objective" in the sense that they often constitute an uncommonly stable and stubborn part of social reality. The state or public morality may, for example, forbid a certain activity but it will take place anyway.

Utopian thinkers, from this perspective, can be defined as thinkers who disregard interests in their work. Actors without official interests (say, students) are ignored by those in power and are also prone to utopianism in their actions and thoughts. Being a "free-floating intellectual" is by no means as positive as Karl Mannheim believed. Having an established interest may tie you to the order of things and tempt you to "sell out"—but it also makes you a contender and anchors you in reality.

I have tried to point out that there exists an attempt by sociologists in Weber's generation as well as today to integrate interests into the sociological type of analysis, and that this approach (as opposed to the nonsociological and nonempirical interest theory of mainstream economics) is what is most congenial to economic sociology. One can summarize this approach as one that takes both interests and social relations into account—as long as it is clear that interests are defined and expressed through social relations. "Far from being an anthropological invariant," as Bourdieu warns, "interest is *a historical arbitrary*" (Bourdieu and Wacquant 1992:116). Another statement by Bourdieu gives a sense of how deeply intertwined interests and social relations are: "Anthropology and comparative history show that the properly social magic of institutions can constitute just about anything as an interest" (Bourdieu 1998b:83).

But even if there exist a number of positive qualities to the concept of interest, it also raises some problems that need to be discussed. One of these has to do with the difficulty of defining what an interest is. Up to this point in this book, for example, I have not supplied my own definition of interest, and the reason is that I have been unable to find one that is satisfactory. But it is often difficult to find good definitions of key concepts in the social sciences (see box).

Nonetheless, it is time for me to advance my own definition of interest, and it is as follows: *interests are what drive the actions of indi-*

INTERESTS

I have been unable to locate definitions of the concept of interest in the works of Hume, Tocqueville, and Weber. Some of the more suggestive and important definitions in the literature, however, include the following:

Arthur Bentley: "An interest, as we shall use the term in this work [*The Process of Government*], is the equivalent of a group" ([1908] 1967:211).

John Dewey: "Interest is impulse functioning with reference to self-realization" (cited in Small 1905:433).

Jürgen Habermas: "I term *interests* the basic orientations rooted in specific fundamental conditions of the possible reproduction and self-constitution of the human species, namely *work and interaction*" ([1968] 1971:196).

John Locke: "Civil interests I call life, liberty, health, and indolency of body; and the possession of outward things, such as money, lands, houses, furniture, and the like" ([1689] 1955:17).

Vilfredo Pareto: "Individuals and communities are spurred by instinct and reason to acquire possession of material goods that are useful—or merely pleasurable—for purposes of living, as well as to seek consideration and honours. Such impulses, which may be called 'interests,' play in the mass a very important part in determining the social equilibrium" ([1916] 1963:1406).

Roscoe Pound: "An interest may be defined as a demand or desire or exception which human beings, either individually or in groups or associations or relations, seek to satisfy, of which, therefore, the adjustment of human relations and ordering of human behavior through the force of a politically organized society must take account" (1959:16).

Jean-Paul Sartre: "Interest is being-wholly-outside-oneself-in-a-thing in so far as it conditions *praxis* as a categorical imperative" ([1960] 1976:197).

Albion Small (following Gustav Ratzenhofer): "An interest is an unsatisfied capacity, corresponding to an unrealized condition, and it is predisposition to such rearrangement as would tend to realize the indicated condition" (1905:433; emphasis removed).

viduals at some fundamental level. Furthermore, interests are intensely social phenomena. Other individuals have to be taken into account when an actor attempts to realize her interests; there is also the fact that interests are socially defined. This definition is broad enough to encompass many different types of interests, not only economic ones. Much hinges, of course, on what is meant by the expression "at some fundamental level." I use this expression because the concept of interest is typically used to capture the major forces that drive human behavior, the ones that really matter. What is imperative in an interest analysis is to situate the analysis at a deeper level, as Weber does in *The Protestant Ethic*. Once the notion of interest has been properly introduced into the analysis, it can also be useful to drop it and replace it with some other, more specific term, which better describes what drives the actor in a specific situation. This is often the way in which Tocqueville, Weber, and other thinkers proceed.

Another issue that needs to be discussed is that of tautology. One of Albert O. Hirschman's articles, "The Concept of Interest: From Euphemism to Tautology," contains the argument that the economists' concept of interest tends to be tautological since it is used to explain everything (1986). Hermann Isay is another scholar who has given voice to this type of criticism, in one of his articles on the jurisprudence of interests:

> In the first place, the notion of "interest" is too colorless and therefore almost devoid of content. It does not become clearer by being defined as man's "desire for the goods of life" [by Philip Heck]. Under this definition, 'interest' comprises everything that affects human beings either as individuals or as a community: not merely material goods but also ethical, religious, moral interests, the interests of justice, of fairness, "the highest interests of mankind," and the like. Oertmann has justly remarked that in this way the concept of interest is being inflated to such proportion that it becomes useless (1948:316).

What Isay argues is that the concept of interest is treated as if it constitutes the philosopher's stone, something that it certainly isn't. If too much weight is put on the notion of interest, it will break. While interest should not be treated as if it was *the* major concept in sociology (similar to the way that, say, "class" is used in Marxism), it nonetheless deserves to be treated as one of the more important sociological concepts—and surely as a concept that is indispensable to economic sociology.

A related topic is the question whether the concept of interest is reductionistic in nature, that is, if it reduces everything to some interest and thereby impoverishes the analysis (Merton 1968c:553–54; cf., however, Merton 1976:82–83, 152–53). This critique has recently been made by Frank Dobbin, who argues that in contemporary Western society people tend to explain practically everything in terms of interest ("the interest frame"). This, however, is no reason for social scientists to do the same, according to Dobbin, who adds that

> when anthropologists observe totemic societies in which local lore has it that frog spirits rule the universe, they do not conclude that frogs are inscribed in plows and circumcision mats because frogs indeed rule this domain. They conclude that the locals have developed a system of meaning that locates authority over social practices in the frog totem. Likewise, when we study modern social practices, we must do what we can to step outside of the frame of reference of the locals [that is, the interest frame] (2001a:78).

Most of Dobbin's argument, it should be noted, is not directed at the concept of interest that is advocated in this book; what he aims his critique at is the concept of self-interest in economics.

As mentioned earlier, the concept of motivation in psychology is equivalent to that of interest in the other social sciences. The parallels between these two concepts comes out well in the following quote:

> Psychologists favor the term *motivation* to describe the wants, needs, and preferences that guide behavior. Without motivation, there would be few conflicts or problems in human life, especially not between people, because no one would care about anything. Then again, without motivation, hardly anything would get done. In fact, without motivation, the human race would not even reproduce itself. Motivation is vital for life to continue (Baumeister forthcoming).

Since there exists a body of research on motivation, why not simply discard an old-fashioned and "literary" term such as interest and replace it with a more modern and scientific one, such as motivation? One reason for *not* doing so is that this would turn the whole analysis into a study in psychology, as opposed to one in sociology. This is a point that both Weber and Parsons have made (Weber [1908] 1975; Parsons [1940] 1954). To this can be added that interests are not exclusively internal; they are at times also located outside of the individual. What makes interest into such a flexible and evocative concept is that it actually often *spans* the individual and the group, the internal and the external, the biological and the social.

A final issue to be discussed is perhaps the most important of all; and it has to do with the way in which the notion of interest can be used in concrete analyses. My own stance is that the concept of interest should be seen primarily as a conceptual tool and as part of middle-range sociology. It should definitely *not* be elevated into some kind of general theory. The idea of creating a "sociological interest analysis" makes no more sense than having a conflict sociology. The concept of interest should be one of the key concepts in sociology—nothing more, nothing less.

Issue # 3: The Role of Objectivity and Reflexivity in Economic Sociology

In the early days of sociology, especially around the turn of the twentieth century, the issue of objectivity was the subject of much heated debate. Today, however, this discussion has largely been replaced by one about reflexivity, which deals with more subtle biases than those that were earlier at issue. The view that the teacher, for example, must not advocate her own political ideals in the classroom, has been replaced by a concern that the teacher should become aware of the social forces that have shaped her thinking (Weber [1904] 1949 versus Bourdieu and Wacquant 1992:36–46).

Neither objectivity nor reflexivity, however, has played much of a role in modern economic sociology. Still, there are good reasons for bringing them up in this context, especially if one believes in the importance of interests. It is, for example, quite obvious that the stance of objectivity is harder to maintain if powerful interests are involved, including economic interests. There exists, in other words, a direct link between objectivity and interests. It is also likely that the stronger the economic interests are, the more they will shape objective reality. There is consequently also a direct link between reflexivity and interests.

As to reflexivity, it is clear that economic sociologists need to take a close look at their own analyses and try to figure out in which way these reproduce existing values in an unreflective manner. Is there, for example, anything to the charge that network theory is an integral part of the neoliberal ideology (Boltanski and Chiapello 1999)? Economic sociology was reborn in the 1980s, at about the same time as neoliberalism was gaining in strength; again, is there any relationship between these events? Another issue that needs to be discussed has to do with the way in which economic sociology is currently being influenced by the ethos of the business schools. As the situation stands today, a sizeable contingent of American economic sociologists work in business schools. Does this make them look at things from the perspective of the managers and the owners, and disregard the perspective of the employees? Industrial sociology has been accused of looking only at the workers, while ignoring the rest of the firm; do sociologists at business schools only look at the top, and ignore the people at the bottom?

Economic sociologists need, in my opinion, to engage in some reflexive work, which should be concerned not only with the way that economic sociology is shaped but also with the way that its practitioners perceive the world. It would also be useful, I argue, if this effort was extended to include the way that economic knowledge is generated and how this knowledge is perceived in society. By the term "economic knowledge" I primarily mean economic theory, economic ideologies, and economic news of the type that is spread via television, radio, newspapers, and other popular media.

While we know something about economic theory and how it is produced, we have very little knowledge of economic ideologies and economic news. A few attempts have been made to study Keynesianism and neoliberalism, but much still remains to be done (Hall 1989; Campbell and Pedersen 2001). What is most surprising, however, is the nearly total absence of knowledge about the role of economics in the news media. The way in which economic news is produced, the rise of economic journalism, the economic sociology of the media—all of these topics would seem ideal for economic sociologists.

While it may well be true that we know something about the production of economic theory, there also exist big gaps in this knowledge, especially from the viewpoint of economic sociology. What needs to be done, as with other structural holes, is first to get a better sense for what is known about this phenomenon in the other social sciences, and then draw up an agenda for research. As to the former task, it is clear that economists and historians of economic theory have produced a large literature on economic theory, which needs to be much better known in economic sociology.

As a small and biased sample of what "reflexive studies" are available, the following works deserve to be mentioned. *The Political Element in the Development of Economic Thought* by Gunnar Myrdal explores in an exemplary manner the way in which values have influenced the key concepts of economic thought, from its beginnings onward ([1930] 1953). A. W. Coats, a historian of economic thought, has tried to develop a sociology of knowledge approach to economics by looking at the formation of national economic associations, the role of economists in international organizations, and the like (Coats 1981, 1984, 1993).

There is also an interesting attempt to look at the various rhetorical devices that economists use to persuade one another (McCloskey

1985; for the use of metaphors in economics, see Mirowski 1994). The history of economic thought has also advanced very quickly during the past few decades, and economic sociologists may want to consult regularly a journal such as *History of Political Economy (HOPE)* as well as take a look at works on such topics as the history of game theory and the early analysis of law in economics (Weintraub 1992; Pearson 1997).

In discussing how to develop a reflexive approach to economic thought it should be noted that some economic theories may be quite helpful. One of these is the idea that economic actors search for knowledge and that this search has a price (Stigler 1961). Another is the theory of signaling and, connected to this, the concept of asymmetric information (Spence 1974, Akerlof 1970). Both of these theories can, with some minor modification, also be used by sociologists to explore the social dimension of economic theory as well as the production of economic knowledge more generally. How, for example, do economists search for topics to explore in their research? How do politicians search for economists to put on their staff? How do economists signal to politicians that they are of the "right" kind? And how do economists signal to each other what should be included/excluded in the "right" kind of analysis?

But there also exist some contributions to the sociology of economics that have been made by economic sociologists. These include a somewhat heterogenous collection of work, such as a comparative study of the rise of economics in Germany, Great Britain, France, and the United States, a study of the state's role in current economic discourse in the United States, and an analysis of the field of economics in France (Block 1996; Lebaron 2000a; Fourcade-Gourinchas 2001). Two general themes can also be discerned, both of which seem promising. The first is the tendency of economic theory to transform reality into its own image—only to find, when it is used to analyze this new reality, that it perfectly fits! There exists, for example, a sociological analysis of the way in which a former student of economics transformed a traditional market for strawberries in a small French town into a modern market, so that it would be more like the kind of market that you can find in an economic textbook (Garcia 1986; cf. Callon 1998). The second theme is an attempt to use recent ideas in the sociology of science, which are associated with the work of Bruno Latour and his colleagues, to analyze economic topics (Knorr Cetina and Brügger 2002). Mathematical models, for example, have a distinct reality to economic theorists, which shapes the way that they relate to these models (Breslau and Yonay 1999).

Issue # 4: Should Economic Sociology Be A Policy Science?

When one takes the step from analysis in social science to an advocacy of how this knowledge can be used in society, one crosses a magic line according to Weber and the traditional doctrine of objectivity. While the social scientist can be held accountable for her analyses, in the sense that she has to follow certain rules of reason, her politics is an entirely different matter. One's political behavior belongs to a realm where everybody has the right to take whatever position she sees fit, according to her values. Just as social science and politics constitute two different realms, they also imply different types of behavior. Weber himself, it can be noted, was active in politics, even if he was considerably more skillful in analyzing political events than participating in them as a practical politician. He always made it clear, however, whether a statement was intended as social science or as an expression of his political values.

The extent to which today's economic sociologists are active in politics is not known. My general impression is that very few devote much time to politics, especially in the United States, and that there is a general feeling that economic sociology should not be used for political purposes. One reason for this political indifference may be the earlier misuse of Marxism; another is perhaps the sense that it would be premature to turn economic sociology into a policy science. Economic sociology, after all, is a fairly new approach. From this last perspective, it is more important to strengthen economic sociology as a distinct type of analysis, than to launch it into politics.

A quick perusal of the main body of writings in economic sociology since the 1980s shows that they do not address the issue if economic sociology has a normative side, and if it can be used as a policy science. A few exceptions, however, exist, and since these have been ignored in the debate about economic sociology they deserve to be presented in some detail. One of them can be found in *Markets, Politics, and Globalization* by Neil Fligstein. After having presented his theory of markets, which is centered around the idea that corporations do not want competition but stability and no surprises, Fligstein addresses the issue of "normative implications of a sociology of markets" (1997:38–41; cf. Fligstein 1996b). Firms, according to this argument, can only operate efficiently if they are supported by society in a number of ways. Employees need to be educated, and there also has to exist an adequate infrastructure as well as a functioning legal system. All of these are paid for by taxes; and "this means that people and governments have the right to make claims back on firms" (1997: 40).

Fligstein states that his argument goes well beyond the idea of stakeholder rights or that not only the owners, but also many other actors who are part of a firm, have similar rights (such as, workers, communities, customers, and suppliers). The key is that society at large has a claim on the corporations. What society has the right to demand, Fligstein suggests, includes the following:

There should be an orderly shutdown of obsolete facilities. Governments and firms should work actively to retrain workers for real jobs. Incentives should be given to firms to keep production local and to promote high value added service and manufacturing jobs. There should be a cutback of subsidies for firms that shift production offshore and any remaining protection given by tariffs or other non-tariff barriers should be removed. Taxes and tariffs on offshore profits and goods are legitimate. Invader firms should not be allowed to operate under different rules. Stakeholders such as workers and politicians should sit on boards of directors to insure that investment decisions are economically driven (Fligstein 1997:41).

Bourdieu also discusses normative issues as part of his sociology, and since these are often related to economic topics they belong in a discussion of economic sociology as a possible policy science. Bourdieu's viewpoint on this topic can be illustrated by *Acts of Resistance: Against the Tyranny of the Market*, a small book that consists mainly of lectures and speeches given at various public occasions, including strike meetings (1998a; see also Bourdieu 2001). The major theme in this work is that the welfare state is under heavy attack from neoliberalism, and that this has to be fought since the welfare state protects people from the ravages of the market. Neoliberalism advocates individualism and fights every kind of collectivism, especially trade unions. In the developing world the IMF and the World Bank are busy imposing neoliberal reforms, with the most dismal results. In the West, people's sense of security is being undermined by dismissals in the private sector as well as in the public sector. Thanks to the success of neoliberal politics since the 1980s, this is just as true for the middle classes as for the workers. "The American middle classes, exposed to the threat of suddenly losing their jobs, are feeling a terrible insecurity (which shows that what is important in a job is not only the activity and the income it provides, but also the sense of security it gives)" (Bourdieu 1998a:36–37).

A true economic science, according to Bourdieu, would look at *all* the costs of the economy—not only at the costs that corporations are concerned with, but also at the crimes, suicides, and so on that are the

"You know what I think, folks? Improving technology
isn't important. Increased profits aren't important. What's
important is to be warm, decent human beings."

result of misguided economic policies. What such an "economics of
happiness" would look like is described as follows:

> Against this narrow, short-term economics [which is dominant today], we
> need to put forward an *economics of happiness*, which would take note of all
> the profits, individual and collective, material and symbolic, associated
> with activity (such as security), and also all the material and symbolic costs
> associated with inactivity or precarious employment (for example, con-
> sumption of medicines: France holds the world record for use of tran-
> quilizers). You cannot cheat with *the law of the conservation of violence*: all
> violence has to be paid for, and, for example, the structural violence exerted
> by the financial markets, in the form of layoffs, loss of security, etc., is
> matched sooner or later in the form of suicides, crime and delinquency,
> drug addiction, alcoholism, a whole host of minor and major everyday acts
> of violence (1998a:40).

Bourdieu's attack on neoliberalism is not very different from what
one can find elsewhere among social scientists who define themselves
as progressive and antiliberal. One part of Bourdieu's criticism, however, is quite unique to my mind and of special interest to economic
sociology: his attempt to introduce a new set of concepts to criticize
neoliberalism and capitalism more generally, which serve both as po-

litical concepts and as sociological ones. These are centered around the idea of theodicy and include concepts such as "sociodicy," "social suffering," and "economic violence" (1977, 1979, 1998a). This strand of Bourdieu's thought goes back to his early studies of Algeria but has also come to more recent expression in his work, especially in his huge study of social suffering in *The Weight of the World* (Bourdieu et al. 1999).

Theodicy—and this is what I find very valuable in Bourdieu's argument—tries to answer questions such as the following: *Why is there suffering in the world, and why do some people suffer more than others?* Bourdieu's position is that the organization of society has much to do with both the creation of suffering, and he therefore speaks of "sociodicy" or "social suffering" (Bourdieu 1998a:35, 43; see also Morgan and Wilkinson 2001). Neoliberalism, for example, is characterized by Bourdieu as a "conservative sociodicy" since it justifies suffering on the ground that it is necessary for economic progress (Bourdieu 1998a:35). Unemployment, from this perspective, represents a form of "economic violence" (Bourdieu 1977:191–92).

Bourdieu refers several times to Weber's argument that people who are successful invariably feel that they deserve their good fortune, while in reality their success is primarily due to good luck ("theodicy of good fortune" in Weber's terminology; cf. Weber [1915] 1946b:271). In modern capitalist society the educational system operates as a theodicy of good fortune, according to Bourdieu, since it justifies the existence of inequality on the ground that those who are successful are more competent and educated than the rest (Bourdieu 1993b:177–79). A corollary of the theodicy of good fortune is the belief that the poor deserve to be poor because they are ignorant, lack education, and so on ("theodicy of misfortune"—Weber [1915] 1946b:276).

It should finally also be mentioned that it may be possible to approach the issue of economic sociology as a policy science not only from the perspective of theodicy but also from an interest perspective. Or, more precisely, it may be possible to address the issue of how to use economic sociology as a policy science from an interest perspective—what values or ideals should be realized can obviously *not* be decided with the help of economic sociology or any other science. As I see it, Weber outlines an interest model for how radically to change people and society, including the economy, in *The Protestant Ethic*. Changes of this type, he says, can be made only by appealing to people's innermost interests. If people feel that their most important interests are involved, they will change their behavior—otherwise not.

Elsewhere in his sociology of religion Weber elaborates on this insight and notes, for example, that very few religions have succeeded in energizing their members as successfully as the ascetic Protestant sects did. Religions that emphasize that the believer should perform good deeds, follow certain rituals, or enter into a mystical reunion with God, all have one thing in common: they do *not* succeed in energizing their followers to change the world. They lead to traditionalism, not to change.

Translated into the issue of economic sociology as a policy science, Weber's message is clear. It is not only people's opinions that matter—that is, their ideals of how the economy should be organized. You primarily have to connect to the interests of people if you want them to change themselves and the world they live in. But there is also a caveat: Weber warns us that things may not turn out the way we want, when we set about to change the world. The ascetic Protestants did not create heaven on earth but helped to usher in modern capitalism.

References _____

Abbott, Andrew. 1988. *The System of Professions: An Essay on the Expert Division of Labor*. Chicago: University of Chicago Press.

Abel, Richard, ed. 1995. *The Law and Society Reader*. New York: New York University Press.

Abolafia, Mitchel. 1984. "Structured Anarchy: Formal Organization in the Commodity Futures Industry." Pp. 129–50 in *The Social Dynamics of Financial Markets*, edited by Patricia Adler and Peter Adler. Greenwich, JAI Press.

———. 1996. *Making Markets: Opportunism and Restraint on Wall Street*. Cambridge: Harvard University Press.

———. 1998. "Markets as Culture: An Ethnographic Approach." Pp. 69–85 in *The Laws of the Markets*, edited by Michel Callon. Oxford: Blackwell.

———. Forthcoming. "Making Sense of Recession: Policy Making at the Federal Reserve Bank." In *The Economic Sociology of Capitalism*, edited by Victor Nee and Richard Swedberg.

Adorno, Theodore. 1967. "Veblen's Attack on Culture." Pp. 73–95 in *Prisms*. Cambridge: MIT Press.

Akerlof, George. 1970. "The Market for 'Lemons': Quality Uncertainty and the Market Mechanism," *Quarterly Journal of Economics* 84:488–500.

Albrow, Martin. 1970. *Bureaucracy*. London: Macmillan.

Alchian, Armen, and Harold Demsetz. 1972. "Production, Information Costs, and Economic Organization," *American Economic Review* 62, no. 5 (1972): 777–95.

Aldrich, Howard. 1999. *Organizations Evolving*. London: Sage.

———. Forthcoming. "Entrepreneurship." In *The Handbook of Economic Sociology*, edited by Neil Smelser and Richard Swedberg. New York and Princeton: Russell Sage Foundation and Princeton University Press.

Aldrich, Howard, and Roger Waldinger. 1990. "Ethnicity and Entrepreneurship," *Annual Review of Sociology* 16:111–35.

Alford, Fred. 2001. *Whistleblowers: Broken Lives and Organizational Power*. Ithaca: Cornell University Press.

Allen, Sheila, and Carole Truman. 1993. *Women in Business: Perspectives on Women Entrepreneurs*. London: Routledge.

Appadurai, Arjun. 1986. "Introduction: Commodities and the Politics of Value." Pp. 3–63 in *The Social Life of Things*, edited by Arjun Appadurai. Cambridge: Cambridge University Press.

Aristotle. 1946. *The Politics of Aristotle*. Translated by Ernest Baker. New York: Oxford University Press.

Arrow, Kenneth. 1968. "Economic Equilibrium." Pp. 376–89 in *International Encyclopaedia of the Social Sciences*, vol. 4, edited by David L. Sills. New York: Macmillan Co. and Free Press.

———. 1972. "Models of Job Discrimination." Pp. 83–102 in *Racial Discrimina-*

tion in Economic Life, edited by A. Pascal. Lexington, Mass.: Lexington Heath.

———. 1974. *The Limits of Organization.* New York: Norton.

———. 1985. "The Economics of Agency." Pp. 37–51 in *Principals and Agents: The Structure of Business,* edited by John Pratt and Richard Zeckhauser. Cambridge: Harvard Business School Press.

———. 1998. "What Has Economics to Say About Racial Discrimination?" *Journal of Economic Perspectives* 12(2):91–100.

ASA (American Sociological Association). 2002. *Economic Sociology: Syllibi and Instructional Material.* Ed. Gary Green and David Myhre. Washington, D.C.: ASA. 1st ed. appeared in 1996.

Aspers, Patrik. 1999. "The Economic Sociology of Alfred Marshall: An Overview," *American Journal of Economics and Sociology* 58:651–67.

———. 2001a. Conversation with author, Stockholm, spring.

———. 2001b. "Crossing the Boundary of Economics and Sociology: The Case of Vilfredo Pareto," *American Journal of Economics and Sociology* 60:519–46.

———. 2001c. "A Market in Vogue: Fashion Photography in Sweden," *European Societies* 3:1–22.

———. 2001d. *A Market in Vogue: A Study of Fashion Photography in Sweden.* Stockholm: City University Press.

Aubert, Vilhelm. 1952. "White-Collar Crime and Social Structure," *American Journal of Sociology* 58:263–71.

———. 1980. *Inledning till rättssociologin* (= *Introduction to the Sociology of Law*). Stockholm: Almqvist & Wicksell.

———. 1983. *In Search of Law: Sociological Approaches to Law.* Totowa, N.J.: Barnes and Noble.

Axelrod, Robert. 1984. *The Evolution of Cooperation.* New York: Basic Books.

Azarian, Reza. Forthcoming. "The General Sociology of Harrison White." Ph.D. diss., Department of Sociology, Stockholm University.

Babb, Sarah. 2001. *Managing Mexico: Economists from Nationalism to Neoliberalism.* Princeton: Princeton University Press.

Bagnasco, Arnaldo. 1977. *Tre Italie.* Bologna: Il Mulino.

Baker, Tom, and Jonathan Simon, eds. 2002. *Embracing Risk: The Changing Culture of Insurance and Responsibility.* Chicago: University of Chicago Press.

Baker, Wayne. 1981 "Markets as Networks: A Multimethod Study of Trading Networks in a Securities Market." Ph.D. diss., Department of Sociology, Northwestern University.

———. 1984. "The Social Structure of a National Securities Market," *American Journal of Sociology* 89:775–811.

———. 1987. "What Is Money? A Social Structural Interpretation." Pp. 85–108 in *Intercorporate Relations,* edited by Mark Mizruchi and Michael Schwartz. Cambridge: Cambridge University Press.

———. 1992. "The Network Organization in Theory and Practice." Pp. 397–429 in *Networks and Organizations,* edited by Nitin Nohria and Robert Eccles. Boston: Harvard Business School Press.

Baker, Wayne, and Robert Faulkner. 1993. "The Social Organization of Conspiracy: Illegal Networks in the Heavy Electrical Equipment Industry," *American Sociological Review* 58:837–60.

Baker, Wayne, and Ananth Iyer. 1992. "Information Networks and Corporate Behavior," *Journal of Mathematical Sociology* 16:305–32.

Banfield, Edward. 1958. *The Moral Basis of a Backward Society*. Glencoe, Ill.: Free Press.

Barbalet, J. M. 2000. "*Beruf*, Rationality and Emotion in Max Weber's Sociology," *Archives Européennes de Sociologie* 41, no. 2: 329–51.

Barber, Bernard. 1977. "The Absolutization of the Market: Some Notes on How We Got from There to Here." Pp. 15–31 in *Markets and Morals*, edited by G. Dworkin. New York: Wiley.

———. 1995. "All Economies are 'Embedded': The Career of a Concept and Beyond," *Social Research* 62:388–413.

Barbera, Filippo. 2002. "Economic Sociology: Past and Present," *International Review of Sociology* 12, no. 1:145–57.

Barley, Stephen, and Gideon Kunda. 1992. "Design and Devotion: Surges of Rational and Normative Ideologies of Control in Managerial Discourse," *Administrative Science Quarterly* 37:363–99.

Barnes, Jay, and William Ouchi, eds. 1986. *Organizational Economics*. San Francisco: Jossey Bass.

Baron, James, and David Kreps. 1999. *Strategic Management Resources: Framework for General Managers*. New York: Wiley.

Baron, James, and Michael Hannan. Forthcoming. "The Economic Sociology of Organizational Entrepreneurship: Lessons from the Stanford Project on Emerging Companies." In *The Economic Sociology of Capitalism*, edited by Victor Nee and Richard Swedberg.

Barzel, Yoram. 2002. *A Theory of the State: Economic Rights, Legal Rights, and the Scope of the State*. Cambridge: Cambridge University Press.

Baudrillard, Jean. 1988. "Consumer Society." Pp. 29–56 in *Jean Baudrillard: Selected Writings*, edited by Mark Poster. Oxford: Polity.

Baumeister, Roy. Forthcoming. "What Do People Want?" In *Human Nature in Social Context*. Manuscript.

Baumgartner, Frank, and Beth L. Beech. 1998. *Basic Interests: The Importance of Interests in Politics and Political Science*. Princeton: Princeton University Press.

Baumol, William. 1993. *Entrepreneurship, Management, and the Structure of Payoff*. Cambridge: MIT Press.

Beck, Ulrich. 1992. *Risk Society*. London: Sage.

Becker, Gary. 1957. *The Economics of Discrimination*. Chicago: University of Chicago Press.

———. 1964. *Human Capital*. New York: National Bureau of Economic Research.

———. 1976. *The Economic Approach to Human Behavior*. Chicago: University of Chicago Press.

———. 1981. *A Treatise on the Family*. Cambridge: Harvard University Press.

Beckert, Jens. 2002a. *Beyond the Market: The Social Foundations of Economic Efficiency*. Princeton: Princeton University Press.

———. 2002b. *Unearned Wealth: The Development of Inheritance Law in France, Germany and the United States*. Working paper, Center for European Studies, Harvard University.

———. Forthcoming. *Negotiated Modernity: Inheritance in France, Germany, and the United States since 1800*.

Bell, Daniel. 1976. "The Public Household: On 'Fiscal Sociology' and the Liberal Society." Pp. 220–82 in *Cultural Contradictions of Capitalism*. New York: Basic Books.

Bellandi, Marco. 1989. "The Industrial District in Marshall." Pp. 136–52 *Small Firms and Industrial Districts in Italy*, edited by Edward Goodman and Julia Bamford. London: Routledge.

Bender, Donald. 1967. "A Refinement of the Concept of Household: Families, Co-residence and Domestic Functions," *American Anthropologist* 67:493–504.

Bendor, Jonathan, and Piotr Swistak. 2001. "The Evolution of Norms," *American Journal of Sociology* 106:1493–1545.

Benet, Francisco. [1957] 1971. "Explosive Markets: The Berber Highlands." Pp. 188–217 in *Trade and Market in the Early Empires*, edited by Karl Polanyi, Conrad Arensberg, and Harry Pearson. Chicago: Regnery.

Bentley, Arthur. [1908] 1967. *The Process of Government*. Cambridge: Harvard University Press.

Berezin, Mabel. 1997a. "Politics and Culture: A Less Fissured Terrain," *Annual Review of Sociology* 23:361–83.

———. 1997b. *Making the Fascist Self: The Political Culture of Interwar Italy*. Ithaca: Cornell University Press.

———. Forthcoming a. "Emotions and the Economy." in *The Handbook of Economic Sociology*, edited by Neil Smelser and Richard Swedberg. 2nd ed. New York and Princeton: Russell Sage Foundation and Princeton University Press.

———. Forthcoming b. "Politics and Emotions." In "Special Issue on Emotions," *Sociological Review Monographs*, edited by J. M. Barbalet.

Berg, Ivar, and Arne Kalleberg, eds. 2001. *Sourcebook of Labor Markets: Evolving Structures and Processes*. New York: Kluwer.

Berger, Brigitte, ed. 1991. *The Culture of Entrepreneurship*. San Francisco: ICS Press.

Berger, Klaus Peter. 1999. *The Creeping Codification of the Lex Mercatoria*. The Hague: Kluwer Law International.

Berger, Peter. 1986. *The Capitalist Revolution: Fifty Propositions about Prosperity, Equality and Liberty*. New York: Basic Books.

———. 1987. *Capitalism and Equality in America*. Lanham, Md.: Hamilton.

Berger, Peter, and Thomas Luckmann. 1967. *The Social Construction of Reality: A Treatise in the Sociology of Knowledge*. New York: Doubleday.

Berger, Suzanne, ed. 1981. *Organizing Interests in Western Europe: Pluralism, Corporatism, and the Transformation of Politics*. Cambridge: Cambridge University Press.

Berger, Susanne, and Ronald Dore, eds. 1995. *National Diversity and Global Capitalism*. Ithaca: Cornell University Press.

Berggren, Christain. 1993. *The Volvo Experience: Alternatives to Lean Production in the Swedish Auto Industry*. London: Macmillan.

Berman, Harold. 1983. "Mercantile Law." Pp. 333–56 in *Law and Revolution: The Formation of the Western Legal Tradition*. Cambridge: Harvard University Press.

Bernoux, Philippe. 1995. *Sociologie des Entreprises*. Paris: Points-Seuil.

Beth, Anne Shelton. 1992. *Women, Men, and Time: Gender Differences*. New York: Greenwood.

Bielby, Denise, and William Bielby. 1988. "She Works Hard for the Money: Household Resonsibilities and the Allocation of Work Effort," *American Journal of Sociology* 93:1031–59.

Biggart, Nicole Woolsey. 1989. *Charismatic Capitalism: Direct Selling Organizations in America*. Chicago: University of Chicago Press.

———, ed. 2002. *Readings in Economic Sociology*. Oxford: Blackwell.

Bird, Chloe. 1990. "High Finance, Small Change: Women's Increased Representation in Bank Management." Pp. 145–66 in *Job Queues, Gender Queues: Explaining Women's Inroads into Male Occupations*, edited by Barbara Reskin and Patricia Roos. Philadelphia: Temple University Press.

Blaug, Mark. 1980. "The Theory of the Firm." Pp. 175–86 in *The Methodology of Economics*. Cambridge: Cambridge University Press.

Blinder, Alan. 1998. *Asking about Prices: A New Approach to Understanding Price Stickiness*. New York: Russell Sage Foundation.

Block, Fred. 1977. *The Origins of International Economic Disorder: A Study of the United States International Monetary Policy from World War II to the Present*. Berkeley: University of California Press.

———. 1981. "The Fiscal Crisis of the Capitalist State," *Annual Review of Sociology* 7:1–27.

———. 1985. "Postindustrial Development and the Obsolescence of Economic Categories," *Politics & Society* 14, no. 1: 71–104.

———. 1987. *Revising State Theory: Essays in Politics and Postindustrialism*. Philadelphia: Temple University Press.

———. 1990. *Postindustrial Possibilities: A Critique of Economic Discourse*. Berkeley: University of California Press.

———. 1996. *The Vampire State—and Other Myths and Fallacies about the U.S. Economy*. New York: New Press.

———. 2000. "Deconstructing Capitalism as a System," *Rethinking Marxism* 12, no. 3: 83–98.

———. 2001. "Introduction." Pp. xviii–xxxviii in *The Great Transformation* by Karl Polanyi. Boston: Beacon.

Blomert, Reinhard. 2001. "Sociology of Finance—Old and New Perspectives," *Economic Sociology: European Electronic Newsletter* 2 (January): 9–14. See http//:www.siswo.uva.nl/ES.

Bodin, Jean. [1576] 1986. *Les Six Livres de la République*. 6 vols. Paris: Fayard.

Boltanski, Luc. 1987. *The Making of a Class: Cadres in French Society*. Cambridge: Cambridge University Press.

———. 1990. "Visions of American Management in Postwar France." Pp. 343–72 in *Structures of Capital*, edited by Sharon Zulin and Paul DiMaggio. Cambridge: Cambridge University Press.

Boltanski, Luc, and Eve Chiapello. 1999. *Le Nouvel Esprit du Capitalisme*. Paris: Gallimard.

Boltanski, Luc, and Laurent Thévenot. [1987] 1991. *De la Justification. Les Economies de la Grandeur*. Paris: Gallimard.

———. 1999. "The Sociology of Critical Capacity," *European Journal of Social Theory* 2, no. 3:359–77.

Bonacich, Edna. 1980. "A Theory of Middleman Minorities," *American Sociological Review* 38:583–94.

Bonacich, Phillip. 2000. Email to the author, May 9.

Boorstin, Daniel. 1974. *The Americans: The Democratic Experience*. New York: Vintage.

Boudon, Raymond. 1982. *The Unintended Consequences of Social Action*. London: Macmillan.

Bourdieu, Pierre. 1963. "Travail et Travailleurs en Algérie: Etude Sociologique." Pp. 257–389 in *Travail et Traveilleurs en Algérie*. Paris: Mouton.

———. 1977. *Outline of A Theory of Practice*. Cambridge: Cambridge University Press.

———. 1979. "The Disenchantment of the World." Pp. 1–91 in *Algeria 1960*. Cambridge: Cambridge University Press.

———. [1979] 1986. *Distinction: A Social Critique of the Judgment of Taste*. London: Routledge.

———. 1986. "The Forms of Capital." Pp. 241–58 in *Handbook of Theory and Research for the Sociology of Education*, edited by John G. Richardson. Westport, Conn.: Greenwood. Reprinted in Granovetter and Swedberg 2001.

———. 1987. "The Force of Law: Toward a Sociology of the Juridical Field," *Hastings Journal of Law* 38:209–48.

———. 1990a. "Symbolic Capital." Pp. 112–21 in *The Logic of Practice*. Stanford: Stanford University Press.

———. 1990b. "The Interest of the Sociologist." Pp. 87–93 in *In Other Words: Essays Towards a Reflexive Sociology*. Stanford: Stanford University Press.

———. 1990c. "The Scholastic Point of View," *Cultural Anthropology* 5, no. 4: 380–91.

———. 1993a. *The Field of Cultural Production*. New York: Columbia University Press.

———. 1993b. *Sociology in Question*. London: Sage.

———. 1995. *The Rules of Art: Genesis and Structure of the Literary Field*. Stanford: Stanford University Press.

———. 1997. "Le Champs Economique," *Actes de la Recherche en Sciences Sociales* 119:48–66.

———. 1998a. *Acts of Resistance: Against the Tyranny of the Market*. New York: New Press.

———. 1998b. "Is a Disinterested Act Possible?" Pp. 75–91 in *Practical Reason: On the Theory of Action*. Stanford: Stanford University Press.

———. 1999. "Rethinking the State: Genesis and Structure of the Bureaucratic Field." Pp. 53–75 in *State/Culture: State-Formation after the Cultural Turn*, edited by George Steinmetz. Ithaca: Cornell University Press.

———. 2000a. "Principes d'une Anthropologie Economique." Pp. 233–70 in *Les Structures Sociales de l'Economie*. Paris: Seuil. For a translation, see Bourdieu forthcoming.

———. 2000b. "Making the Economic Habitus: Algerian Workers Revisited," *Ethnography* 1, no. 1:17–41.

———. 2000c. *Les Structures Sociales de l'Economie*. Paris: Seuil.

———. 2001. *Contre-feux 2. Pour un Mouvement Social Européen*. Paris: Raisons d'Agir Editions.

———, ed. 1991. "La Souffrance," *Actes de la Recherche en Sciences Sociales* 90:1–103.

————. Forthcoming. "Principles of Economic Anthropology." In *The Handbook of Economic Sociology*, edited by Neil Smelser and Richard Swedberg. 2nd ed. New York and Princeton: Russell Sage Foundation and Princeton University Press.

Bourdieu, Pierre, et al. 1999. *The Weight of the World: Social Suffering in Contemporary Society*. Stanford: Stanford University Press.

Bourdieu, Pierre, and Jean-Claude Passeron. [1964] 1979. *The Inheritors: French Students and Their Relation to Culture*. Chicago: University of Chicago Press.

————. [1970] 1977. *Reproduction in Education, Society and Culture*. Beverly Hills, Calif.: Sage.

Bourdieu, Pierre, and Monique de Saint Martin. 1990. "Le Sens de la Propriété. La Genèse Sociale des Systèmes de Préférences," *Actes de la Recherche en Sciences Sociales* 81–82:52–64.

Bourdieu, Pierre, and Abdelmalek Sayad. 1964. *Le Déracinement. La Crise de l'Agriculture Traditionelle en Algérie*. Paris: Editions de Minuit.

Bourdieu, Pierre, and Louïc Wacquant. 1992. *An Invitation to Reflexive Sociology*. Chicago: University of Chicago Press.

Boyer, Robert. 1990. *The School of Regulation*. New York: Columbia University Press.

Boyer, Robert, and Yves Saillard, eds. 2002. *Regulation Theory: The State of the Art*. London: Routledge.

Braudel, Fernand. [1979] 1985a. *The Structure of Everyday Life. Volume I. Civilization and Capitalism, 15th–18th Century*. London: Fontana.

————. [1979] 1985b. *The Wheels of Commerce. Volume II. Civilization and Capitalism, 15th–18th Century*. London: Fontana.

————. [1979] 1985c. *The Perspective of the World. Volume III. Civilization and Capitalism, 15th–18th Century*. London: Fontana.

Braun, Rudolf. 1975. "Taxation, Sociopolitical Structure, and State-Building: Great Britain and Brandenburg-Prussia." Pp. 243–327 in *The Formation of National States in Western Europe*, edited by Charles Tilly. Princeton: Princeton University Press.

Brennan, Geoffrey, and Alan Hamlin. 1998. "Constitutional Economics." Pp. 401–10 in vol. 1 of *The New Palgrave. Dictionary of Economics and the Law*, edited by Peter Newman. London: Macmillan.

Breslau, Daniel, and Yuval Yonay. 1999. "Beyond Metaphor: Mathematical Models in Economics as Empirical Research," *Science in Context* 12, no. 2:317–32.

Brewer, John. 1989. *The Sinews of Power: War, Money and the English State*. London: Unwin Hyman.

Brewer, John, and Roy Porter, eds. 1993. *Consumption and the World of Goods*. London: Routledge.

Brines, Julie. 1994. "Economic Dependency, Gender, and the Division of Labor at Home," *American Journal of Sociology* 100:652–88.

Brinton, Mary. 1993. *Women and the Economic Miracle: Gender and Work in Postwar Japan*. Berkeley: University of California Press.

Brinton, Mary, ed. *Women's Working Lives in East Asia*. Stanford: Stanford University Press.

Brinton, Mary, and Victor Nee, eds. *The New Institutionalism in Sociology*. New York: Russell Sage Foundation.

Brown, Norman O. 1947. *Hermes the Thief: The Evolution of A Myth*. Madison: University of Wisconsin Press.

Brus, Wlodzimierz, and Kazimierz Laski. 1989. *From Marx to the Market: Socialism in Search of an Economic System*. Oxford: Clarendon.

Buchanan, James. 1987. "Constitutional Economics." Pp. 585–88 in vol. 1 of *The New Palgrave. A Dictionary of Economics*, edited by John Eatwell et al. London: Macmillan.

Buchanan, James, and Gordon Tullock. 1962. *The Calculus of Consent: Logical Foundations of Constitutional Democracy*. Ann Arbor: University of Michigan Press.

Buchanan, James and Richard Wagner. 1970. "An Efficiency Basis for Federal Fiscal Equalization." Pp. 139–58 in *The Analysis of Public Output*, edited by Julius Margolis. New York: Columbia University Press.

———. 1977. *Democracy in Deficit: The Political Legacy of Lord Keynes*. New York: Academic Press.

Burawoy, Michael. 1979. *Manufacturing Consent: Changes in the Labor Process under Monopoly Capitalism*. Chicago: University of Chicago Press.

Burt, Ronald. 1983. *Corporate Profits and Cooptation: Networks of Market Constraints and Directorate Ties in the American Economy*. New York: Academic Press.

———. 1992. *Structural Holes: The Social Structure of Competition*. Cambridge: Harvard University Press.

Callon, Michel. 1997. "Society in the Making: The Study of Technology as a Tool for Sociological Analysis." Pp. 83–103 in *The Social Construction of Tecnological Systems*, edited by Wiebe Bijker et al. Cambridge: MIT Press.

———. 1998. "Introduction: The Embeddedness of Economic Markets in Economics." Pp. 1–57 in *The Laws of the Markets*, edited by Michel Callon. Oxford: Blackwell.

Calavita, K., R. Tillman, and H. N. Pontell. 1997. "The Savings and Loan Debacle, Financial Crime, and the State," *Annual Review of Sociology* 23:19–38.

Cameron, Rondo. 1993. *A Concise Economic History of the World: From Paleolithic Times to the Present*. 2nd ed. Oxford: Oxford University Press.

Camic, Charles. 1987. "The Making of a Method: A Historical Reinterpretation of the Early Parsons," *American Sociological Review* 52:421–39.

Camp, John. 1986. *The Athenian Agora: Excavations in the Heart of Classical Athens*. London: Thames and Hudson.

Campbell, Colin. 1995a. "Conspicuous Confusion? A Critique of Veblen's Theory of Conspicuous Consumption," *Sociological Theory* 13 (March): 37–47.

———. 1995b. "The Sociology of Consumption." Pp. 96–126 in *Acknowledging Consumption: A Review of New Studies*, edited by Daniel Miller. London: Routledge.

Campbell, John. 1993. "The State and Fiscal Sociology," *Annual Review of Sociology* 19:163–85.

———. 1996. "An Institutional Analysis of Fiscal Reform in Postcommunist Europe," *Theory and Society* 25:45–84.

———. Forthcoming. "Fiscal Sociology in an Age of Globalization: Comparing Tax Regimes in Advanced Capitalist Countries." In *The Economic Sociology of Capitalism*, edited by Victor Nee and Richard Swedberg.

Campbell, John, and Michael Allen. 1994. "The Political Economy of Revenue Extraction in the Modern State: A Time-Series Analysis of U.S. Income Taxes, 1916–1986," *Social Forces* 72:643–69.

Campbell, John, Rogers Hollingsworth, and Leon Lindberg, eds. 1991. *The Governance of the American Economy*. Cambridge: Cambridge University Press.

Campbell, John, and Leon Lindberg. 1990. "Property Rights and the Organization of Economic Activity by the State," *American Sociological Review* 55:634–47.

Campbell, John, and Ove Pedersen, eds. 2001. *The Rise of Neoliberalism and Institutional Analysis*. Princeton: Princeton University Press.

Carlton, Dennis. 1989. "The Theory and the Facts of How Markets Clear." Pp. 909–46 in *Handbook of Industrial Organization*, edited by Richard Schmalensee and Robert Willig. Amsterdam: North-Holland.

Carroll, Glenn, and Michael Hannah, eds. 1995. *Organizations in Industry: Strategy, Structure, and Selection*. New York: Oxford University Press.

Carroll, Glenn, and Michael Hannan. 2000. *The Demography of Corporations and Industries*. Princeton: Princeton University Press.

Carruthers, Bruce. 1994. "When is the State Autonomous? Culture, Organization Theory and the Political Sociology of the State," *Sociological Theory* 12, no. 1:19–44.

———. 1996. *City of Capital: Politics and Markets in the English Financial Revolution*. Princeton: Princeton University Press.

———. Forthcoming. *On Credit*. New York: The Russell Sage Foundation.

Carruthers, Bruce, and Sarah Babb. 2000. *Economy/Society: Markets, Meanings, and Social Structure*. Thousand Oaks: Pine Forge.

Carruthers, Bruce, and Terence Halliday. 1998. *Rescuing Business: The Making of Corporate Bankruptcy Law in England and the United States*. Oxford: Clarendon.

———. 2000. "Professionals in Systemic Reform of Bankruptcy Law: The 1978 U.S. Bankruptcy Code and the English Insolvency Act 1986," *The American Bankruptcy Law Journal* 74 (Winter): 35–75.

Carruthers, Bruce, and Wendy Espeland Nelson. 1998. "Money, Meaning and Morality," *American Behavioralist* 41 (August): 1384–408.

Castells, Manuel. 1996. *The Rise of the Networks Society*. Oxford: Blackwell.

Castilla, Emilio, Hokya Hwang, Ellen Granovetter, and Mark Granovetter. 2000. "Social Networks in Silicon Valley." Pp. 218–47 in *The Silicon Valley Edge: A Habitat for Innovation and Entrepreneurship*, edited by Chong-Moon Lee et al. Stanford: Stanford University Press.

Caves, Richard. 1964. *American Industry: Structure, Conduct, Performance*. Englewood Cliffs, N.J.: Prentice-Hall.

Chamberlin, Edward. 1933. *The Theory of Monopolistic Competition*. Cambridge: Harvard University Press.

Chandler, Alfred. 1962. *Strategy and Structure: Chapters in the History of the American Industrial Enterprise*. Cambridge: MIT Press.

———. 1977. *The Visible Hand: The Mangerial Revolution in American Business.* Cambridge: Harvard University Press.

———. 1984. "The Emergence of Managerial Capitalism," *Business History Review* 58:473–503.

Chernow, Ron. 1997. *The Death of the Banker: The Decline and Fall of the Great Financial Dynasties and the Triumph of the Small Investor.* Toronto: Vintage.

Chirot, Daniel. 1981. "Changing Fashion in the Study of the Social Causes of Economic and Political Change." Pp. 259–82 in *The State of Sociology: Problems and Prospects,* edited by J. F. Short. Beverly Hills: Sage.

Clark, Gordon, Maryann Feldman, and Meric Gertler, eds. 2000. *The Oxford Handbook of Economic Geography.* Oxford: Oxford University Press.

Clarke, David. 1987. "Trade and Industry in Barbarian Europe till Roman Times." Pp. 1–70 in Vol. 2 of *The Cambridge Economic History,* edited by M. M. Postand and Edward Miller. Cambridge: Cambridge University Press.

Clawson, Dan, Alan Neustadt, and Mark Weller. 1998. *Dollars and Votes: How Business Campaign Contributions Subvert Democracy.* Philadephia: Temple University Press.

Coase, R. H. [1937] 1988. "The Nature of the Firm." Pp. 33–55 in *The Firm, the Market, and the Law.* Chicago: University of Chicago Press.

Coase, R. H. 1960. "The Problem of Social Cost," *Journal of Law and Economics* 3 (October): 1–44.

Coase, R. H. 1988. "The Firm, the Market and the Law." Pp. 1–31 in *The Firm, the Market and the Law,* by R. H. Coase. Chicago: University of Chicago Press.

Coase, R. H. 1991a. "The Nature of the Firm: Origin, Meaning, Influence." Pp. 34–74 in *The Nature of the Firm: Origin, Evolution, and Development,* edited by Oliver Williamson and Sidney Winter. New York: Oxford University Press.

Coase, R. H. 1991b. *The Institutional Structure of Production.* Stockholm: Nobel Foundation.

Coats, A. W., ed. 1981. *Economists in Government: An International Comparative Study.* Durham: Duke University Press.

Coats, A. W. 1984. "The Sociology of Knowledge and History of Economics," *Research in the History of Economic Thought* 2:211–34.

Coats, A. W. 1993. *The Social Professionalization of Economics.* London: Routledge.

Cole, D. H. 2001. "'An Unqualified Human Good': E. P. Thompson and the Rule of Law," *Journal of Law and Society* 28, no. 2:117–203.

Coleman, James. 1970. "Social Inventions," *Social Forces* 49:163–73.

———. 1974. *Power and the Structure of Society.* New York: Norton.

———. 1982. *The Asymmetric Society.* Syracuse: Syracuse University Press.

———. 1984. "Introducing Social Structure into Economic Analysis," *American Economic Review* 74, no. 2:84–88.

———. 1986. "Social Theory, Social Research, and a Theory of Action," *American Journal of Sociology* 91:1309–35.

———. 1990. *Foundations of Social Theory.* Cambridge: Harvard University Press.

———. 1993. "The Rational Reconstruction of Society," *American Sociological Review* 58:1–15.

———. 1994. "A Rational Choice Perspective on Economic Sociology." Pp. 166–80 in *The Handbook of Economic Sociology*, edited by Neil Smelser and Richard Swedberg. New York and Princeton: Russell Sage Foundation and Princeton University Press.

Coleman, James, Elihu Katz, and Herbert Menzel. 1966. *Medical Innovation: A Diffusion Study*. New York: Bobbs-Merrill.

Collins, Randall. 1990. "Market Dynamics as the Engine of Historical Change," *Sociological Theory* 8:111–35.

Commons, John. [1924] 1995. *The Legal Foundations of Capitalism*. New Brunswick, N.J.: Transaction.

Corrigan, Peter. 1997. *The Sociology of Consumption: An Overview*. London: Sage.

Coser, Lewis. 1972. "The Alien as a Servant: Court Jews and Christian Renegades," *American Sociological Review* 37:574–81.

Cotterrell, Roger. 1999. *Emile Durkheim: Law in a Moral Domain*. Stanford: Stanford University Press.

Cournot, Antoine. [1838] 1927. *Research into the Mathematical Principles of the Theory of Wealth*. Translated by Nathaniel T. Bacon. New York: Macmillan.

Crouch, Colin and Wolfgang Streeck, eds. 1997. *Political Economy of Modern Capitalism*. London: Sage.

Crozier, Michel. 1964. *The Bureaucratic Phenomenon*. Chicago: University of Chicago Press.

Curtin, Philip. 1984. *Cross-Cultural Trade in World History*. Cambridge: Cambridge University Press.

Cyert, Richard, and James March. [1963] 1992. *A Behavioral Theory of the Firm*. 2nd ed. Oxford: Blackwell. Published in 1963 by Prentice-Hall, Englewood Cliffs, N.J.

Dahrendorf, Ralf. 1956. *Industrie- und Betriebssoziologie*. Berlin: de Gruyter.

Dalton, Melville. 1948. "The Industrial 'Rate-Buster': A Characterization," *Applied Anthropology* Winter: 5–18.

———. 1959. *Men Who Manage: Fusions of Feelings and Theory in Administration*. New York: Wiley.

David, Robert, and Shin-Kap Han. 1998. "Assessing Empirical Evidence of Transaction Cost Economics: A Meta-Analysis." Unpublished paper, Cornell University.

Davidson, Paul. 1981. "Post-Keynesian Economics." Pp. 151–73 in *The Crisis in Economic Theory*, edited by Daniel Bell and Irving Kristol. New York: Basic Books.

Davis, Gerald. 1994. "The Corporate Elite and the Politics of Corporate Control." Pp. 245–68 in suplement 1 to *Current Perspectives in Social Theory*, edited by C. Prendergast and J. D. Knotterus.

Davis, Gerald, and Douglas McAdam. 2000. "Corporations, Classes, and Social Movement after Managerialism," *Research in Organizational Behavior* 22:195–238.

Davis, Gerald, and Mark Mizruchi. 1999. "The Money Center Cannot Hold: Commercial Banks in the U.S. System of Corporate Governance," *Administrative Science Quarterly* 44:215–39.

Davis, Gerald, and Walter W. Powell. 1992. "Organization-Environment Relations." Pp. 315–75 in vol. 3 of *Handbook of Industrial and Organizational Psychology*, edited by M. D. Dunette and L. M. Hough. 2nd ed. Palo Alto, Calif.: Consulting Psychologists Press.

Davis, Gerald, and T. A. Thompson. 1994. "A Social Movement Perspective on Corporate Control," *Administrative Science Quarterly* 39:141–73.

Davis, Michael, and Andrew Stark, eds. 2001. *Conflict of Interest in the Professions*. Oxford: Oxford University Press.

Dawes, Robyn, and Roberto Weber. Forthcoming. "Behavioral Economics." In *The Handbook of Economic Sociology*, edited by Neil Smelser and Richard Swedberg. 2nd ed. New York and Princeton: Russell Sage Foundation and Princeton University Press.

De Alessi, Louis. 1980. "The Economics of Property Rights: A Review of the Evidence," *Research in Law and Economics* 2:1–47.

Deal, Terrence, and Allan Kennedy. 1982. *Corporate Cultures*. Reading, Mass.: Addison-Wesley.

———. 1999. *The New Corporate Cultures: Revitalizing the Workplace after Downseizing, Mergers, and Reengineering*. Reading, Mass.: Perseus Books.

Delaney, Kevin. 1989. "Power, Incorporate Networks, and 'Strategic Bankruptcy,'" *Law and Society Review* 23, no. 4:643–66.

Demeulenaere, P. "Interests, Sociological Analysis of." Pp. 7715–18 in vol. 6 of *International Encyclopaedia of the Social and Behavioral Sciences*, edited by Neil Smelser and Paul Baltes. Amsterdam: Elsevier.

Demsetz, Harold. 1982. *Economic, Legal, and Political Dimensions of Competition*. Amsterdam: North-Holland.

De Roover, Raymond. 1963. *The Rise and Decline of the Medici Bank*. Cambridge: Harvard University Press.

Deutschmann, Christoph. 2001. "Capitalism as a Religion? An Unorthodox Analysis of Entrepreneurship," *European Journal of Social Theory* 4, no. 4: 379–86.

Dezalay, Yves, and Bryant Garth. 1996. *Dealing in Virtue: International Commercial Arbitration and the Construction of a Transnational Legal Order*. Chicago: University of Chicago Press.

Diamond, Larry. 1992. "Economic Development and Democracy Reconsidered," *American Behavioral Scientist* 35, nos. 4/5: 450–99.

DiMaggio, Paul. 1986. "Structural Analysis of Organizational Fields: A Blockmodel Approach." Pp. 355–70 in vol. 8 of *Research in Organizational Behavior*, edited by Barry Staw and L. L. Cummings. Greenwich, Conn.: JAI Press.

———. 1988. "Interest and Agency in Institutional Theory." Pp. 3–21 in Lynn Zucker (ed.), *Institutional Patterns and Organizations*, Cambridge: Ballinger.

———. 1990. "Cultural Aspects of Economic Action and Organization." Pp. 113–36 in Roger Friedland and A. F. Robertson (eds.), *Beyond the Marketplace: Rethinking Economy and Society*. New York: De Gruyter.

———. 1994. "Culture and Economy." Pp. 27–57 in Neil Smelser and Richard Swedberg (eds.), *The Handbook of Economic Sociology*. New York and Princeton: Russell Sage Foundation and Princeton University Press.

———. 1997. "Culture and Cognition," *Annual Review of Sociology* 23:263–87.

———, ed. 2001. *The Twenty-First-Century Firm: Changing Economic Organizations in International Perspective*. Princeton: Princeton University Press.

DiMaggio, Paul, and Hugh Louch. 1998. "Socially Embedded Consumer Transactions: For What Kind of Purchases Do People Most Often Use Networks?" *American Sociological Review* 63:619–37.

Dobbin, Frank. 1993. "The Social Construction of the Great Depression: Industrial Policy during the 1930s in the United States, Britain, and France," *Theory and Society* 22:1–56.

———. 1994a. "Cultural Models of Organization: The Social Construction of Rational Organizing Principles." Pp. 117–41 in *The Sociology of Culture*, edited by Diane Crane. Oxford: Blackwell.

———. 1994b. *Forging Industrial Policy: The United States, Britain and France in the Railroad Age*. Cambridge: Cambridge University Press.

———. 2001a. "The Business of Social Movements." Pp. 74–80 in *Passionate Politics: Emotions and Social Movements*, edited by Jeff Goodwin et al. Chicago: University of Chicago Press.

———. 2001b. "Why the Economy Reflects the Polity: Early Rail Policy in Britain, France, and the United States." Pp. 401–24 in *The Sociology of Economic Life*, edited by Mark Granovetter and Richard Swedberg. 2nd rev. ed. Boulder, Colo.: Westview.

———. Forthcoming. "Comparative and Historical Perspectives in Economic Sociology." In *The Handbook of Economic Sociology*, edited by Neil Smelser and Richard Swedberg. 2nd ed. New York and Princeton: Russell Sage Foundation and Princeton University Press.

Dobbin, Frank, and Timothy Dowd. 1997. "How Policy Shapes Competition: Early Railroad Foundings in Massachusetts," *Administrative Science Quarterly* 42:501–29.

———. 2000. "The Market that Antitrust Built: Public Policy, Private Coercion, and Railroad Acquisitions, 1825 to 1922," *American Sociological Review* 65:631–57.

Dobbin, Frank, and John Sutton. 1998. "The Strength of a Weak State: The Rights Revolution and the Rise of Human Resources Management Division," *American Journal of Sociology* 104:441–76.

Dodd, Nigel. 1994 *The Sociology of Money: Economics, Reason and Contemporary Society*. Cambridge: Polity.

Donaldson, Thomas, and Lee Preston. 1995. "The Stakeholder Theory of the Corporation: Concepts, Evidence, and Implications," *Academy of Management Review* 29, no. 1:65–91.

Douglas, Mary, and Baron Isherwood. 1980. *The World of Goods: Towards an Anthropology of Consumption*. Harmondsworth: Penguin.

Douma, Sytse, and Hein Schreuder. 1998. *Economic Approaches to Organizations*. 2nd ed. London: Prentice-Hall.

Downs, Anthony. 1957. *An Economic Theory of Democracy*. New York: Harper and Row.

Dreze, Jean, and Amartya Sen. 1990–91. *The Political Economy of Hunger*. New York: Oxford University Press.

Drucker, Peter. 2001. "The Next Society," *The Economist (Supplement)* November 3:3–20.

Durkheim, Emile. 1887. "La Science Positive de la Morale en Allemagne," *Revue Philosophique* 24:33–58, 113–42, 275–84.

———. [1888] 1978. "Course in Sociology: Opening Lecture." Pp. 43–70 in *On Institutional Analysis*, by Emile Durkheim, edited by Mark Traugott. Chicago: University of Chicago Press.

———. [1893] 1933. *The Division of Labor in Society.* Translated by George Simpson. Glencoe, Ill.: Free Press.

———. [1893] 1984. *The Division of Labor in Society.* Translated by W. D. Halls. New York: Free Press.

———. [1895] 1964. *The Rules of Sociological Method.* New York: Free Press.

———. [1895–96] 1962. *Socialism.* New York: Collier.

———. [1897] 1951. *Suicide: A Study in Sociology.* Glencoe, Ill.: Free Press.

———. [1902] 1980. "Georg Simmel, *Philosophie des Geldes.*" Pp. 94–98 in *Contributions to "L'Année Sociologique."* New York: Free Press.

———. [1908] 1982. "Debate on Political Economy and Sociology (1908)." Pp. 229–35 in *The Rules of Sociological Method.* New York: Free Press.

———. [1909] 1978. "Sociology and the Social Sciences." Pp. 71–90 in *On Institutional Analysis*, by Emile Durkheim, edited by Mark Traugott. Chicago: University of Chicago Press.

———. [1912] 1965. *The Elementary Forms of Religious Life.* New York: Free Press.

———. [1950] 1983. *Professional Ethics and Civic Morals.* Westport, Conn.: Greenwood.

Easton, David. 2001. "Consuming Interests [On Social Research, Incorporated]," *University of Chicago Magazine* 93, no. 6:16–22.

Ebers, Mark, ed. 1997. *The Formation of Inter-Organizational Networks.* Oxford: Oxford University Press.

Eccles, Robert, and Dwight Crane. 1988. *Doing Deals: Investment Banks at Work.* Boston: Harvard Business School Press.

Edelman, Lauren. 1990. "Legal Environments and Organizational Governance: The Expansion of Due Process in the American Workplace," *American Journal of Sociology* 95:1401–40.

———. 1992. "Legal Ambiguity and Symbolic Structures: Organizational Mediation of Civil Rights," *American Journal of Sociology* 97:1531–76.

Edelman, Lauren, and Mark Suchman. 1997. "The Legal Environments of Organizations," *Annual Review of Sociology* 23:479–515.

Elias, Norbert. [1939] 1994. *The Civilizing Process: The History of Manners and State Formation and Civilization.* Oxford: Blackwell.

Ellickson, Robert. 1989. "Symposium on Post-Chicago Law and Economics: Bringing Culture and Human Frailty to Rational Actors: A Critique of Classical Law and Economics," *Chicago-Kent Law Review* 65:23–55.

———. 1991. *Order without Law: How Neighbors Settle Disputes.* Cambridge: Harvard University Press.

Elster, Jon. 1989. "Social Norms and Economic Theory," *Journal of Economic Perspectives* 3 (Fall): 99–117.

———. 1998. "Emotions and Economic Theory," *Journal of Economic Literature* 36 (March): 47–74.

———. 2000. "Rationality, Economy, and Society." Pp. 21–41 in *The Cambridge Companion to Weber*, edited by Stephen Turner. Cambridge: Cambridge University Press.

Emerson, Richard. 1962. "Power-Dependence Relations," *American Sociological Review* 27:31–41.

Engels, Friedrich. [1845] 1973. *The Condition of the Working Class in England*. Moscow: Progress Publishers.

England, Paula. 1992. *Comparable Worth: Theories and Evidence*. New York: Aldine de Gruyter.

———. 1994. "Neoclassical Economists' Theories of Discrimination." Pp. 59–69 in *Equal Employment Opportunity*, edited by Paul Burstein. New York: Aldine de Gruyter.

England, Paula, and Nancy Folbre. Forthcoming. "Gender and Economic Sociology." In *The Handbook of Economic Sociology*, edited by Neil Smelser and Richard Swedberg. 2nd ed. New York and Princeton: Russell Sage Foundation and Princeton University Press.

Esping-Andersen, Gösta. 1994. "Welfare States and the Economy." Pp. 711–32 in *The Handbook of Economic Sociology*, edited by Neil Smelser and Richard Swedberg. New York and Princeton: Russell Sage Foundation and Princeton University Press.

———. 1999. "The Household Economy." Pp. 47–72 in *Social Foundations of Postindustrial Economies*. Oxford: Oxford University Press.

Etzioni, Amitai. 1988. *The Moral Dimension: Towards A New Economics*. New York: Free Press.

Evans, Peter. 1995. *Embedded Autonomy: State and Industrial Transformation*. Princeton: Princeton University Press.

Evans, Peter, Dietrich Rueschemeyer, and Theda Skocpol, eds. 1985. *Bringing the State Back In*. Cambridge: Cambridge University Press.

Fama, Eugen, and Michael Jensen. 1983. "Separation of Ownership and Control," *Journal of Law and Economics* 26:301–25.

Farkas, George, and Paula England, eds. 1988. *Industries, Firms and Jobs: Sociological and Economic Approaches*. New York: Plenum.

Faulkner, Robert. 1971. *Studio Musicians*. Chicago: Aldine.

———. 1983. *Music on Demand: Composers and Careers in the Hollywood Film Industry*. New Brunswick, N.J.: Transaction.

Favereau, Olivier, and Emmanuel Lazega, eds. Forthcoming. *Conventions and Structures in Economic Organization*. Cheltenham: Elgar.

Fine, Ben, and Ellen Leopold. 1990. "Consumerism and the Industrial Revolution," *Social History* 15:151–79.

Finley, M. I. [1973] 1985. *The Ancient Economy*. London: Hogarth.

Fligstein, Neil. 1985. "The Spread of the Multinational Form among Large Firms, 1919–79," *American Sociological Review* 50:377–91.

———. 1990. *The Transformation of Corporate Control*. Cambridge: Harvard University Press.

———. 1996a. "Is Globalization the Cause of the Crises of the Welfare States?" Unpublished paper, University of California, Berkeley.

———. 1996b. "Markets as Politics: A Political-Cultural Approach to Market Institutions," *American Sociological Review* 61:656–73.

———. 1997. *Markets, Politics, and Globalization.* Acta Universitatis Upsaliensis # 42. Stockholm: Almquist and Wiksell International.

———. 2001. *The Architecture of Markets: An Economic Sociology of Twenty-First Century Capitalist Societies.* Princeton: Princeton University Press.

Fligstein, Neil, and Iona Mara-Drita. 1996. "How to Make a Market: Reflections on the Attempt to Create a Single Unitary Market in the European Community," *American Journal of Sociology* 102:1–33.

Fligstein, Neil, and Alec Stone Sweet. 2001. "Institutionalizing the Treaty of Rome." Pp. 29–55 in *The Institutionalization of Europe*, edited by Alec Stone Sweet, Wayne Sandholtz, and Neil Fligstein. New York: Oxford University Press.

Fogel, Robert. 1994. "Economic Growth, Population Theory, and Physiology: The Bearing of Long-Term Processes on the Making of Economic Policy," *American Economic Review* 84 (June): 369–95.

Folbre, Nancy. 2001. *The Invisible Heart: Economics and Family Values.* New York: New Press.

Folbre, Nancy, and Heidi Hartmann. 1988. "The Rhetoric of Self-Interest: Ideology and Gender in Economic Theory." Pp. 184–203 in *The Consequences of Economic Rhetoric*, edited by Arjo Klamer et al. Cambridge: Cambridge University Press.

Fourcade-Gourinchas, Marion. 2001. "Politics, Institutional Structures, and the Rise of Economics: A Comparative Study," *Theory and Society* 30:397–447.

Freeland, Robert. 1996. "The Myth of the M-Form? Governance, Consent and Organizational Change," *American Journal of Sociology* 102:483–526.

———. 2001. *The Struggle for Control of the Modern Corporation: Organizational Change at General Motors, 1924–1970.* Cambridge: Cambridge University Press.

Freeman, John. Forthcoming. "Venture Capital and Capitalism." In *The Economic Sociology of Capitalism*, edited by Victor Nee and Richard Swedberg.

Frenzen, Jonathan, Paul Hirsch, and Philipo Zerrillo. 1994. "Consumption, Preferences, and Changing Lifestyles." Pp. 403–25 in *The Handbook of Economic Sociology*, edited by Neil Smelser and Richard Swedberg. New York and Princeton: Russell Sage Foundation and Princeton University Press.

Frey, Bruno, et al. 1984. "Consensus and Dissension among Economists: An Empirical Inquiry," *American Economic Review* 74 (December): 986–94.

Friedman, Lawrence. 1975. *The Legal System: A Social Science Perspective.* New York: Russell Sage Foundation.

———. 1985. *A History of American Law.* 2nd ed. New York: Simon and Schuster.

Friedman, Milton. 1962. *Capitalism and Freedom.* Chicago: University of Chicago Press.

Friedmann, Georges. [1950] 1961. *The Anatomy of Work: Labor, Leisure and the Implications of Automation.* New York: Free Press.

Frisby, David. 1978. "Preface to the Second Edition." Pp. xv–xlii in *The Philosophy of Money*, by Georg Simmel. London: Routledge.

Fukuyama, Francis. 1995. *Trust: The Social Virtues and the Creation of Prosperity.* London: Penguin.

———. 2000. "Social Capital." Pp. 98–111 in *Culture Matters: How Values Shape Human Progress*, edited by Lawrence Harrison and Samuel Huntington New York: Basic Books.

Furubotn, Eirik, and Rudolf Richter. 1997. *Institutions and Economic Theory: The Contribution of New Institutional Economics.* Ann Arbor: University of Michigan Press.

Gallup, John Luke, and Jeffrey Sachs. 1999. *Geography and Economic Development.* CID Working Paper No. 1. Cambridge: Center for International Development.

Gambetta, Diego, ed. 1990. *Trust: The Making and Breaking of Cooperative Relations.* Oxford: Blackwell.

Gao, Bai. 2001. *Japan's Economic Dilemma: The Institutional Origins of Prosperity and Stagnation.* Cambridge: Cambridge University Press.

Garcia, Marie-France. 1986. "La Construction Sociale d'un Marché Parfait: Le Marché au Cadran de Fontaines-en-Sologne," *Actes de la Recherche en Sciences Sociales* 65 (November): 2–13.

Garth, Bryant, and Joyce Sterling. 1998. "From Legal Realism to Law and Society: Reshaping Law for the Last Stages of the Social Activist State," *Law and Society Review* 32, no. 2:409–71.

Geertz, Clifford. 1963. *Peddlers and Princes: Social Development and Economic Change in Two Indonesian Towns.* Chicago: University of Chicago Press.

———. 1973. *The Interpretation of Cultures.* New York: Basic Books.

Gereffi, Gary. 1994. "The International Economy and International Development." Pp. 206–33 in *The Handbook of Economic Sociology*, edited by Neil Smelser and Richard Swedberg. New York and Princeton: Russell Sage Foundation and Princeton University Press.

Gereffi, Gary, Ronie Garcia-Johnson and Erika Sasser. 2001. "The NGO-Industrial Complex," *Foreign Policy* (July–August): 56–65.

Gerschenkron, Alexander. 1962. *Economic Backwardness in Historical Perspective: A Book of Essays.* Cambridge: Harvard University Press.

———. 1971. "Mercator Gloriosus (Review of John Hicks, *A Theory of Economic History*)," *Economic History Review* 24:653–66.

Gibbons, Robert. 1992. *Game Theory for Applied Economists.* Princeton: Princeton University Press.

———. 1997. "Incentives and Careers in Organizations." Pp. 1–37 in vol. 2 of *Advances in Economics and Econometrics*, edited by David Kreps and Kenneth Wallis. Cambridge: Cambrdige University Press.

Gibbons, Robert, and Michael Waldman. 1999. "Careers in Organizations: Theory and Evidence." Pp. 2373–2437 in vol. 3B of *Handbook of Labor Economics*, edited by Orley Ashenfelter and David Card. Amsterdam: Elsevier.

Giddens, Anthony. 1973. *The Class Structure of Advanced Societies.* London: Hutchinson.

———. 1986. "Introduction." Pp. 1–31 in *Durkheim on Politics and the State*, edited by Anthony Giddens. Stanford: Stanford University Press.

———. 1987. "Social Theory and the Problem of Macroeconomics." Pp. 183–202 in *Social Theory and Modern Sociology.* Stanford: Stanford University.

Gilbert, Emily, and Eric Helleiner, eds. 1999. *Nation-States and Money: The Past, Present and Future of National Currencies*. London: Routledge.

Gislain, Jean-Jacques, and Philippe Steiner. 1995. *La Sociologie Economique, 1890–1920*. Paris: Presses Universitaires de France.

Glucksman, Miriam. 2000. "Retailing: Production's and Consumption's Missing Relation," *Economic Sociology: European Electronic Newsletter* 1, no. 3:12–16. See http//:www.siswo.uva.nl/ES

Goffman, Erving. 1951. "Symbols of Class Status," *British Journal of Sociology* 2:294–304.

———. [1961] 1972. "Strategic Interaction." Pp. 83–145 in *Strategic Interaction*. New York: Ballantine.

———. 1961. *Asylums: Essays on the Social Situation of Mental Patients and Others*. Garden City, N.Y.: Anchor.

Goldscheid, Rudolph. 1917. *Staatssozialismus order Staatskapitalismus?* Vienna: Anzengruber-Verlag Brüder Suschitsky.

———. [1925] 1958. "A Sociological Approach to Problems of Public Finance." Pp. 202–13 in *Classics in the Theory of Public Finance*, edited by Richard A. Musgrave and A. T. Peacock. London: Macmillan

Goldschmidt, Levin. [1891] 1957. *Universalgeschichte des Handelsrechts*. Stuttgart: Verlag von Ferdinand Enke.

Goldthorpe, John, ed. 1984. *Order and Conflict in Contemporary Capitalism: Studies in the Political Economy of Western European Nations*. Oxford: Clarendon.

Goldthorpe, John, et al. 1969. *The Affluent Worker in the Class Structure*. Cambridge: Cambridge University Press.

Goldthorpe, John, and Fred Hirsch, eds. 1978. *The Political Economy of Inflation*. Cambridge: Harvard University Press.

Gordon, David. 1975. "Introduction: J. Willard Hurst and the Common Law Tradition in American Legal History," *Law and Society Review* 10 (Fall): 9–55.

Gordon, David, and Sophie Meunier. 2001. *The French Challenge: Adaptation to Globalization*. Washington, D.C.: Brookings Institution.

Gouldner, Alvin. [1954] 1965. *The Wild Strike: A Study in Worker-Management Relationships*. New York: Harper and Row.

———. 1954. *Patterns of Industrial Bureaucracy*. New York: Free Press.

———. 1960. "The Norm of Reciprocity: A Preliminary Statement," *American Sociological Review* 25:161–78.

———. 1970. *The Coming Crisis of Western Sociology*. New York: Basic Books.

Granovetter, Mark. 1973. "The Strength of Weak Ties," *American Journal of Sociology* 78:1360–80.

———. 1974. *Getting A Job: A Study of Contacts and Careers*. Cambridge: Harvard University Press. 2nd ed. published 1995 Chicago: University of Chicago Press.

———. 1982. "Economic Decisions and Social Structure: The Problem of Embeddedness." Unpublished early draft of Granovetter 1985b.

———. 1985a. Luncheon Roundtable on the "New Sociology of Economic Life." American Sociological Association annual meeting, Washington, D.C., August 25.

———. 1985b. "Economic Action and Social Structure: The Problem of Embeddedness," *American Journal of Sociology* 91:481–510.

———. 1986. "Labor Mobility, Internal Markets, and Job Matching: A Comparison of Sociological and Economic Approaches," *Research in Social Stratification and Mobility* 5:3–39.

———. 1987a. "On Economic Sociology: An Interview with Mark Granovetter," *Research Reports from the Department of Sociology, Uppsala University* 1:1–26.

———. 1987b. "Programmatic Statement on Structural Analysis in the Social Sciences." P. [i] in *Intercorporate Relations: The Structural Analysis of Business*, edited by Mark Mizruchi and Michael Schwartz. Cambridge: Cambridge University Press.

———. 1988. "The Sociological and Economic Approaches to Labor Market Analysis: A Social Structural View." Pp. 187–216 in 1988. *Industries, Firms and Jobs: Sociological and Economic Approaches*, edited by George Farkas and Paula England. New York: Plenum.

———. 1990. "The Old and the New Old Economic Sociology: A History and an Agenda." Pp. 89–112 in *Beyond the Marketplace: Rethinking Economy and Society*, edited by Roger Friedland and A. F. Robertson. New York: Aldine de Gruyter.

———. 1992a. "Economic Institutions as Social Constructions: A Framework for Analysis," *Acta Sociologica* 35:3–11.

———. 1992b. "Problems of Explanation in Economic Sociology." Pp. 25–56 in *Networks and Organizations*, edited by Nitin Nohria and Robert Eccles. Cambridge: Harvard Business School Press.

———. 1992c. "The Nature of Economic Relations." Pp. 21–37 in *Understanding Economic Process*, edited by Sutti Ortiz and Susan Lees. Lanham: University Press of America.

———. 1993. "The Nature of Economic Relationships." Pp. 3–41 in *Explorations in Economic Sociology*, edited by Richard Swedberg. New York: Russell Sage Foundation.

———. 1994. "Business Groups." Pp. 453–75 in *The Handbook of Economic Sociology*, edited by Neil Smelser and Richard Swedberg. New York and Princeton: Russell Sage Foundation and Princeton University Press.

———. 1995a. "Coase Revisited: Business Groups in the Modern Economy," *Industrial and Corporate Change* 4:93–130.

———. 1995b. "The Economic Sociology of Firms and Entrepreneurs." Pp. 128–65 in *The Economic Sociology of Immigration*, edited by Alejandro Portes. New York: Russell Sage Foundation.

———. 1995c. *Getting A Job: A Study of Contacts and Careers.* 2nd ed. Chicago: University of Chicago Press. 1st ed. published 1974 Cambridge: Harvard University Press.

———. 1998. "NET-Society: Mark Granovetter on Network, Embeddedness and Trust," *Sosiologi idag (Norway)* 4:87–113.

———. 1999a. "Mark Granovetter on Economic Sociology in Europe," *Economic Sociology: European Electronic Newsletter* 1, no.1:10–11. See http//:www.siswo.uva.nl/ES.

———. 1999b. "Proposal to the Bechtel Initiative: A Network Study of Silicon Valley." Unpublished proposal; 2 pp.

———. 1999c. "Structural Analysis in the Social Sciences." P. [i] in *Legalizing Gender Inequality*, edited by Robert Nelson and William Bridges. Cambridge: Cambridge University Press.

———. 2000. "Introduction for the French Reader (Preface to *Le Marché est Autrement*, Paris: Desclée de Brouwer, 2000)." Unpublished article.

———. 2002. "A Theoretical Agenda for Economic Sociology." Pp. 35–60 in *The New Economic Sociology*, edited by M. Guillén et al. New York: Russell Sage Foundation.

———. Forthcoming a. "Business Groups and Social Organization." In *The Handbook of Economic Sociology*, edited by Neil Smelser and Richard Swedberg. 2nd ed. New York and Princeton: Russell Sage Foundation and Princeton University Press.

———. Forthcoming b. *Society and Economy: The Social Construction of Economic Institutions*. Cambridge: Harvard University Press.

Granovetter, Mark, and Patrick McGuire. 1998. "The Making of an Industry: Electricity in the United States." Pp. 147–73 in *The Laws of the Market*, edited by Michel Callon. Oxford: Blackwell.

Granovetter, Mark, and Roland Soong. 1986. "Threshold Models of Interpersonal Effects in Consumer Demand," *Journal of Economic Behavior and Organization* 7:481–510.

Granovetter, Mark, and Richard Swedberg, eds. 1992. *The Sociology of Economic Life*. Boulder, Colo.: Westview.

———, eds. 2001. *The Sociology of Economic Life*. 2nd rev. and expanded ed. Boulder, Colo.: Westview Press.

Granovetter, Mark, and Vassily Yakubovich. 2000. Conversations on Polanyi with the author, January 10.

Greenfeld, Liah. 2001. *The Spirit of Capitalism: Nationalism and Economic Growth*. Cambridge: Harvard University Press.

Greenstein, Theodore. 2001. "Economic Dependence, Gender, and the Division of Labor in the Home: A Replication and Extension," *Journal of Marriage and the Family* 62:322–35.

Greif, Avner. 1989. "Reputation and Coalitions in Medieval Trade: Evidence on the Maghribi Traders," *Journal of Economic History* 49:857–82.

———. 1993. "Contract Enforceability and Economic Institutions in Early Trade: The Maghribi Trader's Coalition," *American Economic Review* 83:525–48.

———. 1994. "Cultural Beliefs and the Organization of Society: A Historical and Theoretical Reflection on Collectivist and Individualist Societies," *Journal of Political Economy* 102:912–50.

Grusky, David, ed. 2001. *Social Stratification: Class, Race, and Gender in Sociological Perspective*. Boulder, Colo.: Westview.

Grusky, David, and Kim Weeden. 2001. "Decomposition Without Death: A Research Agenda for a New Class Analysis," *Acta Sociologica* 44:203–18.

Guillén, Mauro. 2001a. "Is Globalization Civilizing, Destructive or Feeble? A Critique of Four Key Debates in the Social Science Literature," *Annual Review of Sociology* 27:235–60.

Guillén, Mauro. 2001b. *The Limits of Convergence: Globalization and Organiza-*

tional Change in Argentina, South Korea, and Spain. Princeton: Princeton University Press.

Guillén, Mauro, et al., eds. 2002. *The New Eonomic Sociology: Developments in an Emerging Field.* New York: Russell Sage Foundation.

Gunn, J.A.W. 1968. "'Interest Will Not Lie': A Seventeenth Century Political Maxim," *Journal of the History of Ideas* 29:551–64.

———. 1969. *Politics and the Public Interest in the Seventeenth Century.* London: Routledge.

Guthrie, Doug. 1999. *Dragon in a Three-Piece Suit: The Emergence of Capitalism in China.* Princeton: Princeton University Press.

Habermas, Jürgen. [1968] 1971. *Knowledge and Human Interest.* Boston: Beacon Press.

———. 1984–1987. *The Theory of Communicative Action.* 2 vols. Cambridge: MIT Press.

Haglunds, Magnus. Forthcoming. *The Enemy of the People: A Sociological Study of Whistle Blowing.* Ph.D. diss., Stockholm University, Department of Sociology.

Hahn, Frank. 1981. "General Equilibrium Theory." Pp. 123–38 in *The Crisis in Economic Theory,* edited by Daniel Bell and Irving Kristol. New York: Basic Books

Hall, Peter, ed. 1989. *The Political Power of Economic Ideas: Keynesianism across Nations.* Princeton: Princeton University Press.

Hall, Peter, and David Soskice, eds. 2001. *Varieties of Capitalism: The Institutional Foundations of Competetive Advantage.* New York: Oxford University Press.

Hamilton, Gary, and Nicole Woolsey Biggart. 1988. "Market, Culture, and Authority: A Comparative Analysis of Management and Organization in the Far East," *American Journal of Sociology* 94:S52–S94.

Hannan, Michael, and Glenn Carroll. 1992. *Dynamics of Organizational Populations.* Oxford: Oxford University Press.

Hannan, Michael, and John Freeman. 1989. *Organizational Ecology.* Cambridge: Harvard University Press.

Hanley, Eric, Lawrence King and Janos Istvan Toth. Forthcoming. "The State, International Agencies, and Property Transformations in Post-Communist Hungary," *American Journal of Sociology.*

Hardin, Garrett. 1968. "The Tragedy of the Commons," *Science* 162:1243–97.

Harmon, Amy. 2001. "Is the 'Idea War' A Fight to Control A New World Currency?" *New York Times,* November 11, section 3:1, p. 12.

Harris, Ron. 2000. *Industrializing English Law: Entrepreneurship and Business Organization, 1720–1844.* Cambridge: Cambridge University Press.

Harrison, Lawrence, and Samuel Huntington, eds. 2000. *Culture Matters: How Values Shape Human Progress.* New York: Basic Books.

Hart, Oliver. 1995. *Firms, Contracts, and Financial Structure.* Oxford: Clarendon.

Hayek, Friedrich von, ed. 1935. *Collectivist Economic Planning.* London: Routledge.

———. 1942. "Scientism and the Study of Society (Part I)," *Economica* 9:267–91.

———. 1943. "Scientism and the Study of Society (Part II)," *Economica* 10:34–63.

———. 1945. "The Use of Knowledge in Society," *American Economic Review* 35:519–30

———. [1946] 1948. "The Meaning of Competition." Pp. 92–106 in *Individualism and Economic Order*. Chicago: University of Chicago Press.

———. 1968. "The Legal and Political Philosophy of David Hume." Pp. 335–60 in *Hume*, edited by V. C. Chappell. Notre Dame: University of Notre Dame Press.

———. 1976. "The Market Order or Catallaxy." Pp. 107–32 in vol. 2 of *Law, Legislation and Liberty*. London: Routledge and Kegan Paul.

Hechter, Michael. 1983. "Karl Polanyi's Social Theory: A Critique." Pp. 158–89 in *The Microfoundations of Macroeconomy*, edited by Michael Hechter. Philadelphia: Temple University Press.

Hechter, Michael, and Karl-Dieter Opp, eds. 2001. *Social Norms*. New York: Russell Sage Foundation.

Heckathorn, Douglas. 1988. "Collective Sanctions and the Emergence of Prisoner's Dilemma Norms," *American Journal of Sociology* 94:535–62.

Heckscher, Eli. [1931] 1994. *Mercantilism*. 2 vols. London: Routledge.

Hedström, Peter, and Richard Swedberg, eds. 1998. *Social Mechanisms: An Analytical Approach to Social Theory*. Cambrdige: Cambridge University Press.

Heilbron, Johan. 1998. "French Moralists and the Anthropology of the Modern Era: On the Genesis of the Notions of 'Interest' and 'Commercial Society.'" Pp. 77–106 in *The Rise of th Social Sciences and the Formation of Modernity*, edited by Johan Heilbron and Björn Wittrock. New York: Kluwer.

———. 2001a. "Economic Sociology in France," *European Societies* 3,1:41–68.

———. 2001b. "Interest: History of a Concept." Pp. 7708–12 in vol. 11 of *International Encyclopaedia of the Social and Behavioral Sciences*, edited by Neil Smelser and Paul Baltes. Amsterdam: Elsevier.

Heimer, Carol. 1985. *Reactive Risk and Rational Action: Managing Moral Hazard in Insurance Contracts*. Berkeley: University of California Press.

Held, David, and Anthony McGraw, eds. 2000. *The Global Transformations Reader: An Introduction to the Globalization Debate*. Cambridge: Polity.

Hennis, William. 1991. "The Pitiless 'Sobriety of Judgment': Max Weber between Carl Menger and Gustav von Schmoller—The Academic Politics of Value," *History of the Human Sciences* 41, no. 1:27–59.

Hernes, Gudmund. 1975. *Makt og avmakt. En begrepsanalyse* (Power and Powerlessness: A Conceptual Analysis). Bergen: Universitetsforlaget.

Hicks, John. 1969. *A Theory of Economic History*. Oxford: Oxford University Press.

Hindess, Barry. 1986. "'Interests' in Political Analysis." Pp. 112–31 in *Power, Action and Belief: A New Sociology of Knowledge?* edited by John Law. London: Routledge.

Hintze, Otto. [1929] 1975. "Economics and Politics in the Age of Modern Capitalism." Pp. 422–52 in *The Historical Esays of Otto Hintze*, edited by Felix Gilbert. New York: Oxford University Press.

Hintze, Otto. 1975. *The Historical Essays of Otto Hintze*, edited by Felix Gilbert. New York: Oxford University Press.

Hirsch, Paul. 1972. "Processing Fads and Fashion: An Organization-Set Analysis of Cultural Industry Systems," *American Journal of Sociology* 77:639–59.

———. 1975. "Organizational Analysis and Industrial Sociology: An Instance of Cultural Lag," *American Sociologist* 10 (February): 3–12.

———. 1982. "Network Data versus Personal Accounts: The Normative Culture of Interlocking Directorates." Paper presented at the annual meeting of the American Sociological Association.

Hirschman, Albert O. [1945] 1980. *National Power and the Structure of Foreign Trade.* Berkeley: University of California Press.

———. 1963. *Journeys Toward Progress: Studies of Economic Policy Making in Latin America.* New York: Twentieth Century Fund.

———. 1977. *The Passions and the Interests: Arguments for Capitalism Before Its Triumph.* Princeton: Princeton University Press.

———. 1982. *Shifting Involvements: Private Interest and Public Action.* Oxford: Blackwell.

———. 1986. "The Concept of Interest: From Euphemism to Tautology." Pp. 35–55 in *Rival Views of Market Society and Other Recent Essays.* New York: Viking.

Hobson, Barbara. 1990. "No Exit, No Voice: Women's Economic Dependency and the Welfare State," *Acta Sociologica* 33:235–50.

Hobson, John. 1997. *The Wealth of States: A Comparative Sociology of International Economic and Social Change.* Cambridge: Cambridge University Press.

Hochschild, Arlie. 1983. *The Managed Heart: Commercialization of Human Feeling.* Berkeley: University of California Press.

Hochschild, Arlie, with Anne Machung. 1989. *The Second Shift.* New York: Viking.

Hodgson, Geoffrey. 1988. *Economics and Institutions: A Manifesto for a Modern Institutional Economics.* Cambridge: Polity.

Hodgson, Geoffrey, Warren Samuels, and Mart Tool. 1998. *The Edward Elgar Companion to Institutional and Evolutionary Economics.* 2 vols. Cheltenham: Elgar.

Hodson, Randy. 1993. "Group Standards and the Organization of Work," *Research in the Sociology of Organizations* 11:55–80.

Hollingsworth, Roger. 1997. "The Institutional Embeddedness of American Capitalism." Pp. 133–47 in *Political Economy of Modern Capitalism,* edited by Colin Crouch and Wolfgang Streeck. London: Sage.

Hollingsworth, Roger, and Robert Boyer, eds. 1997. *Contemporary Capitalism: The Embeddedness of Institutions.* Cambridge: Cambridge University Press.

Hollingsworth, Roger, Philippe Schmitter, and Wolfgang Streeck, eds. 1994. *Governing Capitalist Economies.* New York: Oxford University Press.

Holmes, Stephen. 1990. "The Secret History of Self-Interest." Pp. 267–86 in *Beyond Self-Interest,* edited by Jane Mansbridge Chicago: University of Chicago Press.

Homans, George. 1950. *The Human Group.* New York: Harcourt, Brace.

Horwitz, Morton. 1992. "Santa Clara Revisited: The Development of Corporate Theory." Pp. 65–108 in *The Transformation of American Law 1870–1960: The Crisis of Legal Orthodoxy.* New York: Oxford University Press.

Hughes, Everett C. [1931] 1979. *The Growth of an Institution: The Chicago Real Estate Board.* New York: Arno.

———. 1962. "Dirty Work," *Social Problems* 10 (Summer): 3–10.

———. 1971. *The Sociological Eye.* Chicago: Aldine-Atherton.

Hume, David. [1739–40] 1978. *A Treatise on Human Nature*, edited by L. A. Selby-Bigge. Oxford: Oxford University Press

———. [1741] 1987. "Whether the British Government Inclines More to Absolute Monarchy, or to a Republic." Pp. 47–53 in *Essays.* Indianapolis: Liberty Classics.

Hunt, Alan. 1995. "Moralizing Luxury: The Discourse of the Governance of Consumption," *Journal of Historical Sociology* 8, no. 4: 352–74.

———. 1996. *Governance of the Consuming Passions: A History of Sumptuary Law.* New York: St. Martin's.

Hurst, James Willard. 1956. *Law and the Condition of Freedom in the Nineteenth Century.* Madison: University of Wisconsin Press.

———. 1964. *Law and Economic Growth: The Legal History of the Lumber Industry in Wisconsin 1836–1915.* Cambridge, Mass.: Belknap.

———. 1981. "*J. Willard Hurst*: An Interview Conducted by Laura L. Small." University of Wisconsin, University Archives Oral History project.

Huvelin, P. 1897. *Essai Historique sur le Droit des Marchés et Foirs.* Paris: Arthur Rousseau.

Ingham, Geoffrey. 1998. "On the Underdevelopment of 'The Sociology of Money,'" *Acta Sociologica* 41:3–18.

Inkeles, Alex, and David Horton Smith. 1974. *Becoming Modern: Individual Change in Six Developing Countries.* Cambridge: Harvard University Press.

Isay, Hermann. 1948. "The Method of the Jurisprudence of Interests: A Critical Study." Pp. 313–22 in *The Jurisprudence of Interests*, edited by Magdalena Schoch. Cambridge: Harvard University Press.

Izquierdo, A. Javier. 2001. "Reliability at Risk: The Supervision of Financial Models as a Case Study for Reflexive Economic Sociology," *European Societies* 391:69–90.

Jaffé, Edgar, et al. 1904. "Geleitwort," *Archiv für Sozialwissenschaft und Sozialpolitik* 19:vi.

Jagd, Søren. Forthcoming. *The French School of Conventions.* Cheltenham: Elgar.

Jahoda, Marie, Paul Lazarsfeld, and Hans Zeisel. [1933] 1971. *Marienthal: The Sociography of an Unemployed Community.* New York: Aldine.

James, William. [1897] 1956. "The Sentiments of Rationality." Pp. 63–110 in *The Will to Believe and Other Essays in Popular Philosophy.* New York: Dover.

Jameson, Fredric. 1983. "Postmodernism and Consumer Society." Pp. 111–25 in *The Anti-Aesthetic: Essays on Postmodern Culture*, edited by Hal Draper. New York: New Press.

Jensen, Michael. 1998. *Foundations of Organizational Strategy.* Cambridge: Harvard University Press.

———. 2001. "Value Maximization, Stakeholder Theory, and the Corporate Objective Function," *Journal of Applied Corporate Finance* 14 (Fall): 8–21.

Jensen, Michael, and William Meckling. 1976. "Theory of The Firm: Managerial Behavior, Agency Costs, and Ownership Structure," *Journal of Financial Economics* 3:305–60.

Jevons, W. Stanley. [1879] 1965. "Preface to the Second Edition." Pp. xi–liii in *The Theory of Political Economy.* 5th ed. New York: Augustus M. Kelley.

———. 1911. *The Theory of Political Economy.* 4th ed. London: Macmillan.

Jhering, Rudolf von. [1872] 1915. *The Struggle for Law.* 2nd ed. Chicago: Callaghan.

Jonasdottir, Anna. 1988. "On the Concept of Interest, Women's Interest, and the Limitations of Interest Theory." Pp. 33–65 in *The Political Interests of Gender,* edited by Kathleen B. Jones and Anna Jonasdottir. London: Sage.

Jones, Stephen. 1984. *The Economics of Conformism.* Oxford: Blackwell.

Kahneman, Daniel, Jack Kretsch, and Richard Thaler. 1986. "Fairness as Entitlement on Profit Seeking: Entitlements in the Market," *American Economic Review* 76:728–41.

Kanter, Rosabeth Moss. 1977. *Men and Women of the Corporation.* New York: Basic Books.

———. 1983. *The Change Masters: Innovation and Entrepreneurship in America.* New York: Simon and Schuster.

———. 1988. "When a Thousand Flowers Bloom: Structural, Collective, and Social Conditions for Innovations in Organizations," *Research in Organizational Behavior* 10:169–211.

Katona, George. 1957. *Business Looks at Banks: A Study of Business Behavior.* Ann Arbor: University of Michigan Press.

Katz, Elihu. 1960. "The Two-Step Flow of Communication." Pp. 346–65 in *Mass Communications: A Book of Readings,* edited by Wilburt Schramm. Urbana, Ill.: University of Illinois Press.

Katz, Elihu, and Paul Lazarsfeld. 1955. *Personal Influence: The Part Played by People in the Flow of Mass Commuications.* Glencoe, Ill.: Free Press.

Keister, Lisa. 2000a. *Chinese Business Groups: The Structure and Impact of Interfirm Relations during Economic Development.* New York: Oxford University Press.

Keister, Lisa. 2000b. *Wealth in America: Trends in Wealth Inequality.* Cambridge: Cambridge University Press.

Kelly, Erin, and Frank Dobbin. 1999. "Civil Rights Law at Work: Sex Discrimination and the Rise of Maternity Leave Policies," *American Journal of Sociology* 105:455–92.

Kent, Stephen. 1983. "The Quaker Ethic and the Fixed Price Policy: Weber and Beyond," *Sociological Inquiry* 53 (Winter): 16–32

Keynes, John Maynard. 1936. *The General Theory of Employment, Interest and Money.* London: Macmillan.

———. [1943] 1954. "Preface to the French Edition of *General Theory,*" *International Economic Papers* 4:66–9.

Keynes, John Neville, Sr., [1891] 1955. *The Scope and Method of Political Economy.* 4th ed. New York: Kelley and Millman.

Kindleberger, Charles. 1989. *Manias, Panics and Crashes: A History of Financial Crises.* London: Macmillan.

Kirzner, Israel. 1973. *Competition and Entrepreneurship.* Chicago: University of Chicago Press.

———. 1976. *The Economic Point of View: An Essay in the History of Economic Thought.* Kansas City, Mo.: Sheed and Ward.

———. 1997. "Entrepreneurial Discovery and the Competitive Market Process: An Austrian Approach," *Journal of Economic Literature* 35:60–85.

Kiser, Edgar, and Aaron Matthew Laing. 2001. "Have We Overestimated the Effects of Neoliberalism and Globalization? Some Speculations on the Anamolous Stability of Taxes on Business." Pp. 52–68 in *The Rise of Neoliberalism and Institutional Analysis*, edited by John Campbell and Ove Pedersen. Princeton: Princeton University Press.

Knight, Frank. [1921] 1985. *Risk, Uncertainty and Profit*. Chicago: University of Chicago Press.

———. [1933] 1967. *The Economic Organization*. New York: Augustus M. Kelley.

Knoke, David. 2001. *Organizational Change: Business Networks in the New Political Economy*. Boulder, Colo.: Westview.

Knorr Cetina, Karin, and Urs Brügger. 2002. "Global Macrostructures: The Virtual Societies of Financial Markets," *American Journal of Sociology* 107: 905–50.

Kocka, Jürgen. 1981. "Capitalism and Bureaucracy in German Industrialization before 1914," *Economic History Review* 34:453–68.

Kotz, David. 1978. *Bank Control of Large Corporations in the United States*. Berkeley: University of California Press.

Kreps, David. 1990a. "Corporate Culture and Economic Theory." Pp. 90–143 in *Perspectives on Positive Political Economy*, edited by James Alt and Kenneth Shepsle. Cambridge: Cambridge University Press.

———. 1990b. *Game Theory and Economic Modelling*. Oxford: Clarendon.

Krippner, Greta. 2001. "The Elusive Market: Embeddedness and the Paradigm of Economic Sociology," *Theory and Society* 30,6:775–810.

Krueger, Anne. 1974. "The Political Economy of the Rent-Seeking Society," *American Economic Review* 64, no. 3(June): 291–303.

Krugman, Paul. 1995. *Development, Geography, and Economic Theory*. Cambridge: MIT Press.

———. 2001a. "A Bad Week," *New York Times*, September 23:WK17.

———. 2001b. "Fear Itself," *New York Times Magazine*, September 30:36–41, 54–5, 84–5.

Kuznets, Simon. 1966. *Modern Economic Growth: Rate, Structure and Spread*. New Haven: Yale University Press.

La Porta, Rafael, et al. 1998. "Law and Finance," *Journal of Political Economy* 106:1113–55.

La Rochefoucauld, François, Duc de. [1665] 1959. *Maxims*. Translated by Leonard Tancock. London: Penguin.

Lamont, Michèle. 1992. *Money, Morals, and Manners: The Culture of the French and the American Upper-Middle Class*. Chicago: University of Chicago Press.

Lamont, Michèle and Annette Lareau. 1988. "Cultural Capital: Allusions, Gaps and Glissandos in Recent Theoretical Developments," *Sociological Theory* 6 (Fall): 153–68.

Landes, David. 1998. *The Wealth and Poverty of Nations*. New York: Norton.

———. 2000. "Culture Makes Almost All the Difference." Pp. 2–13 in *Culture Matters: How Values Shape Human Progress*, edited by Lawrence Harrison and Samuel Huntington New York: Basic Books.

Laumann, Edward, and David Knoke. 1987. *The Organizational State: Social Change in National Policy Domains*. Madison: University of Wisconsin Press.

Law, John, and John Hassard, eds. 1999. *Actor Network Theory and After*. Oxford: Blackwell.

Lawler, Edward, and Shane Thye. 1999. "Bring Emotions into Social Exchange Theory," *Annual Review of Sociology* 25:217–44.

Lazarsfeld, Paul. 1959. "Reflections on Business," *American Journal of Sociology* 65:1–31.

Lazega, Emmanuel. 2000. *The Collegial Phenomenon: Social Mechanisms of Cooperation among Peers*. New York: Oxford University Press.

Lazerson, Mark. 1993. "Future Alternatives of Work Reflected in the Past: Putting-Out Production in Modena." Pp. 403–27 in *Explorations in Economic Sociology*, edited by Richard Swedberg. New York: Russell Sage Foundation.

———. 1988. "Organizational Growth of Small Firms: An Outcome of Markets and Hierarchies?" *American Sociological Review* 53:330–42.

Lebaron, Frédéric. 2000a. *La Croyance Economique. Les Economistes entre Science et Politique*. Paris: Seuil.

———. 2000b. "The Space of Economic Neutrality: Types of Legitimacy and Trajectories of Central Bank Managers," *International Journal of Contemporary Sociology* 37, no. 2:208–29.

———. Forthcoming. *Les Fondements Symboliques de l'Ordre Economique*.

Leifer, Eric, and Harrison White. 1987. "A Structural Approach to Markets." Pp. 85–108 in *Intercorporate Relations: The Structural Analysis of Business*, edited by Mark Mizruchi and Michael Schwartz. Cambridge: Cambridge University Press.

Lengyel, György and Zsolt Rostoványi (eds.). 2001. *The Small Transformation: Society, Economy, and Politics in Hungary and the New European Architecture*. Budapest: Akadémiai Kiadó.

Lester, Richard. 1947. "Marginalism, Minimum Wages, and Labor Markets," *American Economic Review* 37:135–48.

Lestition, Steven. 2000. "Historical Preface to Max Weber, 'Stock and Commodity Exchanges,'" *Theory and Society* 29:289–304.

Lewin, Leif. 1991. *Self-Interest and Public Interest in Western Politics*. Oxford: Oxford University Press.

Lewis, David. 1986. *Convention: A Philosophical Study*. Oxford: Blackwell.

Lie, John. 1992. "The Concept of Mode of Exchange," *American Sociological Review* 57:508–23.

———. 1997. "Sociology of Markets," *Annual Review of Sociology* 23:341–60.

Light, Ivan. Forthcoming. "The Ethnic Economy." In *The Handbook of Economic Sociology*, edited by Neil Smelser and Richard Swedberg. 2nd ed. New York and Princeton: Russell Sage Foundation and Princeton University Press.

Light, Ivan, and Stavros Karageorgis. 1994. "The Ethnic Economy." Pp. 647–71 in *The Handbook of Economic Sociology*, edited by Neil Smelser and Richard Swedberg. New York and Princeton: Russell Sage Foundation and Princeton University Press.

Lin, Nan. 2001. *Social Capital: A Theory of Social Structure and Action*. Cambridge: Cambridge University Press.

Lindberg, Leon, and Charles Maier, eds. 1985. *The Politics of Inflation and Economic Stagnation*. Washington, D.C.: Brookings Institution.

Lindenberg, Siegwart. 1985. "Rational Choice and Sociological Theory: New Perspectives on Economics as a Social Science," *Zeitschrift für die Gesamte Staatswissenschaft* 141:44–55.

Lipset, S. M. 1960. *Political Man*. Garden City: Anchor.

——. [1967] 1988. "Values and Entrepreneurship in the Americas." Pp. 77–140 in Lipset, *Revolution and Counterrevolution: Change and Persistence in Social Structures*. New Brunswick, N.J.: Transaction.

——. 1989. *Continental Divide: The Values and Institutions of the United States and Canada*. Washington, D.C.: Canadian-American Committee.

——. 1993. "Culture and Economic Behavior: A Comment," *Journal of Labor Economics* 11:S330–47.

——. 1996. *American Exceptionalism: A Double-Edged Sword*. New York: Norton.

Lipset, S. M., and Gabriel Salman Lenz. 2000. "Corruption, Culture, and Markets." Pp. 112–25 in *Culture Matters: How Values Shape Human Progress*, edited by Lawrence Harrison and Samuel Huntington. New York: Basic Books.

Ljungar, Erik. Forthcoming. *Ethnicity and Entrepreneurship in Sweden*. Ph.D. diss., Department of Sociology, Stockholm University.

Locke, John. [1689] 1955. *A Letter Concerning Toleration*. New York: Bobbs-Merrill.

Lockwood, David. 1958. *The Blackcoated Worker: A Study in Class Consciousness*. London: Allen and Unwin.

Löfgren, Orvar. 1994. "Consuming Interests." Pp. 47–70 in *Consumption and Identity*, edited by Jonathan Friedman. Chur, Switzerland: Harwood Academic Publishers.

Longhurst, Brian, and Mike Savage. 1996. "Social Class, Consumption and the Influence of Bourdieu: Some Critical Issues." Pp. 274–301 in *Consumption Matters: The Production and Experience of Consumption*, edited by Stephen Edgell et al. Oxford: Blackwell.

Lopez, Robert. 1976. *The Commercial Revolution of the Middle Ages, 950–1350*. Cambridge: Cambridge University Press.

Luhmann, Niklas. [1970] 1982. "The Economy as a Social System." Pp. 190–225 in *The Differentiation of Society*. New York: Columbia University Press.

——. 1979. "Trust." Pp. 1–103 in *Trust and Power*. New York: Wiley.

——. 1988. *Die Wirtschaft der Gesellschaft*. Frankfurt am Main: Suhrkamp.

——. 1998. "Politics and Economy," *Thesis Eleven* 53:1–9.

Lunt, Peter, and Adrian Furnham, eds. 1996. *Economic Socialization: The Economic Beliefs and Behaviours of Young People*. Cheltenham: Elgar.

Macaulay, Stewart. 1963. "Non-Contractual Relations in Business: A Preliminary Study," *American Sociological Review* 28:55–67.

——. 1977. "Elegant Models, Empirical Pictures, and the Complexities of Contract," *Law and Society Review* 11:507–28.

Macaulay, Stewart, Lawrence Friedman, and John Stokey, eds. 1995. *Law and Society: Readings in the Social Study of Law*. New York: Norton.

——. 1947. "Rejoinder to an Antimarginalist," *American Economic Review* 37:148–54.

Machlup, Fritz. 1946. "Marginal Analysis and Empirical Research," *American Economic Review* 36:519–54.

MacIver, R. M. 1932. "Interests." P. 147 in vol. 7 of *Encyclopaedia of the Social Sciences*. New York: Macmillan.

MacKenzie, Donald. 1996. "Economic and Sociological Explanations of Technological Change." Pp. 49–65 in *Knowing Machines: Essays on Technical Change*, edited by Donald MacKenzie Cambridge: MIT Press.

———. 2000. "Fear in the Markets," *London Review of Books*, April 13, pp. 31–32.

MacKenzie, Donald, and Yuval Millo. 2001. "Negotiating a Market Performing Theory: The Historical Sociology of a Financial Derivatives Exchange." Paper presented at the European Association for Evolutionary Political Economy, Siena, November 8–11.

Macneil, Ian. 1978. "Contracts: Adjustment of Long-Term Economic Relations under Classical, Neoclassical, and Relational Contract Law," *Northwestern University Law Review* 72:854–905.

———. 1985. "Relational Contracting: What We Do and Do Not Know," *Wisconsin Law Review*, 483–525.

———. 2000. "Other Sociological Approaches." Pp. 694–718 in Vol. 1 of *Encyclopaedia of Law and Economics*, edited by Boudewidja Bouckaert and Gerrit De Geest. Cheltenham: Elgar.

Macy, Michael. 1997. "Identity, Interest and Emergent Rationality: An Evolutionary Synthesis," *Rationality and Society* 9, no. 4:427–48.

Makler, Harery, Alberto Martinelli, and Neil Smelser, eds. 1982. *The New International Economy*. London: Sage.

Malecki, E. J. 2001. "Economic Geography." Pp. 4084–89 in vol. 6 of *International Encyclopaedia of the Social and Behavioral Sciences*, edited by Neil Smelser and Paul Baltes. Amsterdam: Elsevier.

Mann, Fritz Karl. 1943. "The Sociology of Taxation," *Review of Politics* 5:225–35.

Mann, Michael. 1988. "State and Society, 1130–1815: An Analysis of English State Finances." Pp. 74–123 in *States, War and Capitalism: Studies in Political Sociology*. Oxford: Blackwell.

Mansbridge, Jane. 1983. *Beyond Adversary Democracy*. Rev. ed. Chicago: University of Chicago Press.

———, ed. 1990. *Beyond Self-Interest*. Chicago: University of Chicago Press.

March, James. 1962. "The Business Firm as a Political Coalition," *Journal of Politics* 24:662–78.

Markoff, John, and Verónica Montecinas. 1993. "The Ubiquitous Rise of Economists," *Journal of Public Policy* 13, no. 1:37–68.

Marshall, Alfred, and Mary Paley Marshall [1879] 1994. *The Economics of Industry*. Bristol: Thoemmis Press.

Marshall, Alfred. 1919. *Industry and Trade*. London: Macmillan.

———. [1920] 1961. *Principles of Economics*. 9th (variorum) ed. 2 vols. London: Macmillan. 1st ed. published 1890.

———. 1923. *Money, Credit and Commerce*. London: Macmillan.

Marshall, Gordon. 1982. *In Search of the Spirit of Capitalism: An Essay on Max Weber's Protestant Ethic Thesis*. London: Hutchinson.

Martinelli, Alberto. 1987. "The Economy as an Institutional Process," *Telos* 73 (Fall): 131–46.

Marx, Karl. [1844] 1978. "The Power of Money in Bourgeois Society." Pp. 101–

6 in *The Marx-Engels Reader*, edited by Robert C. Tucker. 2nd ed. New York: Norton.

——. [1845] 1978. "Theses on Feuerbach." Pp. 143–45 in *The Marx-Engels Reader*, edited by Robert C. Tucker. 2nd ed. New York: Norton.

——. [1852] 1950. *The Eighteenth Brumaire of Louis Bonaparte*. New York: International Publishers.

——. [1857–58] 1973. *Grundrisse: Foundations of the Critique of Political Economy*. New York: Vintage.

——. [1859] 1970. *A Contribution to the Critique of Political Economy*. New York: International Publishers.

——. [1867] 1906. *Capital: A Critique of Political Economy*. New York: Modern Library.

Marx, Karl, and Friedrich Engels. [1848] 1978. "Manifesto of the Communist Party." Pp. 473–500 in *The Marx-Engels Reader*, edited by Robert C. Tucker. 2nd ed. New York: Norton.

Mason, Edward. 1939. "Price and Production Policies of Large-Scale Enterprises," *American Economic Review* 29:61–74.

Mauss, Marcel. [1925] 1990. *The Gift: The Form and Reason for Exchange in Archaic Societies*. New York: Norton.

Mayer, Martin. 1997. *The Bankers: The Next Generation*. New York: Truman Talley.

McCloskey, Donald. 1985. *The Rhetoric of Economics*. Madison: University of Wisconsin Press.

McKendrick, Neil. 1982. "The Consumer Revolution of Eighteenth-Century England." Pp. 9–196 in *The Birth of A Consumer Society*, edited by Neil McKendrick, John Brewer, and J. H. Plumb. London: Europa.

McLean, Paul, and John Padgett. 1997. "Was Florence a Perfectly Competitive Market? Transactional Evidence from the Renaissance," *Theory and Society* 26, nos. 2–3: 209–44.

McLelland, David. 1961. *The Achieving Society*. Princeton: Van Nostrand.

McNamee, Stephen, and Robert Miller. 1989. "Estate Inheritance: A Sociological Lacunae," *Sociological Inquiry* 59 (Winter): 7–29.

Medema, Steven, Nicholas Mercuro, and Warren Samuels. 2000. "Institutional Law and Economics." Pp. 418–55 in vol. 1 of *Encyclopaedia of Law and Economics*, edited by Boudewidja Bouckaert and Gerrit De Geest. Cheltenham: Elgar.

Medema, Steven, and Richard Zerbe. 2000. "The Coase Theorem." Pp. 836–92 in vol. 1 of *Encyclopaedia of Law and Economics*, edited by Boudewidja Bouckaert and Gerrit De Geest. Cheltenham: Elgar.

Menger, Carl. [1883] 1985. *Investigations into the Method of the Social Sciences with Special Reference to Economics*. Translated by Frances Nock. New York: New York University Press.

——. 1892. "On the Origin of Money," *Economic Journal* 2:39–55.

Mercuro, Nicholas, and Steven Medema. 1997. *Economics and the Law: From Posner to Post-Modernism*. Princeton: Princeton University Press.

Merton, Robert K. 1935. "Fluctuations in the Rate of Industrial Invention," *Quarterly Journal of Economics* 49:454–74.

——. [1938] 1970. *Science, Technology and Society in Seventeenth Century England*. New York: Fertig.

————. [1946] 1971. *Mass Persuasion: The Social Psychology of a War Bond Drive.* Westport, Conn.: Greenwood.

————. 1952. "Bureaucratic Structure and Personality." Pp. 361–71 in *Reader in Bureaucracy*, edited by Robert K. Merton. New York: Free Press.

————. 1968a. "Continuities in the Theory of Social Structure and Anomie." Pp. 215–48 in *Social Theory and Social Structure.* Enlarged ed. New York: Free Press.

————. 1968b. "Social Structure and Anomie." Pp. 185–214 in *Social Theory and Social Structure.* Enlarged ed. New York: Free Press.

————. 1968c. *Social Theory and Social Structure.* Enlarged ed. New York: Free Press.

————. [1970] 1976. "The Ambivalence of Organizational Leaders." Pp. 73–89 in *Sociological Ambivalence and Other Essays.* New York: Free Press.

————. 1973. "Priorities in Scientific Discovery." Pp. 286–324 in *The Sociology of Science.* Chicago: University of Chicago Press.

————. 1976. *Sociological Ambivalence and Other Essays.* New York: Free Press.

————. 1984. "Socially Expected Durations: A Case Study of Concept Formation in Sociology." Pp. 262–83 in *Conflict and Consensus*, edited by W. W. Powell and R. Robbins. New York: Free Press.

————. 2001. Email to the author, November 14 and 15.

Meyer, John. 2000. "Globalization: Sources and Effects on National States and Societies," *International Sociology* 15:233–48.

Meyer, John, and Ronald Jepperson. 2000. "The 'Actors' of Modern Society: The Cultural Construction of Social Agency," *Sociological Theory* 18:100–20.

Meyer, John, and Brian Rowan. 1977. "Institutionalized Organizations: Formal Structure as Myth and Ceremony," *American Journal of Sociology* 83:340–63.

Miceli, Marcia, and James Near. 1991. "Whistle-Blowing as an Organizational Process," *Research in the Sociology of Organization* 9:139–200.

Miethe, Terance, and Joyce Rothschild. 1994. "*Review Article*: Whistleblowing and the Control of Organizational Misconduct," *Sociological Inquiry* 64:322–47.

Milgate, Murray, and Shannon Stimson. 1998. "Hume on Law and Economics." Pp. 222–244 in vol. 2 of *The New Palgrave Dictionary of Law and Economics*, edited by Peter Newman. London: Macmillan.

Milgrom, Paul, Douglass North, and Barry Weingast. 1990. "The Role of Institutions in the Revival of Trade: The Law Merchant, Private Judges, and the Champagne Fairs," *Economics and Politics* 2, no. 1: 23.

Milgrom, Paul, and John Roberts. 1992. *Economics, Organization and Management.* Englewood Cliffs, N.J.: Prentice-Hall.

Miliband, Ralph. 1961. *The State in Capitalist Society.* New York: Basic Books.

Milkman, Ruth, and Eleanor Townsley. 1994. "Gender and the Economy." Pp. 600–19 in *The Handbook of Economic Sociology*, edited by Neil Smelser and Richard Swedberg. New York and Princeton: Russell Sage Foundation and Princeton University Press.

Milkman, Ruth. 1987. *Gender at Work: The Dynamics of Job Segregation by Sex during World War II.* Urbana: University of Illinois Press.

Mill, John Stuart. [1848] 1987. *Principles of Political Economy.* New York: Augustus M. Kelley.

———. [1867] 1988. "The Admission of Women to the Electoral Franchise 20 May, 1867." Pp. 151–62 in vol. 28 of *Collected Works*, by John Stuart Mill. London: Routledge.

Miller, Daniel. 1995. "Consumption Studies as the Transformation of Anthropology." Pp. 264–95 in *Acknowledging Consumption: A Review of New Studies*, edited by Daniel Miller. London: Routledge.

Miller, Joanne. 1988. "Jobs and Work." Pp. 327–59 in *Handbook of Sociology*, edited by Neil Smelser London: SAGE.

Miller, Michael. 1981. *The Bon Marché: Bourgeois Culture and the Department Store, 1869–1920*. Princeton: Princeton University Press.

Mingione, Enzo. 1991. *Fragmented Societies: A Sociology of Economic Life Beyond the Market*. Oxford: Blackwell.

Mintz, Beth, and Michael Schwartz. 1985. *The Power Structure of American Business*. Chicago: University of Chicago Press.

Mirowski, Philip, ed. 1994. *Natural Images in Economic Thought*. Cambridge: Cambridge University Press.

Mises, Ludwig von. 1949. *Human Action: A Treatise on Economics*. London: Hodge.

———. 1961. "Markt." Pp. 131–36 in vol. 7 of *Handwörterbuch der Sozialwissenschaften*, edited by E. V. Beckerath. Stuttgart: Gustav Fischer.

———. [1966] 1990. "Catallactics or Economics of Market Society." Pp. 3–27 in vol. 3 of *Austrian Economics*, edited by Stephen Littlechild. Aldershot: Elgar.

Mizruchi, Mark. 1992. *The Structure of Corporate Political Action: Interfirm Relations and Their Consequences*. Cambridge: Harvard University Press.

———. 1996. "What Do Interlocks Do? An Analysis, Critique, and Assessment of Research on Interlocking Directorates," *Annual Review of Sociology* 22:271–98.

Mizruchi, Mark, and Linda Brewster Stearns. 1994. "Money, Banking and Financial Markets." Pp. 313–41 in *The Handbook of Economic Sociology*, edited by Neil Smelser and Richard Swedberg. New York and Princeton: Russell Sage Foundation and Princeton University Press.

Mjøset, Lars. 1985. *Introduksjon til Reguleringskolen* (Introduction to the Regulation School). Aalborg, Denmark: Nordisk Sommeruniversitet.

Mokyr, Joel. 1993. "Editor's Introduction: The New Economic History and the Industrial Revolution." Pp. 1–131 in *The British Industrial Revolution: An Economic Perspective*, edited by Joel Mokyr. Boulder, Colo.: Westview.

Mommsen, Wolfgang. 1974. "The Alternative to Marx: Dynamic Capitalism instead of Bureaucratic Socialism." Pp. 47–71 in *The Age of Bureaucracy*. New York: Harper and Row.

———. 2000. "Max Weber's Grand Sociology': The Origins and Composition of *Wirtschaft und Gesellschaft. Soziologie*," *History and Theory* 39:364–83.

Montesquieu, Charles de Secondat. [1748] 1989. *The Spirit of the Laws*. Cambridge: Cambridge University Press.

Moore, Barrington. 1966. *Origins of Democracy and Dictatorship*. Boston: Beacon.

Morgan, David, and Iain Wilkinson. 2001. "The Problem of Suffering and the Sociological Task of Theodicy," *European Journal of Social Theory* 4, no. 2: 199–214.

Mueller, Dennis. 1989. *Public Choice II.* Cambridge: Cambridge University Press.

———. 1998. "Buchanan, James." Pp. 174–85 in vol. 1 of *The New Palgrave. Dictionary of Economics and the Law,* edited by Peter Newman. London: Macmillan.

Müller-Freienfels, Wolfram. 1978. "Agency, Law of." Pp. 291–95 in vol. 1 of *Encyclopaedia Britannica (Macropaedia)* . Chicago: Encyclopaedia Britannica.

Mullins, Nicholas, and Carolyn Mullins. 1973. *Theories and Theory Groups in Contemporary American Sociology.* New York: Harper and Row.

Murphy, Raymond. 1984. "The Structure of Closure: A Critique and Development of the Theories of Weber, Collins, and Parkin," *British Journal of Sociology* 35:547–67.

———. 1988. *Social Closure: The Theory of Monopolization and Exclusion.* Oxford: Clarendon.

Musgrave, Richard A. 1980. "Theories of Fiscal Crisis: An Essay in Fiscal Sociology." Pp. 361–90 in *The Economics of Taxation,* edited by Henry. J. Aaron and Michael Boskin. Washington, D.C.: Brookings Institution.

Musgrave, Richard A., and Peggy B. Musgrave. 1989. *Public Finance in Theory and Practise.* 5th ed. New York: McGraw-Hill.

Myrdal, Gunnar. [1930] 1953. *The Political Element in the Development of Economic Theory.* London: Routledge and Paul.

Naylor, R. T. 1999. *Economic Warfare: Sanctions, Embargo Busting and Their Human Costs.* Boston: Northeastern University.

Nee, Victor. 1989: "A Theory of Market Transition: From Redistribution to Markets in State Socialism," *American Sociological Review* 54:663–81.

———. 1992. "Organizational Dynamics of Market Transition: Hybrid Forms, Property Rights, and Mixed Economy in China," *Administrative Science Quarterly* 37, no. 1:1–27.

———. 1998. "Norms and Networks in Economic and Organizational Performance," *American Economic Review* 88 (May): 85–9.

———. Forthcoming. "North's Theory of Institutional Change and State Capitalism in China." In *The Economic Sociology of Capitalism,* edited by Victor Nee and Richard Swedberg.

Nee, Victor, and Paul Ingram. 1998. "Embeddedness and Beyond: Institutions, Exchange, and Social Structure." Pp. 19–45 in *The New Institutionalism in Sociology,* edited by Mary Brinton and Victor Nee. New York: Russell Sage Foundation.

Nee, Victor, and David Stark, eds. 1989. *Remaking the Economic Institutions of Socialism: China and Eastern Europe.* Stanford: Stanford University Press.

Nee, Victor, and Richard Swedberg, eds. Forthcoming. *The Economic Sociology of Capitalism.*

Nelson, Richard. 1994. "Evolutionary Theorizing about Economic Change." Pp. 108–36 in *The Handbook of Economic Sociology,* edited by Neil Smelser and Richard Swedberg. New York and Princeton: Russell Sage Foundation and Princeton University Press.

Nelson, Richard, and Sidney Winter. 1982. *An Evolutionary Theory of Economic Change.* Cambridge: Harvard University Press.

Nelson, Robert, and William Bridges. 1999. *Legalizing Gender Inequality: Courts,*

Markets, and Unequal Pay for Women in America. Cambridge: Cambridge University Press.

Niskanen, William. 1971. *Bureaucracy and Representative Government.* Chicago: Aldine.

North, Douglass. 1977. "Markets and Other Allocation Systems in History: The Challenge of Karl Polanyi," *Journal of European Economic History* 6:703–16.

———. 1981. *Structure and Change in Economic History.* New York: Norton.

———. 1990. *Institutions, Institutional Change and Economic Performance.* Cambridge: Cambridge University Press.

North, Douglass, William Summerhill, and Barry Weingast. 2000. "Order, Disorder, and Economic Change: Latin America versus North America." Pp. 17–58 in *Governing for Prosperity,* edited by Bruce Bueno de Mesquita and Hilton Root. New Haven: Yale University Press.

North, Douglass, and Robert Thomas. 1973. *The Rise of the Western World.* Cambridge: Cambridge University Press.

North, Douglass, and Barry Weingast. 1989. "Constitutions and Commitment: The Evolution of Institutions Governing Public Choice in Seventeenth-Century England," *Journal of Economic History* 49:803–32.

Novak, William. 2000. "Law, Capitalism, and the Liberal State: The Historical Sociology of James Willard Hurst," *Law and History Review* 18, no. 1:97–145.

Oakley, Ann. 1974. *The Sociology of Housework.* New York: Pantheon.

Oberschall, Anthony, and Eric Leifer. 1986. "Efficiency and Social Institutions: Uses and Misuses of Economic Reasoning in Sociology," *Annual Review of Sociology* 12:233–53.

O'Connor, James. 1973. *The Fiscal Crisis of the State.* New York: St. Martin's.

Offe, Claus, and Helmut Wiesenthal. 1980. "Two Logics of Collective Action: Theoretical Notes on Social Class and Organizational Form," *Political Power and Social Class* 1:67–115.

Offe, Claus. 1996. "Political Economy: Sociological Perspectives." Pp. 675–90 in *A New Handbook of Political Science,* edited by Robert Goodin and Hans-Dieter Klingemann. Oxford: Oxford University Press.

Oi, Jean, and Andrew Walder, eds. 1999. *Property Rights and Economic Reform in China.* Stanford: Stanford University Press.

Olson, Mancur. 1965. *The Logic of Collective Action: Public Goods and the Theory of Groups.* Cambridge: Harvard University Press.

———. 1982. *The Rise and Decline of Nations: Economic Growth, Stagflation, and Social Rigidities.* New Haven: Yale University Press.

———. 2000. "The Kind of Markets Needed for Prosperity." Pp. 173–200 in *Power and Prosperity: Outgrowing Communist and Capitalist Dictatorships.* New York: Basic Books.

Opp, Karl-Dieter. 1985. "Sociology and Economic Man," *Zeitschrift für die Gesamte Staatswissenschaft* 141:213–43.

Orlove, Benjamin. 1986. "Barter and Cash Sale on Lake Titicaca: A Test of Competetive Approaches," *Current Anthropology* 27:85–106.

Orrù, Marco, Nicole Woolsey Biggart, and Gary Hamilton. 1997. *The Economic Organization of East Asian Capitalism.* London: Sage.

Orth, Ernst Wolfgang, et al. 1982. "Interesse." Pp. 305–64 in vol. 3 of *Geschichtliche Grundbegriffe*, edited by Otto Brunner et al. Stuttgart: Klott-Ketta.

Ostrom, Elinor. 2000. "Private and Common Property Rights." Pp. 332–79 in vol. 2 of *Encyclopaedia of Law and Economics*, edited by Boudewidja Bouckaert and Gerrit De Geest. Cheltenham: Elgar.

Oxford English Dictionary. 1989. "The Market." Pp. 385–86 in volume 9. 2nd ed. Oxford: Clarendon.

Padgett, John. 1981. "Hierarchy and Ecological Control in Federal Budgetary Decision Making," *American Journal of Sociology* 87:75–129.

Padgett, John, and Christopher Ansell. 1993. "Robust Action and the Rise of the Medici, 1400–1434," *American Journal of Sociology* 98:1259–1319.

Pahl, Jan. 1989. *Money and Marriage*. Basinstoke: Macmillan.

Palmer, Donald. 1983. "Broken Ties: Interlocking Directorates and Intercorporate Coordination," *Administrative Science Quarterly* 28:40–55.

Pareto, Vilfredo. [1916] 1963. *The Mind and Society: A Treatise on General Sociology*. 2 vols. New York: Dover.

Parkin, Frank. 1979. *Marxism and Class Theory: A Bourgeois Critique*. New York: Columbia University Press.

Parsons, Talcott. 1935. "Sociological Elements in Economic Thought, I–II," *Quarterly Journal of Economics* 49:414–53, 646–67.

———. [1937] 1968. *The Structure of Social Action*. 2 vols. New York: Free Press.

———. [1940] 1954. "The Motivation of Economic Activities." Pp. 50–68 in *Essays in Sociological Theory*. New York: Free Press.

———. 1947. "Weber's 'Economic Sociology.'" Pp. 30–55 in *The Theory of Social and Economic Organization*, edited by Max Weber. New York: Oxford University Press.

———. 1963. "On the Concept of Influence," *Public Opinion Quarterly* 27:37–62.

———. 1979. "The Symbolic Environment of Modern Economies," *Social Research* 46 (Autumn): 436–53.

Parsons, Talcott, and Neil Smelser. 1956. *Economy and Society: A Study in the Integration of Economic and Social Theory*. New York: Free Press.

Pearson, Heath. 1997. *Origins of Law and Economics: The Economists' New Science of Law, 1830–1930*. Cambridge: Cambridge University Press.

Peillon, Michel. 1990. *The Concept of Interest in Social Theory*. Ontario: Mellen.

Perlman, Mark. 1987. "Political Purpose and the National Accounts." Pp. 133–51 in *The Politics of Numbers*, edited by William Alonso and Paul Starr. New York: Russell Sage Foundation.

Perrow, Charles. 1987. *Complex Organizations: A Critical Essay*. 3rd ed. New York: McGraw-Hill.

———. 2002. *Organizing America: Wealth, Power, and the Origins of Corporate Capitalism*. Princeton: Princeton University Press.

Persky, Joseph. 1995. "The Ethology of Homo Economicus," *Journal of Economic Perspectives* 9, no. 2: 22–31.

Petersen, Trond. 1992a. "Individual, Collective and Systems Rationality in Work Groups: Dilemmas and Market-Type Solutions," *American Journal of Sociology* 98:469–510.

———. 1992b. "Payment Systems and the Structure of Inequality: Conceptual Issues and an Analysis of Salespersons in Department Stores," *American Journal of Sociology* 97:67–104.

———. 1994. "On the Promise of Game Theory in Sociology," *Contemporary Sociology* 23:498–502.

Pfeffer, Jeffrey, and Gerald Salancik. 1978. *The External Control of Organizations.* New York: Harper and Row.

Phillips, Paul, ed. 1980. *Marx and Engels on Law and Laws.* Totowa, N.J.: Barnes and Noble.

Piore, Michael, and Charles Sabel. 1984. *The Second Industrial Divide: Possibilities for Prosperity.* New York: Basic Books.

Pixley, Joycelyn. 2002. "Finance, Organizations, Decisions and Emotions," *British Journal of Sociology* 53:41–65.

———. Forthcoming. "Emotions and Economics." In "Special Issue on Emotions," edited by J. M. Barbalet. *Sociological Review Monographs.*

Pizzorno, Alessandro. 1978. "Political Exchange and Collective Identity in Industrial Conflict." Pp. 277–98 in vol. 2 of *The Resurgence of Class Conflict in Western Europe since 1968*, edited by Colin Crouch and Alessandro Pizzorno. London: Macmillan.

Podolny, Joel. 1992. "A Status-based Model of Market Competition," *American Journal of Sociology* 98:829–72.

———. 1994. "Market Uncertainty and the Social Character of Economic Exchange," *Administrative Science Quarterly* 39:458–83.

Podolny, Joel, and Karen Page. 1998. "Network Forms of Organizations," *Annual Review of Sociology* 24:57–76.

Poggi, Gianfranco. 1978. *The Development of the Modern State: A Sociological Introduction.* Stanford: Stanford University Press.

———. 1993. *Money and the Modern Mind: Georg Simmel's Philosophy of Money.* Berkeley: University of California Press.

Polanyi, Karl. [1944] 1957. *The Great Transformation.* Boston: Beacon.

———. [1947] 1971. "Our Obsolete Market Mentality." Pp. 59–77 in *Primitive, Archaic and Modern Economies: Essays of Karl Polanyi*, edited by George Dalton. Boston: Beacon.

———. [1957] 1971. "The Economy as Instituted Process." Pp. 243–69 in *Trade and Market in the Early Empires*, edited by Karl Polanyi, Conrad Arensberg, and Harry Pearson. Chicago: Regnery.

———. 1977. *The Livelihood of Man.* New York: Academic Press.

Polanyi, Karl, Conrad Arensberg, and Harry Pearson, eds. [1957] 1971. *Trade and Market in the Early Empires.* Chicago: Regnery.

Polanyi-Levitt, Kari, ed. 1990. *The Life and Work of Karl Polanyi.* Montreal: Black Rose.

Polanyi-Levitt, Kari, and Marguerite Mendell. 1987. "Karl Polanyi: His Life and Times," *Studies in Political Economy* 22 (Spring): 7–39.

Polinsky, A. Mitchell. 1989. *An Introduction to Law and Economics.* 2nd ed. Boston: Little, Brown.

Portes, Alejandro. 1998. "Social Capital: Its Origin and Applications in Modern Sociology," *Annual Review of Sociology* 24:151–208.

Portes, Alejandro, and William Haller. Forthcoming. "The Informal Economy." In *The Handbook of Economic Sociology*, edited by Neil Smelser and Richard Swedberg. 2nd ed. New York and Princeton: Russell Sage Foundation and Princeton University Press.

Portes, Alejandro, and Julia Sensenbrenner. 1993. "Embeddednes and Immigration: Notes on the Social Determinants of Economic Action," *American Journal of Sociology* 98:1320–50.

Posner, Richard. 1975. "The Economic Approach to Law," *Texas Law Review* 53:757–82.

———. 1981. *The Economics of Justice*. Cambridge: Harvard University Press.

———. 1990. "The Economic Approach to Law." Pp. 353–92 in *The Problems of Jurisprudence*. Cambridge: Harvard University Press.

———. 1995. "The Sociology of the Sociology of Law," *European Journal of Law and Economics* 2:265–84.

———. 1998. *Economic Analysis of Law*. 5th ed. Boston: Little, Brown.

Pound, Roscoe. 1920. "A Theory of Social Interests," *Papers and Proceedings of the American Sociological Society* 15:17–45.

Pound, Roscoe. 1959. *Jurisprudence*. Vol. 3. St. Paul: West Publications.

Powell, Walter. 1990. "Neither Market Nor Hierarchy: Network Forms of Organization," *Research in Organizational Behavior* 12:295–336.

Powell, Walter, and Paul DiMaggio, eds. 1991. *The New Institutionalism in Organizational Analysis*. Chicago: University of Chicago Press.

Powell, Walter, and Laurel Smith-Doerr. 1994. "Networks and Economic Life." Pp. 368–402 in *The Handbook of Economic Sociology*, edited by Neil Smelser and Richard Swedberg. New York and Princeton: Russell Sage Foundation and Princeton University Press.

Powell, Walter, and Laurel Smith-Doerr. Forthcoming. "Networks and Economic Life." In *The Handbook of Economic Sociology*, edited by Neil Smelser and Richard Swedberg. 2nd ed. New York and Princeton: Russell Sage Foundation and Princeton University Press.

Pratt, John, and Richard Zeckhauser. 1985. "Principals and Agents: An Overview." Pp. 1–35 in *Principals and Agents: The Structure of Business*, edited by John Pratt and Richard Zeckhauser. Boston: Harvard Business School Press.

Puhle, Hans-Jurgen. 2001. "Interest Groups, History of." Pp. 7703–8 in vol. 6 of *International Encyclopaedia of the Social and Behavioral Sciences*, edited by Neil Smelser and Paul Baltes. Amsterdam: Elsevier.

Putterman, Louis. 1986. "The Economic Nature of the Firm: Overview." Pp. 1–29 in *The Economic Nature of the Firm: A Reader*, edited by Louis Putterman. Cambridge: Cambridge University Press.

Raub, Werner, and Jeroen Weesie. 2000. "The Management of Matches," *Netherlands Journal of Social Sciences* 36, no. 1:71–88.

Rauch, James, and Alessandra Casella, eds. 2001. *Networks and Markets*. New York: Russell Sage Foundation.

Rawls, John. 2001. *Justice as Fairness: A Restatement*. Cambridge, Mass.: Belknap Press.

Renner, Karl. [1904] 1949. *The Institutions of Private Law and Their Social Function*. Boston: Routledge and Kegan Paul.

Reskin, Barbara. 2002. "Rethinking Employment Discrimination and Its Remedies." Pp. 218–44 in *The New Economic Sociology*, edited by Mauro Guillén et al. New York: Russell Sage Foundation.

Reskin, Barbara, and Irene Padavic. 1994. *Women and Men at Work*. Thousand Oaks, Calif.: Pine Forge Press.

Riain, Seán and Peter Evans. 2000. "Globalization and Global Systems Analysis." Pp. 1085–98 in vol. 2 of *Encyclopaedia of Sociology*, edited by Edgar Borgatta and Rhonda Montgomery. New York: Macmillan Reference.

Ricardo, David. [1817] 1973. *The Principles of Political Economy and Taxation*. London: Everyman's Library.

Ritzer, George. 1999. *Enchanting a Disenchanted World: Revolutionizing the Means of Consumption*. Thousand Oaks, Calif.: Pine Forge Press.

Robbins, Lionel. 1932. *An Essay on the Nature and Significance of Economic Science*. London: Macmillan.

Roe, Mark. 1994. *Strong Managers, Weak Owners*. Princeton: Princeton University Press.

Roethlisberger, Fritz, and William Dickson. 1939. *Management and the Worker*. Cambridge: Harvard University Press.

Roman, Christine, and Carolyn Vogler. 1999. "Managing Money in British and Swedish Households," *European Societies* 1:419–56.

Rona-Tas, Akos. 1997. *The Great Surprise of the Small Transformation: The Demise of Communism and the Rise of the Private Sector in Hungary*. Ann Arbor: University of Michigan Press.

Rose-Ackerman, Susan. 1992. "Progressivism and the Chicago School." Pp. 14–27 in *Rethinking the Progressive Agenda*. New York: Free Press.

Roy, Donald. 1952. "Quota Restriction and Goldbricking in a Machine Shop," *American Journal of Sociology* 57:427–42.

———. 1958. " 'Banana Time': Job Satisfaction and Informal Interaction," *Human Organization* 18:158–68.

Roy, William. 1990. "Functional and Historical Logic in Explaining the Rise of the American Industrial Corporation," *Comparative Social Research* 12:19–44.

———. 1997. *Socializing Capital: The Rise of the Large Industrial Corporation in America*. Princeton: Princeton University Press.

Rueschemeyer, Dietrich, Evelyne Huber Stephens, and John Stephens. 1992. *Capitalist Development and Democracy*. Cambridge: Polity.

Sabel, Charles, and Jonathan Zeitlin. 1985. "Historical Alternatives to Mass Production: Politics, Markets and Technology in Nineteenth-Century Industrialization," *Past and Present* 108 (July): 133–76.

Sachs, Jeffrey. 2000. "Notes on a New Sociology of Economic Development." Pp. 29–43 in *Culture Matters: How Values Shape Human Progress*, edited by Lawrence Harrison and Samuel Huntington. New York: Basic Books.

Sachs, Jeffrey, Andrew Mellinger, and John Gallup. 2001. "The Geography of Hunger," *Scientific American* March: 71–75.

Saint-Simon, Henri de. 1964. *Social Organization, The Science of Man and Other Writings*. New York: Harper and Row.

Samuelson, Paul. 1970. *Economics*. 8th ed. New York: McGraw-Hill.

Sardiella, Tiziana. Forthcoming. *Renting Out Labor.* Ph.D. diss. Department of Sociology, Stockholm University.

Sartre, Jean-Paul. [1960] 1976. *Critique of Dialectical Reason.* London: Verso.

Sassen, Saskia. 2000. "Territory and Territoriality in the Global Economy," *International Sociology* 15:372–93.

Saxenian, AnnaLee. 1994. *Regional Advantage: Culture and Competition in Silicon Valley and Route 128.* Cambridge: Harvard University Press.

Scherer, F. M., and David Ross. 1990. *Industrial Market Structure and Industrial Performance.* 3rd ed. Boston: Houghton Mifflin.

Schleifer, Andrei, and Robert Vishny. 1997. "A Survey on Corporate Governance," *Journal of Finance* 52:737–83.

Schluchter, Wolfgang. 1989. *Rationalism, Religion and Domination: A Weberian Perspective.* Berkeley: University of California Press.

Schmalensee, Richard, and Robert Willig, eds. 1989. *Handbook of Industrial Organization.* 2 vols. Amsterdam: North-Holland.

Schmitter, Philippe. 1997. "Levels of Spatial Coordination and the Embeddedness of Institutions." Pp. 311–17 in *Contemporary Capitalism: The Embeddedness of Institutions,* edited by Roger Hollingsworth and Robert Boyer. Cambridge: Cambridge University Press.

Schmoller, Gustav. [1884] 1897. *The Mercantile System and Its Historical Significance.* New York: Macmillan.

Schoch, Magdalena, ed. 1948. *The Jurisprudence of Interests.* Cambridge: Harvard University Press.

Schor, Juliet. 1991. *The Overworked American: The Unexpected Decline of Leisure.* New York: Basic Books.

———. 1998. *The Overspent American: Upscaling, Downshifting, and the New Consumer.* New York: Basic Books.

Schudson, Michael. 1984. *Advertising, The Uneasy Persuasion: Its Dubious Impact on American Society.* New York: Basic Books.

Schumpeter, Joseph. 1912. *Theorie der wirtschaftlichen Entwicklung.* Leipzig: Duncker und Humblot.

———. [1918] 1991. "The Crisis of the Tax State." Pp. 99–140 in *The Economics and Sociology of Capitalism,* by Joseph Schumpeter, edited by Richard Swedberg. Princeton: Princeton University Press.

———. [1919] 1991. "The Sociology of Imperialisms." Pp. 141–219 in *The Economics and Sociology of Capitalism,* by Joseph Schumpeter, edited by Richard Swedberg. Princeton: Princeton University Press.

———. [1927] 1991. "Social Classes in an Ethnically Homogenous Environment." Pp. 230–83 in *The Economics and Sociology of Capitalism,* by Joseph A. Schumpeter, edited by Richard Swedberg. Princeton: Princeton University Press.

———. 1934. *The Theory of Economic Development.* Cambridge; Harvard University Press.

———. [1942] 1994. *Capitalism, Socialism and Democracy.* London: Routledge.

———. [1946] 1989. "Capitalism." Pp. 189–210 in *Essays: On Entrepreneurs, Innovations, Business Cycles, and the Evolution of Capitalism.* New Brunswick, N.J.: Transaction.

———. [1949] 1951. "Communist Manifesto in Sociology and Economics." Pp. 282–95 in *Essays*. Cambridge, Mass.: Addison-Wesley.

———. 1951. "Vilfredo Pareto 1848–1923." Pp. 110–42 in *Ten Great Economists*. New York: Oxford University Press.

———. 1954. *History of Economic Analysis*. London: Allen and Unwin.

———. Forthcoming. "Entrepreneur [1928]," *American Journal of Economics and Sociology*.

Schutz, Alfred. [1953] 1971. "Common-Sense and Scientific Interpretation of Human Action." Pp. 3–47 in *Collected Papers. I. The Problem of Social Reality*. The Hague: Martinus Nijhoff.

Schwartz, T. P. 1996. "Durkheim's Prediction about the Declining Importance of the Family and Inheritance: Evidence from the Wills of Providence, 1775–1985," *Sociological Quarterly* 37 (Summer): 503–19.

Scott, Richard. 1998. *Organizations: Rational, National and Open Systems*. 4th ed. Englewood Cliffs, N.J.: Prentice-Hall.

Selznick, Philip. 1969. *Law, Society and Industrial Justice*. New York: Russell Sage Foundation.

Semlinger, Klaus. 1995. "Industrial Policy and Small-Firm Cooperation in Baden-Württemberg." Pp. 15–30 in *Small and Medium-Size Enterprises*, edited by Arnaldo Bagnesco and Charles Sabel. London: Pinter.

Sen, Amartya. 1977. "Rational Fools: A Critique of the Behavioural Foundations of Economic Behavior," *Philosophy and Public Affairs* 6:317–44.

———. 1981. *Poverty and Famines: An Essay on Entitlement and Deprivation*. Oxford: Clarendon.

———. 1990. "More Than 100 Million Women Are Missing," *New York Review of Books* 37, no. 20 (December 20): 61–6.

———. 1999. "Markets, State and Social Opportunity." Pp. 111–45 in *Development as Freedom*. Oxford: Oxford University Press.

Sewell, William. 1999. "The Concept(s) of Culture." Pp. 35–61 in *Beyond the Cultural Turn: New Directions in the Study of Society and Culture*, edited by Victoria Bonnell and Lynn Hunt. Berkeley: University of California Press.

Shand, Alexander. 1984. "The Market." Pp. 63–76 in *The Capitalist Alternative: An Introduction to Neo-Austrian Economics*. New York: New York University Press.

Shapiro, Susan. 1984. *Wayward Capitalists: Target of the Security and Exchange Commission*. New Haven: Yale University Press.

———. 1987. "The Social Control of Impersonal Trust," *American Journal of Sociology* 93:623–58.

———. 1990. "Collaring the Crime, Not the Criminal: Reconsidering the Concept of White-Collar Crime," *American Journal of Sociology* 55:346–65.

Shelton, Beth Anne. 1992. *Women, Men and Time: Gender Differences in Paid Work, Housework and Leisure*. New York: Greenwood.

Shiller, Robert. 2000. *Irrational Exuberance*. Princeton: Princeton University Press.

Shonfield, Andrew. 1965. *Modern Capitalism: The Changing Balance of Public and Private Power*. New York: Oxford University Press.

Shoup, Laurence, and William Minter. 1977. *Imperial Brain Trust: The Council on Foreign Relations and United States Foreign Policy.* New York: Monthly Review.

Simmel, Georg. [1896] 1991. "The Berlin Trade Exhibition," *Theory, Culture and Society* 8:119–23.

———. [1904] 1957. "Fashion," *American Journal of Sociology* 67:541–58.

———. [1907] 1978. *The Philosophy of Money.* London: Routledge. The first German edition appeared in 1900.

———. [1908] 1950. "Quantitative Aspects of the Group." Pp. 87–177 in *The Sociology of Georg Simmel*, edited by Kurt Wolff. New York: Free Press.

———. [1908] 1955. "Competition." Pp. 57–85 in *Conflict and the Web of Group-Affiliation.* New York: Free Press.

———. [1908] 1971. "The Problem of Sociology." Pp. 23–35 in *On Individuality and Social Forms*, edited by Georg Simmel Donald Levine. Chicago: University of Chicago Press.

Simon, Herbert. 1957. *Models of Man.* New York: Wiley.

———. 1991. "Organizations and Markets," *Journal of Economic Perspectives* 5 (Spring): 25–44.

———. 1997. "The Role of Organizations in an Economy." Pp. 33–60 in *An Empirically Based Microeconomics.* Cambridge: Cambridge University Press.

Simpson, Sally. 2002. *Corporate Crime, Law, and Social Control.* Cambridge: Cambridge University Press.

Sitton, John. 1998. "Disembodied Capitalism: Habermas' Conception of the Economy," *Sociological Forum* 13, no. 1:61–83.

Sjöstrand, Glenn. Forthcoming. *Gnosjö.* Ph.D. diss. Växjö University, Sweden.

Slater, Don. 1997. *Consumer Culture and Modernity.* Cambridge: Polity.

Small, Albion. 1905. *General Sociology: An Exposition of the Main Development in Sociological Theory from Spencer to Ratzenhofer.* Chicago: University of Chicago Press.

Smelser, Neil. 1959. *Social Change in the Industrial Revolution: An Application of Theory to the British Cotton Industry.* Chicago: University of Chicago Press.

———. 1963. *The Sociology of Economic Life.* Englewood Cliffs, N.J.: Prentice-Hall.

———. 1976. *The Sociology of Economic Life.* 2nd ed. Englewood Cliffs, N.J.: Prentice-Hall.

———, ed. 1965. *Readings on Economic Sociology.* Englewood Cliffs, N.J.: Prentice-Hall.

Smelser, Neil, and Richard Swedberg, eds. 1994. *The Handbook of Economic Sociology.* New York and Princeton: Russell Sage Foundation and Princeton University Press.

———. Forthcoming. *The Handbook of Economic Sociology.* 2nd ed. New York and Princeton: Russell Sage Foundation and Princeton University Press.

Smith, Adam. [1759] 1976. *The Theory of Moral Sentiments.* Indianapolis: Liberty Classics.

———. [1776] 1976. *An Inquiry into the Nature and Causes of the Wealth of Nations.* 2 vols. Oxford: Oxford University Press.

Smith, Charles. 1989. *Auctions: The Social Construction of Value.* Cambridge: Polity.

Smith, Clifford. 1987. "Agency Costs." Pp. 39–40 in vol. 1 of *The New Palgrave. A Dictionary of Economics,* edited by John Eatwell et al. London: Macmillan.

Solow, Robert. 1990. *The Labor Market as a Social Institution.* Cambridge: Blackwell.

Sombart, Werner. [1911] 1982. *The Jews and Modern Capitalism.* New Brunswick, N.J.: Transaction.

————. [1913] 1967. *Luxury and Capitalism.* Ann Arbor: University of Michigan Press.

————. 1902–27. *Der Moderne Kapitalismus.* 3 vols. Leipzig: Duncker und Humblot.

————. 1930. *Die Drei Nationakökonomien. Geschichte und System der Lehre von der Wirtschaft.* Leipzig: Duncker und Humblot.

————. 1935. *Das ökonomische Zeitalter.* Berlin: Buchholz und Weisswange.

Sørensen, Aage. 2000. "Toward a Sounder Basis for Class Analysis," *American Journal of Sociology* 105:1523–58.

Sørensen, Annemette, and Sara McLanahan. 1987. "Married Women's Economic Dependency, 1940–1980," *American Journal of Sociology* 93:659–87.

Spence, Michael. 1974. *Market Signaling: The Informational Structure of Hiring and Related Processes.* Cambridge: Harvard University Press.

Spitzer, Karl. 1983. "Marxist Perspectives in the Sociology of Law," *Annual Review of Sociology* 9:103–24.

Stage, Sarah, and Virginia Vincenti, eds. 1997. *Rethinking Home Economics: Women and the History of a Profession.* Ithaca: Cornell University Press.

Stark, David. 1996. "Recombinant Property in East European Capitalism," *American Journal of Sociology* 101:993–1027.

Stark, David, and Laszlo Bruszt. 2001. "One Way or Multiple Paths: For a Comparative Sociology of East European Capitalism," *American Journal of Sociology* 106:1129–37.

————, eds. 1998. *Postsocialist Ways: Transforming Politics and Property in East Central Europe.* Cambridge: Cambridge University Press.

Stearns, Linda Brewster. 1990. "Capital Market Effects on External Control of Corporations." Pp. 175–202 in *Structures of Capital: The Social Organization of the Economy,* edited by Sharon Zukin and Paul DiMaggio. Cambridge: Cambridge University Press.

Stearns, Linda Brewster, and Kenneth Allan. 1996. "Economic Behavior and Institutional Environments: The Corporate Merger Wave of the 1980s," *American Sociological Review* 61:699–718.

Stearns, Linda Brewster, and Mark Mizruchi. 1986. "Broken-Tie Reconstitution and the Functions of Interorganizational Interlocks: A Reexamination," *Administrative Science Quarterly* 31:522–38.

————. Forthcoming. "Banking and Financial Markets." Pp. 313–41 in *The Handbook of Economic Sociology,* edited by Neil Smelser and Richard Swedberg. 2nd ed. New York and Princeton: Russell Sage Foundation and Princeton University Press.

Steiner, Philippe. 1992. "Le Fait Social Economique chez Durkheim," *Revue Française de Sociologie* 33:641–66.

————. 1998. *Sociologie de la Connaissance Economique.* Paris: Presses Universitaires de France.

———. 2001. "The Sociology of Economic Knowledge," *European Journal of Social Theory* 4, no. 4:443–58.

———. Forthcoming. *Principes de la Sociologie Economique Durkheimienne*.

Steinmo, Sven. 1989. "Political Institutions and Tax Policy in the United States, Sweden, and Britain," *World Politics* 41:500–35.

———. 1993. *Taxation and Democracy*. New Haven: Yale University Press.

Stigler, George. 1961. "The Economics of Information," *Journal of Political Economy* 60:213–25.

———. 1967. "Imperfections in the Capital Market," *Journal of Political Economy* 75:287–92.

———. 1968. "Competition." Pp. 181–86 in *International Encyclopaedia of the Social Sciences*, edited by David L. Sills. New York: Macmillan and Free Press.

Stigler, George. 1971. "The Theory of Economic Regulation," *Bell Journal of Economics* 2 (Spring): 3–21.

Stinchcombe, Arthur. 1959. "Bureaucratic and Craft Administration of Production: A Comparative Study," *Administrative Science Quarterly* 4:168–87.

———. 1960. "The Sociology of Organization and the Theory of the Firm," *Pacific Sociological Review* (Fall): 75–82.

———. 1983. *Economic Sociology*. New York: Academic Press.

———. 1985. "Contracts as Hierarchical Documents." Pp. 121–71 in *Organization Theory and Project Management*, by Arthur Stinchcombe and Carol Heimer. Oslo: Norwegian University Press.

———. 1986. "Rationality and Social Structure." Pp. 1–29 in *Stratification and Organization*. Cambridge: Cambridge University Press.

———. 1990. "Weak Structural Data [Review of Mark Mizruchi and Michael Schwartz, eds., *Intercorporate Relations: The Structural Analysis of Business*]," *Contemporary Sociology* 19:380–82.

Stinchcombe, Arthur, and Bruce Carruthers. 1999. "The Social Structure of Liquidity: Flexibility, Markets, and States," *Theory and Society* 28:353–82.

Storper, Michael, and Robert Salais. 1997. *Worlds of Production: The Action Framework of the Economy*. Cambridge: Harvard University Press.

Strang, David, and Sarah Soule. 1998. "Diffusion in Organizations and Social Movements: From Hybrid Corn to Poison Pills," *Annual Review of Sociology* 24:265–90.

Streeck, Wolfgang. 1992. "Revisiting Status and Contract: Pluralism, Corporatism and Flexibility." Pp. 41–75 in *Social Institutions and Economic Performance*. London: Sage.

Streeck, Wolfgang, and Philippe Schmitter, eds. 1985. *Private Interest Government: Beyond Market and State*. London: Sage.

Strober, Myra, and Carolyn Arnold. 1987. "The Dynamics of Occupational Segregation Among Bank Tellers." Pp. 107–47 in *Gender in the Workplace*, edited by Clair Brown and Joseph Pechman. Washington, D.C.: Brookings Institution.

Stryker, Robin. 2001a. "Disparate Impact and the Quota Debates: Law, Labor Market Sociology, and Equal Employment Policies," *The Sociological Quarterly* 42, no. 1:13–46.

———. 2001b. "It's the Law! An Agenda for Socio-Economics." Presidential address, Society for the Advancement of Socio-Economics, Amsterdam, October 10.

Styles, John. 1993. "Manufacturing, Consumption and Design in Eighteenth-Century England." Pp. 527–54 in *Consumption and the World of Goods*, edited by John Brewer and Roy Porter. London: Routledge.

Suchman, Mark. 1985. *On Advice of Council: Law Firms and Venture Capital Funds as Information Intermediaries in the Structuration of Silicon Valley*. Ph.D. diss. Department of Sociology, Stanford University.

———. 2000. "Dealmakers and Counselors: Law Firms as Intermediaries in the Development of Silicon Valley." Pp. 71–97 in *Understanding Silicon Valley: The Anatomy of an Entrepreneurial Region*, edited by Martin Kenney. Stanford: Stanford University Press.

Sullivan, Teresa, Elizabeth Warren, and Jay Lawrence Westbrook. 1989. *As We Forgive Our Debtors: Bankruptcy and Consumer Credit in America*. New York: Oxford University Press.

———. 2000. *The Fragile Middle Class: Americans in Debt*. New Haven: Yale University Press.

Sumner, William Graham. [1906] 1960. *Folkways*. New York: New American Library.

Sutton, John. 2001. *Law/Society: Origins, Interactions, and Change*. Thousand Oaks, Calif.: Pine Forge Press.

Sutton, John, Frank Dobbin, John Meyer, and Richard Scott. 1994. "The Legalization of the Workplace," *American Journal of Sociology* 99:944–71.

Sverrisson, Árni. 1994. "Making Sense of Chaos: Socio/Technical Networks, Careers and Entrepreneurs," *Acta Sociologica* 37:401–17.

Swedberg, Richard. 1986. "The Doctrine of Economic Neutrality of the IMF and the World Bank," *Journal of Peace Research* 23:377–90.

———. 1987. "Economic Sociology: Past and Present," *Current Sociology* 35 (Spring): 1–221.

———. 1991a. *Schumpeter—A Biography*. Princeton: Princeton University Press.

———, ed. 1991b. "*Theme Issue*: Talcott Parsons' Marshall Lectures," *Sociological Inquiry* 61 (Winter): 1–114.

———. 1997. "New Economic Sociology: What Has Been Accomplished, What Is Ahead?" *Acta Sociologica* 40:161–82.

———. 1998. *Max Weber and the Idea of Economic Sociology*. Princeton: Princeton University Press.

———. 2000a. "*Afterword*: The Role of the Market in Max Weber's Work," *Theory and Society* 29:373–84.

———. 2000b. "The Social Science View of Entrepreneurship." Pp. 7–44 in *Entrepreneurship: The Social Science View*, edited by Richard Swedberg. Oxford: Oxford University Press.

———. 2001. "Sociology and Game Theory: Contemporary and Historical Perspectives," *Theory and Society* 30:301–35.

———. 2002. "Knut Wicksell as a Classic and as a Social Thinker." Pp. 133–46 in *Editing Economics: Essays in Honour of Mark Perlman*, edited by H. Lim et al. London: Routledge.

———. Forthcoming a. "The Case for an Economic Sociology of Law," *Theory and Society.*

———. Forthcoming b. "The Economic Sociology of Capitalism: An Agenda." In *The Economic Sociology of Capitalism,* edited by Victor Nee and Richard Swedberg.

———. Forthcoming c. "Max Weber's Sociology of Capitalisms." In *Approaches to Varieties of Capitalism,* edited by Mark Harvey and Huw Beynon. Manchester: Manchester University Press.

———. 2003. "A Nation of Stockholders: Conflicts of Interest and the Corporate Scandals of 2001–2002." Paper presented at the University of Constance, May 16–18.

Swidler, Ann. 1986. "Culture in Action: Symbols and Strategies," *American Sociological Review* 51:273–86.

Szelenyi, Ivan. 1988. *Socialist Entrepreneurs: Embourgeoisiement in Rural Hungary.* Cambridge: Polity.

Szelenyi, Szonia, et al. 1998. *Equality by Design: The Great Experiment of Destratification in Socialist Hungary.* Stanford: Stanford University Press.

Tarschys, Daniel. 1988. "Tributes, Tariffs, Taxes and Trade: The Changing Sources of Government Revenue," *British Journal of Political Science* 18: 1–20.

Thomas, Barbara, and Barbara Reskin. 1990. "A Woman's Place is Selling Homes: Occupational Change and the Feminization of Real Estate Sales." Pp. 205–24 in *Job Queues, Gender Queues,* edited by Barbara Reskin and Patricia Roos. Philadephia: Temple University Press.

Thompson, Dorothy, ed. 2001. *The Essential E. P. Thompson.* New York: New Press.

Thompson, E. P. 1971. "The Moral Economy of the English Crowd in the Eighteenth Century," *Past and Present* 50:76–136.

———. 1975. *Whigs and Hunters: The Origin of the Black Act.* New York: Pantheon.

Thompson, Homer A., and R. E. Wycherley. 1972. *The Agora of Athens. The Athenian Agora Volume 14.* Princeton: Princeton University Press.

Thornton, Patricia. 1999. "The Sociology of Entrepreneurship," *Annual Review of Sociology* 25:19–46.

Tigar, Michael. 2000. *Law and the Rise of Capitalism.* 2nd ed. New York: Monthly Review.

Tillman, Rick. 1992. *Thorstein Veblen and His Critics, 1891–1963.* Princeton: Princeton University Press.

Tilly, Charles. 1990. *Capital, Coercion and European States, A.D. 1990–1990.* Oxford: Blackwell.

Tilly, Chris, and Charles Tilly. 1994. "Capitalist Work and Labor Markets." Pp. 283–312 in *The Handbook of Economic Sociology,* edited by Neil Smelser and Richard Swedberg. New York and Princeton: The Russell Sage Foundation and Princeton University Press.

Tilly, Louise, and Joan Scott. 1989. *Women, Work, and Family.* 2nd reprinted ed. New York: Routledge. Originally published 1978. New York: Holt, Rinehart and Winston.

Tirole, Jean. 1988. *The Theory of Industrial Organization*. Cambridge: MIT Press.

Tocqueville, Alexis de. [1835] 1997. *Memoir on Pauperism*. London: IEA Health Welfare Unit.

———. [1835–40] 1945. *Democracy in America*, translated by Henry Reeve. 2 vols. New York: Vintage.

———. [1856] 1955. *The Old Régime and the French Revolution*, translated by Stuart Gilbert. New York: Doubleday.

Toynbee, Arnold. [1884] 1969. *Toynbee's Industrial Revolution: A Reprint of Lectures on the Industrial Revolution*. New York: David and Charles.

Trigilia, Carlo. 1986. "Small-Firm Development and Political Subcultures in Italy," *European Sociological Review* 2, no. 3:161–75.

———. 1995. "A Tale of Two Districts: Work and Politics in the Third Italy." Pp. 31–50 in *Small and Medium-Size Enterprises*, edited by Arnaldo Bagnesco and Charles Sabel. London: Pinter.

———. 2001. "Social Capital and Local Development," *European Journal of Social Theory* 4, no. 4:427–42.

———. 2002. *Economic Sociology: State, Market and Society in Modern Capitalism*. Oxford: Blackwell.

Tullock, Gordon. 1987. "Rent Seeking." Pp. 147–49 in vol. 4 of *The New Palgrave. A Dictionary of Economics*, edited by John Eatwell et al. London: Macmillan.

Udehn, Lars. 1981. "Central Planning: Postscript to a Debate." Pp. 29–60 in *Spontaneity and Planning in Social Development*, edited by Ulf Himmelstrand. London: Sage.

———. 1991. "The Limits of Economic Imperialism." Pp. 239–80 in *Interfaces in Economic and Social Sciences*, edited by Ulf Himmelstrand. London: Routledge.

———. 1996. *The Limits of Public Choice: A Sociological Critique of the Economic Theory of Politics*. London: Routledge.

———. 2001. *Methodological Individualism: Background, History and Meaning*. London: Routledge.

Useem, Michael. 1993. *Executive Defense: Shareholder Power and Corporate Reorganization*. Cambridge: Harvard University Press.

———. 1996. *Investor Capitalism: How Money Managers Are Changing the Face of Corporate America*. New York: Basic Books.

Uzzi, Brian. 1996. "The Sources and Consequences of Embeddednes for the Economic Performance of Organizations: The Network Effect," *American Sociological Review* 61:674–98.

———. 1997. "Social Structure and Competition in Interfirm Networks: The Paradox of Embeddedness," *Administrative Science Quarterly* 42:35–67.

———. 1999. "Making of Financial Capital: How Social Relations of Networks Benefits Firms Seeking Finance," *American Sociological Review* 64:481–505.

Uzzi, Brian, and Ryon Lancaster. Forthcoming. "Social Embeddedness and Price Formation: The Case of Large Corporate Law Firms."

Valenzuela, J. Samuel, and Arturo Valenzuela. 1978. "Modernization and Dependency: Alternative Perspectives in the Study of Latin American Under-development," *Comparative Politics* 10, no. 4:535–57.

Van den Berg, Axel. 1988. *The Immanent Utopia: From Marxism on the State to the State of Marxism*. Princeton: Princeton University Press.

Van den Bulte, Christophe, and Gary Lilien. 2001. "Medical Innovation Revisited: Social Contagion versus Marketing Effort," *American Journal of Sociology* 106:1409–35.

Veblen, Thorstein. 1898. "The Beginnings of Ownership," *American Journal of Sociology* 4:352–65.

———. [1899] 1973. *The Theory of the Leisure Class*. Boston: Houghton Mifflin.

———. [1915] 1966. *Imperial Germany and the Industrial Revolution*. Ann Arbor: University of Michigan Press.

———. 1919. *The Vested Interests and the Common Man*. New York: B. W. Huebsch.

———. [1919] 1990. *The Place of Science in Modern Civilization and Other Essays*. New Brunswick, N.J.: Transaction.

Verlinden, O. 1963. "Markets and Fairs." Pp. 119–53 in vol. 3 of *Cambridge Economic History of Europe*, edited by M. M. Postan and E. E. Rich. Cambridge: Cambridge University Press.

Veyne, Paul. 1990. *Bread and Circuses*. London: Penguin.

Volckart, Oliver, and Antje Mangels. 1999. "Are the Roots of the Modern *Lex Mercatoria* Really Medieval?" *Southern Economic Journal* 65, no. 3: 427–50.

Walder, Andrew. 1986. *Communist Neo-Traditionalism: Work and Authority in Chinese History*. Berkeley: University of California Press.

———. 1992. "Property Right and Stratification in Socialist Redistributive Economies," *American Sociological Review* 57:524–39.

———, ed. 1996. *China's Transitional Economy*. Oxford: Oxford University Press.

Waldinger, Roger, Howard Aldrich, and Robin Ward. 1990. *Ethnic Entrepreneurs: Immigrant Business in Industrial Societies*. Newbury, Calif.: Sage.

Waldrop, M. Mitchell. 1992. *Complexity: The Emerging Science at the Edge of Order and Chaos*. New York: Simon and Schuster.

Wallensteen, Peter. 1971. *Ekonomiska Sanktioner (Economic Sanctions)*. Stockholm: Prisma.

Wallerstein, Immanuel. 1974–1989. *The Modern World System*. Vols. 1–3. New York: Academic Press.

Walras, Léon. [1874] 1954. *Elements of Pure Economics*. Translated by William Jaffé. 4th ed. Homewood, Ill.: Richard D. Irwin. The first edition of this translation appeared in 1926.

Wasserman, Stanley, and Katherine Faust. 1994. *Social Network Analysis: Methods and Applications*. Cambridge: Cambridge University Press.

Webber, Carolyn, and Aaron Wildavsky. 1986. *A History of Taxation and Expenditure in the Western World*. New York: Simon and Schuster.

Weber, Max. [1889] 1988. "Zur Geschichte der Handelsgesellschaften im Mittelalter." Pp. 312–443 in *Gesammelte Aufsätze zur Sozial- und Wirtschaftsgeschichte*. Tübingen: Mohr.

———. [1891] 1986. *Die römische Agrargeschichte in ihrer Bedeutung für das Staatsrecht- und Privatrecht. Max Weber Gesamtausgabe I/2*. Tübingen: Mohr.

———. [1894–96] 2000. "Stock and Commodity Exchanges [*Die Börse* (1894)], Commerce on the Stock and Commodity Exchanges [*Die Börsenverkehr*]," *Theory and Society* 29:305–38, 339–71.

———. [1895] 1980. "The National State and Economic Policy (Freiburg Address)," *Economy and Society* 9 (1980): 428–49.

———. [1898] 1990. *Grundriss zu den Vorlesungen über Allgemeine ('theoretische') Nationalökonomie.* Tübingen: Mohr.

———. [1904] 1949. "'Objectivity' in Social Science and Social Policy." Pp. 49–112 in *The Methodology of the Social Sciences.* New York: Free Press.

———. [1904–05] 1958. *The Protestant Ethic and the Spirit of Capitalism.* New York: Scribner's.

———. [1906] 1994. "On the Situation of Constitutional Democracy in Russia." Pp. 29–74 in *Political Writings.* Cambridge: Cambridge University Press.

———. [1907] 1977. *Critique of Stammler.* New York: Free Press.

———. [1908] 1975. "Marginal Utility Theory and 'The Fundamental Law of Psychphysics,'" *Social Science Quarterly* 56:21–36.

———. [1908] 1980. "A Research Strategy for the Study of Occupational Careers and Mobility Patterns." Pp. 103–55 in *The Interpretation of Social Reality,* edited by J.E.T. Eldridge. New York: Schocken.

———. [1908–09] 1988. "Zur Psychophysik der industriellen Arbeit." Pp. 61–255 in *Gesammelte Aufsätze zur Soziologie und Sozialpolitik.* Tübingen: Mohr.

———. [1909] 1976. *The Agrarian Sociology of Ancient Civilizations.* London: New Left.

Weber, Max. [1915] 1946a. "Religious Rejections of the World and Their Directions." Pp. 323–59 in *From Max Weber,* edited by Hans Gerth and C. Wright Mills. New York: Oxford University Press.

———. [1915] 1946b. "The Social Psychology of the World Religions." Pp. 267–301 in *From Max Weber,* edited by Hans Gerth and C. Wright. Mills New York: Oxford University Press.

———. [1916] 1994. "Between Two Laws." Pp. 75–79 in *Political Writings.* Cambridge: Cambridge University Press.

———. [1917] 1994. "Suffrage and Democracy in Germany." Pp. 80–129 in *Political Writings.* Cambridge: Cambridge University Press.

———. [1918] 1994. "Socialism." Pp. 272–303 in *Political Writings.* Cambridge: Cambridge University Press.

———. [1919] 1946. "Science as a Vocation." Pp. 129–56 in *From Max Weber,* edited by Hans Gerth and C. Wright Mills. New York: Oxford University Press.

———. [1919] 1994. "The Profession and Vocation of Politics." Pp. 309–69 in *Political Writings.* Cambridge: Cambridge University Press.

———. [1920] 1946. "The Protestant Sects and the Spirit of Capitalism." Pp. 302–22 in *From Max Weber,* edited by Hans Gerth and C. Wright Mills. New York: Oxford University Press.

———. [1920] 1951. *The Religion of China.* New York: Free Press.

———. [1920] 1958. "Author's Introduction." Pp. 13–31 in *The Protestant Ethic and the Spirit of Capitalism.* New York: Scribner's.

———. [1921] 1952. *Ancient Judaism.* New York: Free Press.

———. [1921] 1958. *The Religion of India.* New York: Free Press.

———. [1922] 1978. *Economy and Society: An Outline of Interpretive Sociology.* 2 vols. Berkeley: University of California Press.

———. [1923] 1981. *General Economic History.* New Brunswick, N.J.: Transaction.

———. 1923. *Wirtschaftsgeschichte.* Munich: Duncker und Humblot.

———. 1949. *Essays in the Methodology of the Social Sciences.* New York: Free Press.

———. 1972. "Georg Simmel as Sociologist," *Social Research* 39:155–63.

———. 1989. *Reading Weber,* edited by Keith Tribe. London: Routledge.

———. 1999. *Börsenwesen. Schriften und Reden 1893–1898. Max Weber Gesamtausgabe I/5.* 2 vols. Tübingen: Mohr.

Weeks, John. 1991. "Imperialism and World Market." Pp. 252–56 in *A Dictionary of Marxist Thought,* edited by Tom Bottomore. 2nd ed. Oxford: Blackwell.

Weingast, Barry. 1996. "Political Institutions: Rational Choice Perspectives." Pp. 167–90 in *A New Handbook of Political Science.* Robert Gordin and Hans-Dieter Klingemann. Oxford: Oxford University Press.

Weintraub, Roy, ed. 1992. *Toward A History of Game Theory.* Durham: Duke University Press.

Weir, Margaret, Ann Shola Orloff, and Theda Skocpol, eds. 1988. *The Politics of Social Policy.* Princeton: Princeton University Press.

Western, Bruce. 2001. Review of Lisa Keister, *Wealth in America, Contemporary Sociology* 30, no. 4:335–36.

White, Harrison. 1970. *Chains of Opportunity: System Models of Mobility in Organizations.* Cambridge: Harvard University Press.

———. 1976. "Subcontracting with an Oligopoly: Spence Revisited." RIAS Program Working Paper # 1, Harvard University.

———. 1981a. "Production Markets as Induced Role Structures." Pp. 1–57 in *Sociological Methodology,* edited by Samuel Leinhardt. San Franciso: Jossey-Bass.

———. 1981b. "Where Do Markets Come From?" *American Journal of Sociology* 87:517–47.

———. 1985. "Agency as Control." Pp. 187–212 in *Principals and Agents: The Structure of Business,* edited by John Pratt and Richard Zeckhauser. Boston: Harvard Business School Press.

———. 1990. "*Interview*: Harrison C. White." Pp. 78–95 in *Economics and Sociology,* by Richard Swedberg. Princeton: Princeton University Press.

———. 1992. *Identity and Control: A Structural Theory of Social Action.* Princeton: Princeton University Press.

———. 2001. *Markets from Networks: Socioeconomic Models of Production.* Princeton: Princeton University Press.

———. 2002. "Crowded Markets: Allocation with Valuation in Context." Unpublished manuscript.

White, Harrison, and Robert Eccles. 1987. "Producers' Markets." Pp. 984–86 in vol. 3 of *The New Palgrave Dictionary. A Dictionary of Economic Theory and Doctrine,* edited by John Eatwell et al. London: Macmillan.

Whyte, William Foote. 1948. *Human Relations in the Restaurant Business*. New York: McGraw-Hill.

Whyte, William Foote, et al. 1955. *Money and Motivation*. New York: Harper.

Wicksell, Knut. [1896] 1959. "A New Principle of Just Taxation." Pp. 72–118 in *Classics in the Theory of Public Finance*, edited by Richard A. Musgrave and Alan T. Peacock. London: Macmillan.

Williamson, Oliver. 1975. *Markets and Hierarchies: Analysis and Antitrust Implications*. New York: Free Press.

———. 1985. *The Economic Institutions of Capitalism*. New York: Free Press.

———. 1986. *Economic Organization*. New York: New York University Press.

———. 1994. "Transaction Cost Economics." Pp. 77–107 in *The Handbook of Economic Sociology*, edited by Neil Smelser and Richard Swedberg. New York and Princeton: Russell Sage Foundation and Princeton University Press.

———. 1996a. "Calculativeness, Trust, and Economic Organization." Pp. 250–75 in *The Mechanisms of Governance*. Oxford: Oxford University Press.

———. 1996b. "Economic Organization: The Case for Candor," *Academy of Management Review* 21:48–57.

Wilson, Robert. 1993. *Nonlinear Pricing*. New York: Oxford University Press.

Wood, Robert. 1986. *From Marshall Plan to Debt Crisis: Foreign Aid Development Choices in the World Economy*. Berkeley: University of California Press.

Woolcock, Michael. 1998. "Social Capital and Economic Development," *Theory and Society* 27:151–208.

Wright, John. 1996. *Interest Groups and Congress: Lobbying, Contributions, and Influence*. London: Allyn and Bacon.

Wrong, Dennis. 1961. "The Oversocialized Conception of Man in Modern Sociology," *American Sociological Review* 26:183–93.

Wycherley, R. E. 1976. *How the Greeks Built Cities*. 2nd ed. New York: Norton.

Yakubovich, Valery, and Mark Granovetter. 2001. "Electric Charges: The Social Construction of Rate Systems." University of Pennsylvania Working Papers in Economic Sociology.

Zelizer, Viviana. 1978. "Human Values and the Market: The Case of Life Insurance and Death in 19th-Century America," *American Journal of Sociology* 84:591–610.

———. 1979. *Morals and Markets: The Development of Life Insurance in the United States*. New York: Columbia University Press.

———. 1981. "The Price and Value of Children: The Case of Children's Insurance," *American Journal of Sociology* 86:1036–56.

———. 1985. *Pricing the Priceless Child: The Changing Social Value of Children*. New York: Basic Books.

———. 1988. "Beyond the Polemics of the Market: Establishing a Theoretical and Empirical Agenda," *Sociological Forum* 3:614–34.

———. 1989. "The Social Meaning of Money: 'Special Monies,'" *American Journal of Sociology* 95:342–77.

———. 1994. *The Social Meaning of Money*. New York: Basic Books.

———. 2001. "Economic Sociology." Pp. 4128–32 in vol. 6 of *International En-*

cyclopaedia of the Social and Behavioral Sciences, edited by Neil Smelser and Paul Baltes. Amsterdam: Elsevier.

———. 2002. "Enter Culture." Pp. 101–25 in *New Economic Sociology*, edited by Mauro Guillén et al. New York: Russell Sage Foundation.

———. Forthcoming a. "Culture and Consumption." In *The Handbook of Economic Sociology*. Neil Smelser and Richard Sweedberg. 2nd ed. New York and Princeton: Russell Sage Foundation and Princeton University Press.

———. Forthcoming b. "Kids and Commerce," *Childhood*.

Zey, Mary. 1993. *Banking on Fraud: Drexel, Junk Bonds, and Buyouts*. New York: Aldine de Gruyter.

———. 1998. *Rational Choice Theory and Organizational Theory: A Critique*. London: Sage.

Zucker, Lynne. 1986. "The Production of Trust: Institutional Sources of Economic Structure, 1840–1920." Pp. 53–111 in *Research in Organizational Behavior*, edited by Barry Staw and L.I. Cummings. Boulder, Colo.: JAI Press.

Zuckerman, Harriet. 1988. "Introduction: Intellectual Property and Diverse Rights of Ownership in Science," *Science, Technology and Human Values* 13 (Winter and Spring): 7–16.

Zukin, Sharon, and Paul DiMaggio. 1990. "Introduction." Pp. 1–36 in *Structures of Capital: The Social Organization of the Economy*, edited by Sharon Zukin and Paul DiMaggio. Cambridge: Cambridge University Press.

Zysman, John. 1983. *Governments, Markets, and Growth: Financial Systems and the Politics of Industrial Change*. Ithaca: Cornell University Press.

Index

Abolafia, Mitchel, 34, 94, 118, 247, 279
Abott, Andrew, 96
accounting, 90–1
action. *See* economic action; social action
advertisement, 147, 251
agency, 71, 102
agency theory, 83–5
agent. *See* agency theory
agora, 135–37
agriculture, 55–6
Akerlof, George, 115, 299
Alchian, Arman, 85–6
Algeria, 47, 241–43
animals, 233
anomie, 19
anthropology. *See* economic anthropology
anti-Semitism, 233
anti-trust legislation, 100, 210
appropriation, 202–03
arbitrage. *See* tertius gaudens
Aristotle, 57, 137
Aron, Raymond, 46
Arrow, Kenneth, 87, 115, 132
ascetic Protestantism. *See* Protestantism
Aspers, Patrik, 51
ataraxia, 48
Athens, 135–37
Aubert, Vilhelm, 196–97
Austin, John, 194
Austrian economics. *See* economics: Austrian economics
Axelrod, Robert, 86

Bagnasco, Arnaldo, 66
Baker, Wayne, 34, 125–26
banana time, 94
bank control, 152. *See also* financial hegemony
bankruptcy, 212
banks, 97, 99, 151–54, 277. *See also* central banks; markets: capital markets; savings banks
barter, 135
Battle of the Methods, 109

Baumol, William, 287
bazaar, 237–38
Becker, Gary, 32, 116, 243
Beckert, Jens, 51, 205
behavioral economics. *See* economics: behavioral economics
Bentley, Arthur, 186, 294
Berezin, Mabel, 278
Berger, Peter, 36
Berman, Harold, 201
Beruf. See vocation
big firms. *See* firms: big firms
Biggart, Nicole Woolsey, 34, 277
Blinder, Alan, 116
Block, Fred, 167, 299
Bodin, Jean, 173
body, 256, 262–63, 264. *See also* food
Boltanski, Luc, 49–50
Bonacich, Phillip, 290
bona fides. See good faith
Boorman, Scott, 38
boredom at work, 94, 96
Bourdieu, Pierre, xii, 46–9, 99, 127–28, 241–45, 301–03; capitals, 45, 48, 243–44; on culture, 241–45; *Distinction*, 255–56. *See also* field; habitus
Boyer, Robert, 51
Braudel, Fernand, 133–34
Brazil, 185–86
broken ties, 101
broker. *See* tertius gaudens
Buchanan, James, 164–65, 179
Buddhism, 233–34
Burawoy, Michael, 96
bureaucracy, 89–92, 178–79, 185
Burt, Ronald, 33–4, 39–41, 42
business climate, 167
business groups, 40, 100
business schools, 297–98

Callon, Michel, 49
Cameron, Rondo, 150
Campbell, John, 181
Canada, 238

capital, 48, 56–9; cultural capital, 48, 243–44; human capital, 243; social capital, 45, 48; symbolic capital, 48
capitalism, 47, 54–5, 56–65; pariah capitalism, 59, 233; political capitalism, 60–1; rational capitalism, 60–1; spirit of capitalism, 143–46; traditional capitalism, 60–1, 229–30; varieties of capitalism, 63
capital markets. *See* markets: capital markets
care taking, 274
Carlton, Dennis, 116
Carnegie, Andrew, 236
Carruthers, Bruce, 34, 44, 173, 212, 249
cartels, 212. *See also* anti-trust legislation
Castells, Manuel, 70–1
cast system, 234
catallactics, 112
central banks, 152
chaebol, 100
Chamberlin, Edward, 113–14, 121
Chandler, Alfred, 44, 102, 142, 148–49
charisma, 169–70, 178–79
charity, 233
Chicago School, 115–16
children, 247–48, 261–63, 267–71, 272
China, 204, 233–34
Chinese minority, 238
classes, 9, 25, 288–89
classification, schemes of, 256
closure theory, 288
Coase, R.H., 79–82, 105, 117–18. *See also* Coase Theorem
Coase Theorem, 214–16. *See also* Coase, R.H.
Coats, A.W., 298
coercion. *See* force and the economy
Colbert, Jean-Baptiste, 142–43
Coleman, James, xii, 38, 44–6, 53–4, 85, 210, 231, 249, 254–55
collective action, 187
colonies, 61
Columbia University, 253
comfort, 225
commenda, 90–1. *See also* firms
commercial legislation, 200. *See also* the Law Merchant
communal economy, 16, 57
communication, 150
Communism. *See* socialism

comparable worth, 278
comparative approach in economic sociology, 43–4
competition, 113–14, 120, 128. *See also* monopolistic competition; perfect competition
computer industry, 66–8, 185–86
conflict of interest, 188
Confucianism, 233–34
conspicuous consumption, 252
constitutional economics, 165
consumption, 49, 57–8, 146–49, 249–57. *See also* department stores; shopping; stores
contemporary economic sociology. *See* economic sociology: contemporary economic sociology
contingency theory, 102
contract, 19, 206–10
convention, 15. *See also* economics: economics of conventions; norms
convergence, 181, 235
co-operation, 9
corporate culture. *See* culture: corporate culture
corporation. *See* the firm
credible commitment, 165
credit, 139, 249
crime, 236. *See also* white collar crime
Crozier, Michel, 46, 94
cultural capital. *See* capital: cultural capital
culture, 34, 41–3, 218–58; concept of, 218–22, 226–28; corporate culture, 219, 245; culture and economic development, 222–39; *Kulturwissenschaft*, 226; legal culture, 197
culture and economic development. *See* culture: culture and economic development
custom, 15. *See also* traditionalism in the economy
Cyert, Richard, 77–8

Dahrendorf, Ralf, 46, 91
Dalton, Melville, 94
Davis, Jerry, 34
de' Fieschi, Sinibaldo, 210
demand and supply, 122
democracy and the economy, 171
demography, 264

Demsetz, Harold, 83, 85–6, 109, 204–05
department stores, 148
dependency, economic. *See* economic
dependency
development, 59, 218–40
Dewey, John, 294
Dezalay, Yves, 202
DiMaggio, Paul, 34, 37, 43, 220, 247
direct selling organizations, 277
dirty work, 94
discipline, 155
discrimination, 276
disinterest. *See* interest: disinterest
distribution, 57–8. *See also* department
stores; exchange; reciprocity; redistribution; stores
division of labor, 18–9, 266
Dobbin, Frank, 34, 44, 184, 211, 248, 296
Dodd, Nigel, 51
Durkheim, Emile, 18–20, 167–68, 202,
206–07

economic action, 15–17, 37
economically conditioned phenomena,
13, 15
economically relevant phenomena, 13, 15
economic anthropology, 237–38, 250
economic dependency, 275
economic ethic, 134, 227–34
economic field. *See* field
economic geography, 55–6
economic growth. *See* development
economic habitus. *See* habitus
economic history, 131
economic interests. *See* interest: economic
interests
economic organizations, 53–4. *See also*
firms
economic power. *See* power
economics:
Austrian economics, 111–12
behavioral economics, 77
economics of conventions, 51
evolutionary economics, 79, 85–6
game theory, 77, 85–6, 115, 289–90
general equilibrium theory, 115
household economics, 264
neoclassical economics, 108–111, 115–
16
new institutional economics, 78–9, 117,
164–66

organizational economics, 78–9
physiocrats, 8
social economics, 12–3, 24
the word "economics", 264
economic sanctions, 183–84
economic socialization, 261
economic sociology: contemporary economic sociology 32–52; economic sociology as a policy tool, 300–04;
economic sociology in Europe, 46–51;
economic sociology in the United
States, 33–4; history of, 1–52; new economic sociology, 33–52; old economic
sociology, 32–3; term economic sociology, 5. *See also* comparative approach
in economic sociology; historical approach in economic sociology; structural economic sociology
economic sociology as a policy tool. *See*
economic sociology: economic sociology as a policy tool
economic sociology in Europe. *See* economic sociology: economic sociology
in Europe
economic sociology in the United States.
See economic sociology: economic sociology in the United States
economics of conventions. *See* economics:
economics of conventions
economic system. *See* system, economic
economic theory. *See* economics
economism, 49
economistic fallacy, 27–8
economists, 51, 172, 298–99
Edelman, Lauren, 211
education. *See* capital: cultural capital,
human capital
efficiency, 88
electrical utility industry, 35
Elias, Norbert, 158
Ellickson, Robert, 215–16
embeddedness, 27–8, 32, 34, 36–7, 125,
247, 257
emotions and the economy, 7, 225, 278–
81
enforcement. *See* force and the economy;
property rights
Engels, Friedrich, 10, 155, 165
England, 184, 267–72
England, Paula, 34
entrepreneurship, 26, 66–8, 286–87. *See*

entrepreneurship (*cont.*)
  also ethnic entrepreneurship;
  innovations
environment, 55–6. *See also* Coase
  Theorem
ethic. *See* economic ethic
ethnic entrepreneurship, 238, 239
ethnicity and the economy, 233, 238. *See*
  also ethnic entrepreneurship
ethnography, 94
European Union, 128
Evans, Peter, 185–86
evolutionary economics. *See* economics:
  evolutionary economics
exchange, 28, 57–8
externalities. *See* Coase Theorem
external markets. *See* markets: external
  markets

factors of production, 58–9, 76–7
factory, 93–7, 155–56
fairness, 216
fairs. *See* markets: fairs
Fama, Eugene, 84
family, 263–73. *See also* children; firms:
  family firms; household
Faulkner, Robert, 212
Favereau, Olivier, 51
fetishism of commodities, 251
field, 47, 99, 127–28
finance, 151–54
financial hegemony, 152. *See also* bank
  control
firms, 17, 74–103, 237: big firms, 44; family firms, 74, 91, 266; legal personality,
  209–10; multidivisional firms, 148–49;
  small firms, 237; transnational firms,
  151. *See also* bureaucracy; business
  groups; commenda
fiscal sociology, 25, 173–82
flexible specialization, 66
Fligstein, Neil, 33–4, 41, 102, 127–28,
  172–73, 300–01
Folbre, Nancy, 274
food, 250, 256, 264–65, 271, 274
force and the economy, 150, 158, 162,
  169–70, 171, 191
Ford, Henry, 148
Fordism, 66. *See also* school of regulation
formalism, 20
forms of integration, 27–8

Fourcade-Gourinchas, Marion, 299
France, 50–1, 184, 267–72
Franklin, Benjamin, 230
free rider, 187
Friedman, Georges, 94
Friedman, Lawrence, 191, 197
Friedman, Milton, 116
Fukuyama, Frank, 248

Gambetta, Diego, 248
game theory. *See* economics: game theory
Gao, Bai, 34
Garth, Bryant, 202
Geertz, Clifford, 237–38
gender and the economy, 259–82. *See also*
  women and the economy
general equilibrium theory. *See* economics: general equilibrium theory
geography. *See* economic geography
Gereffi, Gary, 34
Gerschenkron, Alexander, 141
Giddens, Anthony, 46
gift, 23, 242
global economy, 70
globalization, 68–72
Goffman, Erving, 203–04, 253, 289, 292
Goldscheid, Rudolf, 174
Goldschmidt, Levin, 11
good faith, 139, 201
Gouldner, Alvin, 93
governance, 81, 128
Granovetter, Mark, 32–40, 42, 67–9, 87–8,
  98–9, 100, 123–25, 129, 245–46. *See also*
  embeddedness
Greif, Avner, 115
growth, economic. *See* development
Guillén, Mauro, 34

Habermas, Jürgen, 46–7, 294
habit, 15. *See also* traditionalism in the
  economy
habitus, 48, 241–42
Haglunds, Magnus, 97
Halliday, Terence, 212
Hamilton, Gary, 34
Hannan, Michael, 41, 100
Hayek, Friedrich von, 60, 75, 111–12
Hechter, Michael, 221–22
Heckscher, Eli, 141
Hegel, G.W.F., 166
hegemony. *See* financial hegemony

Heilbron, Johan, 2, 51
Heilsgüter. See religious benefits
Heimer, Carol, 209
Hélvetius, Claude-Adrien, 2
Hermes, 137
Hicks, John, 141
Hinduism, 234
Hintze, Otto, 142
Hirschman, Albert O., 183, 279
historical approach in economic sociology, 43–4
Hochschild, Arlie, 280–81
Hollingsworth, Rogers, 63–4
home. *See* family; household; household work
homo economicus, xi, 3, 19, 48, 241, 263, 278
honesty, 232. *See also* economic ethic
household, 57, 363–73. *See also* household work
household economics. *See* economics: household economics
household work, 273–74
house work. *See* household work
Hughes, Everett C., 94
human capital. *See* capital: human capital
Hume, David, xii, 197–98, 281
Hurst, Willard, 199
hybrid, 81

IBRD (International Bank of Reconstruction and Development). *See* the World Bank
ideal interests. *See* interest: ideal interests
identity, 122
illusio, 48
IMF (International Monetary Fund), 71
imperialism, 25
incentive, 84, 89, 163–64. *See also* interest
India, 185–86, 234
Indonesia, 237–38
industrial districts, 65–8
industrial organization, 77, 113–15
industrial policy, 44, 184, 187
industrial revolution, 146–47
industrial sociology, 88, 91, 93–7
inflation, 184
informal economy, 155–56
information and the economy, 257, 299
infrastructure, 163
Ingham, Geoffrey, 51

inheritance, 205–06
Innocent IV, 210
innovations, 236, 254–55. *See also* entrepreneurship
institutions, xii, 54. *See also* new institutional economics; new institutionalism; rules
insurance, 209, 247. *See also* life insurance
integration, forms of, 28–9
intellectual property, 201, 204–05
interest, xii, 1–5, 133; concept of, 1–5, 23, 290–97; definitions, 294; disinterest, 244–45, 263; economic interests, 3, 49, 292; emotional interest, 263; family interest, 261, 272; ideal interests, xii, 3, 219; interests of women, 261, 273; material interests, xii, 3, 219; objective interests, 16; regulatory interest, 196; self-interest, 225; sexual interests, 262–63; subjective interests, 16. *See also* conflict of interest; interest groups; motivation
interest groups, 184, 186–88
interlocks, 101. *See also* broken ties
internal markets. *See* markets: internal markets
international market. *See* markets: international market
inventions, *See* intellectual property
invisible hand, 2, 95
irrationality, 278–81. *See also* charisma
Isay, Hermann, 295
Italy, 65–6
Izquierdo, Javier, 51

Jahoda, Marie, 94
James, William, 281
Jensen, Michael, 83–4, 85
Jevons, W. Stanley, 5, 108–09
Jewish people. *See* anti-Semitism; capitalism: pariah capitalism; Weber, Max: Works: *Ancient Judaism*
Jhering, Rudolf von, 196–97
job search, 123–25
justice, 197
justification, 49–50. *See also* legitimation
just price, 129

Kaldor-Hicks concept of efficiency, 57
Kanter, Rosabeth Moss, 97, 277–78, 286–87

Katz, Elihu, 253, 254–55
keiretsu, 100
Keynes, John Maynard, 112–13
Keynes, John Neville, 109
Keynesianism, 298
kinship. *See* family
Knight, Frank, 53
Knorr Cetina, Karin, 51, 299
Krippner, Greta, 37, 131
Krugman, Paul, 55–6, 279–80
Kulturwissenschaft. See culture:
  Kulturwissenschaft

La Porta, Rafael, 216–17
La Rochefoucauld, 2
labor. *See* division of labor; trade unions;
  work
Landes, David, 232
Latin America, 238–39
Latour, Bruno, 49
law and economics, 79, 85–6, 189, 212–17
law and society, 189
law and the economy, 68, 71, 100, 189–
  217. *See also* law and economics; law
  and society
Law Merchant, 139, 198–200
Lazarsfeld, Paul, 94, 253
Lazega, Emmanuel, 51
Lazerson, Mark, 66
Lebaron, Frédéric, 51, 299
legal culture. *See* culture: legal culture
legal personality. *See* firms: legal
  personality
legitimation, 169–70. *See also* justification
Leifer, Eric, 88
lex mercatoria. See the Law Merchant
life insurance, 247
lifestyle, 256, 288–89
lifeworld, 46–7
Light, Ivan, 238
Lincoln, Abraham, 204
Lindenberg, Siegward, 51
Lipset, S.M., 238–39
Locke, John, 163, 294
long-distance trade. *See* trade
Long-Term Capital Management, 154
lord, 267
loyalty, 77–8. *See also* whistle blowing
Luckmann, Thomas, 36
Luhmann, Niklas, 46, 152, 248
Luther, Martin, 230. *See also* vocation

luxury, 148, 150, 228, 232, 250. *See also*
  sumptuary laws

Macaulay, Stewart, 208
MacKenzie, Donald, 129–30, 154
Mandeville, Bernard de, 23
Mann, Michael, 180
manual labor, 94, 228. *See also* dirty work
March, James, 54, 77–8
market research, 253
markets, 104–57; capital markets, 151–54;
  external markets, 134–35; fairs, 138–40;
  internal markets, 135–36; international
  market, 149–51; labor markets, 106–07,
  113, 154–56; mass consumption markets, 146–49; national markets, 140–43;
  production markets, 121–23; world
  market, 150. *See also* sociology of
  markets
Marshall, Alfred, 23, 58–9, 65–6, 76–7,
  109–11, 121
Marshall, Gordon, 231
Marx, Karl, 8–11, 56, 57, 58, 107–08, 166–
  67, 202, 251
Marxism, 180, 189
Mason, Edward, 114–15.
mass consumption. *See* consumption
mass consumption markets. *See* markets:
  mass consumption markets
material interests. *See* interest: material
  interests
Mauss, Marcel, 23
Mayer, Martin, 153
McLelland, David, 231
meaning in the economy. *See* culture:
  concept of; Weber, Max: *verstehen*
Meckling, William, 83–4, 85
Meitzen, August, 11
Menger, Carl, 108
Menzel, Herbert, 254–55
mercantilism, 141–42
Merton, Robert K., 51, 92–3, 205, 235–37,
  253–54, 291, 296
Methodenstreit. See the Battle of the
  Methods
methodological individualism, 38, 350
Meyer, John, 41, 71, 102, 222, 248
middleman. *See tertius gaudens*
Mill, John Stuart, xii, 3, 6, 18, 107, 261
minority. *See* Chinese minority; ethnic
  entrepreneurship

mint, 136
Mintz, Beth, 152
Mises, Ludwig von, 111–12
Mizruchi, Mark, 34
modernization theory, 234–39
Modjokuto, 237–38
money, 22, 95–6, 97, 151–54, 247
monopolistic competition, 113–14
monopoly, 204–05
Montesquieu, Charles de Secondat, 6
morality in the economy. *See* economic
    ethic
mortgage, 201
motivation, 296
multidivisional firms. *See* firms: multi-
    divisional firms
multinational firms. *See* firms: transna-
    tional firms
Myrdal, Gunnar, 298

national markets. *See* markets: national
    markets
nature, 55–6
Nazi Germany, 81
Nee, Victor, 34
neo-classical economics. *See* economics:
    neo-classical economics
neoliberalism, 298, 301
networks, 34, 36–40, 49, 67–9, 70, 100–01,
    123–26, 257, 297. *See also* embeddness
new economic sociology. *See* economic
    sociology: new economic sociology
new institutional economics. *See* eco-
    nomics: new institutional economics
new institutionalism, 41, 101–02, 248
normative issues. *See* economic soci-
    ology: economic sociology as a policy
    tool
norms, 221–22, 223, 235. *See also*
    convention
North, Douglass, 79, 82–3, 104–05, 117–
    18, 164–66

Oakley, Anne, 273
Obershall, Anthony, 88
objective interests. *See* interest: objective
    interests
objectivity, 297–99
O'Connor, James, 180
Oeconomia. See economics: the word
    "economics"

old economic sociology. *See* economic so-
    ciology: old economic sociology
Olson, Mancur, 187–88
Opp, Karl-Dieter, 221–22
opportunitism, 82
organizational economics. *See* economics:
    organizational economics
organizations, 34, 40–1, 53, 89–93, 98–
    102. *See also* contingency theory; firms;
    industrial sociology; new institutional
    economics; new institutionalism; orga-
    nizational economics; population ecol-
    ogy; resource dependency
organization theory. *See* organizations

Padavic, Irene, 276
Pareto, Vilfredo, 23–4, 294
pariah capitalism. *See* capitalism: pariah
    capitalism
Parsons, Talcott, 28–30, 42, 118–19, 152,
    235, 245
Pascal, Blaise, 2
Passeron, Jean-Claude, 243
patents. *See* intellectual property
patriarchy, 267
perfect competition, 109, 132. *See also*
    competition
Perrow, Charles, 87
Petersen, Trond, 289
pharmaceutical industry, 254–55
phenomenology and economic sociology,
    51
physiocrats. *See* economics: physiocrats
piecework, 95
planned economy. *See* socialism
Podolny, Joel, 129
Polanyi, Karl, 26–8, 118, 146, 155
Polinsky, Mitchell, 214–15
political capitalism. *See* capitalism: politi-
    cal capitalism
political economy, 105–08
politics and the economy, 158–88
poor. *See* poverty
population, 264
population ecology, 41, 100
Portes, Alejandro, 34
Posner, Richard, 189, 199, 213–14
postmodernism, 250
Pound, Roscoe, 196, 294
poverty, 55–6, 181–82
Powell, Walter, 34

power, 16, 89, 288
pragmatism, 294
predatory profit, 61
pre-historic times and the economy, 134–
    35
price-fixing, 212
prices, 105–06, 116, 129–30. *See also* just
    price; price-fixing
principal. *See* agency theory
prisoner's dilemma, 86
production, 59. *See also* factors of
    production
production function, 75
production markets. *See* markets: produc-
    tion markets
productivity, 94–6, 156
profession, 96, 277
profit, 57–8, 72, 119. *See also* predatory
    profit
profit-making, 57, 60
property, 163, 202–05, 288. *See also* inheri-
    tance; property rights
property rights, 128, 204–05
Protestantism, 129, 226–34. *See also*
    vocation
psychology and economics. *See* eco-
    nomics: behavioral economics
public choice, 164–66

racism, 7–8
railroads, 44, 184
rate busters, 96
rational behavior. *See* interest; irra-
    tionality; capitalism: rational capital-
    ism; rational choice sociology
rational choice. *See* interest; irrationality;
    rational choice sociology
rational choice sociology, 44–6
Ratzenhofer, Gustav, 294
Raub, Werner, 51
reciprocity, 28, 57–8
redistribution, 28, 57–8
reflexivity, 297–99
regions. *See* industrial districts
regulation. *See* industrial policy; school
    of regulation
reification. *See* fetishism of commodities
relations of production, 10
religion and the economy, 7, 20, 226–34
religious benefits, 230
rent-seeking, 164–65

reputation, 139, 201
Reskin, Barbara, 276, 278
resource dependency, 40–1, 99–100
retailing. *See* stores
revolutions and the economy, 10, 142,
    237
rhetoric in economics, 298–99
Ricardo, David, 107
risk, 209
Ritzer, George, 251
Roy, Donald, 94–5
rules, 82

Sabel, Charles, 66
Sachs, Jeffrey, 55–6
Saint-Simon, Henri de, 6
Samuelson, Paul, 35, 75
Sartre, Jean-Paul, 294
Sassen, Saskia, 71
savings banks, 152
Saxenian, AnnaLee, 66–7
Say, Jean-Baptiste, 6, 18, 113
Schelling, Thomas, 290
Scherer, F.M., 77
Schmoller, Gustav, 18, 141–42
school of regulation, 51
Schumpeter, Joseph, 6, 9–11, 23–6, 174–
    76, 287
Schutz, Alfred, 4
Schwartz, Michael, 38, 152
science, 204–05
Scott, Joan, 267–72
Scott, Richard, 98
secrecy, 204–05
sects, 232–33
Securities and Exchange Commission
    (SEC), 211
segregation, index of, 276–77
self-interest. *See* interest: self-interest
selling. *See* shopping
Selznick, Philip, 194
Sen, Amartya, 263
Senior, Nassau William, 6
sexism, 259, 260, 273–78
sexual harassment, 97
Shapiro, Susan, 211
Shiller, Robert, 279–80
shopping, 250, 253, 257, 274, 277. *See also*
    consumption; department stores; direct
    selling organizations; stores
signalling, 115

Silicon Valley, 66–8, 211
Simmel, Georg, 3, 19–22, 248, 251–52
Simon, Herbert, 77–8
Sismondi, Jean-Charles-Léonard Simonde de, 18
Skocpol, Theda, 43
slavery, 7–8
Small, Albion, 294
small firms. *See* firms: small firms
Smelser, Neil, 29–30, 118, 152
Smith, Adam, xii, 2, 9, 18, 76, 105–06, 140, 161–64, 281
social action, 15
social capital: *See* capital: social capital
social classes. *See* classes
social construction, 34, 36
social economics. *See* economics: social economics
socialism, 266
socialization. *See* economic socialization
sociology of consumption, 249–57
sociology of law, 104–05, 184–94, 210–12
sociology of markets, 118–30
sociology of work, 93–7. *See also* work
Solow, Robert, 155
Sombart, Werner, 24, 233
South Korea, 185–86
Sozialökonomik. See economics: social economics
speculation, 61
Spence, Michael, 115, 121, 299
Spencer, Herbert, 19
spirit of capitalism. *See* capitalism: spirit of capitalism
stakeholder theory, 78
Stark, David, 204
state, 158–88. *See also* fiscal sociology; imperialism; industrial policy; mercantilism; redistribution; welfare state
statistical discrimination, 276
status and status groups, 251, 287–89
Stearns, Linda Brewster, 34
Steiner, Philippe, 1, 51
Stigler, George, 104, 187
Stinchcombe, Arthur, 93
stock exchange, 119, 140, 211
stores, 149. *See also* department stores
stratification, 287–89
strikes, 95, 156
strong ties, 124

structural economic sociology, 37–40
structural holes, 33
structural sociology, 37–40
Stryker, Robin, 210
subjective interests. *See* interest: subjective interests
Suchman, Mark, 211
suffering, 49, 303
Sullivan, Teresa, 212
sumptuary laws, 250. *See also* luxury
supply. *See* demand and supply
Swidler, Anne, 218–20
switchmen metaphor. *See* Weber, Max: switchmen metaphor
syllabi in economic sociology, 34
symbolic capital. *See* capital: symbolic capital
system, economic, 29–30, 46

Tabanan, 237–38
Taoism, 233
taste, 255–56
taxes. *See* fiscal sociology
tax state, 174–76
technology, 58–9, 66–7, 204–05
tertius gaudens, 21
textile industry, 144–45
theodicy, 303–04
Thévenot, Laurent, 49–50
Thompson, E.P., 189
Tilly, Charles, 43, 171
Tilly, Louise, 267–72
time, 47. *See also* time budget
time budget, 273–74
Tirole, Jean, 77
Tocqueville, Alexis de, xii, 3, 6–8, 205–06, 223–25
tokenism, 277
trade, 134–36, 149–51, 266. *See also* exchange
trade unions, 156, 167
traditional capitalism. *See* capitalism: traditional capitalism
traditionalism in the economy, 169–70, 235, 243
transaction costs, 79–83
transmigration, 234
transnational firms. *See* firms: transnational firms
Trigilia, Carlo, 51
trust, 2, 45, 248–49

Tupperware, 277
two-step flow of communication, 253–54

uncertainty. *See* risk
unemployment, 94, 155, 281, 301
unintended consequences, 2
United States, 63–4, 223–25, 235–36, 238
usury, 233
utilitarianism, 3, 49
Uzzi, Brian, 34, 36–7, 39–40, 125

vacancy chain, 125
value, 220, 226–27, 238
varieties of capitalism. *See* capitalism: varieties of capitalism
Veblen, Thorstein, 24, 236, 252
venture capitalists, 67–8
verstehen. See Weber, Max: *verstehen*
Veyne, Paul, 177
violence and the economy. *See* force and the economy
vocation, 91–2, 230

wages, 276–78, 287–89
Wagner, Adolf, 18
Walder, Andrew, 204–05
Wallerstein, Immanuel, 70
Walras, Léon, 108, 110
weak ties, 124
wealth, 288
Weber, Max, xi–xii, 3, 11–18, 59–62, 89–93, 119–21, 129, 134, 143–46, 168–71, 176–78, 191–96, 198–200, 202–03, 205–07, 226–34, 248, 265–67, 279, 287–88, 292–93, 303–04; bureaucracy, 89–93; capitalism, 59–62; economic ethic, 227–34; firm, 89–93; interests, 3–4, 13, 15–16; market, 119–21; switchmen metaphor, xii, 3, 219–20; *verstehen*, 15, 24,

26; Works: *Ancient Judaism*, 233; *Collected Essays in the Sociology of Religion*, 12–13; *Economy and Society*, 12, 15–18; *The Protestant Ethic and the Spirit of Capitalism*, xi, 12–13, 143–46, 229–33; *The Religion of China*, 12, 233–34; *The Religion of India*, 12, 234
Weesie, Jeroen, 51
welfare state, 171–72, 181–82, 272–73
whistle blowing, 97. *See also* loyalty
White, Harrison C., 34, 38, 84–5, 121–23, 125
white collar crime, 211–12
Whyte, William Foot, 94–6
Wicksell, Knut, 165
Williamson, Oliver, 32, 80–2
women and the economy, 259–82; wages, 276–78; women at work, 97, 273–78; women in the home, 273. *See also* household; inheritance; sexual harassment; sexism
women at work. *See* women and the economy: women at work
women in the home. *See* women and the economy: women in the home
work, 9, 154, 228, 273. *See also* boredom at work; household work; piecework; sexual harassment; sociology of work; whistle-blowing; workers
workers, 92–7. *See also* strikes; unemployment; wages
World Bank, 71
world economy, 70
world market. *See* markets: world market
world-systems theory, 70–2

Zeizel, Hans, 94
Zelizer, Viviana, 33–4, 42–3, 118, 246–47, 257
Zukin, Sharon, 37